TANGIBLE
MEMORIES

TANGIBLE
MEMORIES

Californians and their gardens
1800-1950

Judith M. Taylor MD

and the late Harry Morton Butterfield

This book was printed in the United States of America.

COVER LEGEND

Front
Painting of Villa Montalvo , Saratoga, California by Theodore Wores (1927)
Photograph by Henry G. Ring MD
Reproduced by permission of St Francis Memorial Hospital, San Francisco .

Back
Painting of Spring Blossom in Saratoga, California by Theodore Wores (nd)
Photograph by Henry G. Ring MD
Reproduced by permission of St. Francis Memorial Hospital, San Francisco
To order additional copies of this book, contact:
Xlibris Corporation
1-888-795-4274
www.Xlibris.com
Orders@Xlibris.com

17951-TAYL

TO DAVID AND HUGH

CONTENTS

List of Illustrations and their sources

Jacket, front Painting of Senator Phelan's "Villa Montalvo' by Theodore Wores 1927 {St Francis Memorial Hospital, San Francisco}

Jacket, back Painting of a Saratoga road in the spring by Theodore Wores {St.Francis Memorial Hospital, San Francisco} no date

Frontispiece Harry M. Butterfield {Butterfield family}

INTRODUCTION

How this book came about

Serendipity keeps on happening by chance, as Yogi Berra might have said. I was working with Harry Butterfield's papers in the Special Collections department at the University of California at Davis while doing the research for my book about the olive trees in California. Although it was not part of my task, I could not help noticing the two formidable binders with a carefully typed manuscript lying in the bottom of the box. After the book about the olive trees was finished, I went back and looked into Butterfield's papers again. There it was: the manuscript of "California Gardens of Memory", written over a number of years, ending about 1968.

I obtained permission from John Skarstad, university archivist, to make a copy of the manuscript and submitted it to my publisher. At about the same time, I had an opportunity to show the manuscript briefly to Dr Kevin Starr, California State Librarian and a noted historian of this state. He too found it remarkable, commenting that it had become a primary document of California history in the thirty years since it had been written. Much of what Butterfield had described no longer exists. Houses and gardens have been lost to "progress" time and time again.

After Harry Butterfield died in 1970, his daughter, Dorothy Butterfield Rucker, deposited all his papers in the University of California library, according to the terms of his will. She included a little note with this manuscript, saying that her late father had wanted his work to be available to future students and scholars. She added her own address and phone number. In 1998, when I checked the address and phone number in the telephone directory, Mrs Rucker still lived in the same house. Only the area code had changed.

Mrs Rucker was delighted I had found the work and was extremely cordial and hospitable. She and her daughter Lynne Hanson told me many delightful anecdotes about Mr Butterfield the father and grandfather, as compared to the strictly professional horticulturist and garden authority. He was as strong in the one sphere as the other.

The extremely conscientious scientist always had time for his children and grandchildren. He had three children: Dorothy, Harry and Marjorie. It was clear they had all adored him. Mrs Hanson remembers that her grandfather made them wooden versions of board games, carving all the pieces by hand. The photographs which illustrate this section come from the Rucker family albums.

Because Butterfield had bequeathed his papers to the university of California, the latter owned not only the physical property, but the actual copyright too. The university granted me permission to publish the manuscript as a book and the Rucker family also gave me their blessing.

Gardens and California history
Harry Butterfield's ideas and work

Harry Butterfield had a deep and abiding passion for gardens. Only his family meant more to him. Throughout a long life devoted to all aspects of horticulture, he continually collected information about gardens in California. He wrote numerous articles on his discoveries for the horticultural literature. After he retired he collected all his own observations and the reminiscences of others and prepared a manuscript for publication. He had essentially created a new discipline, California horticultural history.

He included almost eighty small black and white photographs, mainly his own work but a few from other sources. They were meticulously attached to sheets of paper with small triangular fasteners and interleaved among the text.

The manuscript is a rather glorious hodge-podge of extraordinary facts pertaining to anything horticultural: gardening amateurs, nursery men and women, exquisitely detailed local history, mission history and so forth. Butterfield entitled it "California Gardens of Memory", meaning that gardens retained memories of life in a former period.

A garden to him was a vector of memory in a continually changing world, but the paradox of course is that gardens themselves constantly change. Butterfield did not think it was necessary to define a garden. It seems to have been self-evident to him that everyone would know what a garden was. His own views on that subject were very open and elastic. A "garden of memory" could range anywhere from an early American ranch garden to a small vestigial collection of trees in a median divider.

Butterfield's indifference to modern great estates

One type of garden Butterfield seldom included was the elaborate estate designed and built by professional landscape architects at great expense for wealthy people. If a rich landowner were interested in horticulture, Butterfield took notice of his garden. He liked the Blake estate in Kensington (now the official residence of the president of the University of California) because Mrs Blake and her sister in law were keen horticulturists. Filoli, a magnificent estate in Woodside, did not pass his rather idiosyncratic test. The manuscript is silent on that garden, yet it is hard to believe he was not aware of it.

Filoli was built for the Bourns, owners of the Empire gold mine in Grass Valley. They commissioned Bruce Porter, one of the pre-eminent garden designers of his day, to work with Willis Polk, designer of the house, and create a garden for them. Today Filoli is on the National Trust list of heritage gardens.

Work on Filoli began in 1916. The estate rapidly became very well known. Butterfield was active from the 1920s through the

1960s. It is highly likely he knew about this garden. In fact he made a point of commenting on how people came to him as soon as they had built a new garden to get his opinion.

Vernacular gardens

None of the glamour or quality of such estates seems to have impressed Butterfield. He wants to tell us about the few square yards of planting around a small dwelling in Riverside or the relics of ancient pear trees near the Carmel mission. Memory is apparently best served by the modest efforts of those who went before us, not by the owners of great wealth.

One could say that Butterfield was most interested in gardens which did not merit formal landscape review, those which are now known as "vernacular" gardens. Houses which somehow just went up without explicit architectural reference, often cobbled together by building contractors who had to work within very tight budget constraints, come under the rubric of "vernacular" building. Strip malls, idiomorphic restaurants (such as the "Doggy Diner" in San Francisco) and gas stations belong in this category too.

In residential neighorhoods, watered down copies of the critically acclaimed Los Angeles bungalow sprang up in their thousands after World War II. Each one of these had some space around it which later became the yard. The space was not usually dignified with the title of garden. (Note the semantic resemblance. *Yard* and *garden* come from the same Germanic root). The owner did whatever he could afford to make it attractive. This is very much a vernacular garden.

A little patch of grass "for the children to play", some foundation shrubs and brightly colored flowers were pretty much what most people laid out in the front of the house. Fruit trees were planted at the back and the home owner might also put out a few tomato plants or other vegetables unobtrusively where no one of any consequence would see them.

If specimen trees were on the property before the house went up, the owner had another asset. Planting large trees was expensive, but many did put in small saplings and wait for them to mature. Trees provided shade. In much of California, this was important.

The person of moderate income could not afford any costly frills, but there were models to be imitated. Home owners also had to adhere to community landscaping rules.

Garden fashion slowly percolated through society, as wealthy people changed from fussy Victorian styles to Mediterranean eclectic and Spanish revival landscapes. One thing ambitious poor people could do was to adopt some of the superficial symbols of fashionable gardens. We may laugh discreetly at garden gnomes, but in their day, they were the one of the signatures of the Victorian garden.

Nostalgia played its part too. Immigrants from Europe or the Americas brought slips, bulbs and seeds of familiar plants with them. A grandmother's flowering vine or climbing rose bush made a new place feel more like home. Butterfield recounted many such charming anecdotes.

To create this yard, the home owner often turned to the local nursery. Butterfield's pioneering review shows us what plants were available and when they may have first been used by the average person.

The begonias and petunias bred by Mrs Theodosia Shepherd of Ventura, and introduced in the early years of the twentieth century, form a perfect example of such an advance. Luther Burbank constantly introduced new varieties of familiar flowers over a longer period, dazzling the public.

Butterfield's view of history

What we regard as "history" is said by some historians to be the result of cumulative action by the many rather than the heroic deeds of a few great men. Local history is sometimes contemptuously relegated to antiquarianism, a pettifogging concern with trivialities. The daily activities of unimportant people are not seen to be significant, but there are many instances where these have generated overwhelming force.

By collecting the memories of ordinary people's gardens Butterfield tacitly came down on the side of cumulative, "micro" history. When walking or driving through a town or city, one sees many more small residential gardens than large estates.

We form a visual impression of that town based on many cues, but the numerous small gardens contribute a great deal to it. One example is the presence or absence of hedges. In England, or facsimiles of England such as Toronto, gardens have hedges. In Vermont or Colorado there are no hedges. The differences in garden style sets the tone of the community.

Attitudes toward ornamental plants

Butterfield's emphasis on the nursery people who introduced plants suggests he meant to comment on the ebb and flow of plant fashion in urban and suburban areas. Flowers which are the most perfectly adapted to a habitat often become *declassé* because anyone can grow them without too much difficulty. "Geraniums" (pelargoniums), the small bedding annuals such as today's enormously improved impatiens, many shrubs, and striking trees like the palm are all *clichés* of one sort or another.

There are plant snobs just as there are social snobs. New and rare plants which have finicky ways will trump old favorites that bloom reliably without fuss year after year. There is also the human desire for change. People get tired of looking at the same old plants and want variety. The nursery industry has always fully exploited this characteristic. Nothing gives rise to more covetousness than the latest nursery catalogue, gleaming and glossy in all its insidious glory.

Another aspect of Butterfield's choices was his profession as horticulturist. He was not a landscape architect, but a plantsman. The content of the garden caught his attention more than the layout and hardscape. Long lists of plants in their

formidable Latin names might defeat all but the most dedicated reader and so have been banished to an appendix. Anyone who wants to learn which plants were grown in a particular place has only to turn to the back of the book.

Butterfield's motives

What is not clear to me is why Harry Butterfield was so
intent on collecting all this information. Now we have it, there
is an inevitability about it which belies Butterfield's original-
ity. Commercial horticulture has long made up a significant
portion of the state's economy, but gardens indicate a lot about
a society's soul. An ornamental garden's sole *raison d'etre* is
beauty, not utility.

The facts needed to be saved. Immense amounts of creative
energy had been spent making gardens. The sum of these efforts influenced the shape of towns and cities, affecting the
urban and suburban landscape of the California we know today.

From the papers in his collection, it seems that Harry
Butterfield started to study old gardens very early in his career
at the University of California. While he was a boy and young
man the population was still small enough for individuals to
make an enormous difference. He wrote papers and compiled
lists of plant origins which are still prized by horticultural experts.

Knowing the past is valuable for its own sake and also for
choosing new ways to go forward. In the plant world, the original source reveals a great deal about evolution and future
progress, yet his manuscript seems to say more than that.

Butterfield displays a keen sense of human involvement and
a deep interest in people in his work, and does not just line up
dry facts. Possibly the devoted attention to the history of gardens was a surrogate cloaking nostalgia for a past which could
never be recovered. Harry Butterfield came from a homesteading family, ever going westwards. He knew the California of
the late nineteenth and early twentieth centuries. It was van-

ishing more and more quickly, not just the gardens, but the people and a way of life.

Gardens were the symbol, a metaphor for that loss. He waited to put the book together until he retired. Old age is an epoch when one dwells on the past and sees things in a different light.

Building on Butterfield's manuscript

In bringing this manuscript back to life, I have made extensive modifications where needed, and added a lot of new material. Butterfield's own narrative is indicated by a single quotation mark at the beginning and end of each section. I have retained the flow of his narrative and the flavor of his style wherever possible. The title had to be changed because nowadays "gardens of memory" denote cemeteries.

Harry Butterfield walked or drove around many of the towns and cities he describes, probably from the 1930s through the 1950s. We do not know exactly when he did this. His children have no recollection of their father being away on trips and they never accompanied him. Unfortunately, much of what he saw has since been erased by urban sprawl and the inevitable effects of time.

While I have been at pains to retain Butterfield's tone, I have added descriptions of some of the handsome large estates and gardens created by wealthy people to make this a more useful, complete text. They exist, some of them are now quite old, and they offer perfectly genuine memories even if slightly different from what was in Butterfield's mind. He was a very serious person, immune to frivolity, but movie stars and tycoons play a big role in southern California history. There is a lot to feed memory in these estates.

What is a garden?

This might actually be a good place for us to ask the seemingly silly question: what is a garden? In different ages, succeeding civilizations have come up with many ways of creating gardens.

There is no simple definition that everyone can agree upon, but even the most argumentative academic accepts the fact that "garden" connotes human intention, human activity, enclosure and some sort of order.

"Garden" also contains the idea of pleasure, maybe relaxation or idleness, not necessarily connected with utility such as growing vegetables or fruit perhaps. One only thinks of constructing an ornamental garden when there is enough to eat and some leisure to contemplate the cosmos.

Ordinarily in the course of such an introduction, the author follows a carefully established historical path, from the beginning of civilization to the present. I will beg the reader's indulgence to turn this upside down and begin with California, then work backward. While there is nothing new under the sun, California's gardens come very close to it.

Kevin Starr has explored the very fruitful theme that California was as much a state of mind as a geographical location in "Americans and the California Dream". [a](1) This dream encompassed the age-old, uniquely American possibility of starting over again with a clean slate, no matter how many mistakes a person had made previously.

California seemed to be the epitome of Eden, with its mild climate, profound fecundity and at least in the earlier epochs, immense room for everyone to have a house and as much land as they could afford. Golden sunshine and golden oranges lured them in their thousands at the beginning of the twentieth century.

The "California garden"

Once a person achieved success, it had to be flaunted, otherwise there was no point to it. If one were going to announce to the world that the former idler or misfit from the provinces was now a millionaire, it had to be couched in the symbols everyone recognized. The new money was poured into old design bottles.

After more than a century of slavishly copying garden design from Europe and the East coast, a truly California garden emerged. This probably reflected a new level of maturity. Revolutionary designers of residential California landscape in the 1940s and 1950s embraced a degree of unity between the house and the garden not seen since the pioneers came in the late eighteenth century.

These developments were going on during Butterfield's career, but he evidently paid very little attention to them. The value in mentioning them is that the end result affected the way ordinary people planned and created their gardens.

Richard Neutra was an architect rather than a landscape designer, but he, with Thomas Church and Garrett Eckbo, decisively transformed the garden in California. The modern California garden accompanied the transformation of the California house.

Normal domestic life now moved out into the garden. Landscape architects intentionally exploited the possibilities of a soft climate, and rainfall predictably restricted to the winter months. These insights accompanied changes in technology, new attitudes to health and the benefits of sunshine.

The difference between the Spanish pioneers' way of life and the post World War II landscape architects' ideas was that eighteenth century households in Alta California had no choice but to use the open air for cooking and other noxious activities because only the most primitive type of ventilation was available, whereas the twentieth century resident chose to do it for pleasure.

With the advent of radical styles of landscape architecture, the boundary between indoors and outdoors was erased more thoroughly. The designers created new transitions between the living rooms and the outdoors, so that it was not clear whether the garden was coming indoors, or the living room was going outdoors.

Putting the garden on the same level as the house was one key to the change. Using the same material for the floor of the living rooms and the patio was another method of blurring the lines. Complex masonry steps and elaborate balustrades which used to delineate garden entry now gave way to flat cement walks extending from patios. Pergolas and other free standing structures were used to create sightlines.

Holes left in the cement allowed trees to be planted wherever an owner desired. The lawn and paving materials were set in sweeping curves closely approximated to each other without defining edges in many cases, thus also diminishing boundaries and joints.

New techniques had made large flat plates of glass much safer. A sliding panel made of glass now replaced the fussy many-paned door or long window through which one previously went outside. Almost total removal of decoration and a stripping down to basic function were the hallmark of the modern style.

One antique technique was not jettisoned, growing plants in pots in order to move them around more easily. Potted plants accented the patio but could go inside the house with equal ease. Plants had always been indoors but not on this scale, standing freely in main living rooms rather than in specially built conservatories etc. This accentuated the idea that outdoors and indoors were becoming fused.

Although these innovations appeared to emerge abruptly, careful consideration of how the California garden had been evolving since the Depression indicates that subtle change had begun about twenty years earlier. Many of the clients who had wanted elegant and historically allusive designs had lost their money. Landscape architects had to scale everything down, use less expensive materials and search for new clients, all the time streamlining design and construction.

This coincided with the peak of the Bauhaus movement, no doubt itself affected by the immense poverty in Germany and Austria after World War I. While a rebellion against classical and romantic models in all the arts began earlier in the century, the need to simplify and work efficiently was reinforced by the lack of resources. These ideas were championed in the United States by men such as Neutra. His exceptional talents had been developed during the Bauhaus period in Austria.

Modern California garden design and Harry Butterfield

The relevance of this for Butterfield's work is that the ordinary family, the type of people he cared about, now had new models to copy. Instead of hankering after the glamorous unattainable gardens of the great stars of the cinema and business tycoons, they could adapt the new style to their modest resources. These changes coincided with the enormous building boom after World War II, but Butterfield's theme was the past and his vantage point was horticulture, not landscape architecture.

Gardening and horticulture in California

California had obediently adopted all the orthodox designs, one after another. The climate and soil lend themselves to growing almost any type of ornamental or food plant, provided enough water is supplied. In the two hundred and thirty years since Europeans and their descendants took up permanent residence in this territory, gardens have flourished.

Nothing could have appeared to be more unpromising at the outset. The initial residents, missionaries and soldiers, faced enormous difficulties just to stay alive. A tour of duty in Alta California was regarded with the same degree of enthusiasm as being transported to Siberia. Obtaining food was the sole priority in worldly matters. No one gave a thought to ornamental horticulture at that stage.

Influence of the Franciscan missionaries

When the pioneers landed, they brought seed for growing food and small rooted plants from Baja California. The Franciscans led the way, but as more colonists arrived, they too brought a little favorite plant material with them.

The idea of cultivating the soil deliberately to grow food, rather than simply foraging for it, is not thought to have arisen among the native population before the Europeans arrived.

Some anthropologists believe that native people had cared for fertile segments in their terrain, fostering the growth of prized food plants in some way, but the evidence for this is slim and conjectural. The missionaries had to work very hard to transmit the idea of daily, repetitive toil in the fields and orchards to the somewhat unwilling people they rounded up for that job.

The few reports left by visitors who reached California before 1800 or soon afterwards indicate that apart from the Franciscan missionaries, almost none of the Spanish citizens living in Alta California grew much beside corn and beans. As soldiers retired onto the land awarded them by the King of Spain, they relied on the natives for the hard labor of digging, watering, weeding and all the other essential tasks that go with tilling the soil. There was nothing to spare for flowers one could not eat.

Limited incomes and a diminution in the numbers of natives due to the deadly diseases introduced by the Spaniards strained the capacity to grow food and meant that they only grew the bare minimum, but Spanish culture abhorred the idea that a soldier should demean his caste by stooping to agricultural tasks. Such work had to be done by someone else.

Some visitors commented on tiny flower gardens maintained by the women. The soldiers' wives often brought a rose of Castile or a favorite vine with them. Water was scarce and had to be applied by hand. This difficulty probably deterred people more than anything else, yet Spanish women were so devoted to the church they overcame their concern about wasting water. It was a sacred duty to adorn the altar with flowers

It is hard to cast one's mind back to the time before vast irrigation projects changed the face of California for ever. Much of the land was uncompromising desert. Cattle raising and cereal growing supported the missionary enterprises. Neither of these required intentional irrigation. They survived completely on natural sources of water.

The Franciscans watered their table vegetables by hand. They grew gourds specifically to use as watering cans. A few of the missions had an irrigation system, usually just simple dams and ditches *(zanjas)*. The Franciscan monk in charge of the crops at Mission San Buena Ventura was an engineer and he created a more elaborate irrigation system. Theodosia Burr Shpeherd, a pioneer in growing flowers for seed in Ventura, recorded the day in the 1870s that the original aqueduct was repaired for the use of the town.

In spite of the difficulties there were beautiful flowers and shrubs as well as fruit in the mission gardens.This seeming paradox, stringent survival conditions and blooming missions, is due to confusion about the topography of the missions and the way time passed. The true mission gardens were sited away from the main buildings, enclosed and carefully cultivated separately. It was almost fifteen years after they settled in Alta California that the Franciscans turned to growing fruit. Flowers were also late in coming.

The Franciscans built the missions in the style they knew best, an amalgam of Moorish and Christian architecture. Many of the priests came from the island of Mallorca, others from Andalusia. They had to adapt their designs to the sites and territory in the new country. Some of them had been in Baja California and had seen the missions there, laid out by Spanish and Italian Jesuits. In all of them a central courtyard and axial pathways were the hallmarks of their outdoor design.

Anachronism due to restoration

At first, the central quadrangles were completely bare. The lovely plantings seen currently in the reconstructed missions are a concession to modern sensibilites and notions of old world charm. The central courtyard was needed for daily activities. Native men cooked there, ate there, consuming the *pozole* (stew) out of huge troughs, learned trades there, and did penance there while women did the spinning and weaving. There was no need to make such a place beautiful.

The priests later built completely separate enclosed gar-

dens with orchard trees and attractive shrubs. Adobe walls or
dense cactus hedges formed the enclosures, keeping out domestic and wild animals and any human marauders. Fragments
of these structures still survive in a few places. For example, a
recent archaelogical expedition unearthed a fragment of the
garden wall at Mission San Buenaventura. Flowers grew here,
shaded by olive trees or pepper trees along the geometric walks.
Quiet constitutionals among the scented blossoms were permitted as a way the fathers could take a brief break from their
busy schedule.

California annexed to the United States

More and more civilians took up residence in California as
it separated itself first from Spain, and then from Mexico. By
the treaty of Guadalupe y Hidalgo in 1848, it became a province of the United States. The towns and villages expanded,
slowly at first and then exponentially with the advent of the
gold rush. The Mexican government had dispossessed the missionaries in 1834, taking over their lands and reducing the
Franciscan monks simply to parish priests with minute sections of their great estates around the church buildings. Some
priests almost starved to death in this phase. The once flourishing and lovely missions decayed inexorably.

The new citizens needed somewhere to live. For many it
was a tent or roughly built shack. Some knew how to make
adobe. There were very few commercial sources of milled lumber to build anything much more elaborate. John Sutter's lumber mill was a new idea at the time, but it was derailed by
finding the gold in the mill race. Eventually, the money the
miners earned enabled them to import better materials and
indigenous industry followed very quickly.

Gold rush in 1848

There were modest attempts to create a garden even in the gold country, but essentially nothing of that remains today. The gold rush made an enormous change in the demographics of California. "Anglos", an omnibus term which included northern Europeans such as French and Germans at that time, became the dominant group. They had a tradition of gardening, and fewer inhibitions about physical labor than their Hispanic predecessors. Food always took precedence, so planting orchards and vineyards came first, but ornamental horticulture was not far behind. In some cases, the now dilapidated mission ochards and gardens supplied plant material to develop new holdings.

The modern California olive industry started with cuttings taken from Mission Santa Barbara and Mission San Diego. Peach, pear and apple trees were also grown from mission seeds and cuttings, as were grape vines. Vineyards and wine making also developed initially from the mission stock.

Tools

The immigrants also brought something else with them, beside plants and skill. They brought tools. Unlike other civilizations which gradually evolved and developed the tools they needed, the builders of America in general and California in particular came armed with the basic equipment. Indigenous people used digging sticks and other objects which came to hand. The immigrants had forged iron or steel tools which improved their productivity and enabled newcomers to cover a lot more ground.

Rise of commercial agriculture and horticulture

Ten years after the California gold rush had peaked and begun to decline, the authorities realized that the state needed new industries and resources to feed and employ all the new residents. Agriculture and horticulture were two important ways to do this. The California

State Agricultural Society was chartered in 1854 and began work in the late 1850s. The California State Board of Horticulture was created later.

The Vallejo family had made a small start even before the great influx. General Mariano Vallejo's brother Jesus had bought the old Mission San Jose from the Mexican government in 1835. He employed an emigrant from New England, E. L. Beard, to manage it. Beard saw an opportunity and soon branched out on his own. He opened a store in the town and set about improving on the peaches inherited from the mission by getting different varieties sent from home. The new peaches were a success and he made money.

Nurseries arise

Nurseries supplying both food and ornamental plants arose soon after the gold rush. The first professional nurseryman to come to California was Colonel J. L. L. Warren. He came and stayed briefly in 1849, bringing with him a proper nursery catalogue from Massachusetts. In 1850, he and one of his sons came back to settle permanently. Warren transformed horticulture in California by his knowledge and energy.

One year later, in 1851, another energetic Easterner, A. P. Smith, opened a nursery near Sacramento. He devoted it to shrubs and flowers. The Lewelling brothers, who had taken the first grafted fruit trees to Oregon in 1847, later brought some of their stock to California. Henderson Lewelling settled in Oakland and is buried there.

Garden development in California

Spanish settlers in the old coast cities such as Monterey and Santa Barbara created gardens based on their memory of life at home. Landscape architects built on those styles, embellishing them according to the wealth and desires of their clients. A.E. Hanson, Florence Yoch, Peter Thiene, Charles Gibb Adams and other notable landscape architects of the 1920s and 1930s worked in a variety of styles all deriving from their view of the "Mediterranean" garden.

After the second world war, servicemen re-entered civilian life. They wanted to marry and raise families and needed houses in which to live. Huge housing developments were built, some planned as communities, some simply allowed to sprawl unchecked. Fashion and necessity merged to bring forth thousands of houses built on an industrial scale, the tiny gardens echoing some shred of Church or Eckbo's work.

Water-sparing gardening

Within the last thirty years, the California garden has undergone another major change, not so much in its design but rather in its plant content. Recurrent droughts had focused the public's attention very forcefully on the chronic shortage of water. At last, the public recognized that lush green lawns and huge "water-guzzling" gardens were irresponsible.

Community leaders began very slowly to adopt the idea of "xerophytic" gardens, spaces planted with native California flowers and shrubs, adapted over millenia to the Mediterranean climate with its annual cycle of rain and dry weather approximately every six months. The trend is still not universal, but such a garden no longer looks bizarre or out of place.

Harry Butterfield did not really take part in either of these two revolutions. His work covers California's gardens from the beginning in about 1780 until 1960.

Harry Morton Butterfield

Harry Morton Butterfield was born in Wilsonville, Nebraska in 1887, the second of eleven children. His mother chose the middle name Morton in honor of the secretary of agriculture at the time. A few years later, they all moved to Orange County in southern California. His father started growing citrus fruit. At first they lived in a tent and later in a sod house. The fruit growing was not a financial success, but the family sustained itself with considerable inner strength. This comes through obliquely in his opening chapter, touching on his own childhood. (Figure 1)

Figure 1 Harry Morton Butterfield as a young man
(Reproduced by permission of Dorothy Butterfield Rucker)

Harry and his elder brother took turns to go to high school in Long Beach, each alternating a year of work with a year of classes. Both graduated, but only Harry went on to college, at the University of California at Berkeley in 1914. He concentrated on the natural sciences, incorporating his love of the outdoors in his studies. Once he was graduated, he worked for a time as a groundsman, but later found the resources to return to college to specialize in horticulture. He obtained a master's degree in pomology.

Just after the end of the first world war, he obtained a position in the University of California cooperative extension service. He served as a "specialist" in that department until he retired. Some of the pamphlets he wrote were extremely popular, such as "Home Floriculture in California". For years he went everywhere on foot, but did eventually buy a model T car.

During the second world war, he concentrated on helping the public grow vegetables successfully. Once the war was over and the food supply was no longer threatened, he picked up his work in ornamental gardening. One of his contributions was the nomenclature for begonias. A few years later, he began to publish the results of his historical research in California horticultural journals.

Butterfield was a loyal member of the California Gardens Clubs Inc, and served on its board for many years. One of his gifts to that group was a succinct pamphlet explaining how to judge the entries at an amateur flower show.

After he retired and his wife had died, he bravely kept his spirits up by working assiduously in his own and his family's gardens. He also wrote this book. One day, after he had worked in the garden all morning and had come in for some lunch, he lay down on his bed for a nap. He never woke up. His daughter was disturbed because he did not answer the phone. She called the family doctor. The doctor went to the house and found Harry Butterfield dead, still wearing his overalls.

Judith M. Taylor

NOTE

Botanical nomenclature has changed considerably in the period since Harry Butterfield was working. The plant names in this text date from his epoch and have not been changed to the modern terminology.

HARRY M. BUTTERFIELD'S PREFACE

The story of many California gardens and their treasured memories is told here for the first time. It is hoped this record covering plants, places, and people will serve as a progress report. Many additional details need to be filled in and perhaps certain statements corrected to cover the facts more adequately, but at least a first step has been taken in the history of ornamental horticulture in California. Documentary evidence supplied by early papers, reports, letters, old nursery catalogs, and other references forms the basis for most of the story. Many old gardens still furnish living evidence.

The writer has had a rare opportunity to study the available literature and follow the footsteps of the pioneers as they developed garden history. Readers may wish to visit the actual gardens and share in this pleasure. If this is not possible, at least the story of gardens of yester years and their treasures can still provide inspiration.

Berkeley, California
1968

Harry Morton Butterfield later in life
(Reproduced by permission of Dorothy Butterfield Rucker)

CHAPTER 1

Early San Francisco Gardens

Harry Butterfield was able to trace gardens back to the days before the gold rush when there were only a few hundred people in San Francisco. He went about his work of reconstructing a very particular sort of history, that of gardens and horticulture, by first setting the scene, grounding it in the larger, general history of the period. We are introduced to the *dramatis personae*, and only then is there a discussion of trees, shrubs and flowers etc.

Essentially nothing is left of the early residences but the information that they existed. One key character was William Leidsdorff. He was the first known African-American entrepreneur to inhabit the village and among the earliest Americans of any kind to take root. He ran a successful business but is significant to this story because he had a garden.

Quoting from Butterfield's original work: 'San Francisco has gardens that date back to Yerba Buena and the Spanish. Potatoes grew at the Portsmouth Square site as early as 1833. Jacob Leese put up the first building at Dupont (now Grant Street) between Clay and Ward in 1836. At that time San Francisco Bay came within two hundred and fifty yards of the location. A small inlet of the Bay pierced Montgomery at Jackson so Montgomery was really the waterfront. The bay receded to the north and barely reached Montgomery at Chestnut.'

William A. Leidsdorff's home faced the Plaza on Kearny near Clay Street, now Portsmouth Square. (Note 1) His was the only house in town with a garden in the eighteen forties. (Figure 2)

Figure 2 Portsmouth Square 1892
(Photograph by Eadweard Muybridge Reproduced by permission of
the California Historical Society)

Going past the other houses and dwellings where the Hudson
Bay Company, Nathan Spear, Captain Hinckley, Captain John J.
Vioget, and others carried on their business, one reached the port
very quickly.

Butterfield then introduced the Gillespies. In 1848 the
clippership *Eagle* arrived from Canton in China. Among other passengers, this ship carried the Gillespie family. Mr. and Mrs. Charles
V. Gillespie, accompanied by one Chinese and one Irish servant,
landed at the dock. They were destined to make important contributions to their new home. Charles Gillespie was about thirty

eight years old and Sarah was thirty three. They had no children. Their arrival coincided with the start of the gold rush.

Gardens may not immediately come into one's mind when thinking about the gold rush. San Francisco was filled with men of all nationalities, there was a lot of crime and violence, and the streets were no more than mud tracks. No sooner was a house or store put up than it burned down. Gardens do not fit into the stereotypes we have of the period, and yet there were many of them.

Sarah Gillespie was an expert gardener. Once settled in her house on Chestnut Street she created a garden in which she introduced new plants to California. We must remember that at this date Robert Fortune had only just returned from his first visit to China to collect plants. Up until that time only a small trickle of Chinese plants had been received in the West. It would be fifty years before the very well-known Ernest ("Chinese") Wilson travelled to China for the first time. If Sarah Gillespie had been a different sort of woman, and not restricted by the *mores* of her time, she might have become quite prominent for her horticultural achievements.

Her husband, C. V. Gillespie, a very worthy soul, served as managing assistant to M. D. M. Howard, Leidsdorff's estate manager. Gillespie was very public-spirited, serving as an inspector of elections in 1848 and in 1853. In 1855 he was on one of the Vigilante Committees. His paper on conditions in San Francisco in 1848 is on file in the Bancroft Library of the University of California, but although Mr. Gillespie was a pioneer of note, he has been eclipsed in history by his wife.

By 1853, or perhaps even earlier, Mrs Gillespie was devoting a lot of time to her greenhouse. One is struck by the amazing speed with which Mrs Gillespie's greenhouse was constructed in the San Francisco of the day. All building materials were in very short supply, and even if they had been plentiful, almost all ablebodied workingmen had gone off to the gold fields. Perhaps the servants built it for her.

Mrs Gillespie is said to have planted the first Australian acacias raised from seed in California. Colonel Warren had grown acacias from seed many years before in Massachusetts but he gave credit to Mrs. Gillespie for being the first person to grow seedling acacias in California.

She also noticed the changes occurring in her adopted city. Families with children were starting to settle there. In 1864 she began what may have been the first Sunday School in the city. Sarah Gillespie was a capable and effective woman.

First state flower show in California

A flower fair opened on Friday morning, October 7, 1853, according to the *Daily Alta California*. Mrs. Gillespie entered some flowers as did Colonel J.L. Warren, of Sacramento. Among the plants she exhibited in 1853 was *Passiflora alata*, one of the passion flowers. (Butterfield's list of plants introduced into California does not mention *P. alata* nor does it appear in his 1964 compilation. The latter list has half a dozen other passion flowers. One of them arrived in 1854, the others twenty years later. He overlooked Mrs Gillespie too.)

The next year, at the same flower show, she exhibited fourteen kinds of fuchsias, fourteen geraniums, ten calceolarias, six acacias, two camellias, and many other ornamentals, a total of a hundred and eight kinds, as listed by Colonel Warren in his *California Farmer* at the time. Everyone of these was an exotic, imported from somewhere else.

No one else came anywhere near her volume of entries. She was probably assisted in the heavy work by her servants, but the Chinese man might also have supplied some of the horticultural knowledge and skill.

In 1856 the Gillespies were living at the corner of Clementia and Second but two years later they moved to the northwest corner of Kearney and Chestnut. Mr. Gillespie was an attorney and later served as a searcher of records. Butterfield assumed he had to move frequently because of his work.

After her dazzling debut Mrs. Gillespie disappeared from the public scene as a gardener. She was still alive as late as 1895. Maybe Mr Gillespie was threatened by her success and "put his foot down", but more probably, money was in short supply. Gardening is an expensive hobby. It is tantalizing to know so very little about a wonderful woman.

Figure 3 Colonel James Lafayette Warren 1805-1896
Unknown artist (Reproduced by permission of the Regents of the
University of California)

Colonel Warren

Colonel James Lafayette Warren was a most remarkable man who deserves some comment. (Figure 3)

He came from Massachusetts, the first professional nursery-man in California at the time of the gold rush. His California career had several "firsts": issuing the first nursery catalog in California while living in Sacramento in 1853 and starting the first agricultural and garden paper in the state, the *California Farmer* , in San Francisco in 1854. (Note 2) This paper was later taken over by the *Pacific Rural Express* but the original name of the *California Farmer* has been resumed under new editors.

Warren (1805–1896) arrived in California on the "Sweden" on August 6, 1849. He soon moved from San Francisco to Sacramento. As a young man of twenty he had been the sergeant and guard of honor for Lafayette at the laying of the corner stone for the Bunker Hill Monument at Boston in 1825, but later adopted horticulture as his life work. He received a prize from the Massachusetts Horticultural Society for growing the first tomato in Massachusetts.

Between 1830 and 1845 Warren ran the "Nonanum Vale Gardens" at Brighton, not far from Boston, Massachusetts. He traveled in Europe at the time of the Irish Famine and met famous men of his day. Traveler, lecturer, and horticulturist, Colonel Warren naturally heard about the discovery of gold in California. His family consisted of four daughters and a son. Together with his son he established the Warren and Son's Garden and Nurseries at 15 J. St., Sacramento.

The Warrens issued their first nursery catalog in 1853. At least two copies of this catalog have been saved, one in the Bancroft Library of the University of California in Berkeley and the other owned by Mrs. Gerald D. Kennedy, who inherited it from her grandfather, Charles Weber of Stockton.

Colonel Warren had listed five species of Australian acacias at his nursery near Boston as early as 1843. In 1853 He had *Acacia armata, A. decurrens* var. *dealbata, A. longifolia,* and variety, *flori-*

bunda. He did not mention the eucalyptus in his 1853 catalog. He had many other Australian plants, such as *Sollva heterophylla, Correa alba, Epacris, Callistemon citrinus,* and *Pimelia decussata.* Special mention might be given to *Agapanthus, Aucuba japonica,* calla, *Camellia japonica, Erythrina crista-galli, Ficus elastica, Fuchsia coccinea, F. magellanica* var. *globosa, Gardenia florida (G. jasminoides), Syzygium jambos (Eugenia jambos), Pittosporum tobira* (as *P. chinensis), Plumbago capensis, Strelitzia reginae* (as *S. ovata*), *Sparaxis tricolor, Tecoma capensis (Tecomaria capensis),* Carolina Yellow Jasmine, *Amaryllis belladonna* (now *Brunsvigia rosea), Ipomoe learii, Lachenalia tricolor, Passiflora edulis, P. alata,* and *P. quadrangularis,* tree peonies, azaleas, and Lisbon lemon. Colonel Warren offered the Lisbon lemon at his nursery at Brighton, MA, as early as 1844. This remained a popular variety in Santa Barbara County.

Once in San Francisco Warren established the *California Farmer* in 1854. It was the first magazine of its kind in California. Baker and Hamilton later took over his store in Sacramento. Colonel Warren had a very broad vision of how horticulture should be conducted and was far ahead of his day. The State Fair which he helped organize is still flourishing. In time the *California Farmer* was merged with *Pacific Rural Press.* The original name has now been restored.

It is not surprising to find a list of hardy ornamental plants common in the eastern states in the 1853 catalog. He had many roses of his day, such as Chromotella, Lamarque, Gold of Ophir, Persian Yellow, Double Yellow Harrison, Sweet Briar, and both the white and yellow Banksia roses.

Warren insisted on the state creating a horticultural board and agricultural commission. He stitched the first linen bag to pack California wheat. California's state fairs sprang from his concern about fostering high quality crops. No task was beneath him. He was the sole staff of the *California Farmer.* That included sweeping the floor, setting the type and binding the issues.

When he died at the age of ninety four, he left behind an extraordinary collection of curiosities and fine memorabilia. The earthquake and fire in 1906 destroyed these treasures.

San Francisco emerges from Yerba Buena

Yerba Buena became San Francisco in 1847, while Washington Bartlett was the first Alcalde under American rule. At that time the population was said to be four hundred and fifty nine. After gold was discovered in California it drew people from all parts of the globe, or as J. S. Holliday put it so vividly, "The world rushed in". (2) San Francisco became a huge melting pot, as we shall see when speaking of nurserymen and gardeners a few years later.

By that time San Francisco was already losing its quiet Mexican character. The rapid rise in population and lack of any established authority allowed criminals and grafters to cause trouble in 1851 and again five years later. Alcohol, greed and prejudice against foreigners were very potent stimuli for crime and misdemeanors. A bell on the old Memorial Fire Company summoned the vigilantes.

The original overland stagecoach, usually known as the Butterfield Stage, took about three weeks to come from St. Louis by way of Los Angeles, covering a distance of a little over 2,600 miles. (Note 3) The first one reached Los Angeles on October 7 and San Francisco on October 10, 1858. At that time Los Angeles was much smaller than San Francisco.

The exciting, short-lived pony express first reached Sacramento in 1860 and the mail was relayed to San Francisco from there. The first street car started on Market Street in 1860 but the cable cars on Clay Street did not come until 1873.

Life was not easy even after money began flowing freely. There was still no direct route between California and the Eastern United States. Communications were slow. In San Francisco the citizens gathered twice a month at the wharf on steamer days to get mail and Eastern papers. A telegraph line between Telegraph Hill (Alta Loma) and Point Lobos in 1853 announced the arrival of ships.

Development of horticulture in San Francisco

Progress in importing ornamental plants was made very rapidly. The population of San Francisco grew to about 25,000 in 1849. A year later some 40,000 more people arrived. This sort of population growth lead to a need for housing. Gardens were the natural accompaniment of the houses.

Professional horticulture already had a long history in the rest of the United States. Nurserymen had had wide experience abroad, as well as in other parts of the United States, and it is not strange that San Francisco, glittering with newly acquired wealth, should be among the first to be filled with rare plant treasures.

Nurseries in California started slowly and tentatively, with A.P. Smith and Colonel Warren in Sacramento. Over the next twenty five years, they increased at an almost geometrical rate as the cities grew mightily. By the late 1870s, there were over a hundred and twenty nurseries in the state.

Early San Francisco Nurseries

Successful miners and their suppliers who had made even more money began to build houses and gardens in San Francisco and surrounding areas as early as the 1850s. Florists and nurserymen began arriving in 1849 and 1850. Until then there were no nurseries as we think of them today. This situation changed quickly.

On January 3, 1854 the *Daily Alta California* carried this advertisement: "Camellias, japonicas and cut flowers of the choicest kinds always on hand. Private gardens and pleasure grounds laid out, ornamented, and kept in order by practical gardener. Flowering plants, ornamental shrubs and shade trees for sale at the greenhouse and nursery, corner of Fourth and Folsom Streets, adjoining the toll house or at store, No. 70 Washington Street." (The japonicas were probably Japanese Quince).

Learning the identity of the nurseryman offering these services was a challenge. Harry Butterfield found that it was one William Connell Walker. He owned a nursery at Fourth and Folsom, the Golden Gate Nursery, and it was he who had inserted the advertisement. This lot is now the home of the Society of California Pioneers, a most fitting transition.

Figure 4 Lone Mountain Cemetery ca. 1854
Lithograph by Kuchell and Dressel
(Reproduced by permission of the California Historical Society)

William Connell Walker

At that time Mr. Walker was a man of forty. He had been an attorney in the southern states before coming to California in 1849. In a few years he became famous as an importer of Australian ornamentals, in fact, perhaps the most famous such importer California has ever had.

Butterfield found Walker's biography, also copies of his initial nursery catalogs and a master copy of the 1858 catalog in presumably his own handwriting. This gave sources of plant materials, plus a check list of his roses added later, naming between four hundred and five hundred roses.

The reader may wonder how it is possible to discover information about the plant materials used in the early California gardens. William Walker can be used as an illustration. The sequence of events was as follows.

During this phase of his work Butterfield was looking up the history of the deodar cedar in California. The *California Farmer* in 1859 noted that this cedar was planted in Lone Mountain Cemetery (Laurel Hill). Cemeteries often contained interesting plantings in early San Francisco, such as those at Lone Mountain (Laurel Hill) Cemetery. (Figure 4)

Mountain View cemetery in Piedmont was perhaps the first one in California to copy the idea of cemetery as park like the one in Mount Auburn, Cambridge, Masachusetts. It had twenty kinds of ornamental trees there before 1860. The Deodar cedar was among them. A beautiful hawthorn tree, *Crataegus pubescens* var. *stipulacea* was imported from Mexico and planted there by Don Vicente Oviedo in 1868 in memory of his son. Other rare plants may also have been planted there.

Butterfield did not know exactly where Lone Mountain cemetery had been and he asked Alice Eastwood of the California Academy of Sciences in Golden Gate Park. She could not say where it was either. (This land no longer serves as a cemetery. First a convent was built nearby, then the University of San Francisco took it over as its Lone Mountain campus.)

Alice Eastwood was a truly remarkable woman. She was an expert professional botanist at a time when most women were still rather dilletantish, and was keeper of the herbarium at the Academy of Science. Her favorite pastime was climbing in the remote hills, looking for undiscovered plants.

During the great earthquake of 1906, at great personal risk, she saved the Academy's priceless collection. Even though the building was perilously damaged, she persisted in executing the plan she had prepared in case such an earthquake struck.

Miss Eastwood told Butterfield she did have an old nursery catalog from the 1850s listing the deodar cedar. This catalog turned out to be manuscript version of the 1858 nursery catalog of the Golden Gate Nursery in San Francisco. This was no ordinary catalog but a master document in what is assumed to be William C. Walker's own handwriting. (The California Historical Society now has this valuable list.)

The handwritten copy had been used to issue the printed edition but it too been saved. The manuscript list contained later entries from 1859, such as where seeds and plants had been ordered. There was a check list of Walker's roses and a list of persons to whom the catalog had been sent. Such information meant far more than an ordinary printed catalog. For the first time there was incontroverible evidence clearly showing the sources of plant materials in California.

Walker noted that he had imported Australian seeds from a certain M. Guilfoyle of Sydney, Australia. Butterfield was curious about M. Guilfoyle. One day when he was reading a book on the eucalyptus by William R. Guilfoyle, former director of the Melbourne Botanical Garden in Australia, it occurred to him that William Guilfoyle might be a relative of the earlier M. Guilfoyle. Butterfield decided to write to the director of the Melbourne Garden. William R. Guilfoyle had died in 1912

The director replied that Michael Guilfoyle had been William C. Guilfoyle's father. The director also forwarded a copy of a letter from Mrs. Agnes Black, daughter, and only surviving child of M. Guilfoyle, then in her late eighties. She related how her father had gone from England to Sydney in 1852 and settled in the suburbs where he started the Double Bay Nursery. She also reported how her brother, William Guilfoyle, had scoured the country for seeds and plants. These were then cultivated in the father's nursery.

William C. Walker had obtained the address and had imported both seeds and plants from M. Guilfoyle. Eucalyptus, acacia, and other plants were imported. Mr. Walker was among the first to introduce the eucalyptus into California, having had it at his nursery by 1856. We now know where he got it, also how he happened to have so many rare plants from Australia.

In another thread of this story, Butterfield's hobby of collecting old nursery catalogs published in California led to him setting up a display at one of the California Spring Garden Shows in Oakland. While he working at the show one day Butterfield noticed a young lady paying a lot of attention to the old garden publications. He spoke to her and found out that she had been settling an estate of her aunt. Among the aunt's papers were many agricultural clippings and some old nursery catalogs.

It transpired that the old nursery catalogs had been collected by the young lady's grandfather, Captain Charles Weber, founder of the city of Stockton. Weber had started to collect the catalogues in the eighteen fifties and continued until his death in 1881. His only daughter had preserved the collection and added others.

Buttefield went to see the nursery catalogs with his new friend, Mrs. Gerald D. Kennedy, Weber's granddaughter. The collection contained copies of William C. Walker's catalogs for 1858, 1859, 1860, and several other editions. Walker's advertisement in the *California Farmer* stated that he had seventy kinds of acacias in 1860. Now it was possible to learn what these seventy varieties were. Mrs Kennedy was a devoted member of the San Francisco Garden Club.

Harry Butterfield continued to make chance work to his advantage by a combination of curiosity and perserverence. He spotted relevant information at such seemingly superficial events as flower shows.

Flower show, 1854

Butterfield found ornamental plants listed at the 1854 flower show in San Francisco reported in the *California Farmer* that he considered modern introductions. Mortimer Ryan from the Simpson Thompson nursery near Suscol in Napa County entered *Celosia cristata* in this show. General M. G. Vallejo of Sonoma hung grapes in festoons for decorations and exhibited several fruit varieties. Joseph Aram of San Jose exhibited two squashes weighing sixty five and seventy eight pounds respectively. More will be said about these people later in the book.

James Saul worked at the Commercial Nurseries at Folsom and Centre Streets, representing Charles Downing's Highland Nursery in Newburgh, New York. He helped to decorate the room. (Center Street is now 16th street.) Mrs.E L Beard and Nellie Ellsworth also came up from Mission San Jose to help. E. L. Beard had taken over the old mission orchard in San Jose and grew Australian acacia as early as 1855.

William C. Walker displayed seven kinds of fuchsias, as well as *Acacia decurrens* var. *dealbata, Acacia verticillata, Mannetia cordifolia, Abutilon striatum, Lilium longiflorum (L. lanceolatum)*, agapanthus, poinsettia, eighteen varieties of carnations, twenty varieties of dahlias, two ivy geranium, six scented geraniums, *Crassula coccinea (Rochea coccinea), Calliandra tweedii (Inga pulcherrima), Datura suaveolens* and *D. knightii, Eccremocarpus scaber, Clyanthus puniceus, Cestrum elegans,* Australian Pea Vine, *Callistemon citrinus, Azalea indica, Pittosporum undulatum,* twelve kinds of sweet violets, twenty three Chinese primroses, eleven flowering verbenas, a Lady Hume camellia, and *Begonia manicata,* in other words almost exactly what one may expect to find in a modern flower show. Many modern gardeners may find it hard to believe, yet the report in the *California Farmer* for 1854 leaves little in doubt.

A full review of all William C. Walker's ornamental plants in the years between 1858 and 1865 is not possible in this story .There is only room for a few highlights of his plant introductions. (See Appendix A)

Walker had 20,000 choice plants in pots by 1859 so when we see his list of greenhouse plants in 1858 we are not surprised except for some of the species: *Abelia triflora, Datura cornigera, Bletilla striata, Cestrum aurantiacum, C. diaurnum, C. nocturnum, Chorizema varium, Cypropedium insignis, Cereus speciossissimus (Heliocereus speciosus), Aporocactus flagelliformis, Zygocactus truncatus, Daphne odora, Eupatorium glabratum, Gardenia florida, Calliandra tweedii, Lantana, Plumbago capensis, Ruellia formosa, Tecomaria capensis,* and others.

The list of conifers in 1858 at the Golden Gate Nursery was very impressive: *Picea excelsa, Cedrus libani, C. deodara,* nine species of pines, and *Sequoia gigantea (Wellingtonia gigantea).* It is quite surprising to find these trees growing more than a hundred years ago in California.

Among the acacias listed were *Acacia armata, A. dodonaefolia, A. melanoxylon,* and *A. vestita.* Walker had a note on his list to get *Acacia pubescens* in a Wardian case for 1859. In that year he also received seeds of *Acacia cultriformis, A. dealbata* var. *mollis.* After some entries he noted "not in Paxton" (Paxton's Botanical Dictionary, 1849). (3) This would be like a present-day horticulturist saying, "not in Hortus II", a leading academic reference source. Evidently Walker tried to become acquainted with the new plants he imported.

Other seeds imported by Walker in 1858-59 are quite surprising for that day. There were five species of *Banksia, Cryptomeria japonica,*

Podocarpus spinulosa, Lagunaria patersoni, Araucaria excelsa, Dorvanthes excelsa, Melaleuca hypericifolia, H. ericifolia, Grevillea robusta, Phormium tenax, Eucalyptus globulus, E. robusta, Ficus macrophylla, Callistemon lanceolatus, Sutherlandia frutescens, Billardiera longiflora, and *Hardenbergia comptoniana.*

Additional seeds planted that year in California included the California Nutmeg Tree (*Torreya californica*), *Libocedrus decurrens,* and *Chamaecyparis lawsonia.* What nurseryman a hundred years later listed so many fine ornamental plants?

William Walker offered Bermuda grass for $5 a flat in his 1858 catalog, unaware of the threat it would pose in the future. Most likely he obtained seed from O. C. Wheeler, Secretary of the California State Agricultural Society. Wheeler had received it in 1856 from the East Indian Agricultural Society. Bermuda grass continues to be planted as a lawn grass but it is far from an unmixed blessing.

In 1860 Walker offered seventy kinds of acacias but some of these are now considered to be part of *Albizzia* or allied genera. He did have the great majority of acacias available in California at the present time. In that year he also had a few rare plants, such as *Tabebuia rosea* (*Tecoma rosea*), *Eucalyptus piperita, Escallonia floribunds, Garrya eliptica, Ficus lucida,* Camphor Tree, *Hakea saligna,* and *Plumbago indica.* In 1861 he added *Eugenia myrtifolia* (as many list the species), the strawberry guava, Cherimoya, tamarind, and coffee tree.

James and William O'Donnell

The O'Donnell Brothers, James and William, ran the United States Nursery just a block west of the Golden Gate Nursery, at Fifth and Folsom. At the 1854 flower show they exhibited thirteen kinds of camellias, thirteen fuchsias, and four varieties of acacias.

By 1856 two of the acacias were so beautiful that they were sold for $25 each. In that same year William O'Donnell decided to move to San Jose where he established the Mountain View Nursery on William Street. In 1858 James O'Donnell received first prize for the best flower garden in California, awarded by the State Agricultural Society. He also had the best exhibit of roses and dahlias at the State Fair that year.

Juan Centre

John Center ("Juan Centre") near Mission Dolores, just off Folsom in early days, ran his business, the Commercial Nursery, at the corner of Folsom and 16th Streets. Mr. Center became president of the Mission Dolores Plank Road Company in 1858. He had leased his conservatory to O'Hara and Company the year before. (Figure 5)

Figure 5 Juan Centre (Hispanicized version of John Center)
(Reproduced by permission of the California Historical Society)

Dahlias from Center's garden had been exhibited at the 1854 flower show. His nursery served as agent for the Highland Nurseries of Newburgh, New York. Butterfield had a copy of the Highland Nurseries' catalog for 1854 with the name of the Commercial Nursery printed on the cover and with the name of James Saul (1828–1881), as agent. Saul, an Irishman, represented the Highland Nurseries at the Commercial Nursery from about 1854 until 1858. (Note 4) He then moved to Sacramento and worked for A. P. Smith. Saul died at Davis (Davisville), California, and was buried in the old Catholic Cemetery there.

This old catalog listed such ornamentals as *Cotoneaster microphylla, C. rotundifolia, C. thymifolia, Ailanthus altissima*, gingko, and *Salix babylonica* var. *crispa (S. annularis* or Ring-leaved Willow).

Henry Sonntag

Henry Sonntag and Company ran the Pacific Nursery on 16th Street above Mission Dolores in 1854 and continued to do that for a few years. Henry Sonntag was noted for his roses and shrubs. His nursery was sometimes called the "Garden of Roses." He exhibited Lamarque, Solitaire, Hermosa, Sofrano, Agrippina, Giant of Battles, and even the green rose (*Rosa chinensis* var. *viridiflora*) at the 1854 flower show. In 1865 Mr. Sonntag sold two pounds of *Sequoia (Sequoiadendron) gigantea* seed in Germany at the rate of $125 a pound, indicating the sort of demand California nurserymen were helping to meet.

Miller and Sievers

Frederick A. Miller of Miller and Sievers, had a nursery opposite Woodward's Gardens on Mission Street between 13th and 14th Streets. There were ten greenhouses, each a hundred feet long. (Note 5) His main conservatory was a hundred and twenty feet by a hundred and thirty feet and contained fine palms, tree ferns, and the water lily, *Victoria regia*. (Figure 6)

Figure 6 Cover of Miller and Sievers' catalog ca. 1880
(Reproduced by permission of the Society of California Pioneers)

The tree ferns included *Cibotium chamissoi, C. glaucum, C. menziesii,* and *Dicksonia antartica,* according to an early listing. There were over two hundred kinds of fern in the fern houses. One greenhouse was devoted to camellias, azaleas, and rhododendrons. Another house contained seventy five varieties of palm. Miller and

Sievers offered roses, carnations, gardenias, heliotrope, camellias, bouvarida, orange blossom, *Hova carnosa*, and ferns for greens as cut flowers.

Miller was a very enterprising man. He exhibited in the Bay District Flower Show in 1872. In 1873 he imported such varieties of cacti as *Epiphyllum album violaceum*, and *E. ruckerianum*, in several separate colors. These were all probably hybrids and not entitled to species rank. As late as 1910 Miller was wholesaling tree and shrub seeds in Fruitvale, a part of present Oakland.

S. W. Moore

S. W. Moore of 110 California Street between Sansome and Montgomery started a nursery in 1850 and by 1862 was listing such bulbs as *Lapeyrousia cruenta* (Anomatheca), *Antholyza aethiopica, Lachenalia, Scilla perviana*, and nine kinds of amaryllis. (Note 6) These initial San Francisco dealers deserve great credit for their early importations.

The rich opportunity to supply the owners of fine houses and estates in early San Francisco encouraged the development of three types of dealers: the well-established nurseryman who grew most of his plants, the dealer who worked on a margin and grew little of what he sold, and the third kind who might have had a tramp steamer loading up rare plants at some foreign port and brought them to San Francisco to sell at auction.

James Welch

A good example of the third type of dealer was James Welch in the Exchange Building on Washington near Battery. (Note 7) He advertised a shipment from New South Wales in 1865. A few of the outstanding plants imported at that time were: *Araucaria cunninghamii, A. bidwillii, A. excelsa, A. rulei,* and *A. columnaris (A. cookii)* which had just been discovered and had been selling for ten pounds in London. *Agathis robusta* was in this lot.

In addition he offered *Cunninghamia lanceolata, Corynocarpus laevigata, Ficus rubiginosa*, the Camphor Tree, *Podocarpus totara, Catinospermum australe*, twenty four varieties of camellia including Waratakh, Alba Plena, and other species of plants that are still unfamiliar to most gardeners in California. There were many kinds of seed, such as *Correa speciosa, Bossiaea, Doryanthes excelsa*, the loquat, and numerous others listed which would require hours of research to translate into terms we now use for plants.

Evidently these oddities and rarities appealed to San Francisco gardeners who wanted something new. Cost was a minor consideration. Wealth from gold itself, or from supplying the gold miners with the tools to dig up the gold, was easily translated into wealth from the plant world.

Coit and Beals at 94 Battery Street offered fifty assorted colors of camellias. P. Sweeny and Company of 108 California Street was another successful nursery with bulbs and flower seeds for sale.

Smaller nurseries

E. Meyer and Company had a nursery during the eighteen seventies out at the edge of Sutro Forest, west of Stanyan Street. He occupied a part of the nursery site of what later became the La Rochelle Nursery of Victor Reiter, Jr. At the flower show in 1871 Meyer exhibited three Araucarias, *Cedrus deodara, C. libani, C. excelsa*, and *Pinus canariensis*.

E. L. Reimer's nursery was at the southeast corner of 19th and Folsom. There he grew popular greenhouse plants and sold vines such as *Pandorea pandorana, P. jasminoides, Campsis sinensis*, and *Pyrostegia ignes*, all of which trumpet flowers are still popular today after more than eighty five years. He offered twelve kinds of eucalypts, *Chorizema ilicifolia, Escallonia rubra, Leptospermum laevigatum, Podalyaria*, and "*Hakea* of sorts."

E. J. Wickson tells the story that after A. P. Smith went out of business in Sacramento in 1862 Reimer bought some of the old camellias and sold these for $100 each in San Francisco. It must be evident to the experienced horticulturist that San Francisco nurserymen had many of the choicest plants that are grown in California today and that San Francisco served as a center of distribution from the 1850's.

R. J. Trumbull of 427 Sansome Street was best known in the early 1870's for his flowers and seeds but he did occasionally grow rare plants. He raised some seedlings of *Syncarpia glomuifera* (Turpentine Tree) in 1874. In 1877 he shipped a tree fern to New York.

Governor Leland Stanford lived at the corner of California and Powell Streets. Stanford's conservatory was almost finished in 1876. His manager, James T. Murphy, secured ornamental plants from Collie and Stuart, nurserymen and florists at 18 Post Street. At first there were the usual greenhouse plants, such as allamandas, hibiscus, passion vines, orchids, and ferns but in time rarer plants were added. For example, in 1877 the greenhouses included six kinds of *Araucaria*, such as those already available at other nurseries, and *A. rulei*. Other plants of interest were *Banksia grandis, Corynocarpis laevigata*, and *Cryptomeria japonica* var. *lobi*.

Woodward's Gardens

The name of Woodward's Gardens was still familiar to people who could recall visiting the park before 1890. (Figure 8) Almost everybody in those early days would make an effort to see it when they visited San Francisco. Robert B. Woodward started building his house in about 1860 and then began to collect a most notable group of ornamental plants. His property was on Mission between 13th and 14th Streets and covered a large area. At present, there is a restaurant on part of the old site called "Woodward's Garden".

The idea of making the garden into a public pleasure ground stemmed from a rather petulant remark made by one of Woodward's daughters. Because the property was so attractive a charitable organization held its gala event there in 1866. The public then began to wander in and out of Woodward's garden unbidden, whenever they felt like it.

Miss Woodward was put out by so many strangers constantly coming and going that she said "we might as well be a public

Figure 7 Woodward's Gardens , Mission and Thirteenth Streets. This garden was opened to the public in 1868 and contained many rare plants.
(Reproduced by permisssion of the Regents of the University of California)

pleasure ground". This comment resonated with her father. Mr Woodward felt that he had a duty to allow poorer citizens to enjoy the plants and grounds. Woodwards' Garden remained very popular until the Golden Gate Park matured. It could not compete with the great scope of that masterpiece.

Late in 1870 Woodward's Gardens had six kinds of Araucarias, and both the Cinnamon Tree and Camphor Tree. There was a twenty foot tall *Acacia verticillata* tree. In 1871 Mr. Woodward apparently had *Billbergia*. *Strelitzia reginae* was ready to bloom in February, 1872. *Eucalyptus ficifolia* was there in 1877. Visitors from that period recalled the Monterey cypress hedge around the Gardens.

In December, 1863, Mr. Woodward bought Oak Knoll Farm north of Napa and planted many fine trees at his country home. This property will be mentioned again in the chapter on Napa County.

At the Second Annual Bay District Fair held in San Francisco in 1872 Woodward exhibited bananas, pineapples, crinums, *Hoya bella, Lobelia cardinalis, Eccremocarpus, Billbergia*, and ivy geranium.

Woodward grew very interesting types of palm tree in 1877. He had *Acanthophoenix rubra, Cycas revoluta, Cocos romanzoffia (Arecastrum romanzoffanum), Pandanus utilis, Trachycarpus excelsa, Pritchardia martii, Phoenix canariensis, Latania commersonii, Roystonea regia*, and *Sabal umbracculifera.* He also exhibited four kinds of pitcher plants in 1877: *Darlingtonia californica* and three kinds of *Nepenthes.*

Mr. Woodward spent $100,000 on his gardens, exclusive of the grounds. The publicity given Woodward's Gardens no doubt had much to do with public interest in new ornamental plants. This "Central Park of the Pacific" was open to the public at 25¢ for adults and 10¢ for children.

San Francisco Chronicle promotions and ornamental plants

Another important contribution, not only for San Francisco, but for all of California, was the distribution of Chilean trees by E .P. Rixford. He was the garden editor of the *San Francisco Bulletin*, and father of the late Dr. Emmet Rixford (a noted agricultural scientist). In the 1870's he decided to reward new subscribers to his newspaper with seeds or cuttings. Among the most notable ornamental plants distributed were *Quillaja saponaria, Maytenus boaria, Peumus boldus, Cryptocarya miersii*, and *Lythraea caustica.* Stephen Nolan of Oakland had listed *Cryptocarvia miersii* as early as 1871 but most of these are comparatively uncommon even to-day. Mr. Rixford also distributed cuttings of the Smyrna fig, later known as the Rixford fig.

Charles Abraham

Charles ("Charlie") Abraham came to California in 1877 and went to work for F. Lüdemann in San Francisco. (Note 8) (Figure 9) He had served the classic apprenticeship of European garden-ers, first at a large German estate, and later in the Crimea, the subtropical region of Ukraine. He developed a love of subtropical plants as a result.

Abraham went to assist Frank Kunz in planting some of the trees in the Capital Park in Sacramento in 1875, but returned to Lüdemann in 1879. In 1881 Charles Abraham started his Western Nursery at 1630 Greenwich Street and continued it until his death in 1929. Toward the end, his niece took charge for him. During that early period there were many fine houses out toward the Presidio not far from his nursery.

Buying plants from Charlie Abraham was an experience. He was a true plantsman and would sometimes ignore customers just to talk to an enthusiastic plantsman friend. How much he im-

Figure 8 Charles Abraham 1851–1929: eccentric and beloved nurseryman
(Reproduced by permission of the Regents of the University of California)

ported from Europe and Eastern nurseries is not fully known but Butterfield had a fine collection of his old nursery catalogs.

These provide some degree of information. Abraham imported succulents from Haage and Schmidt of Erfurt, Germany, and perhaps conifers from European dealers. He had dealings with famous Eastern nurserymen and also leading nurserymen in California in his day, such as R. D. Fox of the Santa Clara Valley Nursery in 1884, E. Gill of Oakland and H. H. Berger, renowned for importing Japanese plants in 1887. Abraham even had catalogs from the Reasoner Brothers of Florida only two years after that firm started business (1886).

Charles Abraham had saved William C. Walker's master copy for the 1858 nursery catalog, the one which later came into Alice Eastwood's possession. He grew *Bomarea caldasiana* and *Pemus boldus* from Chile as well as other rare plants. Charles Abraham was a true friend of California gardeners.

Nurseries in the eastern part of the United States such as Siebrecht of New Rochelle, N.Y., the United States Nursery of Fischer and Panda in Short Hills, N.J., and others were equally well known in the 1880s.

Frederick Lüdemann

Frederick Lüdemann's Pacific Nursery was on Baker Street between Lombard and Chestnut. Lüdemann received first prize at the1872 Flower Show for the largest and best collection of flowering plants, fuchsias, double-flowering geraniums, coleus, and carnations. He claimed he had the largest and most choice collection of greenhouse and open air plants on the Pacific Coast. His nursery catalog of 1874 gives some idea of the many rare plants he grew but only a few can be listed here: *Hakea laurina, Postanthera nivea, Epacris, Ficus repens, Tibouchina, Homolanthus populifolius, Torenia asiatica, Dionella tasmanica,* and over a hundred varieties of fuchsia. (Note 9)

In 1874 and 1875 Lüdemann concentrated on eucalypts. For instance he listed *Eucalyptus risdoni, E. gumii, E. pilularis, E.*

viminalis, E. corymbosa, E. haemastoma, E. maculata, and *E. macrocarpa.* This brief list gives a hint as to the outstanding plants he had in the early 1870's. Later on he standardized his stock, probably growing mostly what his customers wanted. It seldom pays to sell rare plants. In about 1910 he sold out to Paul Von Kempf. The latter continued to run the old Pacific Nurseries at Colma, south of San Francisco.

H. H. Berger

H. H. Berger and Company had a nursery at 315 Washington Street. Mr. Berger established his business in 1878. After his death his wife continued the business in New York. Japanese plants were his specialty. Butterfield had an 1887 Berger catalogue which listed such plants as *Daphne genkwa,* rare azaleas, camellias, *Enkianthus perulatus (E. japonicus), Pterostyrax corymbosa, Cornus kousa (Benthamia japonica), Magnolia stellata,* and other species, *Cedrella sinensis, Cercis chinensis, Fontanesa fortunei, Prunus mume, Aucuba japonica, Illicium anisatum, Nandina domestica, Rosa rugosa, Iris stylosa, Lilium hansoni* and many other lilies grown in Japan.

Berger was probably responsible for the introduction of the loquat known in recent years as Golden Nugget. There were other nurserymen of the 1870's who might be listed but enough has been said to indicate their influence on early gardens.

Residential gardens

With the many activities of early San Francisco nurserymen, it is not surprising that pioneer San Francisco gardens had the rarest plants in the world. Many residents had made fortunes in the gold mines and expressed this wealth through fine houses and gardens.

An insight into some of these gardens may be found in *Vignettes of Early San Francisco Homes and Gardens,* published by the San Francisco Garden Club in 1935. (4) Old roses, fuchsias, daturas, and the dew plant (*Aptenia cordifolia*) stuck in the minds of those who saw these pioneer gardens. There were also the pepper tree and the magnolia but the great wealth of plant materials discussed in this story largely escaped the attention of visitors except for the few trained in horticulture and able to remember plant names.'

The little pamphlet by nine members of the San Francisco Garden Club is still useful and revealing today, even though almost everything they described has gone. (2000). Only Sutro's Cliff House still exists. The pamphlet was compiled by Mrs Silas H. Palmer, and read at a meeting of the club by Mrs E.E. Brownell. The authors were reminiscing about San Francisco in the late nineteenth century, or even before, so they themselves were clearly not young by 1935.

One lady, Anna Beaver, grew up in a house on Market Street between Fifth and Sixth Streets. It had belonged to the unfortunate James King, editor of the "Bulletin" who was shot and killed in 1856 by the "notorious criminal" Casey. Anna Beaver's father bought this house a few years afterwards. She remembered a two storey conservatory, with a central fountain and a mound of dewplant in the centre. Outside, perfumed vines climbed up the sides of the house. There were heliotrope and star-jasmine on one side, and wisteria on another.

At the back there was a large grass plot on which the family played croquet, surrounded by wide borders and fenced off from the street. This area had a single acacia tree. Pink mallow flowers attracted her as a child. The family moved out in 1868, but she recollected this garden sixty seven years later.

Alice Hooper Mckee recalled gardens in Rincon Hill from the 1870s. Her own family garden had numerous varieties of fuchsia, and borders edged by pink oxalis. She was also struck by a large cactus with "white bells" climbing on a fence. The "bells" lasted a long time and were a source of great excitement when they first bloomed each year.

Mrs Evelyn Norwood Brecz liked to recall her grandmother's garden with its laurestina hedge, conical "rockery" containing ferns and shrubs she had seen in Trinidad, Humboldt County, and many delightful flowers. These included floraponda, abutilon, jasmine, white cactus, heliotrope, marigolds, double pink hollyhocks, fuschia and geraniums. It is significant to note how the same flowers appear again, suggesting that these were sold by the local nurseries. Her grandmother also had a lot of Calla lillies, but no bulbs and only a few roses.

Nob Hill was developed by the silver barons and later the first railroad builders such as Crocker, Huntington and Stanford. Front gardens were dignified, with neatly tended grass and some shrubs, but very few annual or perennial flowers. Occasionally a palm tree would be set next to an evergreen in one of these lawns. The author of this vignette recalls an apple orchard attached to a small cottage, right up against the Tobin mansion.

James Phelan bought former mayor McCoppin's house at 17th and Valencia Streets in 1875. The gardens were Phelan's pride and joy. Mayor McCoppin had created a rose garden before he left, with many old fashioned varieties such as the "Black Prince", Moss roses, tea roses and the "Marechal Neil". In other parts of the garden heliotrope, fuchsia and both white and purple lilac were abundant.

Phelan also had an orchard where he grew cherries and trained a fig tree along a vine. There were tall magnolias and graceful pepper trees on his property, but it was the weeping willow whose branches dipped down to the ground which caused the most comment.

The fuchsia and heliotrope often came from Charles Abraham's nursery because these were among his favorite flowers. One had to be careful with him. If he felt that a client was not a true plant lover, he mulishly refused to greet that person at the nursery and did not want to sell anything to her.Veronica Kinzie, in her vignette, recorded him snubbing a very wealthy client by saying in her hearing "My dear, I would not even sell that woman a geranium, she doesn't love flowers".

It is sad that none of these gardens had even survived until the ladies described them for the garden club. Only one such property can still be seen in San Francisco and that is Sutro's Cliff House.

One of his daughters described the events of Arbor Day, November 27, 1886, when thousands of trees were planted. The idea of an Arbor Day came from Joaquin Miller, the poet, and Sutro took it very seriously. He gave 50,000 saplings to be planted by school children in Oakland and San Francisco. Miller was a fanatic about preserving natural beauty.

Golden Gate Park

The land for Golden Gate Park was finally acquired on April 4, 1870 for the City of San Francisco by Frank McCoppin, then Mayor. It had taken eighteen years, starting in 1852, very soon after the gold rush had enlarged the city's population so extraordinarily. During that period, New York developed the Central Park advocated by Frederick Law Olmsted. San Francisco was flexing its civic muscles and could not bear to be outdone by an old East coast city. They wanted a park too. (5)

The city fathers petitioned the US Supreme Court for title to the "Outside Lands" on the west side of the peninsula, and were awarded the tract in 1864. A 1013 acre section of this tract was set aside as a park, even though the soil was thin and sandy, and swept by oceanic winds.

Olmsted, asked to give an opinion, said it would never be any good. He reckoned without the pertinacity and skill of the engineers, landscapers and horticulturists who were employed. In 1870, Order 800 was confirmed and signed by the governor, Henry Haight. He appointed the first Park Commission of three men. S.F. Butterworth was chairman.

William Hammond Hall

Horticultural historians are indebted to Russell Beatty for reviving the reputation of William Hammond Hall. (6) William Hammond Hall submitted the lowest bid for the initial topographical survey of Golden Gate Park, $4860. The commission

accepted his bid and appointed him Engineer and Superintendent of the Golden Gate Park, after he finished the survey.

He undertook the first development and set out the first trees
in the autumn on the "Panhandle." An early report estimated the
cost at $30.75 per acre for grass and $45.95 for shrubs in reclaiming the eastern section, including the Panhandle. By 1872 the
plants were not large but were surviving. Today we may still see
some of the trees, such as eucalyptus, Monterey Cypress, and
Monterey Pine but the acacias and dracaenas are no longer alive.'

The Panhandle was the logical place to start. Hall found that
just over two hundred acres in that section of the land were fertile,
with eight small lakes, a number of underground streams, and
dark sandy loam. Wild willow trees grew around the lakes. Many
small scrub oak trees and scrub lupin, as well as strawberry plants,
had all been all able to survive

Hall, a cousin of John Hayes Hammond, Cecil Rhodes' right
hand man in the African gold and diamond mines, was a civil
engineer who met this immense challenge so well that several years
later Olmsted himself said it could not have been done better.
Hall's engineering training prepared him to understand the terrain thoroughly and he quickly started the grading for roads.

He taught himself about landscape design and horticulture as
he went along. The Bancroft library has all Hall's papers. Copies of
two letters show that he ordered many excellent texts in landscaping and horticulture from booksellers in New York and Philadelphia. The staggering part of all this was the speed and supreme
confidence with which he read, assimilated and acted on this newly
acquired knowledge, at the ripe old age of twenty five.

Long before ecology had become as exact science, Hall understood the importance of micro-climates. No one was allowed to
remove a single piece of brush or any of the unprepossessing stunted
trees which hung on in the "barren" wastes.

The first part of his plan was to improve the Panhandle by
making entry gates, paths and roads and planting thousands of
trees. The second part was to reclaim the sand dunes and the third
was to wall off the park from the beach by constructing two drives

along the edge of the beach. This latter was essential to diminish the rough effect of the wind, both directly upon young plants and indirectly in the continuous blowing of sand.

Hall designed the park in a somewhat eclectic manner. The gates and fences needed for a public place set a tone of formality. There were not too many models for him in the 1870s, but Olmsted had learned that a grand entry underscored the significance of an enclosed space from the first public park built for the residents of Birkenhead, near Liverpool.

Hall offset this by following a "natural" style for the lawns and tree placement. There are echoes of "Capability" Brown in the great sweeps of lawn and clumps of trees planted to look as if they had grown there without the influence of man. Some other sections are more formal, laid out later by John McLaren, with symmetrical plantings and conventional flower beds, as becoming a city park.

Hall prepared a memoir of his work on the park, *"The Romance of a Woodland Park"*, but did not polish it sufficiently to be published. Note the title. He did not consider his park to be merely a city pleasure ground, but a truly rural oasis. He strove all his working life to protect the park's land from depredation, particularly from the construction of large buildings, even though he only had an intermittent consulting role. His attitude did not endear him to politicians.

He wrote: "Destroy a public building and it can be replaced in a year. Destroy a woodland park and all the people living at the time will have passed away before its restoration can be effected." Hall fought a good fight, but the park has not only a conservatory but the De Young Museum, the California Academy of Sciences with its aquarium and various other structures.

Russel A. Beatty commented on Hall's use of existing native vegetation as protection for the new young plants he introduced and numerous other examples of adopting special techniques to fit the unusual site. Hall also ran a tight ship fiscally and was careful in how he spent the public's money.

In spite of all this, state politicians found fault with him and forced him to resign in a most humiliating manner. Early in his grading and planting of the park, Hall had discharged one Daniel Sullivan for peculation. Unfortunately for Hall, Sullivan was later elected to the state legislature and vowed to get even with Hall. The trumped-up charges of neglect of duty, and conflict of interest were resoundingly refuted by both Hall and his supervisors, but the damage was done and he had to resign.

For ten years the park was neglected, with three Superintendents coming and going in short order. They were victims of a short sighted policy which starved the park of funds. No one could function in this situation.

When the authorities finally woke up to the harm they had done, and asked Hall to return, he was no longer available. He had been appointed California's State Engineer. Governor Stoneman insisted he at least become a consultant to the park, but as a state employee Hall was unable to accept any pay. He consulted *gratis* on and off for about fifteen years. It was he who suggested they appoint John MacLaren to be the fifth Superintendent in 1887. There is no formal memorial to William Hammond Hall in Golden Gate Park.

John McLaren

The Conservatory was constructed during MacLaren's tenure. *Victoria regia* bloomed in the Conservatory in August, 1879, grown from seed bought in London. This conservatory burned down in about 1883 but was rebuilt with funds from Charles Crocker. The building was stocked again with *Victoria regia* . This handsome aquatic plant had become a feature by 1888.

The park itself was later badly damaged by the 1906 earthquake. Not only did some of the buildings collapse, but the very grass and trees were destroyed by the enormous number of people housed in tents on its land. The final bill for that destruction was reported to be $174,000.

'Anyone who would like to learn more about the early plantings at Golden Gate Park should read the annual reports of the Park Commissioners. These reports list all the plants grown there, with new additions from year to year. The lists are too long to be adequately covered in any short discussion. There are probably over 5,000 species growing in the park today.'

The reader will certainly be interested in John McLaren, "Uncle John" as his close friends knew him. He was also called "Uncle John" by the gardeners and foremen, but only surreptitiously and behind his back. He had a dour and gruff exterior and was exceedingly demanding, yet the men trusted him and knew he cared deeply about their fates. (Figure 9)

Figure 9 John McLaren. (1846 – 1943) Director of Golden Gate Park 1887 – 1943
(Reproduced by permission of the Regents of the University of California)

It is not generally realized that John McLaren had been in California for many years before he was called to continue the development of Golden Gate Park. McLaren (1846-1943), was born in Stirling, Scotland in 1846. He came to California in 1870 and became Director of Golden Gate Park, San Francisco in 1887. McLaren had worked in the Peninsula for several wealthy men, designing gardens and parks.

It was McLaren who completed the planting of the sand dunes in Golden Gate Park. He was devoted to rhododendrons and imported many new oriental varieties for the Park's rhododendron dell. Many of these had to be replaced in 2001 but they had given yeoman service in their time.

'Much of the east end of the Park had been developed before McLaren came and even part to the westward near the present bandstand, but he organized the work in such a way as to receive general commendation. At the time he came in 1887, most of the western part of the Park was nothing but sand dunes.

John McLaren continued developing Golden Gate Park by introducing Beach or Sea Bentgrass (*Ammophila arenaria*). He used seed imported from Vilmorin Andrieux and Sons Company of Paris, an ancient business founded before 1745. This grass served to bind the blowing sand. '

He decided to plant it after doing some empirical tests with half a dozen other grasses. It was the only grass which stood up to the effects of the encroaching sand. This is hardly surprising, because it was widely used in the low lying countries of Europe for centuries, such as the Netherlands, Belgium, parts of France and England.

'It is said, perhaps apocryphally, that when asked what he wanted for his birthday, he replied "100,000 pounds of barnyard manure". His wish was granted. The manure came from the horse car barns. With the manure as compost he created top soil, and it became feasible to plant acacias (such as *Acacia longifolia*), Australian Tea Tree (*Leptospermum laevigatum)*, Monterey Cypress *(Cupressus macrocarpa)* and Monterey Pine (*Pinus radiata*). As many as 60,000 acacias were set out in a single year.'

The Monterey cypress and pine trees were chosen as windbreaks following more experiments. McLaren tried numerous other types of tree which were said to work in Europe, but all of them failed dismally. Looking back in hindsight, it makes sense that trees which had evolved over millennia on the California coast should be the best for this particular job.

In time perhaps half a million acacia trees were planted in Golden Gate Park, representing sixty species. (7) These plants were raised in the Park nursery located at the site of the present Kezar Stadium. The various species of ornamental trees and shrubs had been introduced several years before by nurserymen already mentioned. W. H. Hall did the first planting of 12,000 acacias representing ten species. He was also responsible for most of the trees in the eastern part of the Park near the Lodge, such as the Monterey pine and Monterey cypress, also species of *Araucaria* and the *Cordyline indivisa.*'

John McLaren became very interested in building up a fine collection of rhododendrons. At the Royal Botanic Garden in Edinburgh McLaren had absorbed William Sawrey Gilpin's philosophy of "picturesque" landscaping. When McLaren said that a landscape was to be "natural" it meant natural in a picturesque manner, such as replicating a Scottish rhododendron glen. Rhododendron and heather were perhaps his favorites.

The National Geographical Society sent an expedition to Siam (now Thailand), Java, and other oriental countries in the 1930s. McLaren made arrangements for the collection of seeds of many species, including such varieties as *Rhododendron falconeri*. Some rhododendrons had been planted before McLaren began his work but his initiative resulted in about four hundred species being added to the collection.

McLaren viewed a garden or a park as the setting for plants and in this way he had a different emphasis from Hall the engineer. He had been trained in gardening, not landscape architecture, and did not quite have Hall's open mind. If he had preceded Hall instead of the other way about, the park might have been quite different. McLaren built on the solid structure left by Hall.

There was no question about McLaren's skill as a manager. In that he had no peer. He had grown up on a farm in Stirlingshire and served the gruelling apprenticeship of all aspiring gardeners in Scotland at that period. No one was allowed to pamper himself with gloves or a jacket and no one could use a long handled spade. Toughness of mind and body were expected of a professional gardener.

His attitude was unyielding. When he interviewed the first woman to apply for work as a professional gardener in the park, Sidney Stein Rich, his main question was whether she could handle a spade. This was in 1929. Mrs Rich noted in an interview later that he restricted her activities to spade work for the whole of her first year. She proved herself to be tough and effective and eventually rose to be Head "Nurseryman" in 1940. (8)

For fifty six years, almost until his death at the age of ninety six in 1943, John McLaren had autocratic control of the Park's staff. One of his methods was to make an arbitrary demand, knowing full well that it was unreasonable, just to reinforce obedience, according to his successor Roy Hudson. (9) Large trees which had just been planted the day before had to be moved six inches, or a whole bed of flowers had to be pulled out. On one occasion the uprooted plants were returned to the nursery because McLaren did not care for *Griselinia littoralis* 'Variegata'.

While he loved almost all plants, he despised statues. He referred to them in a sneering tone as "stukies". He often refused to allow them to be displayed. If he were forced to let one go in, he planted the fastest growing shrubs he knew to obscure it.

When he retired, his colleague and friend, Commissioner E Cummings, had a statue of him created. This was a true dilemma. McLaren liked Cummings but still followed his usual practice of banishing the "stukies". The statue was kept out of sight at his own house, and did not go in the park. Later, the commissioners placed it in the MacLaren Rhododendron Dell, as a tribute to his love of that species.

'Old "Uncle John" took great pride in the Children's Playground. Later projects included the Shakespearean Garden behind the Academy of Sciences Building followed by the Strybing Arboretum to the south of the Japanese Tea Garden under the able direction of Eric Walther. (Note 10)

Butterfield said he could still hear him chuckle as he told about planting eucalyptus trees on Coyote Point near San Mateo in 1876. He had two crews of laborers, one Chinese and the other Irish. He set a competition between the two groups to see how many trees they could plant in a day. The Chinese won but McLaren thought that perhaps the Irishmen were smart enough not to work too hard for a dollar a day.'

One of his great nephews, the Reverend Timothy Aikman, wrote a brief memoir of McLaren. (10) The book contains at least one hilarious anecdote. It had to so with a chauffeur driven automobile available to the superintendent, something he enjoyed a great deal. During a phase of budget tightening, the commissioners thought he should drive it himself so they could dispense with the chauffeur.

McLaren is said to have obligingly started the engine and driven the vehicle straight into the lake. The chauffeur was re-hired the same day. Given that John McLaren was a thrifty Scot and self-made man, one should have some doubts about the veracity of this story. It seems very much out of character that he would ruin an expensive object like a car intentionally.

Almost every day in good weather John McLaren could be seen shortly after lunch riding over the Park grounds, inspecting the results of his efforts. With his spartan Scottish upbringing, he continued to be active after the age at which most men had died.

Japanese Tea Garden (Japanese Village)

The Mid-Winter Exposition of 1894 held in Golden Gate Park led to the development of the Japanese Tea Garden. In 1893, many banks failed in San Francicso and there was a serious financial depression. The city's leaders thought creating the exposition might stimulate new business. The idea for a Japanese tea garden as part of that exposition came from an Australian who lived in San

Francisco and sold Oriental *objets d'art.* in the arcade of the Palace Hotel.

George Turner Marsh was born in Richmond near Melbourne. As a child his family took him to Japan. He was so enchanted by the country that he prevailed upon his parents to let him live there for six years, staying with an English family. He absorbed the language and the culture almost obsessively. One is reminded of Lafcadio Hearne.

After coming to California in 1875 Marsh lived in Pasadena. He built a large garden there that was ultimately sold to H. E. Huntington. It was through his experience in Japan and his knowledge of Japanese gardening that he undertook the development of the Japanese Tea Garden in Golden Gate Park. Once he moved to San Francisco, he lived in the district now known as Richmond, so named because it reminded him of his home in Australia. George Marsh imported skilled Japanese craftsmen and materials directly from Japan to build the tea garden.

The "Japanese Village", as it was called originally, was so popular that the commissioners decided to keep it after the exposition closed. It is interesting to put this popularity into a world context. Japan had only been open to the Western world since 1854 when Commodore Perry negotiatied the first Japanese—American treaty. At much the same time in the 1880s there was a similar exhibition of Japanese culture in London which influenced WS Gilbert. The result was the sparkling "Mikado". Puccini's "Madam Buttterfly" was another work of the period inspired by an exotic society. It was almost as remote as Mars might be today.

Since 1895, the garden has naturally undergone some vicissitudes. In the early years of the twentieth century, the commissioners employed a Japanese master gardener, Makoro Hagiwara, to maintain it and continue its development. He did this with devotion, taking his family to live in a house on the park's grounds.

They remained in charge for thirty four years. His children continued working there with the same philosophy after Makoro's death in 1925. In spite of this spotless record, they too were rounded up in the early years of World War II and sent first to Tanforan, the camp for Japanese residents in San Mateo and then later to Camp Topaz for the duration of the war.

Since the end of the war, a series of other people have managed the garden, and some of them had a more commercial outlook than the Hagiwaras. It is now leased to a Japanese business man who also owns another restaurant. Park gardeners maintain the landscape, thus separating horticulture from the refreshments.

In his article about the garden in the California Horticultural Journal, Robert Morey describes many handsome and unique plants. (11) Some of them were "sculpted" by Makoro Hagiwara. The exotic, twisted looking pine tree inside the gate began life as a small sapling he found near the beach in 1900. Hagiwara made the trestle bridge from eucalyptus trees on the grounds. Monterey pines were pruned by hand and thinned to give them their unusual, more Oriental shape.

The Fraser Section is near the waterfall. When the Hagiwaras were removed to the internment camp, they asked a colleague, Sam Newsom, to sell their private collection of dwarfed pines, junipers and chamaecyparis. He sold it to Dr Hugh Fraser, and the precious plants were taken to the Frasers' property in the East bay.

When Mrs Fraser died her will indicated the collection should be returned to the Tea Garden and it may be found there today. At his own expense Dr Fraser engaged Sam Newsom to create the proper setting for these rare plants in the garden. Building the waterfall was part of that setting.

The original name of "Japanese Village" is really more accurate than tea garden. There is all the paraphernalia of a Japanese garden, with moon platforms and tiny curving bridges, but no sweeping lawns. The collection of small buildings makes it more like a village and the tea house is one of the buildings.

Pruning remains one of the most important aspects of maintaining its trees and shrubs. It may take several days to shape a tree properly. First one side is done, then the other is compared with it and cut the same way. Only then can the centre of the tree be thinned carefully to allow more light and air to circulate.

Strybing Arboretum

Very little personal information remains about Mr and Mrs Christian Strybing. What is known is that the Strybings came from Germany. Helene Strybing was the daughter of a pastor, Ernst Jordon, in Romstadt. Christian was a silk merchant. She was eighty one years old at her death.

No one really knows why she made her bequest. All that is in the record is that Helene Strybing, a wealthy widow, left her entire estate to the city of San Francisco to build the arboretum in her and her late husband's name, primarily for the display of native plants. She died in 1926, and money began to flow from her estate by the mid 1930s. In 1937, construction began, using additional funds from the federal Works Program Administration.

In addition to the native plants, Mrs Strybing wanted the arboretum to contain useful medicinal plants regardless of their origin. Under that rubric, Walther was able to add plants from other places and not only use native ones. Many species are grouped by country of origin in the arboretum. Many are labeled.

Herbarium at the California Academy of Sciences

The best collection of ornamental specimens of any herbarium on the Pacific Coast was assembled in the California Academy of Sciences in Golden Gate Park under the able direction of the late Alice Eastwood. Alice Eastwood had the idea for the Shakespearean garden. She also helped John McLaren with horticultural specifics when requested. (Mclaren is supposed to have said, "I plant'em and Miss Eastwood tells me what to call'em.")

Jose Jesus Noé

Butterfield liked to think about early life in California. His thoughts drifted back more than a century to 1839, when Jose Jesus Noé was granted a tract of land near the old Mission, 14th to 16th Street and Folsom to Mission Street. Woodward Gardens and also Miller and Sievers were on this fertile site many years later. In 1845 Noé became owner of San Miguel Rancho, containing 4,500 acres. In 1854 John M. Horner paid Noé $90,000 for most of his rancho.

Adolph H. Sutro

Adolph H. Sutro (1830-1898) bought the northwesterly portion of Noé's rancho for $240,000 in 1880. He had a strong sense of old fashioned *noblesse oblige* even though he had grown up in a poor family. The owner of a great property should allow ordinary people to come and enjoy it, as long as they accepted his unspoken terms.

The hills must be planted, said Sutro. The planting of "Sutro Forest" began in 1880 and continued through 1881. The Monroe brothers, old friends of Butterfield's, helped with the planting. Sutro continued planting trees to reclaim the shifting sandy soil near the shore, as witnessed by his participation in the Arbor Day festivities five years later.

Sutro was not content with wind break conifer trees only. The street later known as Palm Avenue was also lined with many hundreds of rose bushes. His private conservatory contained rare tropical plants. Everything he did was on a grand scale. To illumine his love of plants he collected antique herbals and other botanical works. He bought Joseph Banks' library to add to his own. Banks was an eighteenth century botanist who had gone around the world with Captain Cook, and the Banksia rose is named for his wife.

Now all that has vanished. The library was amost completely destroyed in the 1906 disasters. The trees he planted have grown so large and thick that the old flower beds are no longer even visible, assuming there were anything interesting left in them to see. In the end his efforts were in vain. Golden Gate Park met the needs of the citizens better.

Small city parks

Even before the imposing Golden Gate Park was conceived, a series of smaller parks and open spaces was envisaged as early as

1850 by Mayor John Geary. He enabled the city to set aside land for Washington Square in 1851. Portsmouth Square predates all of them, but South Park was laid out in 1856, and Union Square in 1860. This latter was important in the Civil War when California sided with the Union. Later, tradesunion leaders made speeches there.

At a slightly later date, in the mid-1860s, three more small but delightful parks were set aside. They still benefit residents in those nighborhoods. Alamo Square, Alta Plaza and Lafayette Square escaped the developers' grip and are cool havens of grass and plants in the midst of bustle and noise.

General Irwin McDowell

Almost simultaneously with the creation of Golden Gate Park, Major General Irwin McDowell used very similar techniques to improve life at the Presidio and later Fort Mason for his troops and their families. (12) They complained frequently of the sand blowing through their houses. To control this nuisance, General McDowell had lattices built with vines trained over them and planted many shrubs as wind breaks.

McDowell clearly had a lot of imagination. He rearranged the access to the houses. The kitchen entrance was oriented to the shore, so the inevitable sand came in at the back, more informal part of the house and not into the parlor. He also laid dozens of disused cannon balls as edging for paths. These had a slight effect on containing grit and sand.

The men made little cottage gardens around their homes. The officers had more elaborate ones. The units stationed on Alcatraz also had gardens and even a tennis court, before the island's buildings were turned into a Federal penitentiary. Later, gardens became a distant memory. Russell Beatty, former chairman of Landscape Architecture at the University of California at Berkeley, has devoted himself to restoring these old garden.,

CHAPTER 2

San Mateo County and the Peninsula

Butterfield wrote: 'The Peninsula between San Francisco and San Jose has interested visitors from the time of the first explorers who passed that way in 1769. In 1792 George Vancouver was impressed by the "Holly-leaved oaks" (*Quercus agrifolia*) which we know as the Coast liveoak. In the spring of 1799 Don Jose Arguello was sent to California to create a government and aid in the construction of missions.

Don Jose had travelled along El Camino Real and knew how beautiful the country was. When given a chance to select land for his rancho he chose a site in San Mateo County and named it Rancho de las Pulgas ("Ranch of the Fleas"). His home, "Valle Tranquillo" was built in what is now San Carlos, five blocks west of El Camino Real. Menlo Park, San Carlos, and Redwood City now occupy part of this old rancho.'

Florence Atherton Eyre recalled her childhood and the natural beauty of the Peninsula, in another delightful small publication of the San Francisco Garden Club, *"Reminiscences of Peninsula Gardens From 1860 to 1890"*, published in 1933. (13) She noted that the region running from San Francisco south was originally sand dune. Scrub oak, chemisal, yerba santa, dwarf eschscholzia and sand verbena predominated, bound by yerba buena.

Further south, the terrain changed and it was very green. Lupin, cream cups, coreopsis, mallow, buttercups and a little more to the south, wild iris, flourished. Theodore Wores painted these wild scenes many times, with faithful representation of the flowers. A collection of his work was bequeathed to St Francis Hospital in San Francisco where the pictures may still be seen.

Jose Sanchez' fifteen thousand acre Buri-Buri Rancho was to the north of Rancho de las Pulgas. Don Jose Arguello owned thirty five thousand acres. The missionaries established a church to the southward on the Buri-Buri Rancho near the present day Burlingame.

When the first Americans arrived and sought desirable sites for their summer homes they immediately saw the natural beauty of the peninsula area. They developed San Mateo, Burlingame, Hillsborough and the adjacent territory. Gardens and orchards were naturally part of these estates.

George H. Howard

George H. Howard's estate near Burlingame was one of the first to be planted. In 1858 the house was described as a capacious structure with verandas, high-ceilinged halls and rooms, a style of architecture that persisted for many years in California. (Note 11) The land still had the native oaks which Viscaino had seen at Monterey and which so impressed Vancouver. A serpentine driveway, gravelled, and bordered with shrubbery led to the house on this six hundred-acre site. Espaliered trees, a green lawn and native ornamental plants greeted the visitor.

John McLaren had come to California early in 1876. Like so many other Scots and English gardeners who were attracted to wealthy estates the twenty year old McLaren found work on the Howard Estate. His training and experience in Scotland greatly improved the Howard landscape.

Darius Ogden Mills

'Darius Ogden Mills built his estate not far from Howard's in what is now Millbrae. He came to California in 1849 as a merchant and opened a banking house later. He became president of the Bank of California in 1864 and started his house about 1865.

He asked a landscaper named Elliot to plan his garden and by 1872 had finished the conservatory. Up to then native oaks formed most of the landscape planting. Mills set out fine ornamental plants and kept on planting for many years.'

'Pictures taken of the young trees in the early years show a great contrast with the same trees in later years. *Eugenia myrtifolia (E. paniculata* var. *australis)* was planted before 1890. By the mid-twentieth century this tree was about sixty feet high. The diameter of the trunk was about fifteen inches. (Note 12)

Palm trees, *Jubaea spectabilis*, similar to those at the old Shinn garden at Niles, were planted in 1898. About forty years later they had reached sixty feet in height with a trunk diameter of nearly four feet. An Atlas cedar tree, *Cedrus atlantica*, was planted in about 1870 and finally reached a height of a hundred and four feet. *Fagus sylvatica* , the lovely European beech, developed a trunk with a diameter of thirty one inches at two feet. It branched at four feet, reaching a height of sixty five feet.'

'*Ligustrum lucidum*, one of the privets often considered a shrub, was planted in 1876 and developed a round head, reaching a height of fifty four feet. The trunk was forty four inches in diameter at one and a half feet. *Dacrydium cupressinum* planted in 1900 grew to about twenty five feet and its trunk had a diameter of seven inches. *Araucaria excelsa* grew to be about a hundred feet tall years after its planting in 1893.

Buxus sempervirens var. *aborescens* , a variety of box planted in about 1870 reached fifteen feet in height. *Pinus pinea*, the Italian Stone Mine, planted in 1888 reached fifty feet in height. Subdivision of the old properties is inevitable. In time all that will survive will be the memories of the gardens.'

William C. Ralston

William C. Ralston, prominent in early San Francisco and once its mayor, was a neighbor of Howard and Mills. They were all wealthy men who were interested in beautifying their landscape. A feature of Ralston's garden was the terracing. Each step of the terrace had a green Chinese vase with geraniums planted in them. Because of the terraces, Ralston had no lawns.

When John McLaren arrived the three neighbors asked him to plant the roadside on El Camino Real along their estates. Eucalyptus, elms, and pines were planted in 1872 to 1875, each property owner standing his share of the expenses. Many of these old trees were removed when the highway was widened but a few may still remain.

McLaren subsequently laid out a number of streets in the town of San Mateo. In 1896, George Howard Jr, a local architect, decided to develop parts of the Howard estate, inspired by the then current "City Beautiful" movement. There is a plan showing the design dated 1903. The entrance into this new residential park would be *via* a grand crescent from El Camino Real leading into a series of gently winding streets. At every intersection there were circles, medians and crescents with individually landscaped groups of native and imported trees.

McLaren varied the shades of foliage and habit of the trees from one island to another, and these in turn contrasted with the gardens around them. All this created masterly diversity with fairly economical means. Monterey cypress, Monterey pine, black locust, native oak, elm, redwood, maple, and poplar alternate with plantings of palm, magnolia, olive and other semi—tropical varieties.

The residents of these streets cherish "McLaren Park" and take extremely good care of it.. The individual houses also have quite imposing gardens, many of which were landscaped either in McLaren's day or soon after. Recently a number of the older trees in the "islands" have begun to deteriorate. Devoted members of the homeowners' associations, such as Mostyn and Sue Lloyd for example, hold local arbor days in which volunteers plant more than fifty replacement trees at a time.

San Mateo Arboretum

Another example of McLaren's work is the San Mateo Central Park or Arboretum. The exceptional planting has filled out in the hundred years since he started it with massive oak trees, coast red-woods, black walnut, two varieties of palm and gingko among others.

The park has been enhanced with an additional site. Thirty five years ago the city of San Mateo commissioned Naga Sakurai to construct a Japanese garden in the park, and it too has matured very well.

Other early estates in San Mateo County

'Over to the west of San Mateo and Hillsborough in the hills and on to Half Moon Bay were several other old houses which had modest gardens, not equal to those just mentioned. Iceplant, a non-native plant, was growing on the beach at Half Moon Bay as early as 1868. Johnston House in Half Moon Bay has been preserved by the San Mateo County Historical Society.'

Captain F. W. Macondray, president of the old California Horticultural Society in 1858, built his summer house in San Mateo. Such men of ability, interested in horticulture, have always helped to organize activities so the entire community and state might benefit. (Macondray's name is commemorated in Macondray Lane, near Union Street in San Francisco)

John Parrott was a confidential agent of the United States at Mazatlan in 1846. Later he settled on the west side of El Camino Real, buying Captain Macondray's house. He changed the name of the estate to "Baywood".

'Stephen Nolan, the famous nurseryman of Oakland, landscaped the Parrott Estate, according to one of Nolan's daughters. (v.i.) The estate was later subdivided, although some of the old trees were still standing many years afterwards, a little south of the main intersection on the highway. A specimen of *Araucaria bidwilli* planted there developed mature cones and seeds in the 1930s.'

Butterfield wrote about the *Araucaria cunninghamii* in Mrs. Thomas Keen's garden at 105 Hayward Street in San Mateo. A specimen of *Cordyline indivisa*, often known as a dracaena, reached an age of well over forty five years in the Keen grounds. A cork oak could be seen on the de Laveaga Estate, 400 San Mateo Avenue possibly dating back to 1870.

The name of Hayward Street may remind a few of Alvinza Hayward. Hayward made his fortune by "watering" Dry Creek to free it of its gold. He too had a fine garden in San Mateo. As early as 1860 he planted a camphor tree, then very new in California. William C. Walker of San Francisco may have supplied it. By 1885 this specimen was forty five feet in height and five feet in trunk diameter at the base line, according to a report from the College of Agriculture.

San Mateo County also included the large estates of the Athertons, Eastons, Redingtons, Barhoilets and Borels in addition to the ones noted above, according to Mrs. Eyre. She also informs us that the Barhoilets developed the "Russian violet" later known as the "California violet". Unfortunately, that is probably incorrect. This successful flower was developed in Berkeley by Emory Smith and the Carbone family.

'Hillsborough, to the west of San Mateo, has beautiful old gardens. A specimen of *Agathis robusta* planted about 1895 and an *Araucaria bidwillii* , the "bunya-bunya" tree, planted in 1890 at the home of R. B. Henderson, 2265 Ralston, could still be seen in the 1930s. An eighty-foot specimen of *Picea smithiana* stood in the grounds of Jean Saint Cyr on El Cerrito.

Somewhat younger but still interesting were specimens of *Puya alpestris* , a showy bromeliad, at the W. H. Crocker Estate. The plants were probably supplied by Dr. E. O. Fenzi of Santa Barbara many years ago. (v.i.) Dr. Fenzi (Dr. Francheschi to many) listed this variety of *Puya* in his 1908 catalog. The plant is native to South America and has odd metallic blue spikes resembling a yucca.

There is a jacaranda tree in San Carlos, at 1200 San Carlos Avenue, planted in about 1900. This tree is only occasionally planted so far north. Another tropical tree was a specimen of the Guadalupe palm (*Erythea edulis*) planted at the Court House in Redwood City perhaps some time before 1900. An *Araucaria bidwillii* tree planted at H. M. Storey's house, in Selby Lane, probably dates back to before 1890. Another historic site in Redwood City is the Lathrop House. Pacifica has the Sanchez Adobe.'

'Continuing south to Menlo Park we come to the place where

George Gordon imported some acacias and oranges from Australia in 1869, only to find that these trees were infested with the Cottony Cushion Scale or White Scale. Less then ten years later this insect pest had spread to Marin County and also to southern California. For several years it threatened the entire citrus industry.'

'The Sunset Seed and Plant Company laid out its growing grounds in Menlo Park in the early 1890s. There was a large field of sweet peas for seed purposes and also seventy six varieties of carnations.'

'The Floods built their estate, Lindenwood, in Menlo Park many years ago. A large redwood tree planted in about 1882 grew to be about a hundred feet tall. There was also a specimen of *Araucaria araucana*, the Monkey Puzzle Tree, planted a little after 1890 and from which seed was collected for distribution. An old Italian cypress tree on this estate is about as old as the redwood.'

'Mrs. W. K. White's house in Oak Grove Avenue has specimens of *Ginkgo biloba*, *Pinus ponderosa*, and *Wisteria* planted about 1873. Oak Grove Avenue represents the former Redington estate, and some of the residual trees may have been on the White property.

In Littlefield Road Mrs. Leroy Nickel had a specimen of *Euonymus japonicus* which reached a height of twenty feet in the 1930s. It had a crown spread of twenty seven feet. This handsome specimen was planted in about 1863.

The J. A. Donahue estate is also on Littlefield Road. It has a specimen of *Cedrus atlantica*, planted about 1868. *Cedrus libani* , Cedar of Lebanon, was planted ten years later. An upright Irish Yew was planted about the same time.'

Faxon Atherton's estate was next to James Shelby's "Almendral". The latter built his house in the 1860s, and had a very large garden. Mrs Eyre remembered roses and honeysuckle covering the walls of the house and syringa and strawberry trees in the grounds. Selby was said to be responsible for introducing two other features into Menlo Park. One was a fountain, the other were the iron gates.

The Atherton estate was also memorable. The drive was an

avenue which wound through the original woods, with oaks and bay trees high over snowberry, chemisal and poison oak. There were also many wildflowers still to be seen: lupin, larkspur, mariposa lily, mallow, pennyroyal and yerba buena among others. Wild honeysuckle and wild roses came out in the fall. Atherton may have introduced the deodar cedar into the county and one of the *Araucarias*, "monkey puzzle".

Referring to Mrs Eyre's pamphlet, we learn that other large notable estates in Menlo Park were those of the Doyles, (friends of the Athertons), Lathams, and Holbrooks among others. Emmett Doyle bought the first house built in Menlo Park, I.C. Woods' "Woodside". The roses were very lush in this garden too, climbing all over the veranda. An old oak tree was enclosed in a circular wooden platform acting as a terrace, shaded by the branches of the tree.

These gardens all had an almost standard design of a large lawn, deodar cedars, maples, poplars and catalpa trees with a circular driveway. Pines, cedars and cypress lined the driveways. These features were very Southern, reminding us that many settlers in California were from the South.

Mrs. Eyre remembered the popular "ribbon beds" and wonderful shrubs: pink oleander, lilac, pomegranate, lemon verbena. By the 1860s different varieties of rose were available : Moss rose, Castilian rose, sweetbriar, Malmaison and the "Cup of Hebe" rose. Clematis, jasmine, fuchsia, heliotrope and jonquils were becoming widespread as nurseries rapidly developed to cater to these very wealthy people.

Stanford University

The corner stone for Leland Stanford Junior University, named in honor of the Stanfords' son who died on a visit to Europe, was laid by Senator and Mrs. Leland Stanford on May 14, 1887. The 7200 acre Palo Alto estate, the Vina Ranch in Tehama County, and the 32,000 acre Gridley Ranch in Butte County were given to support this university. John McLaren helped to plan the grounds under the direction of the Olmsted Brothers.

There were said to have been titanic battles between Frederick Law Olmsted Sr. and the Stanfords about the design for these grounds. As he grew older and learned more about the terrain Olmsted had come to recognize that the new campus needed to take the arid conditions of California into account. He recognized that the rolling lawns and fragile plants the Stanfords wanted were quite inappropriate. Olmsted also planned to site the buildings so that the mountains in the distance were visible across the open space at the center of the campus.

In the event, Olmsted won a partial victory. The campus is essentially Mediterranean in concept, with paved patios and drought tolerant platings. He lost the fight for the open vista. Stanford insisted that the chapel be central in the very sight line Olmsted hoped to keep open. It would have been wonderful if the two large universities in northern California had in fact been laid out in the way Olmsted wanted.

'The trees and gardens on the Stanford Campus are well worth seeing. Of special interest is a specimen of *Abies venusta* (St. Lucia Fir) which was transplanted successfully. (Note 13) Perhaps no more beautiful specimen of this tree is to be found outside its the native forest. A specimen of *Brachychiton acerifolia*, the Australian Flame Tree, planted around 1903 grew to be about fifty feet tall in the Inner Quad.

Elizabeth Gamble Garden

The Elizabeth Gamble Garden Center in Palo Alto was created intentionally as a public resource. It does not truly fit in with the theme of this book. The house was built in 1902, surrounded by about two acres of garden. Since then, the garden has been extensively re-modelled and is staffed by a professional horticulturist assisted by vounteers.

Menlo Park

Butterfield continued: '(Observe) two fan palm trees (*Washingtonia filifera*), which Governor Latham moved to his property at Menlo Park in early days, paying $1,000 for these at Louis Prevost's nursery in San Jose. Major Rathburn had a Camphor Tree at Mayfield in 1885. All down through the years gardeners on the Peninsula and adjacent territory have been planting choice plants. The San Francisco Peninsula Acacia Festival, Inc. was organized at George E. Keith's Rancho Acacia Baileyana at Los Altos in 1940, to celebrate the flowering of the beautiful acacias in January and February.

Woodside

Butterfield loved to visit Woodside tucked away back in the hills behind Redwood City. Early history was made there by a few settlers, and there was still much unspoiled and natural growth in the area when he was rambling through.

He made no mention of the unique property "Green Gables" created for Mortimer and Bella Fleishhacker in Woodside by Charles Greene. A classical Roman / Italian type of garden was connected to an old fashioned English garden in a most unusual manner.

The old Woodside Store at Kings Mountain and Tripp Road were still in existence in the earlier years of the twentieth century. These remnants predictably attracted Butterfield.

Filoli

Harry Butterfield did not comment on the handsome estate of "Filoli" in Woodside during his travels in the area. The owner of the Empire gold mine in Grass Valley, William Bourn Jr, an extremely wealthy man who also owned the rights to Crystal Springs and a great deal of other property, asked Willis Polk to build him an estate in Woodside using a European style. Bourn liked the motto "*Fi*ght, *Lo*ve and *Li*ve", and the name of his estate was derived from these three words. The grounds were designed by Polk together with Bruce Porter, a noted designer of gardens at the time.

The stylistic antecedents of the gardens at Filoli are mixed. Polk created a very formal Georgian style of house, with a double front and central entry. Porter flanked that with a pair of fruit orchards seen as one approaches the main entrance, in accordance with his theory that double orchards bespeak wealth and opulence.

The gardens are essentially separate from the house with no direct access or axial relationship to it. There is a band of foundation planting and some fine old trees adjacent to the house, to soften the bleakness. Standing at the rear of the house one can see directly over the countryside, the so-called "borrowed landscape" of some English and French estates.

In some ways the grounds are a complete throwback to a very early style of Mediaeval garden, inward looking with a series of disconnected "rooms". Espaliered orchards provide additional mediaeval tone.

There is no denying the sumptuous beauty, remarkable planting and rich tapestries of color. Individual "rooms" have Italian, English or French derivations. The sunken pool with its rigidly symmetrical and formal plantings at each corner harks back to Le Notre. The high amphitheatre, with its semicircle of tall evergreen trees, reminds one of old Italian groves.

Some of the borders echo Gertrude Jekyll. The densely flowering plumbago hedge made me feel very jealous. Then there is a native plant section right next to the English borders. Regardless of any criticisms, Filoli is considered to be a heritage garden and is preserved for posterity by the National Trust. Thousands of visitors enjoy going through the gardens every year.

CHAPTER 3

Oakland, Piedmont, Alameda, and Berkeley

'Butterfield wrote: 'Father Crespi and Lieutenant Fages passed an arm of San Francisco Bay in Oakland, now known as Lake Merritt, early on March 27, 1792.' (The lake was originally the San Antonio slough, a muddy, repellent Y-shaped body of water fed by the tides and three streams coming thorugh the marshes.) 'They were traveling north with the hope of redis-covering San Francisco.' At that point he tells us to look forward twenty eight years.

Peralta Rancho

The next relevant event was that 'Rancho San Antonio was granted to Luis Maria Peralta on June 27, 1820. This grant re-mained intact until 1842. It was then that Luis Peralta divided it among his sons at the age of eighty.'

One son, Vicente, received Encinal de Temescal or Temescal; Antonio Maria was given the territory just south, including east Oakland, while Ignacio received the southeastern part bounded by San Leandro Creek. A. M. Peralta was given Bolsa Encinal or Encinal de San Antonio where Alameda is located today. Domingo Peralta inherited the northern part of the old Rancho, from ap-proximately where the Claremont Hotel now stands northward to the creek that borders Albany.

It would be interesting to see how some of the boundaries were established at a time when land was valued primarily for pasture. Domingo Peralta's property was determined on the south by sighting from the mouth of a canyon near present Garber Park looking toward the island of Yerba Buena (where the Bay / Oakland-San Francisco Bridge now tunnels through). Surveyor's transits came later and early Americans were not very scrupulous when they sought to get possession by squatter's rights. Later, modern cities grew up on the former Peralta domain across San Francisco Bay from San Francisco.

There were no American settlers in Alameda County until 1846. There is no evidence that many of the early Spanish and Mexican settlers had gardens, although a garden was developed at Mission San Jose. Some of the early settlers in Berkeley went to Mission San Jose to get seeds of the Wild cherry (*Prunus ilicifolia*), indicating that this ornamental plant had not yet been grown near Oakland.

Oakland was incorporated in March 1852. As late as 1860 there were only 1,543 inhabitants. The Brooklyn and San Antonio districts were not yet a part of Oakland. San Antonio was started in about 1851 "across the ravine," now known as the mouth of Lake Merritt. San Antonio was consolidated with Brooklyn in 1856. In 1860 Brooklyn had a population of 1,546 or about the same as Oakland. Brooklyn was incorporated in 1870 and annexed to Oakland two years later.

Early nurseries in Oakland

Gardens began in the Oakland area when the first American settlers and a few nurserymen arrived. James Hutchinson started his nursery in Alameda in either 1852 or 1853. The date is not certain. W. F. Kelsey started his nursery at about the same time. With such a small population, we could hardly expect nurseries to conduct very large businesses. The vigor with which the first local nurserymen got going is quite surprising.

The American settlers who first went to the East bay lived in the "Embarcadero San Antonio", a village clustering around the site of the bull ring on Peralta's property. It was at the foot of the present 14th street. In the 1850s, this place was probably what was meant by "San Antonio".

Shell Mound Nurseries

The Shell Mound Nurseries and Fruit Garden reported in the early 1850's that they were located near San Antonio, probably to the east of the present Oakland Auditorium. There was an Indian shellmound near their lot, hence the name of Shell Mound Nursery. The nursery was owned by R. W. Washburn who was also connected with the express office. J. L. Sanford was his local manager

The nursery's single sheet 1856 catalog, now in the Bancroft Library of the University of California, listed Australian gum trees for $5 each and Australian acacia for $1 each. This is perhaps the first catalog listing eucalyptus though Butterfield believed that William C. Walker may have grown eucalyptus previously.'

'The trees must have been planted in 1855 to be sold for $5 each in 1856, so we can give this approximate date for the importation of the eucalyptus to California with documentary evidence to support the date.

The nursery advertised regularly in the early issues of Warren's *California Farmer* , listing such plants as *Kerria japonica, Acacia, Eucalyptus, Paulownia*, Japanese Quince, flowering fruit trees, *Ailanthus*, Arbor Vitae, Pride of China (*Malia*), and Osage orange. The 1856 catalog listed gingko at $1.50, oleander at $2 to $3, and also offered calla lilies, fifteen varieties of fuchsias, and a hundred and fifty varieties of roses. In 1860 this nursery was taken over by Graves and Williams.

James Hutchison

James Hutchison bought land in Alameda in the fall of 1853 but some of his nursery catalogs claimed the nursery was started in 1852. He moved to Alameda from San Francisco in January, 1854. Hutchison quickly developed a good stock of ornamental plants. He next made arrangements to auction plants in San Francisco.

The spirited auctioneer called the cinerarias "senoritas." Carnations brought $2.50 to $5 each, *Salvia splendens* the same, and roses $2 to $5 each. A fine camellia brought $2.50, an *Epiphyllum jenksoni* grafted onto an Opuntia stock brought $30, and a well-shaped rose geranium a top price of $34. Hutchison's ability to solve market problems helps explain why he continued in business for many years.

Hutchison had married a Miss Sanborn at Crown Park, New York, and came to California in about 1850. About 1854 he moved from Alameda to Oakland. Finally he opened his nursery on the northeast corner of what is now 26th Street and Telegraph Avenue across from the Sears Company building. For a time his store was at 14th and Broadway, Oakland. That was out in the country in early Oakland. The nursery was still further out of town.

Telegraph Avenue took its name from a telegraph line that ran north and over the hills about where the Fish Ranch Road is today, over the crest of the hills slightly to the north of the low-level tunnel. It joined the present highway about half a mile east of the tunnel entrance. Large teams of horses followed this road to Contra Costa County and hauled coal as well as grain and other farm products. The leading nurseries soon began to appear on this main travel route.

Here is what James Hutchison's "Bay Nursery" was offering in the early days. At least two of his old catalogs are in existence. Butterfield had a copy for 1874–75. As early as 1858 Mr. Hutchison listed the Snail Vine (*Phaseolus caracalla*), also *Crassula falcata,* a handsome succulent with scarlet flowers. In 1869 he had Pampas grass. By 1874-5 he listed many other new and rare ornamental plants.

Among them were Artillery plant (*Pilea microphylla*), *Begonia semperflorens,* English laurel, spotted calla, *Daphne odora,* white Breath of Heaven, *Echeveria metalica (E. gibbiflora* var. *metalica),* *Cestrum elegans, Iochroma tubulosa, Pittosporum tenuifolium, Photinia serrulata, Valotta speciosa,* thirty four varieties of fuchsias, many garden geraniums, including the new double white, "Aline Sisley" just introduced, General Grant, and a long list of roses.

There were eleven kinds of camellia, including *Chandleri*

elegans. He had many varieties of flowering cacti, such as *Hylocereus undatus, Heliocereus speciosus, Cereus peruvianus, Nyctocereus serpentinus, Aporocactus flagelliformis, Zygocacuts truncatus,* and *Selenicereus grandiflorus.* Most of the popular conifers of today were listed. He sold Monterey Cypress seedlings by the flat at a very reasonable price.

In addition to many vines the 1874-5 catalog of the Bay Nursery listed *Mehernia verticillata, Abutilon thompsoni,* eleven varieties of acacias, various begonias, such as *Begonia boliviensis, Corynocarpus laevigata, Crassula perfoliata, Escallonia rubra, Leptosperum laevigatum, Melaleuca decussata* and *M. ericifolia, Melianthus major, Raphiolepis indica,* and *Hebe (Veronica) speciosa.*

His 1878 catalog listed two varieties of fuchsia, Sunray and Avalanche. In 1879 he advertised *Osmanthus ilicifolius.* Butterfield felt that the modern student of horticulture could get a very good basic training in plant materials simply by confining his study to the ornamental plants already listed for nurseries in California before 1880.

Henry Willard Sanborn, Hutchison's brother-in-law, came to California in 1868 at the age of eighteen and went to work for Hutchison at the nursery. In time he inherited the nursery and continued in this work until his death in 1916. Butterfield began to visit Sanborn's Berkeley nursery when he was courting his bride and bought her corsages of orchids there. Henry Sanborn's son Edgar carried on the business for a time after 1916 but finally became Park Forester for the City of Oakland. He continued in that position until his retirement.

There is a specimen of the Italian Stone Pine (*Pinus pinea*) at Don Ignacio Peralta's old home near San Leandro Creek, said to have been planted about 1860. The property passed into the possession of A. C. Peachey about 1875. There were four acres of lawn, fountains, flower beds, ornamental plants, and a sixty five-foot windmill there in 1877. Only the Stone Pine has survived.

W. F. Kelsey

W. F. Kelsey was proprietor of the Oakland Nurseries at 24th and Telegraph Streets, Oakland. He claimed to have started his business in 1852. No doubt there was some rivalry between Kelsey and Hutchison and perhaps Stephen Nolan as well. In 1874 Kelsey advertised, "My stock of Australian trees and plants not equaled in the state." This claim may be discounted after seeing the nursery catalog of the "Bellevue Nursery" operated by Stephen Nolan in 1871, or the nursery catalogs of an earlier date from William C. Walker in San Francisco, but the nursery did attract customers from distant places.

Joseph Sexton of Santa Barbara, who ran a nursery from 1869 and is famous for developing the Santa Barbara soft shell walnuts, bought his araucarias from Kelsey. Reports show that Kelsey had about seventy five acres on Telegraph near Sycamore Street originally. After starting Kelsey House he finally gave up the nursery business.

Lewelling family

The story of the transportation of the first fruit trees to the Pacific Coast by the Lewelling brothers has been told well by others. Henderson Lewelling and his brother, Seth, went to Salem, Oregon, Seth in 1847 with the first grafted fruit trees west of the Rockies, but few people in California know that Henderson Lewelling later came to California and died here. He is buried in Mountain View Cemetery. "The Father of Pacific Coast Horticulture" is inscribed on his tomb stone.

The Lewellings started out from Iowa. They were Quakers and had been part of the anti-slavery "underground railroad."

These two Lewelling Brothers opened the first truly commercial nursery on the Pacific Coast in 1847 at Salem, Oregon, not far from Portland. John Lewelling, another brother, came to California and for a time worked with E. L. Beard at Mission San Jose. Lewelling assisted Beard in establishing an orchard in 1852. (Figure 10)

Figure 10 John Lewelling: early nurseryman in Oakland
(Reproduced by permission of the Regents of the Univeristy of California)

Alfred Lewelling, one of Henderson's sons, came to California in about 1852, perhaps to work with his uncle, John Lewelling, who had settled in San Lorenzo. Alfred Lewelling later ran the Fruitvale Nursery in the Fruitvale Avenue area. This old nursery gave its name to the whole district at that time. Alfred Lewelling was a member of the Alameda County Agricultural Society in 1858.

John Lewelling founded his San Leandro Nurseries in San Lorenzo in 1855. A visit today will find Lewelling Boulevard at the turn of the old highway in San Leandro. Mr. Lewelling listed a few ornamental plants, such as roses, but offered mostly fruit trees.

The Lewelling family was very significant in the history of California's horticulture. "Lewelling" appears under different guises, such as "Luelling" but the name most likely comes from the ancient Welsh "Llewellyn".

A. D. Pryall

'There were other significant horticulturists at that period. One day a tall, gray-haired man with a Van Dyke beard walked into my office and asked if I had ever heard of A. D. Pryall. I replied that Mr. Pryall had lived on Chabot Road not far from the Temescal artificial lake and had had a nursery "about a mile from the end of the horse railroad". The tall gentleman smiled and stated he was the only living child of A. D. Pryall (Figure 11).'

Figure 11 A.D. Pryall: early nurseryman in Oakland
(Reproduced by permission of the Regents of the University of California)

'I asked him if he had a picture of his father. The son shook his head sadly. About two weeks later he came in again and I said, "I have something to show you." I gave him a picture of his father which he liked and kept.'

'A D. Pryall was born in Ireland and came to California in 1851. In 1852 he had started a nursery in San Francisco where the Emporium used to stand. He moved to Oakland in 1858 and settled at the head of the present Broadway near Temescal Creek, at the base of "Pagoda Hill." He specialized in eucalyptus trees and carried a general line of ornamental plants. Pryall is buried in Oakland's Mountain View Cemetery.'

'The gnarled Blue gums near the old Museum on Lake Merritt (1957) are said to have been from Pryall's nursery. Many of the owners of houses in Oakland and Berkeley purchased their trees from Pryall. The gardens on Tanglewood Road (Garber's, etc.) and the old Byrnes property in Berkeley were probably landscaped by Pryall in about 1870.'

'When Luther Burbank came to California as a young man and was looking around for helpful information, A. D. Pryall instructed him in how to pollinate fruits. Pryall had the first water works on Temescal Creek and disposed of these to the French Canadian Anthony Chabot, later well known for his controlling the water supply in early Oakland. Anthony Chabot also grew a great many kinds of Japanese and Chinese ornamental plants. It is quite possible that Luther Burbank secured some of his first plums from Anthony Chabot.'

Anthony Chabot

Anthony Chabot was sufficiently important in his day to warrant a little digression. He was born in 1814 in St Hyacinthe near Montreal. There are conflicting accounts of his early life. In one version we are told he was one of sixteen children of a deeply impoverished farmer who could barely feed his family. In another, the memorial issued by the Society of California Pioneers at his death in 1888, his father was a prosperous farmer and young

Antoine (Anthony) decided to run away at the age of fourteen out of sheer devilry. Whichever is closer to the truth, one thing is clear. He had practically no formal education.

His wanderings eventually took him to the California diggings. Here he teamed up with two other men and developed the process of hydraulic mining. Unlike so many miners, Chabot became very rich from extracting the gold, not through selling supplies. He later settled in Oakland. He controlled the water supply for years, and led the city through a major installation of gas lighting.

Chabot was an extremely canny businessman. As a relaxation, he indulged his considerable passion for plants and flowers. Anthony Chabot was not a professional nurseryman but his horticultural activities were important.' He was once greatly interested in bamboos.

He owned several very large lots at the outskirts of the city and grew about 30,000 camphor trees, 10,00 tea plants (tea of commerce), 1,000 Japanese Wax Trees (possibly Lewelling *Saepium sabiferum* or Chinese Tallow Tree), 4,000 Japanese red and white plums, 2,000 Japanese persimmons, 1,500 Japanese quinces as stocks, 1,000 Japanese oranges, and 1,000 rarest "Japonicas" or flowering quinces at his nursery in Temescal Canyon around 1885. (Note 14)

In Oakland, on Third Avenue between 15th and 16th Streets, Chabot had a semi-commercial nursery occupying half the block. Chabot donated Washington Park, where the telescope was once located, to the city of Oakland.' His name is commemorated in the Chabot Observatory and Space Center.

Domoto family

From Butterfield: ' In 1883 Chabot invited the Domoto Brothers to come over from Japan and teach him how to turn the leaves of the 10,000 tea plants he grew in Temescal Canyon into tea. The tea leaves proved to be of poor quality, so that was a business venture he did not pursue. The Domotos stayed in California but switched to horticulture. They established their own nursery near the gas works in Oakland.

The surviving Domoto brother, father of Toichi Domoto of Hayward, later settled in Krauss Avenue in Oakland where Butterfield met him many years later. (Note 15) It was while he was working in early Oakland that the senior Domoto developed the chrysanthemum variety, "Mae Turner," known to florists as a late variety. When the sons were old enough they took charge of the business.

Toichi Domoto, a graduate of Stanford University, selected a site for a new nursery south of the railroad and about a mile east of Hayward. He followed in the footsteps of his father and specialized in tree peonies and camellias. He also developed the Domoto Strain of double gerberas. Skill and versatility were hallmarks of this family. Toichi Domoto died in 2001 at the age of ninety eight.

George Lee

Lee's Garden was at the gore formed by Telegraph and Broadway in Oakland in the earliest years. George Lee was killed in the explosion of the steamship, "Central America." Previously he had grown many kinds of citrus trees in his garden and also banana and pineapple. Imagine such a garden in the heart of present Oakland.

Charles Potter

'In 1857 Charles S. Potter moved with his bride from San Francisco and settled on the site of Lee's Garden, this same gore at Telegraph and Broadway, Oakland. George C. Potter took charge of the estate shortly after 1860. During those early years Stephen Nolan was the gardener for the Potter Estate. Charles S. Potter had died in 1863 but Mr. Nolan looked after the Potter garden until he was ready to start his own "Belleview Nursery" well out on Telegraph Road. '

'The Potter children were disappointed when 17th Street was cut through from San Pablo to Telegraph because the asparagus and gooseberries had to be grubbed out. The old Potter house was not pulled down until 1878. Stephen Nolan probably planted a Blue Gum that grew to be two feet in diameter by 1872. Several year ago Miss Gray of St. Helena described the Potter garden as "ablaze with flowers and flower beds, landscaped under and between mighty oaks." Evidently Stephen Nolan did a good job.'

Eucalyptus in California

Several writers on eucalyptus in early California noted that William C. Walker of San Francisco and Stephen Nolan of Oakland were the first to grow the eucalyptus in California. Butterfield used to wonder about these men. Who were they, where did they live? How did they import the eucalyptus? He had no idea that one day he would see the nursery catalogs of both Walker and Nolan and that he would have a picture of Stephen Nolan.

The history of the eucalyptus tree in California is quite tangled. Robert Santos, the librarian in charge of special collections at the California State University at Stanislaus, has written a definitive monograph on this subject. (14) The very first event was in 1849. More than 2600 Australian miners came to San Francisco. One of their ships brought a bag of eucalyptus seed.

Once the seed was here, the next question is who was the first commercial nurseryman to offer seedlings for sale. It seems that William C Walker of the Golden Gate nursery in San Francisco and R.H. Washburn at Shell Mound Nursery in Oakland were the very earliest, listing them in the mid—to late—1850s. Santos does not include Stephen Nolan among this number. Later, Ellwood Cooper took up the cause and others also popularized the tree.

Stephen Nolan

In another of his lucky meetings, Butterfield came across two surviving daughters of Stephen Nolan. Rose Nolan, later Mrs. W. P. Snyder, had a nursery catalog of her father's for 1871. This catalog was subseqently given to the library of the University of California.' (Figure 12)

Figure 12 Stephen Nolan (1834-1918), famed importer of Australian and New Zealand plants. Photo shows him shortly before his death.
(Reproduced by permission of the Regents of the University of California)

'Stephen Nolan was born on the island of Jersey in 1834. He was apprenticed to professional gardeners in England. After working for the Potter estate he started his own Belleview Nursery out on Telegraph Road (now Telegraph Avenue) in about 1870. Nolan knew many ornamental plants grown in England and some from Australia. He established his nursery approximately where 34th Street was later built and not far from the old Moss Estate, now Mosswood Park.

Nolan grew twenty seven kinds of acacias by 1871. He had many of the important species of eucalyptus, callistemons or bottle-brushes, brooms, escallonias, fuchsias, *Hakea*, tea trees, pittosporums, *Pomaderris, Prostanthera nivea, Swainsonia, Templetonia*, and palms. He also listed the Chilean tree, *Cryptocarya miersii*, which closely resembles the Grecian laurel. He offered the Deodar cedar at $2.50 each in 1871. Many of the eucalyptus trees were 50 cents each.

Stephen Nolan's grounds were laid out with the skill of a true artist. Patrick Barry, a nurseryman from upstate New York, waxed quite poetical while visiting the Belleview Nursery in 1874 at a season when most eastern trees are quite bare of leaves. Here was *Grevillea robusta*, the Silk Oak tree from Australia, and the Manna gum (*Eucalyptus viminalis*) in all their glory. "The eye of our friend lighted with the enthusiasm of Nature's poet as he pictured the day when that landscape would be relieved by these magnificent trees." This glory had to be denied to Patrick Barry (1816-1880). These Australian trees would freeze in Rochester NY, since they can only stand about 15 degrees above zero. (Note 16)

Stephen Nolan continued his nursery until about 1879 and then worked as a landscape designer. He landscaped the Parrott Estate in San Mateo. One of his reference books was *An Encyclopedia of Gardening*. J. C. Loudon. 1878. His family gave this book to the University of California after his death in 1919.

Nolan had named his daughters after flowers, including Daisy, Rose, and Camellia. Rose Snyder died in the mid 1940s. Nolan spent his last years in her home.

Edward Gill

Edward Gill 's nursery was on 28th Street between Market and Adeline near San Pablo Avenue. The city's horse cars ran close to his nursery where evergreens and roses were conspicuous in 1874. Butterfield had a copy of Gill's 1890 catalog. It listed two hundred and ninety two varieties of rose, and eleven kinds of palms, not counting dracaenas and yuccas. Other plants listed include *Eupatorium ageratoides* and *Templetonia retusa*. Shortly after 1890 Gill moved to a site on San Pablo Avenue now known as the Gill Tract and owned partly by the University of California and partly by the Western Regional Laboratory.

James Stratton

James T. Stratton, father of the late Professor George H. Stratton of the University of California, planted forty eight acres of blue gum (*Eucalyptus globales*) and seven acres of Red gums (*Eucalyptus tereticornis*) in the spring of 1869. By 1875 he had a hundred and ninety two acres of eucalyptus trees near Hayward but continued to run his Gum Tree and Forest Nursery in East Oakland.

Stratton sold 35,000 gum trees to G. P. Jones for planting in the hills north of Berkeley (about 1876), also 25,000 trees to E. C. Sessions on low hills behind Brooklyn. The trees on the crest of the north Berkeley Hills were planted in 1876 but these do not include the younger trees planted by the Havens interest between 1905 and 1914. (Note 17) This very large scale planting of the Berkeley hills long pre-dated Joaquin Miller's Arbor Day in 1887.

Other nurseries

Many other nurserymen aided in building Oakland's gardens. L. M. Newsome, nurseryman and florist, came to Alameda County in 1861. Robert Turnbull, who ran a nursery on East 14th Street two blocks east of Fruitvale Avenue, moved to the county in 1862. David Tisch, born in Bavaria, on March 24, 1849, immigrated to

Figure 13 Pardee family house and garden, 11th Street, Oakland.
(Reproduced by permission of the Regents of the University of California)

California in 1872. He served as foreman for both James Hutchison and W. F. Kelsey but later established his own nursery and flower shop at 479-7th Street. George R. Bailey moved to California with his parents and started his business in East Oakland. He moved to Berkeley some time later.

Residential gardens

Governor George Pardee's father moved to Oakland in 1860 and built a fine house on 11th Street extending north to 12th street and east half a block from Castro. (Figure 13) The grounds were planted to old magnolias, Norfolk pines (*Araucaria excelsa,*) redwoods, a rubber tree (*Ficus elastica*), and native California laurels. Both father and son died many years ago. These and similar estates have all been subdivided for new houses.

"Reminiscences of East Bay Gardens from 1860 to 1890"

Adeline Street, one of the few streets with an actual name, had several fine large houses with memorable gardens. Belle Mahoon

Magee wrote a charming memoir of her childhood and the gardens she remembered, *"Reminiscences of East Bay gardens from 1860
to 1890"*, produced by the San Francisco Garden Club at the same
time as Florence Eyre's work. (15)

Mrs Magee's grandfather lived there. He wore a "Marechal
Niel" rose in his buttonhole each day. Judge Samuel Bell McKee
had a huge oak tree in the garden with a ciderpress beneath it.
This was to make use of the apples from his orchard. There was
also a circular grove of olive trees where the Queen of the May was
crowned each spring.

Other residents of Adeline Street who had beautiful gardens
included Albert Miller, Judge John Garber, a Mrs Downey and a
Mr Fowler. The Fowler house was named "Marathon Park". Judge
Garber, and later his daughter, Mrs Stringham, planted delicate
borders with white Marie Louise violets. White jasmine and heliotrope grew in abundance. The avenue had black cherry
underplanted with pink Castilian roses.

Mrs Magee recalled other inhabitants such as John Howard
who invented an early form of irrigation but regretted it. The water he led to his roses attracted swarms of snails. Frederick Olmsted
designed a garden for Mrs Duncan McDuffie. Lloyd Baldwin grew
rare bamboos and imported exotic trees.

A Mrs de Golia had the first collection of orchids in Oakland,
according to Belle Magee. Colonel John J Hays built "Fernwood"
in the Southern style near a creek edged with fern and wild flowers.

A. C. Dietz built his house at 5403 San Pablo Avenue, Oakland, in about 1863 and had the grounds landscaped. R. J. Boyer,
who married Dietz's daughter, occupied the house in later years.

Robert Woodward of Woodward's Gardens died in 1888. At
the time his estate was settled in 1892, gardeners sought plants
and statues from his old garden.

Mr. Dietz bought three statues, one of a large dog, another of
a gowned woman, and a third of a reclining nude Venus. At one
time this statue of Venus was near the Dietz's front fence. On two
occasions the family came home to find Venus "properly" covered
so she was moved back nearer the old mansion where she could

still have her sun baths unmolested. The old dog lost his tail, yet few would recognize the long steer's horn which served very well in its stead.

Close by the statue of Venus was one of the largest *Myoporum laetum* trees in California. In 1941 its trunk diameter was twenty one and a half inches at four and a half feet. The crown spread had a maximum of thirty eight feet and the tree was about twenty five feet tall. On the north side of the grounds stood an aged *Cordyline indivisa* (often called dracaena) with a flaring base measuring sixty eight inches in diameter at ground level and thirty six inches four feet from the ground. This was one of the largest specimens reported. Unfortunately this old garden has also given way to "progress".

Mills College moved to Oakland from Benicia in 1871. G. T. Mills and his wife were the owners and directors. They planted many eucalyptus trees and other ornamentals in the years that followed.

A. K. F. Harmon's home was a block east of Broadway between Hobart and 21st Street, just east of Webster. His conservatory contained many rare plants during the 1870's, such as species of *Erica*, *Ixora*, *Canna tricolor*, *C. discolor*, *Gymnogramma*, and *Passiflora*. He reported *Odontonera schomburghianum* in 1875. In 1877 he was proud of his rose, "Beauty of Glazenwood", more properly known as Fortune's Yellow. His gift of the Harmon Gymnasium to the University of California will be remembered by older graduates. He had *Prunus persica* var. "versicolor" before 1875. His old greenhouses were given to the City of Oakland but later removed.

Mosswood

J. Mora Moss came to California in 1853. He moved to Oakland in 1860 and developed a fine estate that eventually became Mosswood Park, south of MacArthur Boulevard and west of Broadway. It is now owned by the city of Oakland. Mosswood is a word made up of the two names, J Mora *Moss* and his wife, a former Miss *Wood*.

The eucalyptus trees, old Monterey Cypress and at one time a "monkey puzzle" tree, *Araucaria bidwillii* grew very well on this estate. *Pittosporum bicolor* once grew near the Moss home, also the Grass Tree, (*Xanthorrhoea*) from Australia. Some of these rare plants were removed when the grounds were re-done. Giant boxwoods once greeted visitors. Today the children who use the playground may not know about Mora Moss but they enjoy playing in the park.'

Fruitvale

The visitor to modern Oakland may see a few remnants of old estates in the vicinity of Fruitvale Avenue. All during the 1870's and later, fine horses and carriages would pull up to houses in this area to discharge their passengers. Sight-seeing tours covered the gardens in that part of Oakland. There were also other fine estates in western Oakland.'

Cohen-Bray House

One of the most important houses of the late nineteenth century in Fruitvale has been kept intact and used as a remarkable source of information about life in those days. Members of the original family still live in part of it. The rest of the house has been turned over to the Victorian Preservation Centre of Oakland, an organization founded by this family. In order to ensure its long term survival, the property was placed on the National Registry of Historic Places in 1988.

Alfred Cohen came to California in 1849 for the gold, but stayed to make money as a commission merchant. He was the son of a formerly wealthy coffee merchant in the West Indies. Cohen was born in London, but educated in the United States. He did well in California, and married Emilie Gibbons, daughter of a well known San Francisco physician.

The Cohens bought a hundred acres of land in Alameda County, in Fruit Vale, when it was still quiet and rural. Alfred recognized its potential since there was easy access to transportation across the bay into San Francisco. Not too far away, another successful pioneer, Watson Bray, also had a large estate. What came next was predictable. In 1884, Alfred Cohen's son married Emma Bray, and the families built them a house as a wedding present.

Watson Bray's own house was remarkable for the avenue of black locust trees which reached more than seventy feet in height. This house was later purchased by Mrs. C. Clay, a former President of the Piedmont Garden Club.

Not too much is recorded about the Cohen's garden, but photographs show rich shrubbery close to the house. Orchards, lawns and extensive flower beds were set out by most of the owners of large mansions in that enclave.

Oakland's redwood trees

A noted scholar and scientist , W.P. Gibbons, was far ahead of his time. In 1862, he read a paper to the Academy of Natural Scieces in San Francisco, advocating preservation of a great stand of redwood trees in Oakland. These trees only grow on the California coast ranges along a five hundred mile line. The grove in Oakland lies midway between Muir Woods in Marin County and a stand at Woodside in San Mateo County.

Later John Muir and Joaquin Miller worked with Gibbons to save the trees. The Oakland grove would have formed the basis of a fine botanical garden, according to Gibbons. There were fifteen species of shrubs and over three hundred flowering plants in it. The city and state rejected his suggestions but Redwood Peak is still there as an open area.

James De Fremery Sr.

Between 16th and 18th Street on Adeline west to Poplar is De Fremery Park, where James De Fremery Sr. had built a house long ago. The grounds were eventually sold to the City of Oakland to become a park. Elms, eucalyptus trees, chestnuts, and liveoaks remained until recently.

James De Fremery Sr. was born in Holland in 1844 and immigrated to California in 1867. He prospered by founding the

San Francisco Savings Union, and then bought nine acres of the original Peralta rancho, "The Grove". It had one of the last stands of native oaks. That was where he built his house. De Fremery was devoted to his garden and continually improved it with various shrubs and trees.

Many years later, after his death in 1899, the city of Oakland wanted to buy the property to create a public park. His son, James De Fremery Jr, called in John McLaren to have the property valued.

An inventory showed that there were more than two hundred and seventy five evergreens and live oaks, many of them over fifty feet high and with spreads of more than a hundred feet. Cultivated trees planted more than forty years previously included Lombard poplar, elm, cypress, acacia, ailanthus, elder, buckeye, pine, willow, linden, eucalyptus, ash, prune and boxwood. The city bought the De Fremery estate for $125,000 in 1907.

McDermont estate

Still further west on 8th Street at Cypress and extending a block further west to Center was the old McDermont Estate. With the passage of time the old garden decayed. It contained one of the largest California laurels or Bay Tree planted in California. It also contained yews, cypress, acacias, eugenias, magnolia, pittosporum, olive, eleagnus, Canary Island date palm, Mt. Atlas Cedar, old lilacs, fig trees, dracaenas, locust, purple-leaved plum, pampas grass, agapanthus, and the Mattress vine (*Muehlenbeckia complexa*).

Oakland's parks

A string of small parks extends along 10th Street in Oakland. Jefferson Park, near the site of the old Oakland High School, marks the place where Anthony Chabot once kept his telescope until it was moved out near Mills College. Not much was recorded about this little park until 1890, but then it is known that the city planted black acacias along its borders. The Superintendent of Parks,

Mr Lamond, was very conscientious and anxious to improve all the parks under his control

Old magnolia trees in Lincoln Park near Harrison and 10th Street are still beautiful. Lincoln Park was named for the slain president on his birthday, February 12, 1898. At the ceremony, soil from forty six states and two territories was used to plant a sequoia tree which grew to enormous size by the 1930s. The park later became the playground for the Lincoln Elementary School.

As the visitor drives east over into the San Antonio district other small parks will be seen. Such parks were determined very early in the city's history. Oakland was incorporated in 1852. A map from 1853 shows intermittent blocks of two acres each set aside to be parks along the axis of Broadway, at half a dozen places. Not all of them were landscaped early. Some of them were left unimproved for long periods. As administrations changed and more money became available in the budget, landscaping began. (Figure 14)

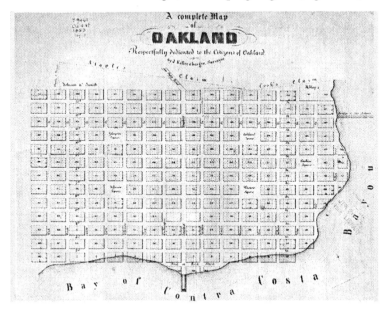

Figure 14 Map of Oakland in 1853, showing space left for future parks.

(Reproduced by permission of the City of Oakland Public Library)
Harrison Square Park was fenced for many years, because its title was unclear. In 1872 the fence was taken down but the Oakland-San Francisco Railroad built part of its track across the land. The local citizens were so angry, they tore the tracks out. It reverted to being a park. Trees were planted in the 1880s and by 1900 the park was said to be much improved. The city allotted $1000 to pay for cement walks, a gardener's salary and gravel.

Fifty years later, in the 1930s, a W.P.A. historian commented that there were an "ancient dropping yew, and very old palm trees". The live oaks may even have preceded the city's activities. These trees were still handsome in the 1930s. The center of the park is a large lawn, with four magnolias as well as the other trees.

The Memorial Plaza is in front of the City Hall. The huge oak tree in its center is named for Jack London. It is possible that the present tree is the one he planted on January 16, 1917.

Francisco Gallindo

'Francisco Gallindo was born in San Francisco on February 24, 1824. He worked in ranching until 1878, when he moved to Oakland and built the Gallindo Hotel with two hundred and fifty rooms. In 1876, at the age of fifty two, he married Inez Peralta, daughter of Antonia and Antonio Peralta.

The Gallindos built a magnificent house at 5401, Telegraph Avenue with a two and three quarter acre garden. The garden had rare trees and shrubs imported from Spain and Italy. It also had a marble fountain imported from Spain. In time the Gallindo property fell a victim to subdivision. Now the garden remains only in memory.'

Hospitals

'Three hospitals have been built on "Pill Hill" near 30th Street and Webster—namely Merrit, Peralta, and Providence. It was in this area that an Academy stood in early Oakland days. The eucalyptus had been planted there by 1860. Today such plants have mostly disappeared and newer trees have been planted, such as the Fern Pine (*Podocarpus elongata*) from Africa, one of the few times where this tree has been planted so far north.'

Joaquin Miller

Joaquin Miller, the poet and environmentalist, had a house up in the Oakland Hills. He was born Cincinnatus Hiner Miller, but after writing an impassioned letter to the press about Joaquin Murieta, he was continually called "Joaquin". He led a complicated life, but was devoted to nature and trees. The first Arbor Day in 1887, the one which so influenced Adolph Sutro, was his idea.

His sixty seven acre property in the Oakland hills was quite bare at first but he planted more than 75,000 trees and shrubs over the years. After his death, the property was acquired by the city of Oakland as a "poet's shrine".

Piedmont

'The early days of Piedmont are still vivid in the minds of a few members of an older generation. William H. Blair planted the Blue gum which stood near the business district in 1878. This tree was later removed to make the street safer. Many will remember the maze of hedges below the business district center where Sunday visitors tried to find their way in and out.'

Mountain View Cemetery

Piedmont was noted for its Sulfur Springs. There is also the old Mountain View Cemetery started in 1863. The cemetery came about as part of a movement which began in Mount Auburn, part of Cambridge, Massachusetts. Dr Jacob Bigelow, President of the newly formed Massachusetts Horticultural Society, believed that a good deal of sickness among the poor stemmed from "miasma" in the ancient cemeteries close to the centre of town. He was a physician at the Harvard Medical School and a social reformer in Cambridge.

Bigelow sought to improve the lives of the populace by moving the cemetery to open space and turning it into a park. The living could mourn the dead in inspiring surroundings. He finally managed to get the funds to start construction in 1831. By 1850, there were another eighteen such cemeteries scattered throughout the United States. That was a long time before Olmsted created Central Park in 1858.

The design looks very much like Central Park in New York, with curving roads and handsome vistas. Olmsted may well have been influenced because Mount Auburn had existed for almost twenty years by the time he started. This new type of cemetery resembled a botanical garden, with rare specimen trees and shrubs. The owners of a plot could plant trees and shrubs themselves but had to adhere to very strict guidelines

Piedmont joined in this movement. Few cemeteries have a more beautiful setting or so many fine trees as Mountain View. Some of the Cryptomeria trees may have been planted in the early 1860's. Henderson Lewelling, the "Father of Pacific Coast Horticulture", is buried in this cemetery, also A. D.Pryall and many early luminaries of San Francisco such as Domingo Ghirardelli, Julia Morgan and Frank Norris.

Berkeley

Butterfield wrote:' Father Crespi and a band of explorers led by Lieutenant Fages visited the area that would later become Berkeley on March 27, 1772. They found wild roses and lilies growing there. Don Luis Maria Peralta, who had been granted Rancho San Antonio in 1820, divided the rancho among his sons in 1842 and Domingo Peralta inherited the Berkeley section. The southern boundary of his domain ran from a point near the mouth of a canyon near the present Garber Park westerly in a line centered on Yerba Buena Island. The northern margin was the creek that separates Albany and El Cerrito, or the Alameda County line.'

Founders of the City of Berkeley

'Francis K. Shattuck (1824-1898) and George M. Blake landed in San Francisco in February, 1850, without dreaming they would help found the city of Berkeley. Later in 1850 James Leonard became Blake's partner digging for gold in the Sierra. When Shattuck started to walk to the Bay region from Marysville he found William Hillegas sick and penniless on the way. He took care of him and stuck with him as a friend all through the rest of their lives.

After reaching Oakland, the two men were joined by Blake and Leonard. Dr.John Marsh, who lived near Mt. Diablo, suggested they mark off a square mile of new ground to start a town. This ground later became the city of Berkeley. Their boundary went from the present College Avenue west to Grove Street and from Addison Street on the north to Russell Street on the south. All this was in 1852. The four men drew lots to see who would get first choice.

They had no right to take this land from Domingo Peralta but Americans were prone to treat the owners of Spanish grants in a highhanded manner. If the land could be held by squatters' rights for a certain length of time, and the holders could prove to the Court's satisfaction that they had been holding the property, title became permanent. This happened many times in Oakland and San Francisco.

Hillegas won the toss. He took the quarter mile strip from College Avenue westward; Leonard had second choice; Blake the third choice. Shattuck ended with the strip between present Shattuck Avenue and Grove Street, then considered the poorest choice of the four, yet today containing the heart of Berkeley business district. It was largely through his own effort and influence with the railroad that he was finally able to dominate this business area.'

'All four men finally built houses and gardens. Former residents may remember seeing Francis K. Shattuck's grounds near the site of the present Berkeley library south of the Shattuck Hotel, also the old orchard south of Addison Street.' (1950s)

A photograph of the Shattuck house in 1898 shows a large lawn in front, with shrubs and a few rose bushes planted rather sparsely, and very little foundation planting around the building. Tall trees are seen behind the house. This garden does not appear to be in any particular style. It was just large.

'Hillegas secured water rights on Strawberry Creek and later donated these to the University of California. This act of generosity greatly helped the University in planting the first trees on the Berkeley campus about 1870-71.'

University of California at Berkeley

The University of California was established as an institution in 1868, but three years before that Reverend Samuel Wiley moved to the College Homestead Tract and built a small cottage at the northwest corner of the present College and Dwight Way. (16) His daughter later explained to Harry Butterfield that her father moved to Berkeley to give the Tract a college atmosphere. He also sought to put a stop to the cutting of liveoaks on the campus site then owned by the College of California.

The Wiley home, northeast corner College and Dwight Way, was just a small rose-covered cottage, like so many seen so often in early days. The garden had a copper beech in which the family took just pride. They also planted a hedge of the wild holly-leaf cherry (*Prunus ilicifolia*) using seeds brought from Mission San Jose.

Reverend Wiley stated in a report to the trustees of the college of California in 1863-64 , "The attempt to obtain seeds and commence the growth of ornamental trees has not succeeded well." A year later he felt more cheerful when he reported, "In anticipation of future wants in the line of trees, I obtained some seeds last fall (1864), some here and some through Mr. Billings in New York and had them planted. From them we now have quite a quantity of young trees growing. A few Cedars of Lebanon, some Italian pines, cypress and Monterey pines, olives, walnuts, pepper trees, magnolias, and a great many locust trees." (Note 18) Such was the humble beginning of tree planting on the Berkeley campus.

Mrs. Gray, Wiley's daughter, told Butterfield later that the nursery where these trees were grown may have been near the Heimbold property, "Oakbrae", in the Claremont Hills district. Frederick Julius Heimbold, a native of Saxony, came to San Francisco on February 14, 1863. He married in 1864. Soon afterwards he went to Oakland where he worked in landscape gardening for the rest of his active life. Heimbold retired to the Claremont Hills home in 1868 and apparently it was there that some of the trees were grown for future planting on the University campus.

Mrs. Gray may have confused the Heimbold location with one near the head of Strawberry Canyon. At any rate the Wiley children remembered walking up the canyon where Mrs. Heimbold would give the girls cookies, very dear to the hearts of two small girls before 1870.

Frederick Law Olmsted Sr.

The campus might have been very different if the authorities had followed Frederick Law Olmsted's suggestions. He must have been very busy when he visited the Bay area in the late 1860s. He recommended a site for the future Golden Gate Park, he laid out a design for the new university at Berkeley and also told the trustees that they had to offer superior housing for the faculty, if they wanted anyone of substance to come and teach at the raw new school. One wonders why they bothered to ask him to submit designs and plans if the minute his back was turned they totally ignored them.

Olmsted's idea for the campus at Berkeley had his usual elegant melding of the terrain with the function of the buildings. He wanted to site groups of buildings in the natural swales along the creeks, allowing for much more careful use of the land. Instead, the trustees turned to the standard Beaux Arts style then current, and imposed large chunky structures without regard for the topography.

Phoebe Hearst played a large role in this decision. She emulated the activities of the "Widow Stanford", to use Kevin Starr's mordant phrase. Mrs Hearst was very generous to the new university, and unlike Mrs Stanford, was extremely interested in the students and their needs.

They did adopt Olmsted's suggestion about faculty housing. The shaping of Piedmont Avenue, just south of the campus, with roads curving according to the rise and fall of the land, still works very well. Handsome houses with pleasant gardens set well back from the road attracted excellent faculty.

The trees of Berkeley campus

Plans for the University of California were so far advanced by 1870 that Reverend Wiley did not see that his services were needed anymore so he went back to preaching and moved away from Berkeley. Eventually the university nursery was located in a hollow near the present south floor of the Stadium in Berkeley. Up to the time that the Wiley family left, no trees had been planted on the Berkeley campus proper.

There may have been one exception, the old redwood tree which grows on the west bank of the creek to the east of Giannini Hall. Core borings of this tree taken in 1921 suggest the tree was planted before 1870, possibly as a young seedling, or else grew from seed scattered by an early camper along Strawberry Creek. (17)

The first two campus buildings were North Hall and South Hall, completed in 1873 and first used in the fall of 1873. South Hall was the first Agricultural Building on the campus and is pictured in the federal Agricultural report for 1874. The late Joseph Rowell, former archivist, told Butterfield that all the eucalyptus trees by the Greek Theatre and along the slope near the Library were growing when he came to the campus in September of 1873. Many years later Reverend Wiley used to refer to the trees on the slope near the Greek Theatre with a sweep of his hand, saying "All of these came from my planting."

Evidently the first trees planted on this campus were set out in 1870 or some time in 1871. Pictures taken in 1873 and 1874 showed the young eucalyptus trees to be several feet in height, although still with juvenile leaves. Joseph Rowell seemed to recall that the eucalyptus trees in the large grove on the western part of the campus were growing when he came in 1873 but he must have been wrong. He did not remember seeing eucalyptus trees planted after he came but there is evidence many trees were planted later on.

Mrs. Jeanne Carr of Pasadena, whose husband Ezra H. Carr taught agriculture at the Berkeley campus for a short time when the University was started, reported to the State Board of Horticulture that more than sixty species of acacia were planted on the University grounds in 1873.

The first propagation houses were constructed in 1874 and a year later contained 10,000 eucalyptus in twenty species, 5,000 acacias in twenty five species, and two hundred conifers, azaleas, magnolias, and other ornamentals. Perhaps the cedars, just a stone's throw from the site of the old propagation houses, were from this early planting, since core boring show them to be quite old.

The remnants of a row of old magnolias still linger east of the creek close by Haviland Hall. The late Clarence Merrill, former postmaster in Berkeley, told Harry Butterfield he picked flowers from these trees for his fiancee in 1880. Even today this area is a beauty spot. The old olive trees were removed years ago. Younger redwood trees were planted along the creek in 1906, all but the one old tree previously mentioned.

Visitors to the Berkeley campus are impressed by the tall eucalyptus trees in a grove to the west of the Life Sciences Building. DeanWickson once reported that these Blue gums were planted in 1884 as a windbreak for the cinder track laid out the previous year, but pictures taken in 1885 and 1887 show these trees too large to have been planted in 1884. Dean Wickson was probably wrong, as was Joseph Rowell. (Note 19)

Later Charles Shinn, son of the Niles nurseryman, and a man who knew trees, reported that these trees were planted in 1877. This date would agree with the size of the trees in photographs taken in 1885. Some of these eucalyptus trees have reached a height of about two hundred feet, perhaps the tallest specimens outside native trees in Australia.

Shinn was a journalist who covered what we would now call environmental issues. In 1902 he even suggested using only native plants in private gardens, or plants which would adapt to the semi-arid conditions of California, rather than plants which required very large amounts of water. This was very forward looking for the time.

Dr. Eugene Hilgard, who became professor of Agriculture and Director of the Agricultural Experiment Station in 1874, as well as dean of the College of Agriculture, reported in 1885-6 that he set out plants of the English oak (*Quercus robur*) five years before. All but one were killed by gophers. The one old tree still growing north of the creek and to the north of the Life Sciences Building is probably this surviving specimen.

Dr. Hilgard also planted an English oak at his home on Bancroft Way in 1876. The Hilgard chestnut (*Castanea sativa*) grew in the depression south of Giannini Hall not far from the English oak just mentioned but it was finally killed by an oak fungus.

Eugene Hilgard was what might today be called a "superstar" academic: brilliant, worldly and polished. He was born in Germany, the tenth child of a politically active legal scholar who had to flee in 1848 because of his liberal views. The family settled in Wisconsin.

Eugene was taught at home, and inculcated with the importance of both science and the liberal arts. He was among the first to insist that farmers needed to use scientific principles and not just age-old wisdom. His specialty was the science of soils.

Dean Hilgard was fluent in English, German and Spanish and married to Dona Jesusa, the daughter of an army officer from Spain.

(For a full account of the trees of the Berkeley campus, described by Harry Butterfield, see Appendix B.)

Residential gardens

'Leaving the campus, going to the east of Liveoak Park, one comes to "The Cedars", built by Napoleon Bonaparte Byrnes in 1868. He and his young wife from Virginia travelled to California by oxcart in 1859. They settled on eight hundred and twenty seven acres in north Berkeley, including the present Cragmont district. "The Cedars" was built in a beautiful southern style.'

' The grounds were originally landscaped by A. D. Pryall of Oakland. An old eucalyptus tree may still remain but a tall Monterey cypress hedge on the east by Spruce Street has been removed. The "Cedars" was sold to Mrs. R. B. Berryman and the Byrnes built another house at 1313 Oxford Avenue in 1880. Mrs. Mendel Melcher later lived in "The Cedars". Subsequently this property became a religious institution.

Driving east on Bancroft Way east of College Avenue one comes to a section where E. J. Wickson and Dr. Eugene Hilgard built their houses on the north and south sides respectively in the 1870's and 1880's. The old Black Acacias growing in the parking strip were planted in 1879. Dr. Hilgard planted two Sierra Redwood trees in front of his home in 1876. Butterfield thought they were still alive in the 1940s. Neighbors in this district, including the Wicksons, Hilgards, Days, Palmers, and Blakes formed an "Association for the Promotion of Neighborhood Improvements" about 1880.'

This neighborhood was established separately from Piedmont Avenue, but clearly the faculty found it suitable. The fine old trees set out as a result of this collaboration survived in several places. They represented one of the first organized efforts for a street tree planting in California.

At the southwest corner of Piedmont Avenue and Bancroft Way is a very old specimen of *Maytenus boaria* or Mayten Tree from Chile. This was still a fine tree as late as 1957. At first glance this tree might be taken for some kind of weeping willow.

The site of the old Blake house is on the east side of Piedmont Avenue to the north of the International House. The Blakes' house was removed to make way for the Stadium. Anson Blake then rebuilt their house about two miles further north, naming it "Adelante", said to mean "further out and and higher up". A fine Deodar Cedar with branches drooping down as much as four feet was still standing there when Butterfield was writing.

The Simons' property was on the north side of Piedmont Avenue where it approaches the former bed of Strawberry Creek. The University later purchased the house.

The LeConte property with a specimen of *Pittosporum undulatum* as tall as the old two-story house once stood where Piedmont Avenue now turns in to Warring. The old house has been replaced by a modern apartment building.

Farther south is the Institution for the Deaf, but the old buildings have been largely replaced with modern structures. A few old trees dating back to about 1870 may still remain. The bear statue by Douglas Tilden, one of the institution's most famous alumni, still stands guard near the main building.

I.Newton Kieruff lived at 2628 Shattuck Avenue where Adeline Street joins Shattuck Avenue. The garden had a handsome red flowering gum tree. This is the story of how he came to grow it.

In 1894 one of Mr. Kieruff's sisters in law visited Sir Herbert Chermside's estate in Nottinghamshire, property formerly belonging to Lord Byron. (Note 20) Sir Herbert had been Governor General of Queensland. He grew ten species of flowering eucalyptus, including *Eucalyptus ficifolia*, the Red Flowering gum, in his park. Kieruff's sister-in-law obtained five seeds of this tree and on return tried to germinate the seeds between two moist blotters.

Only one of the seeds germinated but it grew into the magnificent specimen in the Kieruff grounds not far from Shattuck Avenue. Well preserved cedars and old wisteria suggest age and a garden once loved by its original owner. The house and plantings were replaced by an office building in about 1960.

John Kelsey should be mentioned because he had a large orchard extending for about two blocks east from College Avenue and northward from Russell Street. Old cherry trees still remain in a few gardens. Kelsey Street in this district bears the family name. He may have had a part in laying out the Elmwood District. The first Japanese plum brought to California by Daniel E. Hough of Vacaville was finally named after John Kelsey of Berkeley. He was a brother of George Kelsey of Oakland.

A map of Berkeley in the late 1870's shows that W. B. Thornburg had forty acres where the Claremont Hotel now stands. To the north is Tanglewood Road and along this curving street there were several old houses and gardens, well shaded with fine trees. The Stringhams' property and others which date back to before 1870, deserve special mention. The Garber family lived here. Garber Park in the canyon behind Claremont Hotel is named after them.

While in this district try to visit the grounds of Hotel Claremont. The northern part of the grounds was a private garden until after 1900 when fire destroyed the house, but there are several fine old trees still left, perhaps over a hundred years old.

Nurseries in Berkeley

The Carbone orchid houses used to be in the north hill section of Berkeley. John A. Carbone Sr moved there from West Berkeley. The nursery was later taken over by his son, John Carbone, not far from the late Sydney B. Mitchell's and Carl Salbach's gardens.

John Carbone Sr. came to California from Italy in 1883. He moved to Berkeley in 1890 and worked for his brother who had established a greenhouse the year before (near the present 2200 Fifth Street). His brother George introduced the "California Violet".

George Bailey

George Bailey (Figure 16) started his Forest Nursery in Oakland but later moved to Berkeley on Dwight Way west of Shattuck Avenue. At one time he had three express wagons hauling flats of seedling forest trees across the Bay. (Note 21) Most likely Adolph Sutro of San Francisco secured trees for Sutro Forest from George

Bailey in Berkeley. M. Theodore Kearney of Fresno was another who bought trees from Mr. Bailey.

George Bailey advertised for orders of a million eucalyptus trees and was dubbed "Eucalyptus Bailey." Unfortunately he died when only forty two years of age, leaving a wife with several small children. George Bailey very definitely left his imprint on the landscape of California and many trees still serve as a living memorial to his efforts.

Figure 15 George Robert Bailey (1848-1891), Berkeley nurseryman

Photo: Berton Crandall, Palo Alto.

(Reproduced by permission of the Regents of the University of California)

Berkeley horticulturists

Professor Sydney B. Mitchell, Carl Salbach, and Professor E. O. Essig were three notable horticulturists in Berkeley. The late Professor Mitchell and E. O. Essig made their mark in breeding fine irises, as did Carl Salbach. Mr. Salbach was also known for his fine gladiolus seedlings. Sydney Bancroft Mitchell was a prominent garden writer in the early years of the twentieth century. In spite of his middle name he was not known to be related to the historian. He came from Canada.

Blake estate

Mr. and Mrs. Anson Blake on Rincon Avenue off the Arlington studiously selected and planted the finest ornamental plants over a period of many years. Many plants they introduced were adopted by a broader public.' The house was modelled on an old Tuscan villa, and incorporated Spanish/Islamic concepts. A significant part of the garden emphasised this style, with a central pond leading the way to the house through an avenue of trees, and from which a small rill (narrow channel) originates. Italianate grottoes were built and covered with climbing vines. There is even a "giardino segretto" or secret garden on the estate.

Mr Blake's sister Mabel was the landscape architect. She did not adhere slavishly to the Italian originals, but added Oriental touches at various parts of the garden. There is a minute pagoda at an intersection within the woodland paths. A rose pergola leads to a rose garden which has the four square pattern of the old Persian gardens.

Mrs Blake knew a good deal about irises, and all the planting was expert. There are said to be more than 2500 varieties of plant in the garden. Fortunately the Blake property was given to the University of California and not sold for subdivision. It is now the official residence of the president of the university.

Alameda

From Butterfield: 'Bolsa de Encinal or Encinal de San Antonia was the part of the large Peralta holdings inherited by one of the sons in 1842, A. M. Peralta. Up until that time Alameda had not been developed. Late in 1850 Colonel Henry S. Fitch contracted with Peralta to buy the Alameda property but the deal was not completed. In 1852 W. W. Chipman and Gideon Aughinbaugh purchased the eastern end of the present Alameda and put up forty three lots of four acres each at auction. Those lots facing on High Street sold for $80 apiece. Aughinbaugh lived on Washington Street west of the street called Euclid Avenue in early days.'

Reverend A. H. Meyers

Reverend A. H. Meyers bought one of the four acre lots in 1852 as did William Taylor and his brother, Harvey Taylor. The forty three lots were numbered from the north to the south. G. G. Briggs had lots thirty nine to forty one. Briggs Avenue has been cut through the old Briggs property. Briggs was very important in the orchard and nursery fields.

Reverend Meyers had a nursery on his property in the 1850's. He became County School Superintendent on November 1, 1855 but only served for one year. In 1858 he had 150,000 trees ready for market. Later he became President of the Bay District Horticultural Society. Meyers shipped fruit trees from his Pioneer Nursery to people in the Mother Lode country.

Henry H. Meyers and Dry Creek

Henry H. Meyers, an architect who married a daughter of the wealthy Alameda butcher Augustus Mays, inherited a beautiful piece of land through his wife in what was once Niles/Alvarado. This community is now Union City, and the land has become a section of the Garin Park, "Dry Creek ". Part of this site was once the picnic grounds for the community. Most of it was left unimproved for cattle grazing. The creek runs close to a steep excarpment with a flag pole at the top.

In 1900 Meyers built a cottage in the Craftsman style. It is well placed on the site. The square shape with a green edging to the eaves and weathered shakes over the veranda supports are all perfectly consonant with the wooded background. The house blends in unobtrusively.

He and his wife had three daughters who never married. Each year, the sisters spent the summer months at Dry Creek, working in the garden which Jeannette Meyers had designed. They placed it at the disposal of many charities in Alameda for fund-raising *fêtes* and galas. A consultant to the East Bay Regional Parks service prepared a scrap book for Dry Creek in the late 1990s with copies of all the newspaper articles about the summer charitable events. This is really a garden with many memories.

Jeannette listed herself as a "Floral arranger" on her stationery. One sister, Edith, became a pediatrician in San Franciso, quite an accomplishment in the early years of the twentieth century. The third sister, Sophie, had no particular occupation. All three were graduates of the University of California at Berkeley.

Dr Edith Meyers spent a good deal of her time in Hayward. Maude Gibson, an Australian heiress, had built "La Granja", a large etstate with several smaller houses on her property in Hayward. Edith Meyers and Mis Gibson's friend Dr Anne Martin practiced pediatrics together in one of these outbuildings. The estate later became the California School of Gardening for Women, a pioneering institution. It is possible that Jeanette absorbed some of the ideas about constructing gardens from her sister's friends at the school.

Very old trees are planted close to the Dry Creek house: live oaks, sycamores, an orange tree heavy with fruit, a huge palm, and many tall shrubs. The property slipped after Jeannette died in 1993 and became sadly overgrown, but it is now being restored by the East Bay Regional Parks service. The ranger, Jacqueline Beggs, told me with pride how they have replaced the old armillary sphere which the Meyers had out in the front flower beds. One day the property will be open to the public.

Segmented flower beds surround the front of the house. They are richly planted with many spring bulbs which were just coming back to life when I visited the garden recently (February 2001). The garden is defined by curving gravel walks, passing between high shrubs and trees. Replacing the gravel is a heavy job which Mrs Beggs cheerfully carries out, together with a few devoted volunteers from the Eden Garden Club in the nearby comunity. A central fountain once had wooden picnic tables built around it. The charming arcuate "Monet" bridge over the creek had to be replaced by a straight one after neglect and weather caused the original to disintegrate.

Soft grey perennials edge the beds. An old rose garden is being restored with the varieties originally chosen by Jeannette Meyers. She left a very detailed planting plan which makes it much easier to replace the missing material. The East Bay regional park service is making meticulous plans to do this restoration very accurately.

Alameda nurseries

'Daniel Perkins' property was almost opposite the Pioneer Nursery on High Street. In the 1850's, Perkins was famous as one of the first producers of garden seed in California. The California State Agricultural Society in 1858 awarded him the first prize for the best seeds of ornamental plants, also garden and field seeds.'

'Dr. Henry Haile was an attorney and a member of the Alameda County Board of Supervisors in 1855. Wilson Flint was his partner in the nursery business during the 1850's. In 1858 the nursery included 12,000 fine trees, probably due to Dr. Haile's vast knowledge. He was "a pomologist of no mean ability." (Note 22)

Senator Stow of Goleta purchased budwood of the Lisbon lemon from a "Mrs. Hale" in Alameda in 1873. The tree was already twenty years old at that time, according to reports. Perhaps this budwood came through the efforts of Mrs. Haile. Early settlers reported that the old lemon tree might have been in Abel Thornton's orchard.

Colonel Warren listed the Lisbon lemon in his nursery catalog of 1853. The Alameda tree may have come from him. He listed

Lisbon lemon in his 1848 Massachusetts catalog. The Santa Barbara County strain of the Lisbon lemon differs from the one introduced many years later into Riverside County.

Origin of the loganberry

'Gideon Aughinbaugh of Alameda introduced the Aughinbaugh blackberry which is similar to the Mammoth blackberry. This berry was found growing wild along the creek in old Schutzen Park, later known as Washington Park, Alameda. (Schutzen Park was opened to the public in 1868.) The *California Horticulturist* of 1876 pictures this old variety so we know what its shape was. Judge Logan of Santa Cruz planted the Aughinbaugh on his property and seeds taken from this variety were propagated.

Two different seedlings appeared in the row, one of which became known as the Mammoth and the other as the "Logan". It is probable that the wild berry collected by Gideon Aughinbaugh of Alameda was the seed parent of both the Mammoth and Logan varieties. These seedlings were grown by Judge Logan of Santa Cruz in 1882.'

Bishop William Taylor

'Until October, 1940, a lone spreading Blue gum tree grew between the walk and the curb on Central Avenue, Alameda, just east of High Street where Bishop William Taylor once lived. Some have claimed that Bishop Taylor was the first to grow the eucalyptus in California and pointed out this tree as evidence. It was planted in about 1864.

The fact that Bishop William Taylor went to Australia in about 1863 and sent back eucalyptus seeds to his wife in Alameda seems suggestive but it is equally true that we have documentary evidence showing that the Australian eucalyptus was grown in California at least eight years before Bishop Taylor made his first trip to Australia. (Note 23) The tree was widely planted in central California by 1860.

Starting in 1869 James Stratton used some of the seed sent by

Bishop Taylor but also secured seed from other sources. The old Taylor Blue gum finally died from a scarcity of soil moisture after the street and adjoining property were paved. In October, 1940, a concrete plaque was put up a in honor of Bishop Taylor's son, first mayor of Alameda.'

W. Meyer

'Alameda was incorporated in 1854 with a little over a hundred inhabitants. Woodstock in western Alameda, lying west of Alameda on Pacific, was incorporated the same year. W. Meyer moved to Alameda County in 1853 and settled on a tract extending seven hundred and thirty feet west of Third Street and north two blocks from Pacific Street. There he grew some of the flowers used in his flower shop in San Francisco.'

Colonel Orr

'Colonel Orr's property was at the corner of Third and Spruce Street, not far from where W. Meyer grew his flowers. All of Alameda "Peninsula" was connected with Oakland by an isthmus until about 1884. This isthmus was near 23rd Avenue and finally was dredged away to complete the Estuary formerly known as San Antonio Creek. Today Alameda is on an island. Many fine old houses still stand in Alameda but their days are numbered.' (Written in the 1950s)

Lower Alameda County

San Leandro

From Butterfield: 'Don Jose Joaquin Estudillo settled in San Leandro on January 8, 1836, at Arroyo San Leandro. He built his first house on his rancho in 1836, about two miles south of the present San Leandro. Later he moved nearer the town which he started. As late as 1852 he was the only resident but soon squatters arrived and for a time the place was known as "Squatterville."

San Leandro became the county seat in 1854-55. The old Estudillo home at 1291 Carpenter Street, built in 1850-51, is now the property of Saint Leander's Catholic Church. A very large Mission grapevine once grew there. Old pear trees, a fig tree, and an old pepper tree survive as reminders that here was the first San Leandro garden.

A recent visitor to the San Leandro-San Lorenzo district up might have noticed many old houses dating back to the 1870's and 1880's but only some of the gardens are sufficiently distinctive to justify special mention. A few of the more outstanding ones will be named.

William Meek went to Oregon with nursery stock soon after the Lewellings arrived and married one of the Lewelling daughters. In 1859 he moved to California and became a neighbor of John Lewelling not far from the present Hayward. The Meek house was then purchased by Dr. Ream. The garden used to be much more beautiful than any of the present ones which have remained. William Meek and John Lewelling pioneered in fruit production in the area. They shipped many carloads of cherries in the 1880's.

Following Lewelling Boulevard across the creek we come to 624 Lewelling, home of Miss M. L. Teel. Early Spanish records show that the large native laurel tree (*Umbellularia californica*) growing there is an old timer. We can well imagine this is true when we notice the crown spread of eighty five feet and the trunk circumference of about fifty feet at ground level. The tree is about seventy feet high, but not as tall as other known specimens. The great trunk diameter is outstanding. Reports indicate that this tree served as a canopy for early meetings during the Spanish period.

Jemima Branin

'In 1957 Jemima Branin's old house still stood at the turn of the old highway in San Lorenzo and south from the new freeway. The house and garden are quite different now from when Mrs.

Branin and her family arrived there. She settled in Alameda County in 1865 and lived there continuously until her death in 1935.

Figure 16 Jemima Branin
(Reproduced by permission of the Regents of the University of California)

At first she lived at Alvarado but later moved to this property in San Lorenzo. She began importing varieties of iris from Barr in England before 1900. As early as 1880 she imported the Black calla (*Arum palestinu*) from Scotland to her home near Alvarado. Possibly some of the old plantings of this species date back to Mrs. Branin. (Figure 16)'

'Luther Burbank sent her a trunkless species of Grass tree (*Xanthorrhoea*) in 1904. It took twenty six years to flower. Mrs. Branin was given a medal for her work with irises in 1901 and an iris was planted in her honor in Golden Gate Park. Some of her seedlings in the *Spuria* group were named and at one time a few were grown in the Wayside Gardens of Mentor, Ohio. Butterfield himself grew one of her cream-colored seedlings.

Jemima Branin was born in Kirkaldy, Scotland, on August 18, 1845, and was past ninety at her death. She was elected an honorary member of the California Garden Clubs, Inc. For many years she attended the Alameda County Floral Society.'

Cherries in San Leandro

In 1972, the centennial year of San Leandro, Harry Shaffer, a prominent local historian, wrote a paper about its founding, "A Garden Grows in Eden". (18) An outstanding feature of early San Leandro was its cherry orchards. Robert S. Farrelly was one of the earliest people who grew cherries commercially. Soon apricot and almond orchards were laid out, and many commercial berry and vegetable gardens followed.

The town began to have cherry festivals as well as noted flower shows at the turn of the twentieth century. An important factor in these developments was the influx of Portuguese immigrants, mostly from the Azores. They understood market gardening and the value of hard work.

In March 1964, the Portuguese community commissioned a statue of a "typical" Portuguese immigrant. Numidifico Bessone was the artist.

Shaffer also commented on about a dozen private gardens and estates, such as the Webber house and the Estudillo house. In 1912, Luther Burbank rented a few acres in San Leandro to provide flowers for the Exposition. After two years, he moved to land in Hayward. All that remains of the Burbank endeavor are a few trees at the corner of Breed and Broadmoor Streets.

San Leandro and irises

William Mohr established the wonderful race containing *Iris mespotamica* genes. Mohr's house on the old highway in the Mt. Eden district, just west of the intersection, remained until fairly recently. Orange trees growing in the garden came from Dr. Edwin

Kimball (1831-1896), the pioneer horticulturist of Hayward. An unfortunate railroad accident killed most of the Mohr family.

The late Professor Sydney B. Mitchell took over the iris breeding started by Mohr and made further advances, producing some of the finest yellow irises. Irises such as "William Mohr" are still grown and descendants of this and other irises are still prized.'

Hayward

'In 1840 Don Guillermo Castro was granted the rancho which later became Hayward. Alvinza Hayward arrived in 1851 and built a hotel the next year. He lived across the creek to the west of the present Foothill Boulevard. The farm north of San Leandro Creek near the present Hayward High School belonged to Dr Kimball. The Kimball house was still standing till recently. A large Banksia rose grew near the house, as well as an old California buckeye, and a specimen of Gentile fig.

Dr. Kimball reached San Francisco in 1858 but moved to Hayward four years later, partly for his health. He suggested the name of Eden Township and sold trees to both William Meek and William Mohr. At the end of the Civil War, using funds left over from the Home Guards, he helped establish the old cemetery about a mile east of Hayward.' (Note 24)

'Many do not know that Dr. Kimball imported the Washington Navel orange directly from Washington, D.C. to Alameda County in 1874 quite independently of the navel oranges at Riverside. Most of the old navel orange trees growing in southern Alameda County came from him. Some of these oranges were sold to Crayton Winton who lived on Winton Road.

John Hall came to Alameda County in 1852 and settled on three hundred and eleven acres a mile east of Alvarado. He was a Kentuckian primarily interested in horses and farming, yet he planted some seedling Blue gums imported from Australia in 1865. These trees are still growing near the east end of Hall Station a mile east of Alvarado on the old highway. Mrs Branin noted that she saw the small trees he had brought from San Francisco in 1865.

Washington

George W. Patterson reached California and Alameda County in 1851. The Patterson Ranch once had a wide spread but was later much diminished. In about 1860 he planted the first eucalyptus trees around his house. Some of these reached a height of a hundred and seventy to a hundred and eighty feet and had a trunk diameter of three feet four inches to three feet ten inches, breast high. They are among the oldest living eucalyptus trees in California. (Written in the 1950s) A specimen of *Pinus nepalense* is one of the rare ornamentals planted on the Patterson Ranch.

Washington is a small community between Newark and Centerville. George Patterson built an elaborate house there on his estate "Ardenwood". It had a twenty acre park in which deer roamed freely. They were said to be his wife's pets. One hopes she had a good stout fence between this park and her flower beds, otherwise the deer would have eaten the lot.

Mrs Patterson not only ran her household efficiently but also administered much of the family agricultural business. In 1898, the anonymous contributor to the *Oakland Tribune* year book said she was "the equal of any man in this line".

Fremont

Centerville and Irvington are now a part of a new city, Fremont. Irvington (Washington Corners) to the west of Mission San Jose and Niles at the mouth of Niles Canyon, with Centerville half way between, have many fine old gardens. The " Governor" Cork oak grows between the Holy Ghost Church and the Parish House in old Centerville. It was planted by Father D. D. Governor in the 1890s. The Parish House burned down in 1918 but the old oak was still there at last report, having a crown spread of about fifty feet, as measured by W. Metcalf, former Extension Forester of the University of California.

Niles has been absorbed by the surrounding larger communities such as Union City and Fremont. This is a fitting site for the old adobe hacienda, now found on the California Nursery Company grounds. The roof has been slightly remodeled but the adobe still supplies warm Spanish hospitality on occasions. Scattered through the grounds are old trees first planted in 1885 and 1886 by John Rock and his co-workers. The old fan palms found there must date back to 1885.

John Rock and the California Nursery Company

Johann Fels was a young and energetic German youth who immigrated to America in 1852. He joined the 5th Regiment of New York Volunteers to fight in the Civil War, showing his loyalty to the United States. He also changed his name to John Rock. Rock is the English translation of "Fels". (Figure 17)

In 1863 he moved to California and started a nursery near San Jose in 1865. It was at the northern edge of the city. In 1879 he secured a site out near Wayne Station off Milpitas Road close to Coyote Creek. Twenty years later he merged his business with that of R. D. Fox, of San Jose to create the California Nursery Company at Niles. The combined firm was later purchased by the Roedings from Fresno. Rock Avenue is all that remains of that active business.

By 1889, the California Nursery Company had an extensive stock, the largest on the whole Pacific Coast according to Rock himself. The company introduced many ornamental plants as well as fruit trees. The nursery played a major role in the acclimatization of vast numbers of new olive cultivars imported into California between 1875 and 1900.

James Shinn and his sons

'Several pioneer gardens in the Niles area survived until the mid-twentieth century. James Shinn's property is perhaps best known. Shinn was born in 1807 and came to California in 1855. He died in 1896. Shinn built his house with lumber shipped around the Horn. That house still stands near the railroad on the

Figure 17 John Rock (former Johann Fels) 1836–1904
(Reproduced by permission of the Regents of the University of California)

west side of the Shinn Farm. A shingle roof has been added. Not far away is a large Blue Gum tree which Mr. Shinn had left over from a flat of seedlings. This runt was poked down into the ground with a finger and left to fight its way in life. It did that very nobly.' (Figure 18)

'The gardens surrounding the home of Mr. and Mrs. Joseph Clark Shinn were laid out in 1876 by Dr. Joseph Clark, Mrs.Shinn's brother. In 1937 Mrs. Lucy Clark Schnable, then 93 years of age, remembered helping plan the old Shinn garden when she was a girl. There are two giant redwoods from the Mariposa Grove, a Montezuma cypress, a ginkgo tree with its fan-shaped leaves,

*Figure 18 James Shinn's house, Niles, California. Old Blue gum
growing nearby.
(Reproduced by permission of the Regents of the University of California)*

Castilian roses rooted from cuttings taken from the Mayhew property east of Niles, and a grand Lamarque rose clambering over the porch and veranda.

Planted more recently are a camellia, now about seventy years of age, Japanese maples, a camphor tree, a rubber tree, a fine specimen of *Cryptocarya miersii* from which the University of California distributed seed in 1898, two fine specimens of the Wine Palm (*Jubaea chilensis*) and an old cork oak tree. This cork oak was grown from Spanish acorns in about 1871. The tree has a great spread of seventy five to a hundred feet and the height is about sixty feet. A carob was planted from seed on the spot in March, 1874.

Charles Shinn, one of James' Shinn's sons, must have thought highly of his old home when he wrote in his *Pacific Rural Handbook*, 1879, "The voices of happy children, some of them no longer on earth . . . seem to echo the arching trees (sic). The blue-bells and the violets, the fragrant lilies, and the passion-hearted roses, these carry his dreams back to his boyhood and move the soul to tears. The impulse which led him to found a home is justified." '

Important pioneers

'Joseph Livermore, an Irish sailor who decided to stay in California in the late 1820s, married Josefa Higuera and by that means gained Mexican citizenship. He obtained Canada de los Vaqueros and later, with Jose Noriega, acquired Rancho Pocitas in Livermore Valley. The old town of Livermore has fine plantings of black locust trees and occasionally remnants of old gardens can still be seen.

Agustin Bernal took residence on his property at Pleasanton "Alisal", (*alisal* is Spanish for sycamore) in 1850 but had owned the land since 1839. John W. Kottinger married Bernal's daughter in 1851. The story is told how the king of Spain sent the bride a rose plant, possibly White Cherokee, as a wedding gift. (Note 25) It was planted by the door of the old adobe hacienda, in about 1852. The adobe is gone. The rose remained on a knoll near the corner of Main and Ray Street northeast of the Standard Oil station until the mid twentieth century.'

'Antonio Sunol (1797-1865) came to Monterey in 1816 and started a store in San Jose two years later, becoming the first postmaster there in 1826. He married Dolores Bernal in 1823. Sunol established his 12,000 acre rancho on land granted to him and three of his brothers-in-law. General Naglee of San Jose got title to a third of his tract for helping fight squatters.'

'George Buttner came to this area in 1849 and settled at Sunol.

Old Italian cypress trees near the Southern Pacific Railroad depot and on the back road at the hills, east of the old depot site, grew there till about the 1950s, marking the entrance to the Buttner garden.

Jose Vallejo took over Mission San Jose in 1834 and became postmaster of the small town in 1852. He was granted Rancho Arroyo del Alameda in 1842, a total of 17,705 acres. He received the patent (deed) in 1858.'

'E. L. Beard opened a store near the mission in 1849 and purchased a little over three hundred and sixty seven acres northwest of the mission, west of the highway and as far as Mission Creek.

H. L. Ellsworth, Beard's son-in-law, moved to California in 1850. He took charge of the Beard property in 1858 when Mr. Beard was away with Colonel Fremont in a mining deal. Nellie Ellsworth and Mrs. Beard had helped to decorate the hall for the flower show in San Francisco in 1854. E. L. Beard had a fine garden in which he grew Australian acacia in 1854.'

'Rancho Tularitos was granted to ex-Sergeant Jose Higuera by Governor Arguello late in 1821. The small town of Warm Springs was founded on this land. The hotel owned by Clemente Columbett was not far away in the 1850's. The grounds about this hotel were landscaped by J. B. Lowe of San Jose. In 1850 Mr. A. Beatty leased the hotel, paying $400 a month rent. The hotel accommodated sixty guests. It was known as a fine "watering place." The warm springs were supposed to possess "higeian properties"(sic) and were much appreciated by the hotel guests.'

There are happy memories associated with springs. Guadalupe Vallejo has told about the Vallejo family starting for these springs to wash linens, an occasion something in the nature of a picnic.

The old Spanish *carreta* would rumble along freighted with the smaller children and the laundry itself. In the procession women slowly followed the white-haired Indian driving the poky wagon. Warm Springs means much more than a place on the map. Governor Stanford's brother, Josiah, finally became owner of the property The plants preserve some memories of yesterday.'

CHAPTER 4

Contra Costa County

From Butterfield: 'Contra Costa County once included Alameda County. Ships reaching San Francisco brought spices from the Orient and flowers from far away Australia. China, Japan, and the islands of the Pacific had been scoured for the wealth of the plant kingdom. Rough sailors knew little about the riches they brought, for they lived the life of the sea. They guarded their cargoes well, such as those of La Perouse and those which came to William C. Walker, Colonel Warren, Stephen Nolan, the Vallejos, Peraltas, and others. A hundred years of transformation took place in Contra Costa County. Let us go back to early days for a contrast.'

Nicholas Higuera

Nicholas Higuera and his twelve year old daughter Prudencia lived in his modest hacienda not far from the present Pinole in Contra Costa County. Prudencia and the other children were excited when the first American vessel cast anchor in San Pablo Bay near where they lived . They were even more excited when the captain came ashore.

Higuera knew that the family had been deprived of many ordinary amenities. They had to make do with quite primitive substitutes. Prudencia used a pounded willow twig as a tooth brush. Powdered egg shell was a substitute for face powder. Senor Higuera had hides and tallows to barter and so could afford to get the family the little luxuries they had missed,

The ship carried fishing tackle, but also cloth for dresses. Once Higuera had bought the basic necessities he needed, he added some large brass sailor buttons for Prudencia as a special treat. She was ecstatic.

Dr John Strenzel and John Muir

Dr. John Theophile Strenzel of Alhambra Valley was among many who pioneered the way. Strenzel was born in Poland, on November 29, 1813. (Note 26) He entered the University of Warsaw and graduated as a physician in 1839. (Figure 19) He emigrated to Texas, probably for political reasons, and practiced there for nine years. Poland had many periods of patriotic turmoil and chafed under Russian control. (Joseph Conrad's father was one of the aristocratic rebels who were sent to Siberia.)

Dr Strenzel married Miss Louisiana Erwin in Texas, on December 31, 1843. Soon afterwards Strenzel read Fremont's glowing accounts of California and decided to take the family to California in 1849. (Figure 20)

The overland trip took thirteen months. At first they settled near La Grange, but in 1853 Dr. Strenzel found a site in Alhambra Valley near Martinez. He bought five hundred acres, part hilly and part bottom land. He experimented with 1000 fruit varieties, also many ornamentals plants including flowering fruit trees. Some of his experiments succeeded. Dr Strenzel exhibited muscat raisins at the California State Fair in 1861.

Evereyone has now heard of John Muir, the man who awakened America to the value of its wilderness. Muir managed Strenzel's orchards. Later he married one of Strenzel's daughters. John Muir invited John Swett to settle as a neighbor. Dr. Strenzel died on October 31, 1890.

Harry Butterfield knew John Swett's son Frank very well, since he was an early graduate of the University of California. The Martinez High School is named for John Swett. The Muir property has been made into a state park.' John Muir's house and garden can now be visited on occasion, by appointment.

Figure 19 Dr John T. Strenzel, John Muir's father in law Photographer unknown.
(Reproduced by permission of the Contra Costa Historical Society)

August Hemme

'August Heme (probably Hemme) came to California in 1849 from the South. Remnants of his handsome estate still linger in Contra Costa county. Hemme sold his gold dust in Santa Clara, and bought cattle in the San Ramon Valley to take back to the mines. (Note 27) Later he bought a Spanish grant in San Ramon Valley and built a house in 1854. He stayed there until 1860

Figure 20 Mrs Louisiana Strenzel, John Muir's mother in law
Photographer unknown
(Reproduced by permission of the Contra Costa Historical Society)

when he moved to San Francisco. In about 1880 he decided to move back to the vicinity of Alamo, between present day Alamo and Danville.

Driving south from Alamo to Danville today one comes to a spot on the highway canopied with tall elms and walnuts and a few Blue Gums where the Hemme estate once stood. The designer of the Hotel Del Monte grounds, Rudolf Ulrich, also landscaped this estate. The driveway was planted with an avenue of wild cherry. Many rare ornamental plants were imported from China, Japan, and elsewhere.

The garden seemed to have been constructed all at one time, yet some of the eucalyptus trees may have been set out later. Emory Smith purchased a part of the land in about 1905. After his death the property passed to others. Since Smith played a small role in the development of California horticulture, it is interesting to follow his career.'

Emory Smith

'The boom in California attracted young Emory Smith back in 1887. A versatile and flexible man who cared a great deal about horticulture, he purchased land from E. J. (Lucky) Baldwin. (v.i.) He wanted to develop a perfume farm but when offered many times what he paid for the land he sold the property and invested elsewhere. A year later he lost practically everything when the boom broke.

This did not seem to slow him down. Smith next went to Santa Barbara and started the *California Florist and Gardener* magazine in 1888. As copies of the first edition lay on the back steps of the printing office, a goat came up and chewed the corners. One might say Smith was "accident prone".

Fortunately the printer helped him to finance a reprint. In spite of this reprieve there were too few subscribers in Santa Barbara at that time and he decided to move to San Francisco. He started again, this time with the assistance of Dean Wickson, now editor of the "Pacific Rural Press", in founding the California State Floral Society. They started the society in order to encourage people to become garden minded, incidentally leading to larger numbers of magazine subscribers.

This Society first met on September 21, 1888. Emory Smith was the first president and Dean Wickson the first secretary. The two alternated these posts for fourteen years. Smith's publication ran for about two years, then merged with the Pacific Rural Press.

Emory Smith became assistant editor of the new joint publication.

In spite of everything that persisted in going wrong, his activities were very important to the future of horticulture in California. For years he was interested in the possibilities of producing cork in California. Smith also imported the original spineless cactus from which Luther Burbank developed his special variety of spineless cactus. (Although Burbank succeeded in propagating the cactus as a year round cattle feed when grass was scarce, the cattle did not thrive on it and its use had to be given up. Spineless cactus plants still grow at the Burbank gardens in Santa Rosa.)

The beautiful Blue Gum in front of the Emory Smith house south of Alamo was planted in about 1880 and measures more than eighty inches in trunk diameter breast high. A specimen of *Pinus nepalense* has reached a height of about sixty feet and measured seventeen and a half inches diameter breast high many years ago.

Large Valley oaks on the property are as much as ninety seven feet high and have a spread of a hundred and ten feet, with a trunk diameter as large as six feet. The Golden Deodar Cedar, Ohio Buckeye, spineless cactus, and many other interesting ornamental plants which Smth collected grew on the estate established by August Hemme.

California poppy as California State Flower

In 1891 Sara Allen Plummer Lemon persuaded the California Legislature to adopt the California poppy as the official California state flower. In 1902 Emory Smith published *The Golden Poppy*, used as a reference in many public schools. Smith also helped John Carbone's brother introduce the "California" violet. In 1901 he arranged for the Pacific States Floral Congress.

Danville

'The oldest settlers in Danville may remember the Sycamore School. The Wood family gave property for a school to be built on condition that if it were discontinued the property would revert to the family. George Wood had been proud of the very large Blue Gum planted near the school in 1876.

Mount Diablo, once known as Sierra Bolbones on the map of 1826, stands on the old land grant of Rancho Arroyo de las Nucces y Bolbones. Old residents like to tell about the ghost towns of Nortonville and Somersville which were lively mining towns in 1860.'

Black Diamond Mines Regional Preserve

The site of the old towns has been preserved by the East Bay Regional Parks District as the "Black Diamond Mines Regional Preserve". 4,000, 000 tons of coal were excavated during the forty years the mines operated. This was the leading coal mining area in the state. Steam trains and steam ships were only some of the customers for this fuel. Modern Californiams are astounded to learn that such places ever existed in the Bay area.

The principal stockholder and President of the Black Diamond Mining Company was Alvinza Hayward. Once coal mining ceased to be lucrative in the early years of the twentieth century, the owners simply dismantled all the buildings and shipped them on to the next region, up in Washington state. The land was more or less empty when the regional parks district turned it into a park.

Two graves in the towns' Rose Hill cemetery have been maintained by the Daughters of the Golden West. A lone Italian cypress tree still stands sentinel. This cemetery was Protestant, because so many of the miners were Welsh. Hayward's daughter, Emma Rose, donated the cemetery land to Contra Costa County in 1972. Catholic miners and their families were buried elsewhere.

Dr John Marsh

It is possible to drive via Marsh Creek Road toward Brentwood and see Dr. John Marsh's house. Dr. Marsh reached California in 1835 after a very colorful life. By 1838 he had a small vineyard.

The stone house was built in 1852. He was the first "Anglo" to to live in the somewhat hazardous San Joaquin Valley. (Note 28)

John Marsh was a graduate of Harvard College, but had never studied medicine. In those freee-wheeling days, he was able to get away with this deception quite successfully. The imposing diploma from Harvard reassured the illiterate people who sought his care. The nature of medical practice back then was such that it made very little difference which unscientific and basically useless treatment was applied. Alas, he was murdered by a disgruntled former employee for completely different reasons.

Dr. Marsh welcomed many pioneers who came overland such as John Bidwell, Charles Weber, and others, some of whom who later constructed handsome gardens.' He had an irascible temperament. He was perhaps justifiably annoyed because the Bidwell party killed his best trained working ox for dinner when they first arrived, but he had not told them which animal to choose. Bidwell recorded that Marsh made a great fuss, out of all proportion to the offence.

Although he was a very solitary man in California, he had had quite a romantic past. During his wanderings through the middle west, he had married a native woman, formerly attached to a French trapper. He had a son with this woman. During a very bad winter he had been under the impression that they both died, and so continued to move west. After he had lived in California for a number of years, his son found him and moved into the house with him. Shortly afterwards, Marsh was murdered. There are plans to restore the Marsh house as a state landmark.

'Many of the modest homes in early Contra Costa County had small gardens with cherished plants. Up until recent years a large wisteria vine grew near Concord. It was about seventy five years old with a trunk of over twelve inches in diameter when it was removed in about 1940.

Elam Brown lived near Lafayette and represented that area at the first Constitutional Convention in Monterey and in the first Legislature in San Jose. He planted black walnuts near his home in about 1848. For a time he served as *juez* of Contra Costa County.

Nathaniel Jones bought a portion of Rancho Acalanes granted to Candelario Valencias, a soldier, in 1834. He set out black locust trees which provided the name of "Locust Grove" to his homestead. Contra Costa county has had its share of wonderful plantings.

CHAPTER 5

Santa Clara and Santa Cruz Counties

Here is Harry Butterfield setting the scene:'A little less than a year after the Declaration of Independence, the Mission of Santa Clara was founded. Services were held on January 12, 1777 under an *enramada*. On November 9 of the same year, five soldiers and five of Anza's *pobladores* or colonists with their families, about sixty seven persons in all, settled the pueblo of San Jose de Guadalupe, the first pueblo to be founded in Alta California. The old hall or *juzgado* was on Market Street near El Dorado, San Jose.

The success of Mission Santa Clara is well known in early California history. George Vancouver visited the mission during his 1792 voyage to the Pacific and was surprised to see so many fruit trees doing well. In 1828 the herds contained 30,000 animals. The neophyte population by that time had increased to 1,464. Forty years later, in 1834, secularization ushered in a shameful decline which persisted until the first Americans arrived a few years later.

American settlers began to arrive in San Jose and in other parts of Santa Clara County as early as 1841. The quality of these early settlers speaks well for the gardens that followed. Joseph Aram is a perfect example.

Santa Clara County nurseries

Joseph Aram

Sarah and Joseph Aram came to California overland in 1846. For a time they travelled with the Donner party, but subsequently left them and took a different route. Aram was thirty six.

On one occasion the Sioux Indians stole some badly needed supplies from the travellers. Aram suggested to another member that they capture the old Sioux chief the next time he showed up and threaten to turn him over to the Pawnees with whom the Sioux were at war. They carried out their threat successfully and were no longer troubled by thievery.

Later on during the trip, Sarah Aram was washing clothes at the edge of a stream in the Sierra and noticed some yellow grains in the wet sand. These proved to be gold. It was two years before the Gold Rush.

When the party arrived at Sutter's Fort in Sacramento Aram and his family were told to go to San Jose where they could find living quarters. Colonel Fremont commissioned him as Captain Joseph Aram to help defend the city. (Figure 21) Proving himself to be a leader, Captain Aram was appointed a delegate to the first Constitutional Convention in Monterey in 1849.

He also represented San Jose at the first Legislature in his home city a little later. After California became a state and conditions were more settled, Joseph Aram turned to fruit growing and the nursery business. When these ventures prospered, Aram was elected to the city council and to be a trustee of the College (now University) of the Pacific.

Joseph Aram's Railroad Nursery was on the northeast corner of San Pedro and Hobson Streets. Later he moved to a site south of the Creek, west side, on Milpitas Road, about a mile north of San Jose of today. The property was taken over by the Walter B. Clarke and Company Nursery. 'The very large blue gum at Coyote Creek is often known as the Captain Aram Blue Gum. It was planted in

Figure 21 Captain Joseph Aram
(Reproduced by permission of the Regents of the University of California)

about 1856. A camellia in front of the new office building bears about 5,000 blooms every year and is believed to have been planted in 1876.'

Bernard S. Fox

After Commodore Stockton obtained his large ranch north of Santa Clara he needed an experienced nurseryman to help him.

Figure 22 Bernard S. Fox (1816-1881)
(Reproduced by permission of the Regents of the University of California)

He asked Dana Hovey in Massachusetts to suggest an assistant. A young Irishman had been working there for five years and came from a family of nurserymen. Hovey sent Bernard S. Fox (1816-1881) in 1852. (Figure 23) Within two years of his arrival Fox decided to go out on his own. He opened a nursery on Milpitas Road opposite Joseph Aram. His Santa Clara Valley Nursery (Figure 22) produced more than a million trees in 1860. (Note 29)

Bernard S. Fox had no family of his own but he adopted one of his nephews from Ireland, R. D. Fox, and put him through the University of Santa Clara. After B. S. Fox died in 1881 the nephew took over the nursery and was very successful. He married and had a family of children. Butterfield had Fox's 1884 nursery, a catalog in which three hundred and fifty varieties of roses were listed. (See Appendix C for more detail)

Figure 23 Bernard. S. Fox Nursery, San Jose, in 1876. Founded in 1854.
(Reproduced by permission of the Regents of the University of California)

In 1884 R. D. Fox joined with John Rock and others to found the California Nursery Company at Niles. Each continued to issue his own nursery catalog for a time.

Senator Johnson of Hood , a small town below Sacramento, bought seedling camellias from Rock in 1872 and planted these near his home close to the banks of the Sacramento River. These plants developed into probably two of the largest camellia plants in California, one with a spread of thirty feet.

In 1877 Rock advertised 10,000 palms, including the Washington fan palm and the Japanese fan palm. He planted the cypress, *Cupressus chinensis* var. *torulosa,* from the Himalayas at his nursery north of Rock Avenue. It has reached ninety five feet in height and has a trunk diameter of about forty five inches. He also planted Japanese pagoda trees, *Sophora japonica,* along Rock Avenue. Some of the trunks measure twenty inches in diameter.

The entrance to his home was lined with tree myrtle, *Myrtus communis*, now tall enough to walk beneath. In his1884 catalog Rock listed the glossy shrub *Skimmia japonica* and many other plants of equal interest. After he helped start the California Nursery Company at Niles he continued to excel in growing fine plants for which he received high awards at expositions. Most of the California Nursery Company catalogs from 1893 on have been preserved.

Where Milpitas Road approaches the north edge of San Jose, just to the north of the new Bayshore Highway, the traveler passes between two rows of old trees, many being tall sycamores. It is reported that B. S. Fox planted these. Highway plantings of this sort will be found on Euclid Avenue in Ontario and on both Magnolia and Victoria Avenues in Riverside. Pepper trees were also planted along old Anaheim Road east of Long Beach. Such fine trees dignify a highway.'

William O'Donnell

William O'Donnell ran the United States Nursery in San Francisco with his brother James, up until 1856. (See p. 49) William then moved to San Jose and established the Mountain View Nursery on William Street. In 1870 he lived at 532 William Street, but the almost twelve acre nursery extended as far east as 11th Street. O'Donnell's Zoological Gardens and Park was patterned after Woodward's Gardens in San Francisco.

In the 1850s, William O'Donnell was growing acacia and English ash. By 1858 he had 5,000 acacias, 6,000 roses, 6,000 evergreens, 10,000 ornamental trees, and 1,000 arbor vitae.

Early visitors noticed a circular hedge of *Fabiana imbricata*. In 1860 O'Donnell was awarded first prize by the State Agricultural Society for the hedge. He was a life member of the Society. If you ever drive down William Street think of William O'Donnell with his Zoological Garden and Park and his Mountain View Nursery dating back to 1856.

Louis Prévost

Several French nurserymen were very prominent in San Jose at that time. Louis Prévost arrived in San Jose one day in 1849 and was destined to be recorded both in the history of San Jose and of Riverside. Fortunately Captain Weber saved some of his nursery catalogs so we know what Prevost grew.

Prévost's nursery extended from the "New Bridge on the Guadalupe River" just above City Mill, possibly Park Avenue Bridge of today, west to Spencer Avenue and within a hundred and thirty eight feet of San Carlos in 1856. The Charles C. Navlet Company was on part of this old property . This company was founded in 1885. (Note 30) (Harry Butterfield's daughter, Dorothy, worked at Navlet's as a young woman.)

Louis Prevost is best remembered for his roses. In 1857 he had 17,000 roses, comprising more than eighty varieties, at his nursery. He also grew 25,000 mulberry trees for raising silk worms. There were catalpas, locusts, privets, lilacs and a willow hedge. By 1858 his nursery included 150 date trees, 7,000 potted plants, 2,000 catalpas, 2,000 black locust trees, 1,500 honey locusts, 1,000 lilacs in five varieties and four varieties of basket willows.

Prévost was among the first to grow fan palms while he lived in San Jose. In 1858 he raised fifty specimens of *Washingtonia filifera* and distributed these over California. (Note 31) (also see page 397) Governor Latham bought two of these twenty five feet palms for $1,000 and moved them to his property in Menlo Park. By 1878 these trees were thirty feet high. W. E. Hopping, County Judge in Shasta County also planted two of these palms in 1858. Possibly John Rock and Bernard S. Fox developed their enthusiasm for these palms after seeing Prévost's garden.

Prévost's interest in silk production accounted for his visit to Riverside to form a silk colony but unfortunately his death on August 16, 1869 ended this venture. The State also discontinued its support of tree planting needed to feed the silk worms.

Antonio Delmas lived quite near Louis Prévost. His French Garden Nursery occupied approximately eleven acres. Delmas' son D. M. Delmas was an early San Jose attorney.

Louis Pellier

Louis Pellier was widely known for his introduction of the "French" or "Petite" prune to San Jose in 1856. He lived on Devine Street between Terraine and Santa Teresa streets. His brother, Pierre, was the one who brought back the scions of the French prune and also of the Pond plum, in December, 1856. The two brothers worked together in the nursery. The City of San Jose maintains the remnants of his property as the Pellier Park.

It is strange that early fruit growers did not obtain trees from the Sauls' Highland Nurseries in New York. We have seen that James Saul was attached to Juan Center's nursery in San Francisco very early, clearly indicating their recognition that Calfornia was an important new market. (See page 47) Highland Nursery listed this French prune as early as 1854, but California settlers were unfamiliar with what to grow and where to buy plants.'

'Many other nurserymen opened businesses in San Jose. The Hannay Brothers (J. and J. Hannay) had a nursery in eastern San Jose during the late 1860s. In 1877 they advertised pine, acacia, pepper, and poplar trees. L. F. Sanderson ran the Riverbank Nursery on Milpitas Road at the north edge of San Jose. He grew palms, magnolias, ferns, potted plants, trees, shrubs, and vines. (Note 32)

Residential gardens

The Townsenda lived next door to Captain Aram. Mrs Townsend planted her rose garden in 1873. Some of the old roses were still flowering in 1950 and deodar cedars and silk oaks planted about the same time also flourished until then.

General Henry Naglee

General Henry Naglee came to California in Company D of Stevenson's Regiment in 1846. His garden was famous in early San Jose, a source of delightful memories. Naglee owned about a hundred and forty acres in the eastern part of San Jose, Tenth Street to Coyote Creek on the east, and Santa Clara to William on the south.

His house and garden were near the present corner of 14th Street and San Fernando. At the end of the Civil War he was ready to start landscaping his grounds on a large scale. He started his orchard and vineyard in 1878. Naglee must have done considerable planting before the Civil War ended because Ellwood Cooper, who settled most of Goleta in Santa Barbara County, visited his property in 1866. Cooper saw a ten year old Blue Gum measuring eighteen inches in diameter and between eighty and ninety feet high.

General Naglee probably planted Blue Gum trees within five years of their introduction into California. The sight of these trees on General Naglee's estate inspired Ellwood Cooper to make his large planting about 1872. Cooper also wrote a book on the eucalyptus and forest trees. (See discussion under Santa Barbara County.)

Vignettes of the Gardens of San Jose de Guadalupe

There was an article about General Naglee's grounds in the *San Jose Pioneer* of 1877, according to Helen Weber Kennedy. She wrote this account in *Vignettes of the Gardens of San Jose de Guadalupe* published by the San Francisco Garden Club in 1938. (19) The *Vignettes* were edited by Mrs Kennedy and Veronica Kinzie, both members of the club. This fifty one page pamphlet is an invaluable source of detailed information. Harry Butterfield contributed a brief history of San Jose's horticulture.

Mrs Kennedy and Mrs Kinzie assembled twenty one accounts of old gardens in San Jose, from descendants of the early settlers. Some of the accounts were about a single garden, but a few described more than one.

Veronica Kinzie died in 1972 at the age of ninety four. Her father was Patrick Kennedy, an Irishman who came to San Francisco in 1851. He owned a store on Market Street and participated in the city's politics. She married Robert Kinzie, a mining engineer and general manager of the Portland Cement Company for many years.

Here is Mrs Kennedy's essay: "On entering the grounds I was somewhat reminded of an English nobleman's park; there was such a wealth and variety of foliage in so small a space. The roads, twenty two feet wide, macadamized as perfectly as those of Central Park, were lined on both sides with Monterey cypress. At one approach to the grounds these cypress trees have arms across the avenue forming a dense elliptical arch fifteen feet over the roadway, an evergreen tunnel two hundred feet long. Here I found evergreens from every clime, the Deodar Cedar from Himalayan Mountains; Cedar of Lebanon from Palestine; Chinese, Japanese, and Oregon Cypress; the *Sequoia Washintonia gigantea* (now properly *Sequoiadendron giganteum*, the Sierra Redwood or Big Tree); every conceivable variety of the arbor vitae and seventeen varieties of acacias. Monstrous century plants were dotted here and there in all their majesty. Enormous dracaenas, laurestinus, and all plants from New Holland (Australia) flourish there in the open."

Heliotrope, fuchsia, geranium, oleander, jessamine, ivy, and honeysuckle gave the garden estate rich color and scent. General Naglee introduced the Trousseaux and other varieties of grape for making wine here but in time the property was sold off and subdivided. All that remain are a few redwoods and palms near 14th Street.

Samuel J. Hensley

Samuel J. Hensley came to California in the J. P. Chiles Party of 1843 and helped fight Indians at Bloody Island in the Sacramento Valley. Later he had a command under Stockton. Next we hear of him on a twenty-acre tract of land in old San Jose, bounded by First Street on the west, Fourth Street on the east, and Empire Street on what later became the railroad right of way on the north. Hensley built a large house here in the comfortable southern style. The grounds were landscaped by James R. Lowe, an English landscape gardener who did fine work on several early Santa Clara County estates, starting in 1852.

To meet the standards of those days, most of the ornamental gardens were in front of the home. Passersby could see the garden was beautiful, elegantly laid out, and spacious. Today home gardeners think more of privacy and may have much of the garden in the rear. The Hensley grounds were landscaped like Lowe's own property. After Hensley's death in 1865 the land containing his gardens was subdivided.

James R. Lowe

James R. Lowe had a small property next to Major Hensley in San Jose. There were a rustic summer house and large arbor as well as an ornamental shrubbery. In the words of the Visiting Committee of the California State Agricultural Society, "The finely arranged grounds of forest trees; the wild romance of the rustic summer house; the graceful curves of the serpentine avenues, drives, and foot-ways; the luxuriant growth and abundant fruiting of long rows of espaliers; the rare collection of exotic trees, shrubs, vines, and rich fragrance of perennial bloom combine to make this one of the loveliest places on the Pacific Coast" (1858). (Note 33) This was the beginning of well designed residential property in early California.

Ryland Park

Very imposing residences grew up on north First Street when California became a state in 1850. Peter H. Burnett, first governor of California under American rule, together with C. T. Ryland and William Wallace, purchased a tract on the west side of First Street, San Jose, just to the north of where the railroad passed in recent years. Governor Burnett reserved a section for himself and moved his house in from Alviso in 185, according to Mrs. Kennedy:

"When Mr. C. T. Ryland married Miss Letitia Burnett, the Governor's daughter, they built adjoining the Burnetts. This house was a dignified one, typical of the period, set well back from the street. Lawns and large shade trees surrounded the home. The orchard extended to Guadalupe (Creek) . . . After their daughter Ada Ryland died the heirs decided to deed the property to the City as a memorial park."

One of the largest black locust trees in California grew in Ryland Park. It was said that a sea captain gave Mrs. Ryland a belladonna lily bulb which he had brought from abroad in 1850. Colonel Warren and others grew this bulb at about the same time in California, by 1853.

Over on Third Street there was a veteran pepper tree, (at least up until the 1950s). It probably dated back to 1870. Pepper tree s were taken to San Jose during the 1830's.

Mrs. Cora Older told Harry Butterfield that a cousin of Doña Sepulveda Mesa, Sebastian Moulloza, brought the pepper tree from southern California in the late 1830's. (Note 34) Dona Sepulveda's mother sowed the seed but only two seedlings came up. One was the old Paul Mason tree now cut down but famous until about 1920. Senora Mesa was born in San Jose in 1826.

The Older estate at "Woodhills"

Neither Harry Butterfield nor Mrs Kennedy included Cora Older's own garden in their work. Cora Older was married to Fremont Older, a welknown editor. They spent the first years of their marriage in a San Francisco hotel suite, but later bought property in Saratoga, facing the Los Altos hills. Here Mrs Older indulged her dream of having a rose garden. (19) At the end of the 1920s, the Older rose garden was at its peak. John Gordon photographed it in 1930, showing the central pool, the immaculate standard roses and elegant flagstone paving. The minute figure in the distance is Mrs Older herself. (Figure 25)

Figure 24 Cora Older's rose garden
Photograph by Gordon Commercial photographers
(Reproduced by permission of the San Francisco Garden Club)

Mrs Older also wanted to share her love of roses with the larger public. In 1926, she persuaded the City of San Jose to set aside and maintain land for a Municipal Rose Garden which is still in existence today. She worked with the president of the Santa Clara Valley Rose Society, Mrs Charles Derby, a tireless proponent of beautiful roses. (See Figure 24)

Mrs Derby and Mrs Older took cuttings of the old roses at the mission. The "Mission" roses have not survived, but many others have been planted in their place. Modern hybrid tea cultivars abound. Architecturally, this garden is very similar to Mrs Older's personal rose garden, with a central pool and fountain.

It often takes a visitor to pick out the unusual. This may be the case at the old Flickinger property at 467 East San Carlos Street in San Jose where a Japanese privet grew to about fifty feet in height, (June 1941).

A very fine specimen of evergreen Chinese Fringe tree (*Chionanthus retuse*) could be seen not far away, at Judge Lorigan's house, at the corner of San Salvador and Fifth Street. It had three forks beginning about a foot above the ground.

Donald MacKenzie

Donald MacKenzie's house in early San Jose faced the center of the Plaza and was set well back from the road. It was built in 1859. Isobel D. MacKenzie, writing in *Vignettes of the Gardens of San Jose de Guadalupe* gave a very good word picture of this early garden. " . . . . formal in character, our garden was always regular, and there was a very definite idea of balanced planting; white hawthornes across the front, palm trees on opposite corners of the land, magnolia trees in pairs, and laurestinus grouped on either side of the porch. Nevertheless, when the shrubbery and flowers were in bloom, all the regular outline became softened. Syringas, white and pink oleanders, Mock Orange (*Philadelphus* sp.), and purple lilac formed the high shrubbery in the long beds which were bordered by lavender, whose blossoms were gathered, 'before they were too ripe,' for placing in linen chests; periwinkle, valerian (probably *Centranthus*), hollyhock, feverfew, sweet briar (rose) which grew in great profusion, pomegranate and orange trees; lemon verbena bushes, tree-high. In the south garden, heliotrope grew to great height, as did the fuchsias, Sweet William, mignonette, roses and wallflower. The Lamarque (rose) grew about the library window as well as Paul Neyron, the Marechel Neil, the Homer, Sweet Briar, and Cabbage roses." (Note 35)

Judge Lieb

S. L. Lieb was a partner of D. M. Delmas. After Mr. Delmas moved to San Francisco Judge Lieb bought his property, together with that of Samuel Bishop, to add to his own. This ended the friendly rivalry between the families over whose garden was the more splendid. If Delmas put a fountain in his front garden, then so did Lieb. Some years after the merger of the properties, both the Delmas and Bishop houses burned down.

Judge Lieb had married a woman from Kentucky. She was determined to make her property resemble the Blue Grass state as much as she could. The Lieb garden comes to life in Lida Leib Armstrong's description in the *"Vignettes"*. ' Mrs Lieb planted a loquat tree, an almond, a row of palms, a smoke tree, and dug three small flower beds. Her granddaughter commented on the exquisite *Rosa rouletti* which still flowered prolifically sixty years later in one of those beds.

The Lieb garden contained a fine collection of rare trees, some dating back to when San Jose was just a pueblo. An old Celeste fig tree, Castilian, Damascus, Safrano and Marechal Niel roses, Blue gum, basswood, *Quercus borealis* var. *maxima, Acer saccharinum, Pterocarya stenoptera* (Wing-Nut), and many others of equal interest were growing in the Lieb garden until the 1950s. Judge Lieb was a friend of Luther Burbank. (Note 36)

Agriculture and Horticulture Societies

The Santa Clara County Agricultural Society was formed on May 6, 1854 with Dr. L. H. Bascom of Santa Clara as President. The Horticultural Society was started on August 13, 1854 at Louis Prévost's nursery, according to report. In 1856 the California State Fair was held in San Jose. Three years later the name of the Agricultural Society was changed to the Santa Clara Valley Agricultural Society. The society acquired twenty six acres on the Alameda and planted 2,600 forest trees and ornamentals.

Matilda Hill

It was some time after 1860 that Mrs. Matilda Hill built one of the largest houses in San Jose on her twelve acre property, north of the Hester House. This property changed hands several times but was finally sold to Mr. and Mrs. William Leet. Years later John McLaren re-designed the landscaping in such a way as to help display the fine old trees: elms, Deodar cedars, Monterey pines, eucalyptus, laurels, cypress, pepper trees, and yews. Three old black figs grown from cuttings taken at Mission Santa Clara flourished near the service area. These were the remnants of a family orchard.

Jensen wisteria

One of the largest and oldest wisteria vines in California grew in the Jensens' garden at 917, Asbury Avenue, several blocks east of the University of Santa Clara. Butterfield visited the old failing vine in 1941. It had been planted in about 1861 and at one time occupied perhaps an acre, but was cut back to make way for a trellis. By 1941 it was beginning to fail.

Stockton ranch

Commodore Stockton's ranch occupied several thousand acres between the cities of Santa Clara and San Jose. The nursery on the Stockton ranch was a limited venture. In 1854 many of the vines were sold at auction. Nurserymen often resorted to an auction in those days as a means of selling nursery stock. Fruit growers may be interested to learn that the Stockton nursery had the Corinth grape as early as 1854.

Once Hopkins, Flood, Newhall, and Crocker built the railroad to San Jose in 1864, it was necessary to secure a terminus near San Jose, so John and Charles Polhemus purchased the Stockton Ranch. Part of this ranch was retained by the Newhalls and part by the Pohlhemus family. The main residence of the ranch was on Alameda property recently owned by the Lieb family, according to Edward Polhemus.

Polhemus family

John Polhemus lived in the house he called "Maple Hut." The grounds were laid out by Nellie Polhemus, his eldest daughter. After the old house burned down in 1870 the family moved to a new location on Polhemus Street and Stockton. The new house had been constructed of hardwood in sections back in Massachusetts and taken to California in a sailing ship by Commodore Stockton.

The timbers were secured with wooden pegs rather than nails. It included ten bedrooms, which no doubted provided accomodation for many visitors as well as the family. "Polhemus" was the name of the new home. Nellie Polhemus planned this garden too, as well as the one on the Alameda.

The house burned down again in 1914 and another new house was built. At that time a few old trees were left and some new ones

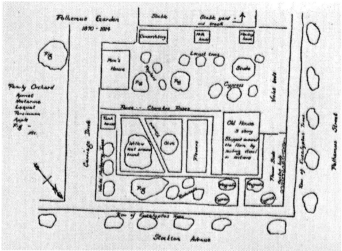

Figure 25 Plan of Polhemus garden in San Jose
(Reproduced by permission of the San Francisco Garden Club)

planted. Magnolia, cypress, redwood, Banksia rose, and a Cherokee rose were planted in the garden, one of the oldest in the San Jose area.

Edward Polhemus recalled every detail about the old garden and drew the accompanying plan from memory. (Figure 25) In 1938 the garden was still maintained and open to visitors.

Still other houses which Commodore Stockton had shipped around the Horn were erected near Stockton Avenue in the 1850's. A piece of the property was bought by Judge A. L. Rhodes and his house survived until about 1927. The old grape arbor and morning-glories remained to remind the visitor of a fading past.

Judge Belden and his little joke

Many substantial citizens of San Jose had handsome properties with memorable gardens. The Beldens, the Morrisons, the Bradleys, the Clays are just a few whose grandchildren recalled early visits nostalgically in the *"Vignettes"*. Judge Belden was quite a wit. Katharine Hall remembered his invitation to come and sit under his oak trees, not telling the recipient that the trees were about six inches tall, just emerging from the acorns.

In 1896 the *San Jose Mercury* published a yearbook showing numerous houses and gardens of prominent citizens, "*Sunshine Fruit and Flowers*". (21) This promotional volume was intended to lure prospective resdents to San Jose. It was re-issued by the newspaper in 1986.

Santa Clara Mission

A few old ornamental plants still remain at Mission Santa Clara. One is the interesting large white double Banksia rose (*Rosa banksia alba-plena*). (Figure 26).

An old Mission fig, which supplied many cuttings for early settlers, is about forty feet high. A Mission lemon grafted or budded on an orange stock measured thirteen inches in trunk diameter.

Some of the ornamental plants were planted more recently but a Tree of Heaven (*Ailanthus altissimia*) on the Mission grounds was fifty inches in trunk diameter in 1941, clearly a survivor from earlier days. This is a fine staminate tree which does not set seed and apparently does not put out suckers from its roots. It has a crown spread of seventy by seventy five feet.

Foster garden

Another fine specimen of *Ailanthus* on the Foster property, at the corner of San Antonio and 13th Street, may have been planted in about 1875, since it was a large tree before 1900. Usually the *Ailanthus* trees mark early settlements in California, as at Chinese Camp in the Mother Lode County, but the tendency for the trees to put out suckers prevents their use very often.

Records show that willows (*Salix laevigata*) from the creek were planted on the Alameda in 1799. There are those who would have us believe the two old specimens there in recent years with a

Figure 26 Double white Banksia rose (Rosa banksia alba plena),
eighty years old, at Mission Santa Clara, in 1941. Mrs. Charles
Derby, noted rosarian, is standing next to the rose trunk.
Photographer unknown
(Reproduced by permission of the Regents of the University of California)

marker date back to the original planting. That could not be, for willow do not live very long. Core borings showed these trees to be not more than seventy years old in 1941.

William Lent

A drive south in Santa Clara leads to a rather forbidding wall and one might wonder why there is a desire for so much conceal-ment. The high wall was built to ensure privacy in the grounds of an order of Carmelite nuns but of more interest to the gardener is the fact that William B. Lent once owned this property. He planted a lane of maple trees leading to the dwelling. There were also lin-dens, Pride of China (*Melia azerderach*) or China Berry, English hawthorns, and an enormous grape arbor leading from the rear of the house to the stables. "No English pleached walk was ever finer," wrote Mace Beaver. "It was so wide five carriages abreast could drive through it.

Smaller grape arbors were built on the axes, and squares formed by these arbors were planted to fruit trees. In the autumn the grapes hung in rich clusters from the arbor. The variety was the popular American grape, Isabella, so familiar to settlers from the eastern states. When J. P. Pierce bought the Lent property in 1866 he named it "New Park" in honor of his grandfather's home in England.

The conservatory on the old Lent property had the popular greenhouse plants of the day, such as *Stephanotis*, gloxinia, rare ferns, and begonias. Jack London, in writing of "New Park" said, "It stood back from the road, half hidden among trees through which glimpses could be caught of the veranda that crosses it on three sides. The house was approached by a gravel highway which wound through the spreading lawns and under interlacing boughs of tall trees." This is the pleached driveway already mentioned.

Mr. Lent planted Isabella grape vines. After Mr. Pierce took possession, he noticed that the children were eating some grapes from a vine that differed in size from the true Isabella. (Note 37) Canes from this vine were taken and rooted. Ultimately the new variety was called Pierce's Isabella. Some people know it as "Isabella Regia" or just "California Concord" but it is a large-fruited form of Isabella and not Concord.

Santa Clara gardens

'South of the business section of Santa Clara there were some interesting ornamental plants in Butterfield's day. There was a specimen of *Erythrina crista-galli* or Coral tree in D. Rusconi's garden which dated back to about 1900. It was one of the largest in California. Out at Headen Park Farm on El Camino Real near Gould Street there was a Douglas fir (*Pseduotsuga douglasii*) that was seventy seven years old in 1941. Specimens of the Coast redwood of the same age and an olive tree survived until the late 1950s.

Gould Street was named for A. L. Gould. Gould had his fruit orchard and nursery in Santa Clara before 1860, covering about ninety six acres. In 1858 he had two hundred rods of osage orange (*McClura*) hedge, a concrete barn, and an artesian well. He joined with other leading nurserymen to establish a code of fair prices for nursery trees that year.

To the south of Santa Clara, Dr. L. Bascome had a hundred and sixty acres. At one time he was treasurer of the California State Agricultural Society. In 1852-53 he was county supervisor. We have a word picture of his property in 1858 in the California State Agricultural Society report for that year. "The arrangement of this place is so unique that an idea of it cannot fail to interest. A circular driveway, nearly a mile in length, is constructed with osage orange hedge for its inner, and a double row of trees (in great variety) for its outer line. Within the circle, the orchard of 5000 trees of choice assorted fruits is planted. At the front of the circle, the gates open into the highway, and immediately opposite, on the rear stands the dwelling, surrounded by a great variety of our native trees and shrubbery, among which are not a few of our choice evergreens."

This use of native plants has been continued and is most fitting for many rural areas, although very few farmers now have a curved entrance a mile long, neither would modern farmers care to plant osage orange. Dr. Bascombe had a Cherokee rose and Kentucky Coffee tree to remind him of his home in Kentucky.

One of the largest camellia trees seen in this county grew in R. F. I. Raymond's garden in Saratoga. It was in Senator Phelan's former estate, "Montalvo", and must have been many years old. Possibly it is still alive (written in the 1950s).

There are other remnants of former splendor. Mortimer Lovenbritt of Oak Knoll, Los Gatos, had a large European chestnut tree planted in 1865. Frank Duvaneck of the Hidden Villa Ranch grew a fine specimen of an old *Magnolia grandiflora*. These magnolias survived for many years in Santa Clara County gardens.'

Laurelwood Farm

'Laurelwood Farm was formerly near the old Santa Clara mission in 1858. It was started in 1853. William B. Thornburg bought it from Stephen A. Franklin. During the 1850's and later the entrance to the farm was about three-quarters of a mile long, lined on either side by black locust and other ornamental trees. James R. Lowe landscaped it. There were 3000 ornamental plants and shade trees as well as native and foreign shrubbery, clematis, and others . Butterfield noted that there was a thriving pear orchard on the property when he visited the area. Shortly after the big earthquake of 1868 the Polhemus brothers moved to this farm with their families.'

Riverside Farm

'Just to the north of the Laurelwood Farm site and south of the Alviso Hospital Riverside Farm still stands, owned in the 1850's by Mr. John Southworth . (1941) A long lane leads to the house from the west. There is still an air of lingering luxury from the days gone by when the estate must have been very beautiful. The old lightposts are not in good repair, but there is still a pool, and an old grafted ash tree dominates a lawn area. Behind the house is an old Araucaria.

Immense cottonwoods border the stream bed near the old mansion, one measuring seventy five inches in diameter in 1941. As the visitor stands at a distance and views this garden of memory, he sees the signs of age, yet there is a grandeur that suggests beauty and refinement in the days of the 1850's and 1860's.'

James Lick

'James Lick, founder of the Lick Observatory on Mt. Hamilton, (at a cost of $700,000), once ran a nursery near South First and Willow Street in San Jose. He also had a flour mill four miles north and not far from Agnew, as well as a 200 acre farm. In time the flour mill was converted into a paper mill and still later the property was transferred to the Lane Memorial Association of Boston. After fire destroyed the buildings, people still were able to enjoy the lake.

He is said to have spent $200,000 on California Laurelwood to finish the inside of his house. Lick's house with its surrounding lawns, ornamentals, conservatories, flowers and fountains was finally moved to a new location south of San Jose.

The San Jose Scale insect was found for the first time in Lick's garden. Some say it came from South America and others that is was borne on flowering peach trees from Japan.'

New Almaden

There were gardens near the quicksilver mines at New Almaden. Men who had lived in that community as children remember playing in the gardens. There were also many other old gardens in Santa Clara County that were full of beauty. Until recent years two old black walnut trees still stood on the highway about a mile south of Gilroy, on the east side. (1940s)

These two trees were planted in 1856 or 1857 by a Mr. Reeve, according to Judge Lieb of San Jose. In 1888 the larger tree measured sixty six inches diameter and both had to be topped to about ninety five feet to clear a power line. A gasoline service station built near them prevented the roots from getting enough water. As a result the trees died, although the site is visible where the power line still stands high as it did previously.

Santa Cruz

According to Butterfield: 'Had Gaspar de Portola and his group of men found Monterey in 1769, it might have been many years later before Santa Cruz would have been discovered. By missing the object of their journey, the party continued on around Monterey Bay to the vicinity of Santa Cruz. The area had fertile land, plenty of water, and abundant timber. No wonder this country appealed to the Spanish explorers, yet it was not until twenty two years later that the Mission of Santa Cruz was founded.

Six years after that, the pueblo of Branciforte was started and this Spanish settlement continued until the American occupation. Many tales have been told about the village and the great hardships that faced the settlers. A more cheerful picture is that of the old Mission and the gardens of early settlers.

One of the oldest avocado trees in California was in an enclosure near the Santa Cruz mission, according to the late Professor G. W. Hendry of the University of California . He specialized in studying the adobe bricks and the plant materials they contained. This old avocado tree may have been planted before the American period and has not been given much publicity.

In 1866 Amana Gray crossed the Isthmus of Panama on his way to California, taking a seedling oak in a flower pot with him. This was a Massachusetts oak, commonly known as the Swamp White Oak. It was planted at 32 Union Street in Santa Cruz and had reached over sixty two feet in height with a crown spread of seventy feet by the middle of the twentieth century.

In about 1888 a young *Juniperus chinensis* var. *alba* was planted at the Bishop Warren property on Cliff Drive. A tulip tree of similar age is growing at 61, Garfield Avenue. Other old Santa Cruz homes had their choice ornamental plants. Mr. Bern, an early nurseryman, sold fuchsias, pampas grass, the Lamarque and Sofrano roses, deutzia, and euonymus before 1870. *Cordyline indivisa* originally brought him $10 each in early days but on short notice the price dropped to $1.50. Gardeners had learned that nurseries could sell at a lower price and were quick to demand more moderate prices.

Judge J. H. Logan, who developed the Loganberry, had his garden of memory where the Methodist parsonage recently stood in Santa Cruz. He sent away for magnolia trees to plant in this garden. Both the Logan and Mammoth varieties of berries originated in the judge's garden and are still grown today after seventy fiveyears. The story about the Loganberry now shifts to the Pajaro Valley.

James Waters arrived in San Francisco on the brig, "Osprey," in 1848, at the age of twenty one. He moved to the Pajaro Valley in 1860 but lost everything in the flood of the winter of 1861-1862. With J. A. Blackburn he began to grow nursery stock in 1867. Six years later he became the sole owner of the nursery at Watsonville. He was a member of the Santa Cruz branch of the Society of Pioneers.

After the loganberry was developed, Mr. Waters began to sell it. Later the College of Agriculture at the University of California in Berkeley distributed the variety from its test garden. Perhaps older people still living in Santa Cruz County will remember some of the fruits and ornamentals taken from Water's Pajaro Valley Nursery.'(Written in the 1950s)

The story is also told that the judge had a neighbor, Albert Knott. He sold fruit and vegetables from a stand near Logan's garden. This was the begininning of the enterprise known as Knott's Berry Farm, now in Los Angeles.

San Benito County

San Benito is a small county but has its share of garden history. In 2000, Janet Bryan, a devoted local historian, introduced me to Charles Turner's stories and articles about Hollister and San Juan Bautista. The Culp family's property was a fairly typical example of a large rural garden.

The buildings at Mission San Juan Bautista have been restored. There is also a historically accurate and careful plan to re-create a nineteenth century garden at the old Plaza Hotel and Castro Breen House across the way. The groundkeeper, Virginia Navarro, showed me the heirloom plants she tends so carefully. One unusual feature of this program is that they are also backbreeding the poultry. Specially bred hens and chickens run about in their pens, secure against the hungry foxes which lurk about in hopes.

The roses are a highlight of the garden plan. Frances Grate, the garden historian from Monterey who drew up the plan, features roses which would have been available in the 1860s, such a *Rosa banksia lutea, Rosa californice,* Noisette and Bourbon roses.

The Ferry Company, a nursery which began in San Benito County and ran for almost ninety years later merged with Morse. The resulting firm of Ferry Morse was subsequently bought by another, larger company.

CHAPTER 6

The Native California Garden and the Gardens of Childhood

California before the coming of the Europeans

Butterfield began his book as follows:'Four hundred and sixty years ago, Juan Rodrigues Cabrillo, the Portuguese pilot, first sighted Point Pinos on November 6, 1542. It lay on a vast bay where the Spanish were to found their first capital many years later. He did not come in to land but recorded the sighting in his log. He emphasised the pine trees in his entry. One of the first features to be noted about California was its trees.

Next came Sebastian Viscaino, a hundred and fifty years later in 1602. He too saw the California coast line. He went ashore briefly at San Diego and Santa Barbara, but was actually looking for a more northerly harbor.

Viscaino sailed across the huge shimmering bay which Cabrillo had seen. It must have been one of the few days without fog. This time he landed. He saw the sandy white beach, and pine trees at the crest of Point Pinos. His ship came in where the Monterey Presidio now stands. There was an oak tree which a few years ago we knew as Viscaino's oak. Father Ascension said mass under this tree.

Here in what would later become old Monterey, Viscaino tells us there was a "noble harbor" and an abundance of wild flowers, even though it was a December day. To the south he named a river the Rio Carmelo. This river flows by the mission which was built almost two hundred years later, San Carlos de Borromeo, sacred to Father Serra.

Cabrillo and Viscaino had each been at sea for months. The sight of trees and wild flowers was restorative, but it also set the tone for the future of the territory. This was a place where things would grow. The Spanish crown, which officially owned these lands, had never done very much about them, but once they saw other nations showing considerable interest in them, decided to develop this territory.

In 1769, after gruelling journeys both by land and by sea, a group of Spanish Franciscan missionaries, and a small detachment of soldiers, landed at San Diego and founded the first Mission. They also made plans to push on to the Bay of Monterey, later in 1769, the year before the Boston Massacre.

On this overland journey, the explorers passed through mile after mile of natural beauty, "Nature's garden". Other historians have recounted the journey of Portola, Palou, and Crespi and their privations, but did not comment on the wild bushes and flowers on all sides.'

Native plants

'The Spaniards followed the hills of chaparral, and climbed over slopes covered with chemise, (*Adenostema fasiculatum*) . Ruddy larkspurs (*Delphinium nudicaule*) bloomed near the bank in the wild. There were fields of golden poppies (*Eschscholtzia californica*)) seen by Johann Friederick Eschscholtz in 1816 near the Presidio in San Francisco. His colleague Chamisso later named the poppies Eschscholtzia in his honor.

There were hills where lupines grew (*Lupinus nanus* and others), golden fields of baeria (*Baeria chrystoma*), and sometimes innocence (*Collinsia bicolor*). Tidy tips (*Layia platyglossa*), baby blue eyes (*Nemophila insignia*), or masses of meadow foam (*Limnanthes douglasii*) also blossomed at times. The large blue gilia (*Gilia capitata*) and cream cups (*Platystemon californicus*) grew there, also the large flowered godetia (*Godetia grandiflora*).

The cream and blue grass-like iris (*Iris douglasii*) nestled in shady nooks.

Monterey peninsula

The trip to find Monterey in 1769 was a failure. The Spanish contingent had marched right past the bay of Monterey because it was shrouded in fog that day. In 1770 another trip was more successful. They were able to found the Presidio at Monterey.

Monterey Peninsula was important to Butterfield personally. He and his wife spent some happy spring days there. That same scene later caused him a great deal of sorrow. One of his brothers had drowned in the Pacific Ocean trying to save someone's life. Their mother received a posthumously awarded Carnegie medal.

In Point Pinos, close by the sea-hammered rocks wet with spray there was what Butterfield liked to call a "wild garden". Beach asters (*Erigeron glaucus*) and white-rippled sand dunes still stretch for miles along the beach.

Butterfield's childhood

Butterfield grew up in Southern California, in an unspoiled rural region near the coast. When he commented on children's activites, he was describing the newly arrived Americans at the end of the nineteenth century . The Spanish and "Californio" children probably had had the same untramelled experience.

As children Harry Butterfield and his friends wandered down by the sand dunes, where the tide left its margin, looking for mosses and sea shells and starfish. Sand verbenas (*Abronia umbellata* and *A. latifolia*) and the ice plant (*Carpobrotus chilensis*) were draped over the sand dunes. They ate the ripe fruit of the ice plant.

Moving further away they came to tall willows where cawing crows objected to their presence. They climbed to the top of the willow trees to look at the crows' blue eggs and dark nestlings. Not far away they could see the Bixby hacienda built by Don Abel

Stearns on his Los Alamitos Rancho. The Bixbys' descendants lived there in a house dating back to the eighteen forties.

As youngsters they could not distinguish between the native and the exotic. None of them knew that the tree mallow (*Lavatera assurgentiflora*) was native to California and grown in early Spanish gardens, but that the round disks of gazania flowers they called "Gold Dollars," came from South Africa. It never occurred to them that the mossy portulaca was from Brazil. They grew it for its velvet texture and varied colors. Butterfield cherished a simple sunflower was as much as the choicest of ornamental plants.

Today the scene is changed. Most of the places Butterfield loved as a child have been destroyed to make way for new houses. There are still a few relics. Driving east from Long Beach on Seventh Street instead of Anaheim Road one may still see the old house on the bluff. Pepper trees still line the old roadway, probably planted by John Bixby in the eighteen seventies.

Near the old adobe, one can picture Mrs. John Bixby, Fred Bixby's mother, carefully planting her garden. Her daughter Mrs. Sarah Smith tells the story in her book and mentions "Deafie," the old deaf fence rider Butterfield saw as a child. (Note 38)

CHAPTER 7

Spanish California Gardens

Harry Butterfield had the romanticized and sentimental view of California history typical of his period. What follows is how he described events we now see in a very different light. (See Limerick and White for modern views: { bibliography})

He chose to tell of the old Spanish and mission gardens; not clerical and ecclesiastic history. That aspect of the mission experience has been well told by others. The Franciscans created the first gardens of memory, to continue to use his term, but he saw no point in repeating other material that had been thoroughly rehearsed many times.

Unlike some modern scholars Butterfield believed that the settlers did have some sort of ornamental garden. They were probably quite basic. Expatriate Spanish life had very few margins for luxury or excess of any kind. Survival was uppermost in their minds.

Domestic life in Spanish California

'An atmosphere of peace prevailed in the Spanish hacienda and in the patio which it surrounded. A bare and spreading veranda or *correodore* was typical of many houses, running along the front of the white-walled adobe or next to the patio, serving as an outdoor living room.

The food was somewhat monotonous. It was enlivened by a modest number of fruits and vegetables. (These were presumably grown in the province. Shipping was far too uncertain to import perishable items.) Red peppers added warmth and flavor to the *tortillas*. Peas, carrots, garlic, onions, sometimes potatoes, cabbage and a few other vegetables were served. On occasion there were melons. Pears, tunas (cactus fruit), and other fruits in season were available. Surrounding the house there might be a few trees, perhaps some olives, Mission figs, or a small orchard cordoned off by willow trees to deter wandering cattle from damaging the fruit trees.

Near the coast in mild districts the pepper tree (*Schinus molle*), Arbol del Peru, as the Mexicans called it, and at times the cypress, (*Cupressus macrocarpa*) furnished greenery. Some rancheros went to the hills and brought back the wild cherry (*Prunus ilicifolia*). A few had jasmine, possibly Roman jasmine, (*Jasminum grandiflorum*) to twine around the supports of the veranda.

Cestrum nocturnum, the night-blooming jasmine, shed its evening fragrance. Later the settlers grew orange and lemon trees, the perfume of whose blossom served to remind the exiles of old Mexican or Spanish gardens. The pioneers also grew tree tobacco, *Nicotiana glauca*, known to the Spanish as "buena moza", loosely translated as lovely girl.

In time the true shrubby myrtle, *Myrtus communis*, the huisache (*Acadia farneshiana*) and lemon verbena (*Lippia citriodora*) made an appearance. Perhaps they grew the Floriponda or Mexican trumpet (*Datura suavelens*), known to pioneer children as Chinese lanterns. The first American gardeners knew this as *Brugmansia*. (Brugman was a great German botanist and this plant commemorates his name). Periwinkle can still be seen today, scrambling over adobe ruins.

In spite of the difficulties they had in maintaining a garden, the Spanish settlers prized rare plants. At Arroyo Hondo in Santa Barbara County, one of the Ortega places near Gaviota, there are three old trees known as "Capolini". This simply means cherry, but not our common sweet cherry. Tradition says they were planted by the mission fathers. When Don Hugo Reid planted his orchard by his adobe at Arcadia in 1840 he included a few of these capolini trees. This tree, *Prunus capuli* (Figure 28) was probably not listed by the first American nurserymen.'

Figure 27 Old cherry tree (Prunus capuli) from tropical America, planted by the Russians at Fort Ross, California about 1820. The trees were still alive early in the twentieth century. These trees were also planted in Santa Barbara County by Spanish settlers and by Hugo Reid at Arcadia.
(Reproduced by permission of the Regents of the University of California)

The oleander (*Nerium oleander*) and pomegranate (*Funica granatum*) were typically Spanish and Mexican but they were not common up to 1850. Only the Franciscans grew pomegranate frequently. The Castilian rose, (*Rosa damascina* var. *rigintipetala*), not the California rose which Portola's expedition called Castilian, was planted in some Spanish gardens.

Original Spanish gardens: an oxymoron?

Some writers have skipped over the Spanish gardens, saying that they were either non-existent or very bare. To a great extent that is true, but it appears fairly certain that the women did find some protected space in the patio, away from the herds, to plant a few precious flowers for color and fragrance. (22)

We get some evidence of this from Guadalupe Vallejo. The mission garden at Mission San Jose was taken over by Don Jose Jesus Vallejo in 1834. Guadalupe was his fourth child. She told this story later when she was an old lady in San Francisco. (Note 39)

Dona Guadalupe mentally pictured the flowers: roses, chiefly pink ones known as Castilian, also white (possibly White Cherokee) and pinks, sweet peas, and hollyhocks which some Spanish knew as *Vara de San Jose*: (St. Joseph's Staff). Nasturtiums came all the way from Mexico. White lilies were also planted in this garden.

CHAPTER 8

Monterey County

'The gardens in Old Monterey, the "City of Adobes" as well as a city of charm and romance, were neglected for many years and decayed badly.' Writing in the mid years of the twentieth century, Butterfield said that it was possible still to catch a faint glimpse of those first efforts. He travelled west from Highway 101 by way of Fort Ord or west from Salinas, past old ranchos and hills covered with oak or buckeye (*Aesculus californica*).

Butterfield quoted Lieutenant Fages in this story. Fages had seen buckeyes with white trunks resembling a fig tree. Small stream beds were lined with native sycamores, cottonwoods, or willows. In time the trees on the hills change to Monterey pines as one gets closer to the Spanish city. '

Hotel del Monte

'Moche Buena, near what was once Hotel Del Monte, is in the vicinity of that disappointing trip made by Crespi and others in 1769 searching for Monterey Harbor. Country houses in this area are half hidden by wild plantings. Toward the coast as one nears Monterey one passes by the grounds of the former Hotel Del Monte tucked away in an area landscaped about 1880.'

Rudolf Ulrich, who came to the United States from Germany after an apprenticeship in landscape gardening, designed the Hotel Del Monte grounds as well as those of the two other major resorts in California. He originated the idea of a garden comprised solely of succulents. The property now belongs to the U.S. Naval Post Graduate School.

Butterfield wrote: 'The same old araucarias are still in the grounds. There are large oaks stuffed with acorns by the woodpeckers, the native trees of the area and Grecian laurel. One of the features of those grounds were the "Arizona gardens". Huge succulents gave the garden a wonderful primitive feel.

Old Monterey

In order to trace the rise of Monterey, one must start with that long trip overland made by Portola and his followers. It was not until March 24, 1770 that they reached Monterey. This was not the Monterey we see today, just the liveoak dear to Father Serra, *El Estrero*, the inlet, and of course, the blue sky and blue waters. On May 31 the "San Antonio" arrived.

Solemn mass was held beneath "Viscaino's oak" three days later, the same place where Father Ascension had said mass and given his blessing. The joy of the occasion was slightly diminished by the memory of the previous year when Portola and his followers, worn out, sick, and hungry, had trudged on, yet failed to reach their goal.

On June 5, 1770 the Royal Presidio Chapel, (the Church of San Carlos) was founded. In 1771 Mission San Carlos de Borromeo de Monterey del Carmelo was founded. Then came adobes and haciendas, as one reaches the time of James McKinlay, Thomas C. Larkin, and William Tecumseh Sherman.

The Soberanes, Vallejos, and Don Jose Amesti all settled there at about the same time, joined by Juan Batista Alvarado, Jose Abrego, and Esteban Munras. One has to include the names of Don Jose de la Torre, Florencio Serrano, and General Jose Castro. There were about two hundred souls besides the troops of the Presidio viewed in 1844 by John Bidwell. (Note 40)

Garden lovers will find little distinctly Spanish in the Monterey gardens of today and very little that is early American. Here and

Figure 28 Casa Soberanes before restoration
(Reproduced by permission of the Monterey State Historic Park,
California State Park Service)

there is an old fig tree, an olive, or a lingering cottonwood and occasionally an old rose or cypress. This is hardly surprising. The original inhabitants had very few resources for creating gardens, and water was always very scarce in the summers. If the civic groups in charge of restoring Monterey to its original condition had adhered to stict authenticity, the town would seem very dreary to us now. (Figure 28)

Restoring Monterey's gardens

Knowing that they were perpetrating some degree of anachronism, the devoted citizens decided to sacrifice the strict interpretation of the past and create attractive gardens. They compromised by planting only those plants which might have been available to the residents of Monterey at the designated epochs. By the 1860s, there were quite a few possibilities and indeed, some of the houses from that period did indeed have their own gardens.

"The Path of History"

'Perhaps the best way to see early Monterey gardens is to walk around the town, following "The Path of History." (Note 40) Enormous effort has gone into making the garden tour accessible and pleasant. Privately sponsored groups and the California State Park Service both participated. (Turn to Appendix F to follow the full walking tour.) What follows is a partial version of the tour.

The city of Monterey built a delightful small park at one corner of the grounds surrounding Colton Hall, "Friendly Plaza".As with other important spaces in the city, the land for this garden was donated to Monterey by the Misses Jacks on May 7, 1929. Several small houses were on the site. The occupants were distressed at having their homes demolished. By October 1930, Myron Oliver, a local artist and devoted citizen, had prepared a plan of the prospective garden. He lived in the De La Torre house just around the corner . Money to construct the brick walls and paths came from the WPA.

The grounds are mainly open lawn, with a few shrubs and smaller trees. Oliver was not an horitcultural historian and the ideas he submitted were not strictly according to current views about reviving planting in Monterey. He wanted contemporary rose beds, not "Las Flores de Antes" or "La Rosa Castilla".

The plaza contains many old trees. Three mature redwood trees grow in the upper terraces. Further down there are a fine cork oak, some Washington palms, a row of olive trees, a linden tree, a Catalina ironwood and a number of London plane trees.

Lagunaria patersonii (cow itch tree) is also there. It is not perhaps the best choice for a public garden, as its fruit causes a contact dermatitis, rather like poison oak. The garden does have a quince tree, an integral part of Spanish life, but no fig or orange trees. Japanese flowering cherry and flowering maples grow in the park too.

A charming circular fountain in a hexagonal base adds more period character. Beds with Japanese anemones, calla lilies, geraniums, many spring bulbs, iris of several varieties and numerous others continue this mood. It is a restful place where people sit on the benches in the shade to eat their sandwiches and children can run about and play.

Across the street on the west side of Dutra almost opposite Colton Hall is Casa Vasquez, originally a one-story adobe and reported to be the birthplace of Tiburio Vasquez, the almost legendary bandit. The old garden which surrounds the adobe is shaded by a large Monterey cypress. The Maidenhair vine, *Muehlenbeckia complexa*, grows on the cypress. Nearby are aloes, close to the front gate. In the garden is a fine specimen of *Acacia baileyana*.

Further north on the west side of Dutra is Casa Alvarado, built in 1839 by Juan Batista Alvarado, Governor of California from 1836 to 1842. A large Monterey cypress in front is accompanied by a tree mallow, aloes, and other shrubs, possibly camellias. 'The building has a wooden jacket, as if ashamed of its dirty adobe. Also notice the old misshapen cypress tree on the east side of Dutra, claimed to have been used for hangings.'

At the northwest corner of Pierce and King Streets is the Gordon House, built in 1849-50 with lumber said to have been brought from Australia. It has a narrow veranda covered with fuchsias, black locust at the east side, also broad-leaved *Acanthus*.

Drive north on Pierce from Colton Hall Park to the southeast corner of Pierce and Jefferson where Casa de la Torre is located. This adobe was built in 1849 for Don Joaquin de la Torre, once Alcalde for the old Mexican capital. Cactus plants grow in the rear. A pepper tree, weeping poplar, purple plum, and fuchsias made up the garden planting.

Half a block north of Jefferson on the west side of Pierce is Casa Soto, owned by Jesus Soto during the early eighteen fifties. An old Monterey cypress grows there. This adobe has since been remodelled and is now used as offices.

Casa Serrano (or Estrada) is further north on the west side of Pacific Street. This house was built in 1849 by Don Florencio Seranno, alcalde under the Mexicans. Don Felicio Soberanes lived there until 1920. The overhanging balcony greets those who come to eat at the restaurant on the site. Still further north on the west side of Pacific just past Franklin is the Merrit house, built in the 1860s.

One block north of Franklin, facing Pacific, is Casa Soberanes, the "House of the Blue Gate", built in about 1842 by Rafael Estrada. Dona Maria Isadora Vallejo married Mariano Soberanes. The Soberanes family occupied the house from 1860 to 1920. There is a Monterey cypress hedge in front on Pacific. Behind may be seen a toyon and *Piitosporum tenuifolium.*'

Casa Soberanes has been very carefully restored, first by Jean and Reuben Serrano in the 1920s and 1930s, then by William and Mayo Hayes O'Donnell in the following decade. (See Figure 30) In 1954, the O'Donnells donated the property to the California State Department of Parks .

The garden was created in 1907. It is terraced and many of its beds are whimsically outlined by upended bottles, abalone shells and even pieces of whalebone. Near the house itself is a gigantic old oak tree, with one or two limbs exceedingly low to the ground. In the rear of the house there is a classical Spanish courtyard, flat and dusty, with an apricot tree, a few oleanders and a small herb patch further back. The garden has an authenticity all its own and a haunting atmosphere.

'The Henry House, girlhood home of Mrs. Herbert Hoover, is at the southeast corner of Pacific and Jackson' (The Henry House was demolished several years ago.) 'At the southwest corner of Scott and Pacific is the First Theater, where players revive the performances of an earlier day. A Monterey cypress at the southwest corner and clinging ivy on the Pacific side soften this copy of an old building. Whale bones near the walk serve as an edging.

The Old Whaling Station with its overhanging balcony is near the southeast corner of Pacific and Decatur. The garden has a border of echeverias, fuchsias, a climbing rose, and a young avocado tree, very charming and evocative.

Near the middle of the same block on the south side is the first brick house built in California, constructed in 1847 by the Dickenson family, survivors of the Donner tragedy.' Between the First Brick House and the Whaling Station, there is a modern

garden which nevertheless has a remarkable feeling of age and se-
renity . The brick walks wind around raised beds, with many fragrant roses, stocks and other aromatic plants contributing to this
mood. It is maintained by the Junior League of Monterey.

'Going east, Casa Verde is at the corner of Decatur and Oliver.
Charles Warren Stoddard wrote many of his stories and poems
here.

Moving to the southeast corner of Scott and Oliver we come
to Casa de Oro, the House of Gold, built in 1845 and now a State
Historic Monument. The miners stored their gold in it. From the
House of Gold go east to the southeast corner of Scott and Main
Street where the Old Pacific House is located. At one time soldiers
were housed in it. At the rear is the Memory Garden where the
State's birthday is celebrated each September 9. The restored garden might well represent an earlier garden and the setting is most
fitting.'

The Memory Garden was created by the Misses Jacks starting
in 1925. These two sisters inherited very large amounts of property from their wealthy father, David Jacks. Part of his estate contained the Old Pacific House (noted above) and the land around
it. They chose to use some of this land to re-create a Spanish garden which eventually was donated to the State of California.

The Jacks sisters retained the Olmsted brothers to design and
lay out their garden. One of the first things the Olmsteds did was
to add heavy arches in the mission style to the back porch. The
small library in the Monterey State Historic Park offices nearby
contains all the documents pertaining to the creation of the garden. At one time, long before the Jacks family was involved, bear
and bull fights were held in the corral behind the Pacific House.

Now the grounds are quiet and shady, with orange, lemon,
and magnolia trees carefully spaced across the flat dusty courtyard
surrounded by a high stucco wall. There are wisteria vines, a fuchsia hedge and numerous pots with brightly colored annuals spark-
ing the scene. The old bear pit is now a tea garden. A glittering
tiled fountain is in the center of this section and near it is a dwarf
pomegranate tree. This garden really offers a sense of memory, and

yet it was made long after the city had been settled and already changed to the modern era.

'Walk across Main Street to the Old Custom House and Museum. The building was started in 1814 and the north end completed in 1822. All trading began here and customs duties were assessed. Sad days of decline and ruin were to follow, but finally the building was restored from 1903 to 1905.'

' After viewing the old relics, the black lacy mantilla, and perhaps some old papers, walk to the east in the garden and see two old Monterey cypresses at each corner of the building. The small garden is all that is left of Plaza de Muelle.'

Later in the twentieth century, after Butterfield visited the city, the whole plaza was skilfully redesigned to reflect Monterey in its Spanish period. There is a mixture of antiquarian restoration with some modern license. The Monterey Maritime Museum is anachronistic, but a valuable resource for the casual visitor as well as scholars. Not far from the Custom House is a restoration of the "Jos. Boston" store, in the Casa del Oro shell. At one side of the store is a minute herb garden, filled with the sort of plants, "physic", that a nineteenth century apothecary or physician might have needed. The Historic Garden League maintains this store and garden.

The huge open plaza gives one the feeling of being at the edge of a continent, dependent on the sea for all outside supplies and news. Cool wind blows from the bay, accentuating the maritime atmosphere.

Francis Doud house

One private house whose garden Butterfield did not describe is Francis Doud's house. The garden was designed by a well known landscape architect, Florence Yoch, in the 1920s. Miss Yoch created the landscape at Tara for the film "Gone With The Wind". She made gardens for Hollywood celebrities such as George Cukor and David O Selznick, but Butterfield was silent on her efforts.

Doud's house was a typical New England clapboard structure. Miss Yoch put in an elegant pergola covered with wisteria and "Belle of Portugal" roses, and other signature touches, just is if it were in the same league as a movie star's estate. Members of the Historic Garden League of Monterey continue to care for it.

Asilomar

Close by to the south is Asilomar, (designed and built by Julia Morgan, architect of San Simeon) It now belongs to the State. Then comes the start of the Seventeen Mile Drive to Carmel by the Sea. Here is the scene with the pines and the cypress, and the white sand dunes. The sea still pounds against the rocks.

Along the peninsula between Pacific Grove and Carmel stands the forest of pine and cypress. These trees grow nowhere else as natives. On arrival at Carmel, visit the old mission which Father Serra loved so well and where he lies buried.

Mission San Carlo de Borromeo del Carmelo

The mission has been restored to something like its original condition. One may call the mission by its official name, San Carlos de Borromeo de Monterey del Carmelo, to be proper but to many it will remain just Carmel Mission. A Catholic parochial school occupies much of the old mission quarters. No old garden exists to greet the visitor, yet below on the flat near the highway are old pear trees now in their dotage, a reminder of what more than a century of living can mean to a pear tree.' (Figure 29)

There is a handsome garden now at the Carmel Mission, (Spring 2000). It was laid out all around the buildings, leaving a large open quadrangle at the back of the church, but enveloping the front, sides and most of the old churchyard. Although the courtyard at the missions was typically empty, some large trees were known to be planted for shade. Olive, pepper and oak trees have been used at Carmel for this purpose.

At some entrances, bougainvilllea and climbing roses soften

the lines. The gardens are punctuated by palm trees, numerous shrubs, and sprawling perennials such as lantana, and rosemary. Kniphofia gives vertical emphasis and color.

Figure 29 Old pear trees at Carmel Mission (Photograph ca. 1940) (Reproduced by permission of the Regents of the University of California)

CHAPTER 9

Napa County

H arry Butterfield wrote: 'General M. G. Vallejo founded Vallejo in 1850. There was increasing interest in the country to the north of Napa County from 1850. The route north was familiar to the Spanish, Kit Carson, and others. Nacional Rancho Suscol once supplied cattle and horses for the Mexican government in California. Vallejo took over the ranch during secularization.

The Spanish explorers were surrounded by Indians at this site but managed to send a rider for help. In time the soldiers arrived and saved the explorers from possible massacre. Native thistles growing on the land are reported to have given the name of Suscol to the area. Today there is an airport to the south and lingering reminders of early homes and a nursery.

After crossing the Napa County line on the way north from Vallejo there was an old brick house at the turn of the old highway. This old brick house was built by Peter Fagan in about 1860. A very large Monterey Pine and the Funeral Cypress (*Cupressus funebris*), an oleander, and remnants of an old garden persisted there into recent years.' This house has since been torn down.

G. W. Watson

Butterfield continued: 'Only curious minded gardeners would take the trouble to search out old gardens back from the main roads and highways, yet I recall visiting the old home of G. W.

Watson several years ago. The house was built in 1854, some distance east of the old highway. Grandfather Watson was visited by Kit Carson and no doubt many other early travelers.

Watson's grandmother brought a Matrimony vine (*Lycium chinense*) from her old home in Contra Costa County to plant in her garden of the 1850's. What else but such a tough vine could have withstood all the years of depredation of sheep and other livestock? New houses have been built by the younger Watson generations and yet when G. W. Watson rode up on his horse, "Nugget" and began to tell about old times, I could see that he had seventy years of memories about that old house and its garden. It was being kept as a sort of family heirloom.'

Thompson Brothers nursery

When Butterfield secured a copy of the old nursery catalog of the Thompson Brothers Nursery at Suscol for 1861 he wondered how a famous nursery could have been started there. Napa County history finally gave the answer. It seems that William Neely Thompson had come to San Francisco in 1849 with a nephew and started a lumber yard on Market Street at a time when sawn lumber was scarce.

General Vallejo wanted to build a State House in Vallejo to attract the new State Legislature. He had more acres than money so offered Mr. Thompson three hundred acres of land at Suscol in exchange for enough lumber to build the State House.The land was traded for lumber and the State House was built in Vallejo.' (Note 42)

'William Neely Thompson, the new owner, was a lumber man, not a farmer. His brother, Simpson Thompson, arrived in May, 1852, with the idea of manufacturing coal gas in San Francisco but with coal costing $50 a ton at that time, gave up this idea. (Figure 30) (This pre-dates the development of the Black Diamond Mines at Antioch. Presumably the coal had to be imported into California,thus accounting for the high price.) William sug-

*Figure 30 Simpson Thompson settled on his brother's land at Suscol,
Napa County. The brothers established a famous early nursery.
(Reproduced by permission of the Regents of the University of California)*

gested to his brother that he go up to Suscol and see what he could
do with the land. Simpson Thompson obtained peach pits from
Yount and began to grow nursery trees for sale when fruit trees
were still scarce. '

'At that time young fruit trees had to be ordered in the East
and shipped around the Horn. (Note 43)Transportation to the
Suscol nursery site was not difficult since the Napa River runs
close by to the west, and is easily reached from the San Francisco
Bay by smaller boats. Simpson Thompson had Australian acacia
before 1860. In 1858 locust trees, maples, elms, larch, and Nor-
way Spruce were planted along the different lanes and in the garden, about 3000 specimens in all.'

'Simpson Thompson's nursery catalog for 1861 proudly listed

the Southern Evergreen Magnolia (*Magnolia grandiflora*) as the "most beautiful of evergreen trees." Many of the old trees were still standing in 1957. The old specimen of *Pinus ponderosa* no longer scatters its large cones but the Holly-Leaf cherries (*Prunus ilicifolia*) still flourished in the mid 1950s. The Swamp Cypress trees (*Taxodium distichum*) have reached about eighty feet in height and four feet in trunk diameter. They are beginning to show their "knees." ' (1940s)

A grand old Atlas Cedar (*Cedrus atlantica*) still flourishes. Even a Sassafras tree (*Sassafras albidum*) holds a place along the lane. About six hundred acres still remain in this old estate. The present house was built around 1880 but the early buildings were burned leaving only the rock-walled basement. Not many gardeners have heard of this nursery that was once known over the entire Pacific Coast in 1860.

Napa State Hospital

'Traveling on north toward Napa one comes to the State Hospital east of the highway. The visitor has to slow down as he comes to the hospital entrance. The buildings were started in 1872, and were dominated by a seven story Gothic type of edifice, surrounded by spacious gardens and lawns. A long, wide promenade set the buildings back from the road.' This approach has not been changed.

'In time wonderful trees grew up, including several of the finest cork oak trees in California. One of these specimens is considered to be the largest cork oak in the state.' (The name was changed to Napa State Hospital from Napa State Hospital for the Insane in 1922. Much of the complex is still the way it was when Butterfield saw it, but the Gothic "castle" was replaced by more modern structures in 1949.)

City of Napa

'The City of Napa was laid out in 1848 by two men, Nathan Coombs and Terrill Grigsby. The old Nathan Coombs property is just over a mile west of the High School on Lincoln near a bend in the road. The old house built in 1850 is gone but there are two privet trees (*Ligustrum lucidum*) that remained up until the 1950s. Mr. Coombs planted many rare trees in his garden after he returned from Japan in the 1870s.

Fuller Park in Napa is not old and yet there are few small parks that are more beautiful.' (The park is at the confluence of Oak, Laurel, Jefferson and Seminary Streets. Land was purchased by the city in January 1905 and the park was named for Mayor C. H. Fuller. One of the earliest references to it was in Tom Gregory's *"History of Solano and Napa Counties"* 1912) 'A Pin oak (*Quercus palustris*) growing there is about fifty feet high.

Butterfield suggested that the visitor should try to see a triangular grassy parkway at Second and Wilson Street where a rare Christmas tree grew. It was planted in April, 1922. The tree was decorated every year. It has been identified as an Algerian Fir (*Abies numidica*) from the mountains of northern Africa. The specimen was bought at the California Nursery Co. at Niles for $120, considered to be a special price. John Hartley, Frank Hunt, and Frank T. Ames were on the committee that did the planting. It is the finest of its kind in California.' (This tree was removed many years ago)

'There are still many old houses in Napa and some of the old garden plantings remain. Unfortunately buildings need to be modernized and it is often cheaper to replace them than try to modernize a building.' Butterfield remembered the old building occupied several years previously by Judge Percy King and his wife. It was said to have eleven fire places and mantles.

(According to Dorothy Soderholm, a volunteer at the Napa County Historical Society, the judge moved from 1562 Third Street to 1721 Pine Street in 1930. Mrs. Soderholm searched through the records of the Napa County Historical Society but failed to find a house fitting this description.) 'An Eastern persimmon (*Diospyros virginiana*) grew in the garden. A large eucalyptus, old dwarf boxwood hedges, and many fine roses may still greet the visitor. It is easy to understand why the whole community loved the Kings.'

Cayetano Juarez

'Persons interested in adobes may wish to visit the Cayetano Juarez Adobe built in 1841 and owned in more recent years by Mrs. Metcalf.' (There have been other owners since Butterfield visited the adobe. At present it is known as the "Old Adobe Bar and Grille", operating as a bar and restaurant. It is at the intersection of Soscol Avenue and Silverado Trail.)

'Cayetano Juarez built his house in 1840 on two square leagues of land granted to him. The Harbison Adobe north of Napa was built by the Berryessas. Salvadore's old house hass gone but two grand old trees are still growing near the former entrance.

Marjorie Albert

Marjorie Albert's old home is also interesting and well kept. This house was built in the 1840s by Salvador Vallejo in the Spanish style. It was on the north side of Monticello Road, just east of the Little Trancas.' (It was later named "Longwoood".) 'The upper part was built over the original adobe.' (Unfortunately, this house burned down in November 1970. Miss Albert had just completed the arrangements to have it registered as a permanent state landmark, and it was due to be listed a few days after the fire. After torrential rain in 1971, two of the weed seeds in the adobe bricks sprouted. These plants have been dried and may be seen in the Napa County Historical Society's premises. At the present time, the property is all vineyard.)

'Marjorie Albert's house and the Maxwell house illustrate the transition from the Mexican to the modern American period. The houses rather than their gardens impress us, yet the gardens are pleasing. The Timber bamboo (*Phyllostachys reticulata*) planting near the north edge of Napa was furnished by the San Francisco nurseryman Charles Abraham many years ago.'

Guadalupe cypresses

A grand specimen of the Guadalupe cypress (*Cupressus guadalupensis*) is on the old Fischer property, owned in the 1950s by the California Lands, Inc. It is in the Union District, half a mile west and an eighth of a mile north of Union Station. In 1939 this tree was about seventy two feet tall. Another specimen of this cypress is found on C. J. Buhman's property one mile east of Union Station. It was eighty feet tall in 1939.

The reader may be interested in these two specimens and also in the Guadalupe cypress trees planted in early days in Capital Park, Sacramento at a time when the species had not yet been named. The two trees above Napa are even larger than those in Capital Park and may have been planted around 1865, possibly from seed.

Oak Knoll Farm

Oak Knoll Farm to the west of the highway north of Napa was originally owned by Joseph W. Osborn. This ranch was sold to R. W. Woodward of Woodward's Gardens in San Francisco on December 27, 1862. The property was described by the Visiting Committee of the California State Agricultural Society in 1858 with these words, "The home of 1858 is new, large, convenient, unique, plain, rich, droll, labyrinthian (sic), and unfinished. The English Elizabethan style, applied to a Swiss suburban villa, (is) surrounded by East Indian verandas, and topped by a touch of Burmese pagoda, covered with a Chinese-built root."

Such was the house of Joseph Warren Osborn. Tragically Mr. Osborn was later murdered. The murderer was said to have had had the somewhat melancholy distinction of being the first person to be legally hanged in Napa County. Robert Woodward did more planting after he bought the property and he probably did some new construction.'

Woodward's daughter married a man named Drury Melone, and her son Harry inherited the property after his father died.

Since then, it has changed hands several times. Part of this property later became the Eschol Ranch [see below]. Woodward's granddaughter, Alice Malone Hooper, was an early member of the San Francisco Garden Club. She described her grandfather's activities in the club's "*Vignettes of Early San Francisco Homes and Gardens*". The house remains a very handsome place.

'Stately avenues of black locust trees are still growing after more than a hundred years. A ginkgo tree growing near the house measured seven feet seven inches in circumference breast high about 1939. A Blue Gum is ten feet. seven inches in circumference. Immense boxwoods and English Holly date back to Woodward's time. The statuary which once adorned the place has long ago disappeared.'

Judge Percy King told Butterfield that Mr. Woodward gave a large pink tree peony to his mother-in-law, Mrs. J. A. Klam, then a neighbor in the early 1870's. It was believed to have come originally from Woodward's Gardens in San Francisco.

Grigsby brothers

Almost opposite Oak Knoll Farm on the east side of the Napa valley was the Grigsby brothers' property. Captain Grigsby and his brother lived there in the late 1850's. Captain Grigsby was among those who helped raise the Bear Flag in Sonoma.

Mr. Coombs and one of the Grigsbys laid out Napa City. Magnificent oaks were growing on this farm in 1858.' (There were several Grigsby properties in early Napa. It is unclear which one is meant here. Terrill Grigsby owned the Occidental Winery which is still standing. Another brother, J. W. Grigsby, had a dairy farm.)

Emerson Farm

'A little further north from Oak Knoll Farm and on the east side of the highway is the farm once operated by the Emersons and later by Clark Fawver. Pecans, eastern black walnuts, and butternuts are planted along the road leading to the Eschol Ranch house, very likely reminding the original owner of his home in the Middle West.' (Trefethen Vineyards and Winery now occupy this land.)

Magnolia Farm

'Just north of Eschol Ranch is what was once well known as Magnolia Farm, purchased on November 11, 1866 by William H. Nash after he moved from his former Walnut Grove Farm six miles north of St. Helena. (Note 44) William H. Nash and Ralph Kilburn imported and planted the first grafted fruit trees in the Napa Valley in the spring of 1850.'

Mrs Josephine Tyler later owned Magnolia Farm. She was the daughter of James David who bought the property about in 1880. The old dwarf boxwood hedge, a good specimen of California Nutmeg Tree (*Torreya californica*), gingko, and many other trees still remain a tribute to more than one of the early owners.'

Walnut Grove farm

Walnut Grove Farm originally belonged to an eccentric, some-what alcoholic English surgeon, Dr E.T. Bale. Bale was chief surgeon in a Mexican regiment, so evidently he continued to function effectively regardless of his drinking. In spite of his very public drunkenness and frequent social misdemeanors, he was gladly accepted as a husband for one of Mariano Vallejo's sisters.

'Bale built the old mill north of St. Helena on the west side of the highway, in 1846. He also built a large adobe house on Whitehall Lane, St. Helena, in 1839. Ralph Kilburn built a saw-mill on the Napa River. It was this mill that cut the lumber for Bale's Mill on the highway.

Leonard Coates

Leonard Coates, who later started the Leonard Coates Nursery in Morgan Hill, learned his craft as a young man working on Magnolia Farm. While there in 1882 he sent seed of *Fuchsia procumbens* to the University of California in Berkeley. The year before he had supplied seed of *Arthropodium cirrhatum*, *Pittosporum ralphii*, *P. tenuifolium*, *P. eugenoides*, and *Dodonaea viscosa*.

The *Pittosporum ralphii* was still growing on the campus at the University of California at Berkeley in the 1950s. On old Magnolia Farm Eastern Black walnuts alternate with California Black walnuts along the entrance. These probably date back to the 1860s.

General Miller

General Miller's property northeast of Napa was typical of some rural homes in California. General Miller bought it from a Spaniard and remodeled the original adobe in about 1859. Later his daughter inherited the property and her family used it as a summer home. R. P. Maxwell came into possession of it and removed many of the old statues about 1932. Long rows of trees bordering the narrow roadway entrance and the use of many statues on the spacious grounds about the old mansion helped furnish a note of wealth and refinement.' (Miller's property is now the Silverado Country Club and Resort. The grounds have been very well maintained and remain very beautiful.)

William Alexander Trubody

'William Alexander Trubody (1839-1933) went to ranch on his father's property north of Napa when he was seventeen years old, after attending the University of the Pacific. (Note 45) His father purchased most of the ranch for $480 from Levi Schlosser. He bought the upper piece from Hiram Smith. All this property was originally owned by Salvador Vallejo, General Vallejo's brother.

At one time this old ranch had twenty seven acres of blackberries. The fruit was picked by Chinese workers and sold in the San Francisco market. It took the owners a day make the round-trip of seventeen miles to Napa by horse and buggy. A Blue Gum (*Eucalyptus globulum*) planted on this farm in 1867 had reached a height of thirty feet in 1870. In the 1950s it measured more than eight feet five inches inches in trunk diameter, perhaps the largest trunk of any eucalyptus tree in California. The tree was a hundred and thirty seven feet tall..

George Calvert Yount

George Calvert Yount (1794-1865) went to California with William Wolfskill of Los Angeles in 1831 and finally settled at what is now called Yountville. (Note 46) Until 1837 the town was called Sebastopol. His wife Elizabeth Yount had travelled to California with the Chiles party. Chiles received his grant in Napa County in 1845.

Yount lived in an adobe about a mile north of Yountville and two hundred yards west of the old Yount Mill. Many early settlers got peach pits from Yount's orchards to plant their own trees. Yount's old log house was at the end of the adobe building. He built it in 1837 when he first settled on his land. Yount used spaces between the logs to shoot at intruders while protecting his property. This log house is said to be the first such dwelling erected in California by an American. Yount used the power generated in his mill, built before 1845, to churn butter.

Later his widow Elizabeth lived in a house at 423 Seminary Street. This house had a garden and was still standing in Butterfield's time. The log cabin had no garden of any consequence.

When approaching Yountville from the north, the traveler will notice some fine old eucalyptus trees on the east side. The white-barked kind is the Manna gum (*Eucalyptus viminalis*).

Soldiers Home

The Soldiers Home is west of the highway near Yountville where *Lagunaria patersoni* and other interesting trees grow. Yount gave the property for the old cemetery at the north edge of town to the city. The Soldiers Home, now the California Veterans Home, was incorporated in 1882. It cared for men who had fought in the

Mexican, Civil and Spanish wars and who had been honorably discharged

Old wineries dot the landscape north of Napa. The vine-covered castle entrance to Inglenook on the west side of the highway near Rutherford is one of the most beautiful to be seen. Wooden buckets used in Germany during the fourteenth century are on display there.

Captain Niebaum

Captain Gustave Niebaum, a German sea captain, settled in the foothills near Rutherford around 1890. His house lies west of the winery on a knoll, pictured in the tracery of mammoth oaks. A modern garden takes shelter beneath. Niebaum's property was owned previously by W C Watson, and called "Inglenook". In 1994, Francis Ford Coppola bought it and re-created the Inglenook Winery complex.

St Helena

St. Helena was founded on the original land grant but was not incorporated until 1876. About five years later, on September 26, 1881, the city was lined with crape on Main St. from Adams to Pope. Citizens marched to the cemetery to plant an Italian Cypress as a memorial to the murdered President James A. Garfield, who died on September 19. This cypress tree thrives in the center of a newly-planted green lawn and displays a new plaque that may be viewed by the many who pass through the valley.

John Lewelling, formerly of Mission San Jose and San Lorenzo, spent his last years near St. Helena. Descendants of the Lewelling family still reside in Napa, but their garden is not open for visits.

Walnut Grove Farm, a few miles north on the highway, belonged to William H. Nash. The fine redwoods which stood there in 1858 are gone but we still have the story of the Nash Family and the memory of their garden. Nashville, Tennessee, was named after an uncle of William H. Nash.

Henry Hagen's property

Harry Butterfield did not mention two other properties in Napa which still have old gardens. One has been very well maintained, the other is sadly very dilapidated and now in ruins. At 4301 Hagen Road, the house and garden constructed by Henry Hagen more than a century ago has just recently been sold. Successive owners have cared for the property very well and the gardens remain handsome. Hagen was a very early resident, moving to the Napa Valley in 1852. He planted more than a hundred acres of vineyards, choosing early Riesling and other imported varieties of grape, rather than persisting with the then standard "Mission" grape.

In an 1881 account of Northern California, published by the Lewis Company, the reporter noted three acres of park, with streams, fish ponds and deer. The gravel avenue leading to the house from the street was shaded by "a bower of over-arching cypress".

Napa Soda Springs

The fate of a famous pleasure and health resort, Napa Soda Springs, has not been so good. It occupied more than a thousand acres at its peak in the 1880s. The orignal owners built a very small, rudimentary hotel on this lot back in 1855, to take advantage of the mineral springs. There were many battles about the title but it really became a resort when Colonel J. P. Jackson took it over. "The grounds are artistically arranged and flowers and shrubs grow in profusion. In the forks of a great oak there is a platform with seats and railing around it, which is known as 'Lovers' Retreat'." (from a 1891 history of Napa.) Colonel Jackson was man of parts from Ohio, lawyer, journalist and politician.

The earlier chroniclers waxed rhapsodic about the views from this property: eg " . . . lofty proportions of Mt Tamalpais piercing the sky, like a giant sentinel on some grand old Titan fortress on the outer bulwarks of creation." On the ground, other writers noted "groves of patriarchal tree—the live oak, the black oak, festooned with gray Spanish moss or mistletoe, the eucalyptus, the mountain pine, while the Italian cypress lends an exotic charm to the natural scenery."

Many tourists visited the resort in its heyday, but by the early 1920s, the increased ease of travel meant that people could go much further afield for their holidays. When the complex burned to the ground in 1944, it was never replaced. For almost sixty years it has remained a ruin, with wild flowers and creepers covering the old stones and erasing the presence of man. This land is still in private hands and no one is allowed to enter it.

Calistoga

Butterfield noted: 'Calistoga, so well known for its hot geysers, also had old gardens. *Phormium tenax*, pampas grass, yuccas, araucarias, dracaenas, and *Livistona australis*. were reported to be growing at Calistoga Springs. The redbuds, old lilacs, the Smoke Tree, European euonymus, as well as other old ornamentals, still flourish and add their color to the landscape. There is a shaded cemetery by the highway that leads westward through Knights valley where William H. Nash and his family are buried. The green boughs of the fir trees and native plants present a scene of tranquillity and restfulness'

CHAPTER 10

Solano and Yolo Counties

Butterfield wrote: 'Benicia, named in honor of General M. G. Vallejo's wife, was once a strong competitor of San Francisco for city honors. Few visit the old gardens there or talk with early settlers. Mrs. Maria Fischer Quinn and others told interesting stories about the old days, of the Castilian rose which Mrs Quinn grew, and of men and women who made history. (Stephen De Benedetto recovered this early history.)

A Captain Walsh grew Australian acacia there before 1856. Old cork oak trees are to be found in the city's park, probably planted during the 1860's and 1870's. Conception Arguello is buried in the old Benicia cemetery . Ancient Monterey pines grace this cemetery.

Vallejo

To the west is the old town of Vallejo, briefly the capital of California. Vallejo (Eureka) and its State House have already been mentioned in connection with the Thompson Brothers and their nursery at Suscol in Napa County. General Vallejo founded the town in 1850. The Naval Shipyard on Mare Island was started very early.'

Mare Island

Admiral Farragut brought a plan with him for Mare Island to set off the officers' quarters by three small parks or "pleasure grounds". Only one of these may still be found. It is named Alden Park after a commander who only served eight months in all, during 1868. Local historians have often wondered how his name was attached to a landmark after such a short period of service.

The secret may lie in an old map from 1859, showing that Commodore James Alden had been part of a Navy detail which surveyed Mare Island in order to prepare it to be an important shipyard. It was totally barren at the time. (Sue Lemmon) When he became commandant, he immediately began to ask sea captains to bring him trees and flowering shrubs from every part of the world. The impression is that he wanted to improve the site over the next ten years.

The Vallejo Naval and Historical Museum has a newspaper article from December 1868 recording the arrival of pine, locust, poplar and Balm-of-Gilead trees in a schooner. These were planted in the avenues and small gardens of his island and did very well.

Butterfield visited many old gardens on this island in the 1950s and saw old street trees, such as Blue gums, the European ash and many others. Young families grew up and moved away, only to create new gardens elsewhere, leaving this quiet precinct to its own devices.

Old communities

A glance at a California map will show Cordelia, Suisun and Fairfield, and Vacaville in Solano County. Further north are Winters and Woodland in Yolo County. The town of Winters was laid out by the Vaca and Clear Lake Railroad, and named for Theodore Winters, a well known breeder of fine horses. Dean Wickson wrote about this whole area, which he referred to as the Vacaville-Winters district, in 1888. (Note 47)

A. T. Hatch

A. T. Hatch, born in Indiana in 1837, made the Suisun Valley famous for his seedling almonds. Every modern almond grower knows about the Nonpareil, IXL, and Ne Plus Ultra varieties, all seedlings originated by Mr. Hatch in the Suisun Valley from seed planted in 1872 and 1878.

He began his fruit farming near a modest cottage, almost hidden by a large climbing rose. Gradually he added many other farms to his holdings and moved into a fine new house, but with Dean Wickson, we may say that this rose-covered cottage "will always remain a cherished feature" of the many Hatch properties. (Figure 32)

Figure 31 A.T. Hatch, noted breeder of almond varieties
(Reproduced by permission of the Regents of the University of California)

Vacaville

The City of Vacaville was laid out in 1852. Gradually many families drifted there. Ansel W. Putnam came to California in 1854 and worked for Simpson Thompson at Suscol. Finally he moved his family from Suscol to Pleasant's Valley where he, together with John Dolan, had bought a settler's claim. He probably introduced the first budded fruit trees into Vacaville Township.

Daniel E. Hough (1816-1876) moved from Oakland to the Longmire farm five and a half miles out of Vacaville in the 1860's. In 1870 he imported the first Japanese plum tree into California. This variety later named the Kelsey after John Kelsey of Berkeley. The names of such men were associated with a movement to establish better homes and gardens in this large area. Fruit raising became a dominant feature and yet all about Cordelia, Vacaville, and in the adjacent valleys history was made in residential gardens. Here is an example.

L. J. Harbison's father lived a short distance northeast of Vacaville and 1854 planted an Arizona black walnut (*Juglans rupestris*) there. The Harbison house was built in 1876. Today the traveler may notice a sign, "The Nut Tree Inn", near which this old walnut tree grew until about 1952. Old trees in this area mark the homesites of many early fruit growers and farmers.' Sadly the modern travellers' complex which occupies the same site and has the same name has been closed for a long time.

Jerome C. Davis

Butterfield noted in the 1950s:'Few of us would expect a stockman to be especially interested in a garden and perhaps Jerome C. Davis on Putah Creek near the present Davis in Yolo County was not outstanding. Those of us who knew the University of California campus at Davis in earlier years do recall seeing remnants of an old fruit orchard probably dating back to the 1860's. Jerome C. Davis had about 12,000 acres along the north bank of Putah Creek in 1858. There were 7,000 acres fenced with redwood posts and boards, in all twenty miles of fencing. By 1858 he had seeded 1,200 acres of alfalfa.

There were an orchard and vegetable garden near the house which stood a little west of a sharp bend in the creek. The old fig and olive trees have remained on the campus up until recent years.' (There are still a few very old olive trees probably dating back to the time of Jerome Davis in the courtyard in front of the Sproul building at UC Davis.)

George C. Briggs

George C. Briggs (1824-1885) is best known as a fruit grower who settled near Marysville about 1850 but was forced to give up in the terrible floods of 1861-1862. In 1869 he acquired property just south of Davis across to the south of the creek. Part of his property was crossed by the railroad. He planted a famous vineyard there. In 1880 he dehydrated a million pounds of raisins.

Mr. Briggs came to California overland and settled there in 1850 . The State Agricultural Society awarded his orchard first prize in 1858. Three years later his orchard was ruined by floods so he moved to the Santa Paula District of Santa Barbara County, now in Ventura County. Later he returned to Oakland and finally settled at Davisville (Davis).'

Briggs also planted pecan trees in his Sutter county orchards. They were still bearing fruit as late as 1924, when Peter Delay wrote his history of Sutter county. Commercial orchards were very important in this county from an early period. The Phillips cling peach, immensely popular with canners, was first developed by John Duke Phillips, starting in 1888. Cherries were another significant crop.

John Wolfskill and Juan Vaca

On August 15, 1841, Juan Felipe Peña and Juan Manual Vaca came to Vaca Valley as the new owners of Los Putos Rancho. J.T. Rivers married one of Peña's daughters and Jose Demetrio Peña built a new house.' In 1842, a year after the settlement of Peña and Vaca, John R. Wolfskill secured possession of Rio Los Putos Rancho lying on both sides of Putah Creek, near Winters of today. This rancho included the territory tributary to Winters and extending southward toward Vaca Valley.

Juan Manuel Vaca disputed John Wolfskill's claim to his Putah Creek property and they battled in court for many years. Vaca felt very strongly about it because he had received provisional title to the land from Vallejo himself. The fact that the town is named for Vaca says a lot. President Buchanan finally signed the patent for him in June 1858. John Wolfskill's patent for his section was signed in December of that same year.

Butterfield wrote; ' Mrs. Elise P. Buckingham bought the old Peña property in 1884 and called it "Lagunita Rancho." Pears, figs, and walnuts were planted in 1853 and an old olive tree remained for many years as the largest in Vaca Valley. Mrs. Buckingham was "not content to linger in the shade of historic trees" . She improved the old farm by planting fruit trees.

William Wolfskill, of Los Angeles, John's elder brother, originally owned the Putah Creek property, but gave it to his brother when the latter came to California from their old home in Ohio. John and his wife finally built a house on the south bank of the creek and established their garden and orchard there. John told the story of how he survived the first few days he lived out in that wild area. He had to sleep in a tree to avoid the bears. (Note 48)

'Orange, lemon, lime, citron, and Chinese chestnut planted in 1854 grew in this orchard. Dates were planted as early as 1859 and ripe fruit from a palm was exhibited at the Mechanics Institute in San Francisco in 1877. Some grapes were planted as early as 1842, figs in 1851, almonds in 1853, shellbark hickory in 1873, pecans in 1876, and old Northern California black walnuts were top-grafted to English walnuts in 1875.

Many early settlers obtained olive cuttings from Wolfskill's orchard. They recorded the sale of more than 124,000 cuttings in one season. He also imported Mexican apricots from Mexico and marketed the fruit, thus pioneering the way for the early fruit district of his area, but that is another story.'

John Wolfskill's daughter Frances died in 1934. She bequeathed over a hundred acres of the property to the University of California at Davis and the university used it as an experiment station. More recently the U.S. Department of Agriculture has developed the National Germplasm Cloning Repository on the grounds. In spite of these changes, the great avenue of olive trees leading up to the original house still stands.

Winters and Woodland

'Few detailed records have been saved about the other properties in Winters and Woodland, but the R. B. Blowers vineyard near Woodland in the 1870's and 1880's was famous for its raisins. A picture of Mr. Blowers hangs in a hall in the State Capital Building in Sacramento. A. D. Porter, associated with a Woodland bank for many years, had a fine house and garden where he grew banana trees and harvested fruit from them in a sheltered spot as early as 1888. A neighbor had an old tree peony (*Paeonia suffruticosa* var.*banksii.* John D Stephens' house and garden occupied almost a block. Woodland was garden-minded.

Early Yolo County offered extensive opportunities for farming. William Gordon, who came with the Workman-Rowland Party in 1841, settled ten miles west of Woodland. In 1856 James Moore built the first irrigation ditch. David Quincy Adams, early alfalfa grower, started a dam in 1857 to irrigate his property. The dam was two miles west of Capay. There was a Chinese garden on his farm in the early 1850's. Chinese workers looked after the gardens on many early farms and and in the cities. They often planted seeds of familiar vegetables and crops, such as large gourds. Some planted Ailanthus trees.'

CHAPTER 11

Sacramento

From Butterfield: 'Gabriel Noriega made a trip to the Sacramento Valley in 1808 and admired the large Valley Oak trees. John A. Sutter reached California in July, 1839, and settled at "New Helvetia" about a month later. The townsite for Sacramento was surveyed in 1848-49 under the direction of Samuel Branin and on Feb. 27, 1850 the City was incorporated. Sacramento became the permanent State capital in 1854.

Like many early cities affected by the gold rush, Sacramento grew almost instantaneously from a town of four houses in 1849 to a metropolis when 10,000 people arrived in the summer of 1850. John Sutter had helped make the city safe in the Mexican period by acquiring the old Russian cannons from Fort Ross with the help of John Bidwell. He mounted them at Fort Sutter in 1841.' Although Sutter was a romantic rascal who put out all sorts of misinformation about himself when he thought no one was looking, he used what little military training he had actually had quite effectively.

Judge E. B. Crocker

Judge E. B. Crocker first lived at the corner of 7th and F Street in early Sacramento . Later his residence adjoined the Crocker Art Gallery near 216 O Street. Mr. and Mrs. Crocker directed the Art Gallery in 1870-73 at the corner of 2nd and O Street. After the judge's death on June 24, 1875 his wife gave the Art Gallery to the City of Sacramento. The residence has since been acquired by the

California Museum Association and combined with the Art Gallery.

The old garden was replanted by the Sacramento Garden Club. Among Judge Crocker's roses were "Gloria de Rosamene" which we commonly call Ragged Robbin, Lamarque, Multiflora, Cloth of Gold, Sufrano, Persian Yellow, and Sweet Briar. The *Passiflora caerulea* of his garden is still grown. Among his shrubs were *Camellia japonica* , oleander, lemon verbena, sweet-scented shrub, deutzia, Jerusalem cherry, Australian heather, Bridal wreath, Cape Jasmine, and tree peony, *Euonymus japonicus,* strawberry tree, eight varieties of fuchsias, and *Cestrum (Habrothamnus*).

No doubt Mrs. Crocker was pleased with the Lady Washington geranium, also rose, apple, and nutmeg scented geraniums which are still grown. His bulbs included *Lilium longiflorum, L. rubrum,* and *L. candidum* plus six varieties of gladiolus. Like many gardeners of his day, Judge Crocker planted the Pride of China (*Melia azederach*), catalpa, American Elm, and cottonwood, all for shade. His portulacas were in bloom by April 20, amaryllis from May 1 to November 1, and the gladiolus from June 1 to December 1. This old garden has all the qualities we associate with the past. (Note 49)

Nurseries

A.P. Smith

Among the new settlers in the Sacramento area was a young man of thirty six who arrived on the barge, "William Ivy," by way of the Horn in 1848. He bought fifty acres from Captain Sutter about two and a half miles above Sacramento on the American River, paying $100 an acre. He formed the firm of Smith, Baker, and Parker, nurserymen and gardeners.

This young man was Anthony Preston Smith, (1812 – 1875), He was joined by his brother, Sydney Smith, in 1853. Sydney looked after the store at 44 J Street between Second and Third St.

while A. P. Smith looked after the nursery. Smith's Pomological Garden and Nursery was "two and a half miles from the steamboat levee and stage office" near where the Tivoli was built many years later. Smith was a canny business man and had made quite a lot of money by careful gambling on the long voyage to California.

At first he concentrated on seed production and some fruit but later turned to the production of ornamental plants together with other specialties. He irrigated his grounds with eight-inch pipe, four-inch laterals, hydrants and a hose. In 1856 he reported he had 15,000 roses. In 1857 he had 2,000 camellias, and some say he had two hundred varieties.

Butterfield owned a copy of Smith's nursery catalog for 1856 listing many fruits and ornamental plants. In 1858 Smith received a prize from the California State Agricultural Society for the best greenhouse.

Readers who are familiar with early rose varieties will probably not be surprised to find him listing such roses at Géant des Batailles, Hermosa, Sov. de la Malmaison (sic), Aggrippina or Cloth of Gold, Lamarque, Ophire, Solfaterre, Baltimore Bell, Prairie Queen, and Multiflora in 1856. Most of his ornamental shrubs were those common to the Eastern States.

A. P. Smith once raised a Pound pear weighing four pounds nine ounces for which he was awarded a medal by the American Pomological Society. The heavy floods that came in December of 1861 and January of 1862 practically ruined his nursery, yet his influence on early gardens and orchards of his day will never be forgotten. He and Colonel Warren were largely responsible for making Sacramento the "Camellia City."

O. C. Wheeler

Reverend O. C. Wheeler, who established Wheelers Gardens on 10th Street, also served as Secretary of the California State Agricultural Society in the 1850's. He arrived in San Francisco by steamer on February 28, 1849. Samuel Wiley of Oakland and

Berkeley was on the same boat. He grew Swiss pines, sugar maples, and fruit trees.

Bermuda grass

J. R. Scupham, who worked as Assistant Engineer for the Central Pacific Railroad, gave a report in 1877 before the California Academy of Sciences in San Francisco describing the introduction of Bermuda grass into California. The State Agricultural Society received Bermuda grass seed in 1856 or 1857 from an East Indian agricultural society. Secretary Wheeler sent seed to his friends in Sacramento and elsewhere for testing.

The grass grew rapidly from the seed and when the heavy winter floods of 1861-62 came, it was spread over the bottom lands below Sacramento. (Note 51) William C. Walker of the Golden Gate Nursery in San Francisco listed Bermuda grass at five dollars a flat in 1858. George Rich, who lived six miles below Sacramento, was another who tested this grass and helped distribute it.

Kulau and Co,

There was a plank road extending ten miles east of Sacramento in 1855. Two miles out on this road were the gardens of Kulau and Company in which grew Sweet William, petunias, violets, dahlias, hollyhocks, geraniums and verbenas. There were also fine roses and "japonicas" which we know as flowering quinces.

Empire Nursery

Peter Kunz had worked for Peter Henderson in New York before coming to California in 1854. After arriving in San Francisco he worked for Thomas Hayes in Hayes Valley for two and a half years, then went to Sacramento where he rented property on 3rd Street between S and T streets. There he went into partnership with his brother-in-law, Charles Schiminger, founding the Empire Nursery. By 1861 the Empire Nursery was worth $50,000.

Kunz's cousin Frank Kunz also worked for Peter Henderson and various others in New York for a few years before going to California in 1856. In time he reached Sacramento and started the Union Nursery.

Terrible floods throughout the Sacramento basin in the winter of 1861-62 became legendary. Peter Kunz lost his nursery stock in that flood but was not entirely discouraged. At night during the flood he would row a boat up to the second story window, crawl in and go to bed. Finally he was able to buy a lot at the corner of 3rd and B Street in 1864. Many years later, in 1878, this nursery was also damaged.

In 1860 the Empire Nursery listed such plants as *Callistemon citrinus*, *Pandorea jasminoides*, ten kinds of acacias, and crape myrtle. Schiminger and Kunz continued to run their nursery in partnership until 1877. Frank Kunz sold flowers and ornamental plants. He won many prizes at the California State Fair in 1879. Governor Frank Perkins appointed him State Gardener and he hired Charles Abraham of San Francisco briefly to help in the planting of Capital Park.

W. B. Strong and Co.

W. B. Strong and Company established the Capital Nursery and Seed House in 1857. W. B. Strong and Robert Williamson were in partnership at their nurseries at 16th and U Street in 1875 and near the river on J. Street in 1878. Finally Robert Williamson became sole owner. James A. Andrews purchased Strong's interest. This company dealt largely in fruit trees but also imported rare trees from China and Japan. Pioneer fruit growers recalled the Orange Hill Nursery at 7th and J Street in the late 1870s.

Capital Park

Planting in Capital Park, lying between 9th and 15th Streets and between L and N Streets, began in about 1870. The capital building was first occupied late in 1869 but was not completed until 1874. Its Corinthian style gives the building a sense of classical dignity

There is a story that Major Pierson. B. Reading supplied seeds for the deodar cedars growing in Capital Park in 1869 but according to William Vortriede (in a discussion with Butterfield several years ago) we have more accurate dates for many of the tree plantings. In 1871 *Cedrus deodora* were planted near the walk at the west end of the Park, together with *Cryptomeria japonica, Cupressus gudalupensis* (probably planted before botanists had named the species), *Picea excelsa, P. canadensis, Picea glehni, P. sitchensis,* and the two different redwoods native to California.

The next big planting was made in 1887. Trees set out at that time include *Acer saccharinum, Acer negundo* var. *californicum, A. palmatum, Aesculus hippocastanum, Araucaria bidwilli, A. araucana (A. imbricata), Arbutus menziesi, Arbutus unedo, Buxus japonica, B. balerica, B. sempervirens, Callistemon speciosus, Catalpa bignonioides, C. speciosis, Cedrus libani, Citrus aurantiacum, C. maxima, Crataegus monogyna* var. *pauli, Erythrina crista-galli, Ginkgo biloba, Juniperus communis, Lagerstroemia indica, Prunus laurocerasus, Laurus nobilis, Libocedrus decurrens, Liriodendron tulipifera, Magnolia grandiflora, Magnolia conspicua, Melia azederach* var. *umbraculiformis, Morus nigra, Myrtus communis, Olea europaea, Paulownia tomentosa, Phoenix canariensis, Phoenix datylifera, Pinus halapensis, Pinus pinea* (near West Walk), *Pittosporum eugenoides, P. tobira, Pseudotsuga douglasi, Quercus agrifolia, Quercus macrocarpa* (northeast of Capital Building), *Quercus suber* not far away, *Rhus cotinus (Cotinus coggygria), Robinia pseudoacacia, Schinus molle, Tamarix gallica, T. parvifolia, Taxus baccata* var. *fastigiata* (along path east of Capital), *T. floridana, Ulmus campestris (U. suberosa),* and *Washingtonia filifera.* (Figure 32)

Fraximus americana, Ulmus americana, Ulmus alata, and *U.*

crassfolia and a rather extensive group of native species were planted in Capital Park in 1912, including palms, conifers, and broad-leaved trees. The acacias and eucalyptus trees were killed in the freeze of 1932. Planting dates for most of the other trees are lacking. Measurements have been made of many of the old oaks on the grounds as well as of other trees for records. The native plants in the southeastern part of the Park and the Civil War trees from battlefields are interesting to some visitors.

Figure 32 Deodar Cedar, Capital Park, Sacramento, west side of Capital building. Planted in 1871.
(Reproduced by permisssion of the Regents of the University of California)

Sacramento County Gardens

'George Rich, who lived six miles southeast of Sacramento, was among the first to plant Bermuda grass. He came to California in 1855 and some plants in his garden date back as far as 1860. There were acacias, pampas grass, English yews, Monterey pine and Monterey cypress, and English box.'

Rosebud Farm

'Rosebud Farm is about a mile north of Hood on the Sacramento River, east bank. State Senator William Johnson built his house here in about 1874. Mrs. Mary Edinger and her sister lived on the property surrounded by beautiful ornamental plants. One of the finest specimens of the southern evergreen magnolia (*Magnolia grandiflora*) still flourished near the adjacent levee in the mid-twentieth century. A camellia purchased from John Rock of San Jose was planted when the grounds were laid out and now (1940) has a crown spread of thirty feet. A sister seedling is also about thirty feet in height.'

Runyon properties

'Down the Sacramento River a few miles below Courtland are the Runyon properties. Armistead Runyon had about 720 acres of land which he divided for his sons Oron and Solomon Runyon. They both had farms in this area. Armistead's daughter married a man named Dorsey. Old palms flourish at the white house. Solomon Runyon's house is slightly south of where Mrs. and Mrs. Amick lived. (Note 52) A specimen of camellia, "Warratah", said to have been imported about 1885, grew on this old farm. A very large oak tree and a cedar grow near the home. Other similar fine houses from the early days may still be found in this river district.'

Hock Farm

'John A. Sutter has often been mentioned in connection with Sacramento and Sutter's Fort but less has been said about his home and gardens on Hock Farm, about eight miles below Yuba City.

(Note 53) Sutter secured eleven leagues of land on which he established Hock Farm. An adobe was built in the winter of 1841-42. John Bidwell, who arrived in 1841, acted as Sutter's foreman and bookkeeper for a year and a half, between 1843 and 44. It was during this time that the old cannons of the Russians were removed to Fort Sutter.

Sutter's house was built in 1850, not far from the old adobe. There with the aid of his son, Colonel E. Sutter, he established a fine garden that is now only a memory. Perhaps a state marker will be all that is left of this famous garden of the 1850s.

The Sutter family was among the first to use fruit trees as ornamental plants. A large portion of the trees were set out on either side of broad avenues, opening through the extensive grounds in various directions. The ornamental garden occupied a gentle slope from the front of the house to the river. (Note 54) Within the space of an acre orange, citron, *Firmiana simplex (Sterculia platanifolia), Paulownia, Laurus nobilis,* ginkgo, *Cotoneaster microphylla,* Silk Oak, *Coronilla,* hawthorn, *Calianthus,* live oak, cypress, *Eurphorbia splendens,* oleander, lilies, and various conifers were all growing.

The fruit trees were arranged to present a unique landscape effect. This garden so impressed the Visiting Committee of the California State Agricultural Society in 1858 that they gave John Sutter a silver medal, his garden ranking only second to that of James McDonnell of San Francisco.

Sutter loved peace and contentment but was denied these most of his life. Only three years later the terrible floods of 1861 ruined the garden, leaving it covered with debris and mud. For a while people used this space for picnics but in time it disappeared altogether. A tablet was placed on the grounds in 1927 to let the visitor know where a pioneer's garden had once stood.' At present

Figure 33 Eleanor Holmes, current owner of Hock Farm
Photograph: Gerald Tsuruda (Reproduced by permission of Eleanor
Holmes)

the Holmes family lives on part of Sutter's old Hock Farm. The only surviving building from Sutter's time is an old shed in a corner of the property. (Figure 33)

New England Nursery

'George H. Beach's New England Nursery was four miles below Marysville on the east bank of the Feather River. The farm was half grassland and half river bottom. Fifty acres were devoted to orchard, vineyard and nursery. It was irrigated by means of a steam pump lifting 10,000 gallons of water per hour from a well and distributing it through wooden flumes.

Mr. Beach depended on his ornamental nursery very largely to increase sales during the winter months. He grew 6,000 Pride of China (*Melia azederach*), 10,000 black and honey locust trees, 1000 Ailanthus, and 2,000 miscellaneous trees, such as elm, ash, and acacias in 1858. (Note 51)In 1856 he had 5,000 roses and many flowering shrubs and vines. We can well imagine that some of the early gardens in the Marysville area were started from plants grown by George H. Beach.

Marysville

'M. C. Nye purchased the old rancho land at the site of Marysville in 1848. The town was laid out and named Yubaville in 1849, but after Covilland came, he chose the name of Marysville in honor of his wife Mary. Mary Murphy, later Mrs Covilland, had been in the Donner Party. In 1858 John C. Fall had a greenhouse and ornamental garden surrounding his mansion, "with few equals and perhaps no superiors in the State," as reported by the State Agricultural Society.

Theodore Cordua leased land from John A. Sutter in 1842. In 1848 he employed Charles Covilland to help him. Charles Covilland's farm was about a mile above Marysville. In 1858 the house was two hundred yards from the driveway, near the Feather River. There was a path on either side of the driveway, skirted with a double row of ornamental trees intermingled with both standard and climbing roses. Luxuriant clematis vines, both native and exotic, surrounded a broad verandah. The garden and fruit orchard were very well laid out. This property was also irrigated by mechanical means from a well twelve feet wide and twenty feet deep.

Men like John C. Fall, G. N. Swezy, John A. Paxton, and Rev. Walsworth had fine gardens in spite of the gravelly soil. The indomitable energy and perseverance of these early gardeners made the town a "very gem among our California cities" as early as 1858.

Yuba City

Yuba City also had its gardens. Butterfield remembered the large Paradox Hybrid Walnut tree that once grew at the home of Mrs. R. S. Lyman, 229 B St., a tree that was planted in the 1870's by J. L. Wilbur. Before it was removed it measured six feet in trunk diameter and was a hundred and five feet tall. The crown spread was a hundred and thirty eight feet.

CHAPTER 12

Sacramento Valley

Glenn County

Colusa was an ancient Indian town on the Sacramento River. The beautiful site was bordered by oaks. Major Stephen Cooper lived about a mile west of town in 1858 on an eighty-acre farm with 8,000 trees in his nursery. He had created the first trail across the mountains to Santa Fe, New Mexico, in 1822.

The modern town of Colusa was founded in 1850 and became the county seat in 1854. The work of the early gardeners "imported a beauty which could be obtained by no work of art." The few hundred inhabitants living there in 1858 enjoyed a very pleasant home life. Glenn County became a separate entity in 1891.

The early history of San Francisco and Benicia includes the name of Robert Semple. Dr. Semple purchased Rancho Alamo six miles west of Williams in 1853 with his uncle. He died there in 1854.

Butte County

John Bidwell discovered gold at Bidwell's Bar on July 4, 1848. Mining there forced early settlers to move down to Ophir City, now Oroville, named in 1856. The old seedling orange tree growing by the bridge at Bidwell's Bar is famous in the history of the Sacramento Valley. (Note 55)

Jesse Morrell planted the seed in Sacramento in 1855. The

tree was sold to R. Van Norden in 1859 and was set out by the south side of Howard Burt 's office at Bidwell's Bar. This seedling Acapulco orange first bore fruit in 1865. The crop was about forty oranges. It is not the oldest orange tree in California but is perhaps the oldest growing so far north.

Chico

Chico is famous as the early home of General John Bidwell. Few know that John Bidwell started his nursery in 1851 and that he continued to run it until his death in 1900. How did John Bidwell come to settle in the Chico area?

When Bidwell, Charles Weber and others arrived in 1841 they stayed for a time at Dr. Marsh's compound, and several members of the party went to Mission San Jose to get their papers. During the stay in central California in 1843, Bidwell's horses were stolen. He learned that a party going to Oregon Territory was probably guilty. He accompanied Peter Lassen and John Burheim's group in an attempt to get the horses back. and found them in Red Bluff.

It was during this trip that John Bidwell must have been impressed by the fine Valley oaks at the site of Chico. Later he returned and bought the old rancho in 1844. Rancho del Arroyo Chico consisted of 24, 200 acres. (Note 56) Bidwell set aside twenty seven acres to be a nursery and garden by 1858.

Pierson B. Reading accompanied Bidwell on several of his trips.' The City of Redding, an early mining town, was originally named Reading in his honor but was later changed to Redding. This was done to honor another important citizen, Benjamin B. Redding. B. B. Redding was an official with the Southern Pacific railroad which came through the town. He was also a skillful amateur scientist in an age when educated men could still perform serious scientific study on their own.

William Dickey and Edward A. Farwell were first granted Rancho Chico on November 29, 1844. Bidwell bought it from these grantees. He built the stone mansion now used by the Cali-

fornia State University at Chico.' In its day this was a most innova-
tive house. Every bedroom had running water in the wash basins.

He wanted to impress his future wife, the very religious and
serious Annie Ellicot Kennedy. She came from Washington DC
and was very loth to go out and live in the wilds of Northern
California. Bidwell hoped that if she saw how much effort he put
into meeting her needs, it would change her mind. It did.

Among Bidwell's many excellent qualities was deep concern
for the environment and the plight of the terribly depleted and
tormented native people. He supported John Muir's ideas on preservation of the wilderness very early.

' In 1886 he gave land for the State Forestry Experiment Station, now owned by the City of Chico and known as Bidwell Park.
This park was given to the City July 10, 1905. The Park includes
the Hooker Oak. (Note 57) Mrs. Bidwell added three hundred
and one acres on May 11, 1911.

Sir Joseph Hooker, famous son of a famous father, Sir William
Hooker, both directors of the Royal Botanic Garden at Kew in
their day, had visited Rancho Chico in 1877. An oak tree, already
said to be very large at a hundred and ten feet tall, was named in
his honor. At one time this tree had a spread of a hundred and
ninety seven feet.

The grounds about the Bidwell mansion were not planted
until after the building was completed. Trees planted at that time,
such as the Turkey oak (*Quercus serris*) and *Quercus nigra,* are still
to be found on the grounds. There are old Italian cypress trees in
the cemetery and beautiful large camellias and magnolias growing
elsewhere in Chico.

Buutterfield wrote that 'A few years ago a Claro walnut tree
stood beside the home of Dr. H. I. Voorhies. This walnut tree was
presumably planted by John Bidwell in 1871. When the tree endangered the home of Dr. Voorhies, it was removed. The lumber
was purchased by a veneer manufacturer. The wood weighed 65,000
pounds and made 5,000 board feet or 160,000 feet of veneer and
was valued at $12,000.

Neither John Bidwell nor anyone else could have predicted

the outcome when this tree was planted in 1871. Sometimes pioneer tree planting does pay in the end.' (This commercial triumph is an odd sentiment to our modern attitudes, but it bespeaks Harry Butterfield's tough upbringing in a homesteading family.)

Tehama County

'Tehama County has a number of towns and cities, such as Corning, Tehama, and Red Bluff. Shasta County is also connected with the history of the area. In 1843 Samuel J. Hensley, later of San Jose, accompanied Major Pierson B. Reading on a trip and recommended land in this area be settled. Major Reading finally settled near Cottonwood in Shasta County where he secured a grant. (Note 58) His orchard had a mixture of fruit trees, with grapevines and seedling Indian Cling peaches among them. He surrounded his home with many ornamental plants, such as Pride as China, locust trees, osage orange, and flowering cherries (in 1858).' Major Reading also produced some crops of olives, unusual so far north in California. His olives were mentioned in the *Alta California* in January 1854.

'Tehama was the first important town in Tehama County. During the 1850's the streets were lined with trees. Rancho de los Sucos (ranch of the elders) was granted to Robert Hasty Thomas in 1844, a man who came in the same party as John Bidwell. He built an adobe in 1847 and a frame house in 1858. R. H. Thomes gave Albert Thomes the land for the site of Tehama. A Paradox Hybrid walnut was planted here in Tehama in about 1870. By 1940 it was seventy feet tall with a spread of a hundred and twenty feet.'

Red Bluff was established by 1858 and there were high hopes for its future. Warren Woodson, a self-made man who became a major realtor and land owner in Corning, began his career as the post master in Red Bluff in the late 1880s. He is worth noting as he created the olive industry in Corning almost inadvertently, planting many of the then new variety of olive tree, the Sevillano, on lots he sold to newcomers from the eastern United States. He did this in order to promote sales.

Shasta

'Gardens were well established in Shasta by 1860. It was one of the finest of the mountain towns. (Note 59) Benjamin Swasey used 5000 feet of lead pipe varying in diameter from a half to one inch in diameter to irrigate his orchard and garden on his five acre property in 1858. D. D. Harrill had a flower garden and nursery "arranged with taste and worked with fidelity." He planted mulberry trees from seed in 1857.

Dr. Benjamin Shurtleff had five acres on a hill to the west of town where he started his garden in 1856. He showed taste in the cultivation of shrubbery and flowers in spite of the granite bedrock which came near the surface.' Dr Shurtleff was an early member of the faculty of medicine at the new University of California at Berkeley.

'A. L. Downer had a two and a half acre fruit garden started in 1853. It included apricots, apples, plums, peaches, cherries, pears, figs, and almonds, showing no bounds in the kind of fruit trees tested by these early pioneers. Future generations profited from this early experience.

Tower House, about twelve miles above Shasta on the Weaverville Road, was started by Levi H. Tower who settled there in 1853. In 1858 he had fenced in fifty acres but used his house as an hotel. Its garden was mostly planted with fruit trees. He had several sparkling fountains. With a fifty-foot hose and nozzle he could throw water a hundred feet high.

Tower planted a specimen of *Juglans sieboldiana* (Heart Nut) in about 1860 but the tree was not identified until late in the 1880s by G. P. Rixford. Most readers have never seen this nut unless they have traveled in Japan. One wonders where he obtained the seed.

CHAPTER 13

Stockton

'A group of French trappers settled the site of French Camp below the present City of Stockton during Mexican days. (Note 60) When the Bartleson Party came that way in the fall of 1841, Charles M. Weber, a member of the party, was impressed with the fine Valley oaks growing in this area. (Figure 34) A few years later General Fremont camped under the oaks in the valley .

One of several old oaks where Fremont camped is near the Calaveras River not far from the Waterloo Road leading to Lockford. This particular oak bears a tablet placed there in 1923 by the Daughters of the American Revolution, indicating that Fremont passed that way on March 26, 1844.

William Gulnac

William Gulnac (Don Guillermo Gulnac) settled in Baja California in 1819 but moved to the Santa Clara Valley in 1833. For a time he was *Major Domo* at Mission San Jose. When Charles Weber came in 1841, Don Guillermo was forty years old and was quite familiar with Spanish and Mexican ways in California. The two men became partners in a store. Through this partner, who was a Mexican citizen, and who had secured a grant of Rancho Campo de los Franeses containing 48,747 acres on January 13, 1844, Weber was finally able to get a foothold in what later became the Stockton country.

Figure 34 Captain Charles Weber (1814-1881), founder of the City of Stockton
(Reproduced by permission of the Regents of the University of California)

Captain Charles Weber

It is reported that Weber got possession and title to this property for canceling a grocery bill of about $60. Attempts were made to settle this rancho in 1844 but few settlers had yet arrived. Later Captain Weber gave away many acres to attract new settlers. He moved to "Tuleberg" in 1847 and laid out the town site a year later, the City of Stockton we know today. The name of Stockton was not accepted until 1849. Weber built a house on Weber Point and moved there with his young wife (formerly Helen Murphy of San Jose) in 1849.' (Note 61)

His generosity also included minority communities. The Jewish cemetery in Stockton, the first consecrated Jewish cemetery west of the Rockies, was a gift from Weber. When Solomon Friedländer died in 1851, a miner far from his native village in Germany, the members of his congregation were frantic about burying him properly, in accordance with Jewish tradition. They turned to Weber, who did not disappoint them. His only condition was that the land remain as a cemetery, and never revert to any other use. The congregation respected his wish, and it is still the community's cemetery today. The state of California has put this cemetery on the list of pioneer heritage sites.

Weber may have learned his somewhat liberal attitudes from his family back in Germany. The Webers and the Hilgards were related. Eugene Hilgard, the great professor of agriculture at the University of California, was his cousin.

According to Butterfield , 'The Webers planted a garden with fruit trees, shrubs, and flowers. Fruit in those days sold at a phenomenal price. In 1854 they planted an Australian acacia in their garden. Knowing that Captain Weber left a fine collection of early nursery catalogs, including a copy of Col. Warren's nursery catalog for 1853, we may assume that Weber purchased the acacias from Colonel Warren. The latter had listed several species of this tree. Charles Weber also loved native oaks.

Because of his interest in gardening he accumulated one of the best collections of nursery catalogs available in his day. These were inherited by his granddaughter, Mrs. Gerald D. (Helen Weber) Kennedy.

Weber's house in Stockton burned down shortly after his death in 1881. Later the family rebuilt on the southeast corner of the property facing Stockton Channel. Still later the house was moved to West Lane beyond the Diversion Canal outside the City. Everything original has gone, including the garden, except for a few shrubs that linger on the site.

An interesting footnote to the story of Captain Weber is that his attorney, a Mr Hall, was the father of the man who later built Golden Gate Park, William Hammond Hall. The Halls moved from Baltimore to California in 1852, when William was seven. After a brief period in San Francisco, the family went on to Stockton where the boy spent the rest of his childhood.

William A. West

William A. West was born in Massachusetts in 1824. Because of poor health he was advised to go to sea. As a boy he had been interested in nursery stock. Gold presumably attracted him to California in 1848. In 1850-51 he was at Campo Seco. Later, he and his brother George started a nursery in 1853.

They purchased young fruit trees from Dana Hovey and Co. of Cambridge, Massachussetts.' At that time, making sure that young trees survived the taxing journey from the Eastern states to California was a serious problem. Eliza Farnham, an enterprising woman who tried ranching in Santa Cruz at the same period, lost almost all the fruit trees she had paid to be sent around the Cape. She was not alone.

'West's nursery was about two and half miles out from the Courthouse off Calaveras Road on West's Lane. In 1856 William West took over his brother's interest in the building. Gradually the nursery became more profitable. Many think of the Stockton Nurseries as a source of grapes but William West did pioneer work with evergreen trees for the inland valleys.'

West also took more than a passing interest in the craze for olive trees which swept California at the end of the nineteenth century. He made at least one trip to Spain and Italy, looking into the sources of new trees. He wrote about this journey in a San Francisco weekly in 1879 . West 's remarks showed he had a lot of good sense.

'His catalogs contained a very fine list of such trees as deodora, eucalyptus, and acacias. (Note 62) In 1881 he advocated growing more evergreen trees in the inland valleys, "The only requisite is to raise them from seed and nurse them through first and second years. They then become hardy, grow thriftily and will do with less water than any ornamental tree. We think the day will come when they will be cheap and plentiful so that we may adorn our dwellings, make hedges, and use them freely. The want of them is sadly felt in our landscape."

Before West left his nursery in 1885 to assist the Fancher Creek Nurseries at Fresno in the introduction of the Smyrna fig, he had seen a vast change in plantings in the inland valleys. His faith in evergreens for gardens in the warm interior valleys was fully vindicated. We know that what he advocated is appreciated to this day. Many fine old trees in the Stockton area date back to the time of George and William B. West, and also to Captain Weber.'

Residential Gardens

'There were many fine houses and gardens in Stockton near the Insane Asylum. Dr. E. S. Holden, a physician at the asylum, had walks and avenues in his garden bordered by acacias, China trees (*Azederach*), ailanthus, elm, walnut, tree tobacco, black and honey locust, catalpa, hedges, and tropical plants and shrubs. He lived there for thirty years.

Dr R. K. Reid's house adjoined the Asylum. He had fruit trees and vines mingling harmoniously with roses, passion vines, jessamine, clematis and eglantine (*Rosa eglanteria*), the sweet briar so dear to the hearts of the first American gardeners in California.

B. W. Bourse of Stockton grew a great variety of roses and geraniums. He imported the oleander from Mexico in 1852, showing that at that time it was not common in California. He also brought in species of Mexican cacti. Several other early settlers in Stockton, such as Dr. Bateman, Judge Brown, C.C. Burton and R. B. Parker, also created gardens.

Other old houses and gardens may be of interest. The J. H. Cole House just north of the Eight Mile Road was built in 1863. Old elms and Italian cypress have survived till the present.' (1940s) 'Once there was a climbing rose on the dwelling.

The Carson House, about four miles north of Stockton on the lower Sacramento Road, had a fine grove of oaks. That house was built in 1852 but was later torn down. Ivy and myrtle vine as well as ailanthus mark the site of the original garden.

J. O. Malley built a house along the French Camp Road near Simms before 1860. Old olive trees and walnuts, and beautiful old black locust trees reflect the glory of an earlier day. Members of the local garden club may know of other heirloom gardens which can be added to those mentioned above.'

CHAPTER 14

Gardens of the San Joaquin Valley

Butterfield commented that there are very few old gardens in the San Joaquin Valley. There was no particular inducement to settle there until the railroad was built in the 1870s. One of the few who did go there was Colonel Thomas Baker.

Colonel Thomas Baker

Baker arrived in Benicia in 1850, and then went on to Stockton. By 1852 he was in the southern part of Tulare County where he helped found one of the very first towns, Visalia. At that time Tulare Lake was an important if intermittent body of water, used as a commercial conduit when it was full. The whole valley was populated by huge herds of wild deer and literally millions of birds flocked there, darkening the sky in their squadrons.

Baker represented Visalia in the State Assembly in 1855. He became a senator in 1861 while Visalia was still a small hamlet. Inyo and Kings counties were formed in 1866 and Bakersfield was named in honor of Colonel Baker in 1869. Baker also helped get Santa Monica started by encouraging development.

The Butterfield stagecoach stage went viâ several small San Joaquin towns on the way from Los Angeles to San Francisco. It took about three days to go from Los Angeles to San Francisco. The coach turned through Pacheco Pass to reach the coast after reaching Firebaugh.

Tulare County

Tulare County traces its garden history back to the 1850's. The Election Tree, seven miles east of Visalia near an old quarry, bears a tablet stating that beneath the tree an election was held on July 10, 1852, to organize Tulare County. Another tree near Dinuba is interesting but for a different reason. The McCubbin Bum, a specimen of *Eucalyptus viminalis*, is about sixty five years old. Old trees of this sort often show garden possibilities.

Visalia set aside a wonderful park of oak and other native trees in their original habitat, Mooney Grove. There are many modern "improvements" for picnics and sport, but the park itself remains fairly authentic. The citizens find it very refreshing and enjoyable on a warm summer evening.

There is a fine planting of the Giant Timber bamboo, *Phyllostachys reticulata (Phyllostachys bambusoides)*, on the William Tevis property, recently owned by the Stockdale Country Club near Bakersfield in Kern County, perhaps the largest single planting of this species in California.

Fresno County
M. Theodore Kearney

There was another notable exception to the paucity of settlers. M. Theodore Kearney arrived in San Francisco in the early 1870's and helped develop Fresno as the manager of the Central California Colony. Fresno was founded by the railroad in May, 1872 and became the county seat in 1874. It was not until 1875 and later that there was any big expansion of the vineyards.'

Theodore Kearney was a fascinating, self-made man, who is worth a brief digression. He was born into a poor Irish family in England, but after moving to Massachusetts in 1854 he worked his way up to becoming the manager of an important company by dint of immense efforts in self—improvement. When he came to California in 1868, he was an established figure on the social scene in Boston. He and his family travelled to England and France frequently.

By investing in property in and around Fresno, he became very rich. Kearney intended to build a perfect copy of the Chateau Chenonceaux at his estate just outside Fresno. In the end this chateau was not built. The surviving house, which was later given to the University of California as an agricultural research station, is an adobe built for the superintendent of the estate.

The extensive grounds were planted with numerous exotic trees and shrubs, later to be named "Chateau Fresno Estate", but perhaps the handsomest feature of all was the eleven mile boulevard lined with eucalyptus and palm trees, leading from the estate to the city of Fresno proper. The estate was landscaped by F. D. Rosendale and the trees came from George Bailey of Berkeley.

Roeding family

Continuing with Fresno, there is another very significant pioneer.'Frederick Christian Roeding was born in Hamburg, in 1824. After visiting Chile and Peru he arrived in California in 1849. He must have prospered for in 1869 he joined a group of men to buy 80,000 acres in Fresno County. This was the Fresno Colony. Roeding, who was a banker, became interested in horticulture in 1884 and established the Fancher Creek Nurseries in Fresno.

Roeding showed excellent judgment when he took on William West of Stockton in 1885 to help as propagator. West was sent abroad to help introduce the Smyrna fig. The 1885 catalog of the Fancher Creek Nurseries listed such evergreens as *Araucaria bidwillii*, *A. cunninghamii*, *A. excelsa*, and *A. graucana*. (Note 63) The Red Flowered gum (*Eucalyptus ficifolia*) and *Sophora scundiflora* were included. A fine list of shrubs could be ordered to start a beautiful garden. Fancher Creek Nurseries practiced what they preached.

Roeding Park was given to the City of Fresno in 1903 and it still has the trees and plants which should make any pioneer proud. When Kate Sessions of San Diego was attending a state garden club meeting in Fresno she was shown a specimen of *Agathis* for identification. She frankly admitted that after many years in the nursery business she had never seen this plant growing.

George Christian Roeding, born in San Francisco on February 4, 1868, carried on the nursery which his father had started. Later he bought the California Nursery at Niles, the business started by John Rock and R. D. Fox in 1884-5. An amazing Swedish scientist, Gustav Eisen, was his nursery manager for a short time.

Eisen was expert in anthropology, horticulture, zoology and some other disciplines. At one time he was a colleague of Alice Eastwood at the California Academy of Sciences where his incisive questioning and criticism goaded her into excelling even further.

George Roeding's son, George Roeding, Jr., continued to run the nursery at Niles. The younger Roeding worked with the University of California in trying out new crop plants. The horticulturists and extension officers used his nursery as well as various others as an adjunct to the five university trial grounds. His work with olive trees was exemplary. He, alone or possibly with Gustav Eisen, wrote very detailed and scholarly commentary on each variety for sale in his catalogues. Similar pamphlets on the culture of grapes were known to be written by Eisen.

The story of the Smyrna fig has a lot of drama behind it. The Shinn family maintains it was the first to find out about "caprification", the process by which the specialized fig wasp promotes pollination. Until this time, Smyrna fig trees in California had not produced fruit, and Turkish growers were understandably not too keen on publicizing this essential ingredient of fig growing. The Shinns and the Roedings feuded rather nastily in public for many years over this priority. It is still not clear who was the first one to use the fig wasp.

Butterfield stated ' . . . . we might go back about sixty five years to picture the Fresno landscape. Gustav Eisen, who had worked there in 1885, was familiar with the gardens. "The place shows uncommon taste and refinement, and is beautified by avenues of poplars, magnolias, by groves of acacias and umbrella trees, by palms and flowers, and by roses and climbing plants. A pond with lilies overhung by weeping willows and shaded by stately elms is an unusual sight, even in this country of abundant irrigation."

In time such cities as Modesto, Merced, Madera and others copied this style of landscaping so that today both the city and country gardens contain shade plants as well as plants for color. The city parks are especially appreciated in summer.

Travelers on Highway 99 from Bakersfield to Los Angeles may wish to stop about eight miles north of Lebec to see an oak tree west of the highway at the northeast corner of Fort Tejon Parade Grounds. (See State Marker #129 for Fort Tejon established June 24, 1854.) Camels were introduced to California in 1858 in Lebec. Peter Lebec was killed by a grizzly bear on October 17, 1837, and is buried beneath this old tree. Beside this historical record, it is interesting to see the other native oaks.

CHAPTER 15

The Mother Lode Country

Butterfield recorded: 'Gold was discovered on January 24, 1848, at Coloma where John Sutter had established a mill on the river. This was not the first time that gold had been found in California but the reports sent out seemed to inflame the whole world. The lust for gold left little room for sober thoughts in a garden. Previous strikes had been minuscule. This one indicated a great abundance of easily obtained metal, and that was the difference.

In spite of this mass loss of reason, a few men and women here and there throughout the Mother Lode country planted small gardens. An old town square with its plantings or tree-lined streets, large or small, bears evidence that some still thought of beauty. Secluded cemeteries with moss-grown tablets showing the effects of age, also bear witness to this fragile attempt to create a civilized environment for the miners and their families.

A trip over the Mother Lode Highway , now Highway 49, reveals scars of the gold-mining communities, with iron-barred buildings often crumbling into ruin. A surviving shrub or tree may survive, or an ancient vine clinging to the walls of an old building. A note of sadness dominates the scene. With the return to reason, time is restoring the terrain as the miners found it.' (Butterfield could not have seen the Malakoff Diggings, irredeemably scarred beyond recall.)

One marvels at how men moved huge quantities of supplies over primitive or non-existent roads, to reach the improbable places in which the gold was found. The miner then lived out in the open until it was possible to build houses. Nothing was done easily. If the miner did not carry something with him, then he did without.

'Sleepy towns are half hidden or tucked away in a mountain valley, perhaps only the name surviving for memory. All that may be left could be a Tree of Heaven (*Ailanthus*) nurtured in spare moments by a miner's wife, some old ivy clinging faithfully to a church or dwelling, or the myrtle vine in a grass-grown cemetery.' Chinese laborers brought the Ailanthus tree with them and planted the trees in their gardens. The tree naturalized itself and became very widespread.

'Occasionally one finds a fragrant rose, forgotten, but still blooming. Dedicated, even obsessive, rosarians have found places like this to be a wonderful source of old species roses, totally forgotten or neglected by modern nurseries. At times we see an apple tree, or pear tree near a mining stream, forlorn and far away from present civilization. There are abandoned fig trees, black locust, elm trees, and cottonwoods.'

Mariposa

Mariposa, county sea of Mariposa County, lies on the way to Yosemite. The old courthouse, erected in 1854, is perhaps the oldest still being used in California. Just beyond the main store buildings, turn north from the highway to reach Mt. Bullion. Mt. Bullion (Princeton) has its old stores and rusted safe, still gaping. An old adobe store is guarded by two cottonwoods. Next one goes through Mt. Ophir and on to Bear Valley.

Bear Valley

In Bear Valley notice a pine tree on the west side of the road growing in a ruined building. Coulterville has its Hangman Tree in the middle of the public square but nothing else unusual. Big Oak Flat, about a mile east from Priest's Flat, has a monument and the remains of the oak tree that grew to be over eleven feet in diameter. This tree gave the name to the district, Groveland, once referred to as First Garrotte, to distinguish it from Second Garrotte. Bret Hart wrote the sad story of "Tennessee's Partner" in the cabin there. Second Garrotte had another Hangman's Tree, but all that remains is a name to bring up memories.

Jacksonville

Jacksonville was founded in 1848 and is the site of the first orchard in the district. Next one comes to Chinese Camp, almost out of the mountains. Many small ailanthus trees grow there and the Cory Thornless blackberry was developed there. Woods Crossing marks the site where gold was first discovered in Tuolumne County.

Jamestown and Sonora

Jamestown was founded in 1848 by Colonel James Billington. The old adobe was covered with lumber which was brought around the Horn. Sonora, also settled in 1848, comes next. St. James Episcopal Church is perhaps the oldest in California'. Sonora was the epicentre of the South American mining community. Quite a few of the French lived there too, yet no Catholic church seems to have been built or has survived. The riot over the foreign miners' tax began in Sonora.

'Wander down the side streets and alleys. There are moss-covered stone walls, old trees, and cherished gardens. The narrow streets common to many mountain towns in the Mother Lode have their own charm, and in the back country, as at Colombia, there are fine old roses and other ornamental plants left over from miners' gardens.

Shaw's Flat

Mandville Shaw planted an orchard at Shaw's Flat in 1849. Old black walnut trees are to be found at Caldwell's Gardens.

Next drive on to Tuttletown, founded by Judge A. A. H. Tuttle. He built a log cabin there in 1848. Also see the old cork oak tree opposite the Patterson mine on the outskirts of this village.

The visitor may wish to take a short trip to Jackass Hill, just west of Tuttletown not far from the highway. There is a replica of Mark Twain's old cabin and the oak close by it where he wrote some of his stories, such as "The Jumping Frog of Calaveras."

Calaveras County

Calaveras County is at the other end of the Mother Lode, and it had a flourishing population soon after the gold rush began. By the early 1850s, French immigrants had also established households and planted gardens in Tuolumne County near Sonora. The "keskidees" (a nickname given to the French miners because of their irritable way of continually asking "Quesqu' il dit?" when they did not understand English or Spanish) brought formidable gardening skills with them.

The next arrivals, Italians mainly from Genoa, also quickly settled in to follow their previous occupations. Once they realized that they were not going to get rich quickly with gold, they started truck gardens, orchards and vineyards. Because it was hard for them to find enough water for the commercial crops through the long dry summers they could not spare too much for ornamental gardens.

The Genovese, as they thought of themselves before the unification of Italy, re-created their ancestral environment in the foothills of the Sierra. One can still see faint outlines of terracing in Calaveritas. This section of San Andreas is quiet now, but during the gold rush was a centre of commerce.

Luigi Costa

Luigi Costa came to Calaveritas in 1852. He built a house and a store. About ten years later, he replaced the house with another one bought ten miles away. Costa dismantled the new house, labelled all the components and had it put back together on his own property. The second house has also gone, but the third house built in 1890 still stands. His great granddaughter, Louise Greenlaw, lives there and cherishes her domain.

Luigi Costa was a merchant, or at least became one in his new circumstances. He built a store just next to the house, and that sturdy old structure with its two steel doors is still in place. In the recent past, neighbors and friends have used the cool empty building to make and store their wine.

Across the garden is a small cottage which had been the midwife's residence. The presence of a midwife belies the notion that only men went to the gold rush. There is also a small one room school house not too far away, similarly supporting the fact that women and children were part of the immigration.

Mrs. Greenlaw is devoted to the garden, which still has some of the old trees from the last century. The garden wraps around the buildings in all sides, with small terraced lawns, many perennial beds, shrubs and charming areas where poppies grow up between old paving stones. Old mining implements are used as decoration. The veranda is shaded by a monster ivy which has been there from the beginning.

Mrs. Greenlaw told me how her grandmother, Luigi's daughter, met her grandfather, a Mr Cuneo, at the Malaspina store over in Douglas Flat. The Malaspina store has also survived and is in equally loving hands as the Costa store. Annie and Barden Stevenot bought the property a few years ago and are continually restoring and upgrading their treasures.

Douglas Flat is noted for the ivy-covered old cabins and shrubbery. The one room school still survives here. Wells Fargo used Malaspina's store as a collecting station for the bags of gold dust. Picture the scene in the old building used as a store and bank. It had small windows, and iron-shutters for protection against robbers.

Annie and Barden Stevenot

The Stevenots are maintaining the old store. Barden showed me its security feature. A marksman was stationed in a little booth discreetly hidden among the shrubbery while the gold was piling up in a strong box. He aimed his rifle through an almost invisible slit in the wall toward the box in the opposite corner. This was probably an effective deterrent.

Annie Stevenot, a pediatrician and woman of many skills, is restoring the overgrown garden to its more authentic state. She is also adding new features which echo the style of the past, such as an herb garden with flagstone partitions, and raised vegetable beds. The orchard is very old, but fig and other deciduous fruit trees still bear. Bulbs are everywhere, blooming vigorously in season. Mature vinca fills many gaps and deeply toned blue bells surround the house, under the shade of the ancient trees.

Amador County

Jackson, county seat of Amador County, has its hanging tree and there are many stores with barred windows. The Native Daughters of the Golden West started their organization there in 1886. The mine whistle blown each morning reminds visitors that this is mining country.

Pine Grove lies nine miles to the east on the Alpine Highway. This could be called the "Deserted Village." Not far away is Volcano with its St. George Hotel built in 1854. Volcano has old black locust trees and an Express Office.

Placerville

Placerville (Hangtown or Dry Diggins) was incorporated in 1854. Ivy House, with its overhanging balcony, is on the main street. Beneath the balcony is an old English ivy vine. The old Methodist church is near the bend in the street to the east . It is draped with tangled ivy. This church was dedicated on September 8, 1861.

There is a Coast Redwood on Coloma Street planted in 1865, which is almost a hundred and fifteen feet tall. On Highway 48, two blocks north of the main street is a Port Orford cedar (*Chamaecyparis lawsoniana*) a hundred feet tall.

Georgetown

In Butterfield's day, one left Placerville to go to Georgetown through what seemed to be an alleyway, leading north. This narrow alleyway leads through a winding down-grade, then up a zig-zag trail until finally there is a crest line. In time the small town of Kelsey is reached with its pioneer museum. Not far away is Garden Valley (Johntown), named for its old gardens. The native planting is interspersed with the aggressive Scotch broom, now a nuisance.

Georgetown is a very characteristic mountain village of its period. The only thing missing are those gaudy Saturday nights when miners came to town. Nowadays the village is so quiet that one wonders if it is real. Alice Eastwood once told Butterfield about staying at the local hotel in Georgetown.

The owner's family wished to go to a dance. They asked Miss Eastwood if she minded staying alone in the hotel. No, she did not mind for she was tired. There were fine furnishings in the main room from miner days, antiques by now. She had a very pleasant time in her solitude.

Shannon Knox

Shannon Knox's old home stands where the highway intersects the main street, at the northwest corner. The old fruit garden contains sour cherries, pears, apples, walnuts, and a butternut. Spireas and lilacs also thrive in the garden. Along the streets there are black locust trees, incense cedars, old roses, and lilacs.

Miners' cemetery

A stop at the cemetery north of town is revealing. Lilac, rose, boxwood, euonymus, mock orange, and black locust trees are what one might expect. Treading lightly on fern brakes, Butterfield recalled reading an old tombstone with a mother's anguished epitaph, "Oh, Thou Jewel of truth and consolation. 10 years. 1885."

Pilot Hill (Centerville).

About a mile away on the driver's right and off a short distance from the highway is the old Pilot Hill Cemetery. Large black locust trees stand guard at the family plot of the Kirchners. In another day a mother may have longed to visit that grave of Samuel R. Weller, age 22. He died in 1850. All about are the spreading pastures, made golden in summer with St. John's wort or Klamath Weed, a species of *Hypericum*.

Nevada City and Grass Valley
Felix Gillet

Felix Gillet, pioneer French nurseryman, settled in Nevada City before 1870. Gillet was a self made man. He was born in France, but could not afford to go school after the seventh grade. That did not stop him from reading widely and continuing to learn all his life.

In 1852, he came to the United States to meet Julia Ward Howe after corresponding with her about slavery. He was seventeen years old. Very little is known about his plans or motives. He worked as a barber in San Jose once he came to California, but there is no record of why he chose to move to California in 1859.

It is not clear how he learned so much about horticulture, but presumably it was after he left school and before he came to the United States. It is also not clear why he chose Nevada City at a time it had begun to decline from the peak of its prosperity and importance.

Gillet was very thrifty, and saved all his money from running a barber shop on North Pine Street. The town was startled when he bought a barren hillside in 1870 with the intention of making it

into a nursery. He had to truck in great quantities of top soil to make it fertile, but in ten years, it had become a show place. In addition, Gillet found time and energy to play a major role in civic politics. He called his nursery "Barren Hill".

He was already a prominent citizen when he decided to marry Therese J. Berness in 1891, a woman of twenty two. Gillet was extremely short. His bride stood much taller than he did, another striking discrepancy. They did not have any children.

One of the keys to his success was in knowing what to order from France. Most of the fruit and nut trees he imported did very well in California. Beside nuts, he also contributed to the development of the prune, chestnut and almond industries.

He kept meticulous records of the weather for years, making the observations in a series of ledgers which Mr Gallagher showed me. (See below) Gillet wrote idiomatic English. The notes in his nursery catalogues and his many papers on the cultivation of fruit are clear and easy to read. Charles Parsons, who had bought the nursery from Felix Gillet's widow in 1913, told Mr Gallagher he had watched Gillet write carefully in longhand, rather than use a typewriter.

'The land around Barren Hill Nursery may have been barren when Gillet started it in 1870 but today the nursery, which is still run by others, is interesting and well planted. Old trees, such as walnuts, lindens, and other shade trees make us wonder what is next. Gillet died in 1908.'

The term "others" refers to Charles Parsons. Mme. Gillet had tried to run it herself but was not successful. Parsons worked on his twenty acres for over forty years. In 1954 his land was subdivided into lots. Parsons died in 1969. Parts of the house and old greenhouse built by Gillet are still in use, though much modified.

Mr. and Mrs. William Gallagher went to live in the Nursery Street house with Mr Parsons in 1968. They still reside there. Mr. Gallagher was very cordial during a recent visit and most knowl-

Figure 35 Felix Gillet Residence
Sunken Garden (Old wine cellar entrance) c. 1923.
(Photographer unknown. Reproduced by permission of William
Gallagher)

edgeable about his property and his predecessors. He has a number of rare old photographs. (Figures 35 and 36) Miners had decimated the trees all over that district for fuel and to use in innumerable other ways. The Sierra foothill ecosystem is normally wooded, but that section of it on the outskirts of Nevada City had indeed become completely barren after they got through with it.

A few of Gillet's original trees are still thriving in the garden around the house. Some of them are so mature they affect the light and shade in wholly new ways. There is a wonderful old Atlas cedar, one of the three varieties of true cedar. The Atlas cedar arose in the Atlas mountains of Morroco. The others are the deodar from India and the cedar of Lebanon from Lebanon. Other trees which became gigantic over the last few decades are the redwoods Gillet planted.

Figure 36 Felix Gillet Nursery c. 1951
Charles Parsons standing by weeping redwood.
(Photographer unknown. Reproduced by permission of William
Gallagher)

Gillet was very interested in nut trees. He may be said to be the father of the commercial walnut industry in California. In the

Nursery Street garden hazelnut trees bearing filberts are still healthy. A Kentucky hickory remains vigorous. An ancient "Winter Nellis" pear tree stands close to the house. In winter it appears to be dead, but each spring returns to life and bears a crop of fruit. Mr Gallagher took out the diseased centre in order to prevent the trunk from splitting completely open and finally killing the tree.

Main Street

Butterfield gave a brief, rather impressionistic picture of the gardens in Nevada City and Grass Valley. 'About a block away is the old mansion of an early settler, perhaps landscaped during the 1870's when it was stylish to place an iron dog or antlered deer in the open lawn. All about are old shade trees. Going further up the main street one comes to the hotel built in 1863 (National House). The silver sugar casters and cruets await us at the tables, just as in grandmother's day.'

He may not have had too much time to spend there. In a recent visit to augment the text, the present author was privileged to meet several people with very different gardens going back many years, beside William Gallagher mentioned above. Memory is important in each of these, but perhaps not necessarily in the way Butterfield had in mind.

Margaret Steele and Hazel Whitford

Back in Nevada City, two sisters, Margaret Steele and Hazel Whitford, built adjoining gardens up in the hills. Margaret Steele started hers about twenty five years ago, when their mother was still alive. Everyone in the family helped to build the house from the ground up, and then they created the garden. Their mother adored gardening. After she died, Margaret came back to live in the same house and maintains the garden almost completely by herself. Hazel began about forty years ago. Both of these gardens are works of art.

More than one other member of their family lives in adjoining properties, forming a compound. One niece has inherited the love of gardening, but the others are content to enjoy someone else's flowers.

Margaret Steele told me she had once lived in Seattle and the style of garden there had been a strong influence. There is a sort of inevitable flow to the property. It depends on structure and form and shades of green as much as on the color and pattern of flowers. Mature conifers, dogwoods, oaks and maples form the backdrop. Massed shrubs with varying foliage are everywhere, particularly rhododendron with its dark glossy leaves and many varieties of azalea.

Even late in the year when the blossom is over, the subtle gradation catches and holds the eye. I saw photographs of the shrubs in spring and fall and the rich color was astounding. One can see tall hills in the distance from the terrace and the lawns. A former swimming pool is being turned into a sunken garden. Margaret does almost all this hard work herself.

Hazel Whitford and her husband Fred transplanted a handsome variegated ivy vine to the outside of their garage when they built their house. That vine has now twined itself all around the supports of the garage but nothing touches the ground except for the primary root. Each of the Whitfords has different sections of the property which they cultivate, but the total effect remains harmonious.

Although they own many acres, only one or two are in cultivation. The rest has been left natural with many pine trees and other Sierra vegetation. A large circular bed in front of the house holds an enormous coast redwood they planted from a small slip. It provides numerous progeny and anyone is welcome to have a young tree. In this garden too, the rhododendron and azalea have pride of place. Both sisters grow many perennial and annual flowers, but these are serious gardens with strong statements about structure and form.

Restoration of Nevada City

Nevada City has been through many cycles. At one time it was more important than San Francisco but that did not last very long. Through a long period of quiescence and even incipient decay in the town proper, the wooded hill areas were so lovely that former foresters retired there, to remain in tune with Nature. Now it has come back to vigorous life thanks to two changes, which also encompass Grass Valley.

Town officials recognized it had potential as a tourist destination, and revived all the old charming buildings intentionally to attract vistors. In December, the whole town becomes one huge decoration for a "Victorian Christmas". The other, more adventitious change has been an increasing influx of people seeking to retire to a lovely, still unspoiled region. They bring many talents and abundant energy to this new home.

One example is that of my friends Tom and Annabel Straus. Tom is an engineer who retired from the aerospace industry in southern California. Annabel has dived into Nevada City life enthusiatically. She devotes time to the Nevada County Historical Society in very practical ways as a docent at the museum. It was entirely due to her efforts that I met the owners of all the gardens described above.

Empire State Mine

One very large and imposing property in Grass Valley which Butterfield neglected is now the State of California Empire Mine State Historic Park. It was formerly a private mining company with a so-called "cottage" in the grounds where the owner, William Bowers Bourn Jr, lived at times. This house was designed by William Polk, as were all Bourn's residences. It is possible the garden was designed by Polk's associate Wright.

Butterfield's indifference to big estate gardens may have been at work here. The Bourns built Filoli some years later, a place he also ignored. The garden in Grass Valley pre-dated that estate by twenty years at least, giving plenty of time for memories to develop. These were both personal and communal.

The Bourns themselves did not spend too much time at their handsome country residence, but the general manager, George Starr, and the families of succeeding managers, the Nobbs and Manns, lived there continuously in the house built for them. George Starr was Mr Bourn's cousin. Mrs Bourn was said to be distressed by the constant pounding noise of the stamp mills. The manager's house burned down many years ago. There are plans to re-build it and use it as a visitors' centre. (23)

The Nobbs were enthusiastic horticulturists and planted numerous trees and shrubs. A few of their modifications were not completely pleasing, such as removing beloved roses over an arbor and replacing them with grapes, but at least they were sufficiently involved to feel like changing things. One of Mr Nobbs' grandsons studied horticulture at the University of California in Berkeley.

In the late 1920s, Mr Bourn became very depressed. He had had a stroke in 1923 and remained very disabled. His only daughter, Maude died in 1929. Because of these distressing events he sold the Empire mine to the Newmont company. This company also bought the other important mine in the area, the North Star.

Comparing the fates of these two properties after that is very instructive. Empire continued to supply gold. After World War Two, when the government fixed the price of gold at $35 an ounce, and it became unprofitable to bring the gold up to the surface, Empire remained in fairly good condition even before the state of California acquired it.

The local citizens had a lot to do with that acquisition. Their memories of the estate's beauty as well as the significance of its gold mining history fuelled the drive to get the state involved and keep the pressure up until a decision was made. It became state property in 1975. Since then, the grounds have been skilfully managed by well trained gardeners, assisted by a few devoted volunteers. The present head gardener is Richard Figuerdo. At one time he did a tour of duty at San Simeon, so is very familiar with grounds on the grand scale.

North Star Mine

The North Star mine has not had that good luck. At one time Bourn owned it. He sold it to James D. Hague, but afterwards bought it back again. When John Hayes Hammond (famous as Cecil Rhodes' mining engineer) managed it, the mine performed well. Later it too became unprofitable. Newmont subsequently sold it to a developer. One of the Hague relatives hoped it could be donated to the Univerity of California for preservation, but the family did not agree.

A series of developers made unfortunate decisions and the house, an early work by Julia Morgan in the "craftsman" style, is now in an advanced state of decay. One developer made the unwise change of taking out the back staircase, creating a fire hazard, but the house still did not fit the use he intended. In spite of a high fence, or perhaps because of it, the local vandals use it as a drug haven and for other asocial purposes.

Instead of being a garden of memory, North Star house and its garden have shrunk to being a memory only. If it were not for Evelyn Foote Gardiner, granddaughter of the manager, George Foote, and some grainy pictures she treasures, almost nothing would be known about this once handsome home.

Mrs Gardiner was one of the people the author met in Grass Valley. No one has lived in that house since the late 1960s. George Foote's wife was Mary Halleck Foote, a noted artist and writer, and author of "A Victorian Gentlewoman in the Far West: the reminiscences of Mary Hallock Foote". (This work was adopted by the late Wallace Stegner as the basis of "Angle of Repose" with rather perfunctory acknowledgement).

Mrs. Gardiner recalls that her grandfather was an avid amateur gardener, and planted many things himself. When the mine was profitable, four gardeners were employed, but after he retired and the company gave him a hundred and thirty acres he maintained the cultivated section of the grounds with only one helper.

During Mrs. Gardiner's childhood, there were a double row of white "wild" azaleas, a hawthorn hedge along the road, a semi—

formal rose garden and a huge bed for the so-called "cutting flowers" beloved of hostesses: iris, chrysanthemums, columbine, amaryllis, Michaelmas daisies and many others. Washingtonia palms
surrounded part of the property. Large orchards held every kind of
fruit a child could desire. Mrs. Gardiner said that some of the fig
tree and persimmons still bear fruit. A really charming conceit had
been encouraging a climbing white rose to grow up into a pine
tree. The flowers looked like a waterfall as the rose bloomed.

The family had left woods close to one side of the house, keeping it shaded and cooler in the hot summers, but at one time the
subsequent owner logged very extensively and the woods disappeared. In the cultivated part of the garden, there were poplars,
maples and magnolia trees which still stand.

Not far away, at the Empire Historic Park, things are very
different. A fragment of the actual Empire mine has been preserved, but visiting the park to see the house and garden has a
special meaning. Polk and / or Wright sited the house carefully
along an axis giving the best views. The land is fairly high, about
3000 feet. In the beginning, one could see across the Sacramento
Valley and other attractive areas, but the evergreen trees have grown
so large those views no longer exist.

The house was started in 1897. In a hundred years, trees grow
to astonishing heights, but nowadays the idea of cutting anything
down is anathema. Although it would be historically accurate,
there will be no view in the near future. The front of the house has
a smooth lawn with two symmetrically placed classical fountains.
At the edge of the lawn, there is a series of "water steps", an Italianate
conceit, going down to a reflecting pool. It is possible to glimpse
the origin of the landscaping concepts which were used later at
Filoli.

At the back of the house, there are terraced flower beds and
shrubs at each side of shallow steps marching down toward the
driveway. Two traditionally styled urns filled with plants are at the
top of the steps. Trellises arch over the steps and old world climbing roses cover them. Originally, these beds held cutting flowers
too, and at one time, there were a lot of geraniums (pelargonium).

One of the docents, Ben Braly, showed the author many photographs which corroborated these historical facts. Mr Braly is a true enthusiast, and conducts a special guided walk around the grounds each week pointing out these features and many others. Horticultural riches are on every side.

Now the beds are devoted to antique roses, showing the chronological progression from Rosa gallica, Rosa alba, hybrid perpetuals, rugosas and many others in the chain of rose history. This minor degree of historical inaccuracy for the garden is completely eclipsed by the charm and beauty of the old roses. The garden is used by rosarians to teach and instruct students.

Approaching the gardens from the parking lot takes one through cool avenues of tall cedars, magnolias and maples among many other specimen trees spaced out over extensive lawns. Mature shrubs are as large as many trees. The deutzia have mounded out, as have the philadelphus and other fragrant bushes. In this garden there is also an unexpected "marriage" between a climbing vine and tall evergreen tree. (Maybe this idea was copied from the North Star house, or perhaps it was the other way around.) At Empire, it is a wisteria which dates back to the very early period. The trunks of the wisteria are massive.

Aaron Augustus Sargent

Lacking the resources of a personal gold mine, other families in the two towns still created gardens of extraordinary beauty. Two of them go back much further even than Empire or North Star. One was started by Aaron Augustus Sargent, newspaper editor and later state lawmaker, in 1856. He eventually became a senator and even briefly ambassador to Germany. His house on Broad Street in Nevada City has been preserved, and updated as an inn.

The front and back gardens contribute a great deal to the period charm emanating from the house. A delicately traced wrought iron fence separates the plot from the street. Symmetrical lawns are punctuated by brick paths and attractive low shrubbery with flower beds on each side of the concrete walk approaching the front door. The restoration of the front garden was supervised by Carolyn Singer, owner of the Foothills Cottage Gardens Nursery and a most helpful guide to old gardens in the town.

The back garden has a totally different appearance, steeply sloped, and very irregular with brick and stone stairways dividing the sections of lawn and flower beds. All this work was done by Chinese stone masons attracted to the region by the gold. Some of the rock was rough cut from the mines, but in one or two instances, the masons had used smooth river stones. Mature linden, holly, and walnut trees are still in good condition, as are a deodar cedar and Amazon smooth spruce. The manager of the inn told us that weddings are sometimes held in this garden.

Across Spring Street, behind an apartment house built in about 1960, Carolyn pointed out that there is a continuation of the Sargent garden with the same signature stone work as in the Broad Street one. The terrain is much wilder, forming part of an extensive ravine behind several Spring Street properties. A small stream runs through the bottom of the rocky area.

The Chinese masons built a set of elaborate staircases, walls, bridges and paths around the water, an arbor, and an open barbecue here. There are also a cistern and covered well. Although the planting has run wild, one can still see remnants of ornamental shrubs, together with two palm trees which survive in spite of the chilly Sierra winter. The ornamental young ladies of the era would have been less likely to roam through this section unchaperoned though it must have been tremendously romantic. Now it is home to ferocious brambles and decidedly unromantic weeds.

Sonntag property

The other very old property which once belonged to the Sonntags now belongs to Carolyn Singer. She allowed me to visit her garden on Sonntag Road about ten miles outside Grass Valley. Carolyn bought the property in 1977 and became a nurseryperson a few years later. Originally she sought the peace and refuge of a quiet country spot to help her son recover from a chronic illness.

Now he is well and launched into his own career, she still gets deep pleasure from the nursery.

The Sonntag family had homesteaded on a thousand acres in the 1860s. They had pear and walnut orchards and large vineyards. A few of the original English walnuts are still bearing and there are some grafted Bartlett pear trees left.

The house they had built burned down in the 1920s. A new one was built in the 1930s. The lawns were alight with species daffodils and numerous violets from the original period when Carolyn took over. These had all naturalized themselves. Carolyn also pointed out an old maple tree, an alder tree and native black oak which came from the homestead period. One of the Sontag granddaughters, Ardis, an artist, still lives in the county, married to a writer and publisher, David Comstock. She likes to visit her grandparents' home.

Convent of Mount St Mary

In Grass Valley, the former convent of Mount Saint Mary, at one time an orphanage, is now a community centre, St Josephs. The Grass Valley Museum is housed there and the nuns' chapel is now a community hall. Mount Saint Mary was started in 1866. There is a garden in the front which was built during the early years of the twentieth century. St Patrick's church once stood across the street, but it was razed about fifty years ago. A new one has taken its place. Mount Saint Mary's is a state historic landmark.

An old rendering of the property shows an open, rather "picturesque" landscape with informally placed trees and shrubs. The only formal planting was of two large conifers, one on each side of the front gate. In the 1880s, the order planted a peach orchard which lasted about twenty years. Some of the peach trees survived through the later years.

The director of the St Josephs Center, Joseph Guida, generously spent a lot of time with me going over photographs of the building at different epochs, to show me the evolution of the garden. In 1900 no garden existed. A high wall had been built around

*Figure 37 Garden at Mount Saint Mary's Convent. Grass Valley
(Reproduced by permission of St Joseph's Center {Joseph Guida})*

the front in the 1890s, and the garden was created inside this
space. The sisters chose a formal design with four parterres, each
shaped like a Celtic harp, defined by boxwood hedges. A fountain
and sundial were added in about 1935. Subsequently, topiary
shrubs were replaced by rose bushes. Two religious statues have
been in place for a very long time. (Figure 37)

Apart from the religious statues, this is a very classical "Paradise" or four square garden inherited in almost a straight line from
the early Persian structures. The four paths represent the four rivers in Paradise, water, milk, honey and wine. The equivalent He-
brew myth is in the book of Genesis, where the water in the garden of Eden flows into four rivers.

Everything is somewhat overgrown now, but one can still see
the shape of the "rooms" and understand how the garden is meant
to augment the spirit of the foundation. Viewed from the higher
floors of the former convent, the outlines are very clear. Many former
residents of the convent, the orphanage and the town had memories of this garden.

CHAPTER 16

North Coast Counties

Marin County

The San Rafael Mission was the "hospital" of the mission chain because of the warmer climate in Marin. Living in San Francisco took its toll of the missionaries and some of their converts. The persistent cool temperatures and chilly fog not only had physical effects but psychological ones too. They could not just turn up a thermostat to get warm.

There was no escape from the depressing effects this had. The Spanish and Mexican-born men needed to see the sun frequently to be sure they were really alive. Days went by in the colony by the bay when the sun was hidden by the marine layer. Even the strict Franciscan order had to do something to mitigate these symptoms, as otherwise the work would slow down too much. They allowed a few ailing workers to stay in the San Rafael mission long enough to recover their zest and energy.

Mission San Rafael

Mission San Rafael Archangel was built in 1817. After secularization, the mission property was sold to "three Califorrnios" in 1834. When the French diplomat De Mofras travelled around California in 1841, he found it a total ruin. He did record the presence of many "superb tobacco plants" in the garden. A man named Murphy and about twenty native people lived on this property. James Byers, a local carpenter, bought the ruins in 1861 just to get the timber in its roof.

Margaret Kittle Boyd (Mrs. George Boyd) noted in her *"Reminiscences of Early Marin County Gardens"* that the last surviving pear tree from Mission days was cut down in the late 1930s. (24) She remembered playing in them as a child, and that they had an odd "twisted" bark. In her childish way, she thought the missionaries had twisted the seeds before planting them.

The only image of the mission in its original form is a sketch drawn by General Vallejo. No one ever took a photograph of this mission, or at least, none has ever been found. After its sale, six acres were returned to the church for the parish priest.

The mission had a very large orchard on the site where Macy's later built a department store. Macy's has since been replaced by a modern office block. The orchard was surrounded by an adobe wall. Bancroft noted that the inventory of the property in 1834 assessed the value of the orchard at $968. When John Bidwell went to buy fruit trees in San Rafael in 1847, he presumably purchased them from the men who now owned the property. It appears that no traces of any of the original buildings remain but no consistent, professional archaeological study has been carried out, such as the one at Lompoc, for example.

The Marin Historical Society has records of at least one lawsuit about water rights to this land. The water came from springs higher up on the Boyd property. Water for the San Rafael parks still comes from this source. In 1949 a replica of the old mission was built. This is the building now seen in San Rafael.

Olompali Ranch and the Burdells

The earliest known residential garden in Marin County was at Olompali Ranch. In 1776, a group of Spaniards was travelling north and stopped at a native rancheria (settlement) next to a spring. They camped there for a few days and were made welcome by the native people. In return for this hospitality, the Spaniards taught the natives how to make adobe bricks and build with them.

Camillo Ynitia's father, the last chief of the Olompali tribe, built himself an adobe using his new skill. This was the first private dwelling built north of San Francisco. Later Camillo's son built another house, encompassing the first one. The property was acquired by James Black. Dr Burdell, a dentist, married James Black's daughter and Mr Black gave his daughter a house as a wedding gift. The original adobe was incorporated in a larger house built by the Burdells when they moved there in 1863.

When the adobe house was torn down years later, the adobe bricks sprouted many plants and unexpected weeds. The same phenomenon was noted in several places, such as Lompoc and later in Napa. The Olompali bricks produced "wild" oats, filaree grass and burr clover. Alice Eastwood, Curator of the Herbarium at the California Academy of sciences, was consulted about this. She believed that the oats had come with a European immigrant because oats were not indigenous to California.

Mrs Burdell laid out a magnificent garden. She understood perspective, grading extensively in front of the house, with long graceful terraces leading down to the sea. The Burdells took a wedding trip to Japan and she brought back numerous oriental plants for her garden. She did not copy Japanese garden design, but stuck to the usual plans of her period. A formal central bed had brick paths radiating out from it, ending in a circular bed to make a "wheel".

The planting was completely unconventional for the time. Japanese maples, magnolias, oleanders, and camellias survived until the 1930s when Margaret Boyd was writing. The avenue approaching from the road consisted of handsome eucalyptus and pine trees, with amaryllis in the understory. In the centre of the round flower bed a tall spiral palm was dominant. Next to the front entrance of the house, there were four other very tall palms.

Margaret Boyd draws the reader's attention to two large specimen trees in the garden. One was an old oak with a cross carved in its bark commemorating the only person to die in the Bear Flag revolt. The other was a redwood tree grown from a seed found in the crop of a quail killed at Fort Ross. Another handsome feature of this garden was a rich pomegranate hedge.

While Mrs Burdell had powerful resources to make her garden unusual, the rest of the ranch gardens from that period were in much the same style, a long avenue of cypress with eucalyptus and a wide circlular bed with a solitary palm tree in its centre. Almost nothing of these gardens remained at the time Margaret Boyd was writing. Occasionally a few roses could be seen, but almost all the orchards disappeared rapidly. Once in a while, Mrs Boyd found an isolated misshapen old pear or apple tree, without any connection to a house.

Mrs Boyd was writing almost seventy years ago. Olompali Ranch is now a state park in Novato and close to the Sonoma County line. The gardens have fallen into decline but there is talk of reviving them.

City of San Rafael

The City of San Rafael was not laid out until 1848 and there were only two houses besides the Mission at that time. Captain William A. Richardson owned Rancho Saucelito (original spelling) in this area and there seemed to be no need to build more than the three houses in San Rafael in 1849.'

' San Rafael was in such easy reach of San Francisco that it was just a matter of time until many homes were established'. Butterfield had met his future wife on a trip to Muir Woods over forty years previously.

Butterfield was travelling and writing about Marin county for some time before the Golden Gate bridge was built. He and his wife probably crossed the water by ferry, unless he always drove round the top of the bay along what is now Highway 37. There were far fewer people living in Marin county at that epoch. It was still rural and open. Rich men's properties covered a lot of space, allowing for glorious park—like grounds. Because there were fewer places to see, each one assumed more significance.

Estate gardeners

Gardeners abounded, but the best people did not employ just any gardener. Gardeners were not interchangeable the way a housemaid might be. Only cook had the same latitude. Gardeners (and cooks) might be surly and ornery, but the employer bit his or her tongue and put up with it for the sake of their reputation in the social / horticultural stakes. There was a not so subtle rivalry among all these society ladies as to who had the best roses, the greatest variety of rhododendrons, the earliest strawberries and most abundant peaches, for example.

Ah Sing

There is the wonderful story of Ah Sing, Mrs Louise Boyd's Chinese gardener at Falkirk. He was a virtual tyrant for fifty years, from 1885 to 1935, allowing no one else to make any decisions about what was grown and how to do it, not even his employer. Only gardeners could tell their employer home truths and get away with it, (oh yes and possibly a gentleman's gentleman). In an age when servants were invisible and anonymous, Ah Sing stood out. Someone took a photograph of him, an extraordinary departure from normal practice. (Figure 38). The Marin County Historical Society has a print of it.

Mrs Boyd wanted to reward him for these years of devotion. She knew that his religion demanded that he die in his native land. When he retired, she prevailed upon her friends, the Dollars, who owned a shipping line, to give him a free passage back to China. Ah Sing sailed back to China to die, and the garden was never the same again.

Falkirk

Louise Boyd's property, currently known as "Falkirk", is now owned by the City of San Rafael, and used as a community center.

While Mrs. Boyd's family owned it the garden was developed by

Figure 38 Ah Sing, Mrs Louise Boyd's gardener, ca. 1930
(Reproduced by permission of the Marin County Historical Society)

two of her uncles, Daniel and Seth Cook. They brought a noted landscape architect from Boston to design it, another first for San Rafael.

The Cooks called their place "Maple Lawn" because the garden had a fine collection of Japanese maples. Large clumps of bamboo, and numerous specimen trees added to its splendor. A unique and perfect *Araucaria robusta*, an *Araucaria brazillana*, a cedar of Lebanon, and a *Grevillea bidwilli* were all in very good condidion for many years, quite probably because of Ah Sing's devotion and unremitting attention. He also maintained oleanders, orange trees and dozens of fragrant vines around the house.

(Butterfield wrote the following at some remove from the events. Margaret Boyd was probably more accurate about the Cook family. 'At San Rafael, Ira Cook and his son planted *Araucaria excelsa* in May, 1876, *Grevillea robusta* on September 11, and a blue gum on October 25 of the same year. There was an old blue gum not far from the old Hotel in San Rafael which is said to be one of the largest in California.')

Fortune's Yellow Rose

'A fine specimen of the rose, Fortune's Yellow, was so outstanding that it was renamed Beauty of Glazenwood and also listed simply as San Rafael Rose.' This rose has also gone by the name of "Rose of Ophir" according to some experts. The specimen in San Rafael had come directly from China. Robert Fortune originally sent his find back to England with his other botanical specimens in 1846, but James Walker had this particular specimen brought by a friend who was travelling in China.

Planted in about 1880, a specimen of this rose at 126 Corte Madera Avenue grew to a size of about twenty feet across the front of a tree, looking like an enormous bridal wreath. It entwined itself in a large redwood tree and everyone could see it. For many years the driver on the Tamalpais Railroad stopped the train leading to the top of the mountain so passengers could view the fifty year old rose while it was in bloom.

'Many subtropical trees flourish in Marin County but the lush acacias growing there in the late 1870's fell prey to the White Scale introduced on oranges and acacias at Menlo Park a few years before.

Marin Art and Garden Center

Many rare plants were found in the leading gardens of Marin County. Butterfield wondered what a future visitor would say when he visited the Art and Garden Center at Ross, started by a group of enthusiastic women in the 1930s.

Fine old trees of a past generation and more blend with the Dawn redwood, *Metasequoia glyptostroboides* imported from China in the early 1940s. Flower shows and displays at the Art and Garden Center should give the visitor a good excuse to make a trip to see specimens from an old garden still display their prime beauty.'

In spite of Butterfield saying he had a soft spot for Marin, he did not have time to do its old gardens justice. With the devoted assistance of the librarian at the Marin County Historical Society, Jocelyn Moss, I have ferreted out information about numerous gardens of immense beauty and significance in this broadly diverse county.

Bolinas

Bolinas is a quaint little village now. Its current residents belligerently try to keep it unchanged, preventing tourists and would-be settlers who want material things from coming there, ie they are opposing "gentrification". The townspeople even go to the length of tearing down the road sign pointing to the village every time the state erects one.

This was not always the case. Very early in California history Bolinas was a busy port for the lumber industry, not at all a sleepy backwater. Rafael Garcia settled there in 1834. Before that the men who hunted sea otters used it as their port, until that section of the bay silted up. Bolinas became the port for shipping lumber down to San Francisco. (25)

Bolinas still had rows of tall cypress trees and a ten foot high cypress hedge in the 1930s. The cypresses were said to have come round the horn from Portugal. In the 1870s, a Captain Mckinnon planted cypress trees he had bought in Sausalito.

Bolinas' climate supported ornamental and market driven horticulture extremely well. Wealthy merchants built large houses and laid out gardens to match. Poorer citizens grew vegetables there for the San Francisco market. Many years later, history repeated itself. Bolinas is currently one of the sites where organic vegetables are cultivated for discerning Bay area residents, both individuals and restaurants.

Many cottage gardens contained roses, fuchsias, lemon verbena and datura which grew abundantly in the moist cool climate. Fruit trees planted before 1850 were still bearing as late as 1935. The apples had been particularly prized in the early days, before more sophisticated orchard produce was available.

Olema and Fairfax

From Bolinas one reaches Olema through the Olema Valley. Judge James Mcmillan Shafter owned a very large estate at the end of the nineteenth century. He numbered his ranches "A", "B", "C" etc in order. The porch around his house was festooned with climbing roses. (26, 27)

The Sir Francis Drake Highway, named for the sixteenth century English freebooter, (a polite term for pirate), goes east from the coast through Fairfax, home of another Englishman, "Lord" Fairfax. The Fairfaxes planted an English type of garden with many evocative flowers and shrubs. The estate was surrounded by native forest still rich with madrone, laurel and oaks, home to many bears.

San Rafael
Paul D'Heiry

San Rafael grew slowly. A notable early resident came from France, M. Paul D'Heiry. He bought a large tract of land behind the ruined old mission, and created a flourishing garden with many flowers and fruits imported fom France. Mrs Boyd remembered he had a lot of grapevines.

D'Heiry was very generous. Anyone who wanted a slip or cutting from his garden was welcome. The village physician, Dr Taliaferro, took many such slips. His house was almost totally obscured by the Marechal Niel roses brought by D'Heiry earlier. This warm hearted Frenchman moved up to Oregon where he had mines, and all trace of his house and garden vanished.

The D'Heiry land was sold in 1863 to Henry Wilkins. An important feature of the property was the old Mission spring running through it. Mr Wilkins enjoyed swimming and constructed the first artificial swimming pool in Marin in the late 1860s. The sides and surrounding deck were made of wood.

Maillard estate

One small boy, John Maillard, often jumped into this water. He lived near the Wilkins house in a house built by his father. The Maillard family raised thoroughbred horses and Jersey cattle, the first in Marin. Mrs Boyd spoke both to Mr Wilkins and Mr Maillard herself, so the facts are correct.

The Maillard estate was a rather utilitarian establishment and only had the standard cypress and eucalyptus lined driveway. After it changed hands twice more, and was bought by Mrs. William Butterworth, a fine garden was constructed there.

Mrs. Butterworth built a fish pond with a central fountain. She planted lilac of every sort, orange trees, crepe myrtle, magnolias and numerous fragrant vines. Margaret Boyd remembers luscious figs, but did not know where Mrs. Butterworth bought the trees. Fifty years later, the fig trees were still producing fruit profusely.

In 1886, Mrs Butterworth sold the estate to A. W. Foster, a man who was also very interested in horticulture and garden design. He named his property "Fairhills". One feature which he changed markedly was the long straight driveway. He made it curved, and lined it with palm trees. Foster also laid out many more flower beds, and filled them with both annuals and perennials.

Immediately after the great earthquake and fires of 1906, John McLaren asked Mr. Foster to take in six Japanese gardeners and masons from the Golden Gate Park at the estate in San Rafael, until they could return to work in the park. The Japanese men spent their time very profitably. By the time they returned to San Francisco, Foster's estate had a waterfall, summer house and bridge in the Japanese style added to it, as well as handsome azalea and rhododendron beds, with tree ferns as an accent.

Margaret Kittle Boyd had her sixteenth birthday party in this newly refurbished garden. No one can gainsay the fact that the Foster garden held memories for Mrs. Boyd together with many other people who were privileged to visit it. She also comments wrily on the house her family lived in and its garden. In his enthusiasm for rare trees, she says that her father crammed twice as many plants into a small garden as it could tolerate.

Several other large estates were built in the late 1880s, but at the same time Mrs Boyd recalls dozens of small cottage gardens with Banksia roses and wisteria climbing around the porch. One such cottage housed Miss Murrison's elementary school. Miss Murrison taught the children in the garden when the weather was fine and took them on botany walks along the country lanes around San Rafael.

The population of Marin remained very low until the 1870s, when wealthy families began moving over there for the summer, establishing many of the handsome estates noted by Mrs. Boyd and later by Butterfield. The Gerstle and Sloss families were part of that movement. Young Margaret Kittle, as she was then, was allowed to wander round their flower gardens while her mother paid the obligatory calls.

Eastern section of San Rafael

W. T. Coleman bought much of the eastern section of San Rafael as an investment. A number of large estates grew up there in time. The DeYoungs owned "Meadowlands". Dominican College was chartered in 1890, and had numerous fine trees planted on its campus. The Anderson family grew exceptional blue hydrangeas. Mrs Boyd comments that other houses had simple gardens with many flowers but few "distinguishing features".

William Babcock

She did however remember one garden in that part of the town for its style. It belonged to William Babcock. He personally supervised where each tree and shrub was to be placed. As the garden matured all the plants had the proper room to grow. He delighted in magnolias, catalpas, hawthorne, English holly, camphor and many types of evergreen. These trees surrounded extensive lawns. There was an elegant air of restraint about this approach to the house, but in other parts of his garden, brightly colored flowers abounded. Babcock always had brilliant arrangements inside the house.

San Rafael Improvement Club

Margaret Boyd participated in the San Rafael Improvement Club, an early forerunner of the garden club. The women planted the road to San Anselmo with shade trees, carefully staking each one and tying them to prevent them from falling. To their amazement, the trees were continually untied, no matter how often they redid them. The assumption was that it was the work of mischievous young boys, but the culprit turned out to be an elderly pillar of local society, Mrs. William Barbar. Mrs. Barbar could not bear to see the little trees so tightly tied and felt sorry for them!

Ross

The town of Ross was named for James Ross who settled on the ten thousand acre Rancho Punto de Quentin in 1859. Since that time, the rancho has been divided into Ross Valley, Kentfield and San Anselmo. By the time Margaret Boyd was writing, the occupants of the old Ross house were his granddaughters, the Misses Worn. They had clear memories of the garden at their grandfather's house. It had " . . . . an old wild cherry tree in one corner, pomegranates and datura, around the center bed little 'Virgin's tears', ... how we loved to pick them. (There were also) a lovely pink Castilian rose, English currants and bushels of great fat hairy gooseberries."

Dibblee property

There was another garden in Ross which Margaret Boyd believed was the finest in Marin county at that time. Albert Dibblee bought a large part of the Ross estate in 1870, and built a typical "New York Hudson River" style of house with a fourteen foot veranda across the entire front. Roses abounded. Banksias covered two sides of the house and 'Marechal Niel' grew along its southern exposure. Mr Dibblee had moved to Marin from New York, and named his new home "Fernhill". This is the site of the present Branson School.

Trees dotted the lawns and there were immense beds of "old fashioned" flowers: asters, cannas, wall flowers, chrysanthemums, marigold and stocks. It is amusing to see the term "old fashioned" used to describe these flowers, planted in the 1870s and 1880s, back in the early years of the twentieth century. These flowers are timeless and continue to be grown and cherished today.

It is also interesting to see how Mr Dibblee used trees, as individual specimens or small groups in his lawn. He may have seen this is his travels, perhaps to England where many estates were influenced by "Capability" Brown, or he may have consciously or unconsciously been reflecting the appearance of Marin county's wild landscape.

Dibblee was passionate about trees. He planted many of them in the streets of Ross. Some survived until the mid-twentieth century. In his own garden, there were dozens of trees which had been obtained for him in China, Korea and Japan by his friend Admiral Shufeldt. The admiral had "opened" Korea and had been the first American minister under Grant. Other trees and plants had been sent from nurseries in New York and various parts of the United States.

The inventory of the trees and plants in his garden is long. It included American elms, linden, horsechestnuts, hickory, and an astonishingly tall *Liriodendron tulipifera* (the Southern tulip tree). His daughter, Nellie, had visited Yosemite and in keeping with the custom of young ladies at that time, had brought back a handful of sequoia seed wrapped in her handkerchief. One of these seeds grew into an outstandingly large and healthy *Sequoia gigantea*.

Dibblee also planted an orchard. The trees were still actively producing fruit fifty years later. He had Bellflower, Newtown pippin and little "Christmas" apples, pears, cherries, quince, walnut, pomegranate, persimmons, figs and olives. Like Louise Boyd and other landowners, Mr. Dibblee employed Chinese gardeners.

After Albert Dibblee died in 1895, his widow decided she wanted a quite different house. Mrs Dibblee built her new house on Upper Road in Ross. It was intended for her daughter one day, but the daughter, an artist, preferred to live more simply. Eventually Mrs. Dibblee's son Benjamin inherited the house. Descendants of Albert Dibblee still live in Marin: Thomas Dibblee, Wendel Nicolaus, and his sister Polly Nicolaus Wolff.

In its heyday, the garden occupied seven acres, densely filled with rare plants. There were many formal beds and elegant shrubs. Thomas Dibblee told me that the camellia walk, with camellias on both sides, and ending at a seat, and the "little garden" outside the dining room, were both designed by the Olmsted Brothers of Massachusetts. (Figure 39) The house and garden looked toward Mount Tamalpais, with an incomparable "borrowed landscape".

Benjamin Dibblee was an inveterate hands on gardener, vigorously digging, fertilizing and planting together with the hired staff. He could be touchy about his treasures. One relative coveted some of his exceptional blue pansies but he did not want to share them

Figure 39 Garden at the Benjamin Dibblee estate, Ross, Marin County
(Reproduced by permission of the San Francisco Garden Club)

with her. She was very resourceful, cajoling the gardener in the greenhouse. When he found out, he was said to be extremely irate. Mrs. Kirkham, Thomas Dibblee's sister, verified this story. She had heard it from the "culprit", her grandmother, Mrs. Harrison Dibblee.

William Kent

A year after Albert Dibblee arrived in Ross, another influential family followed, the Kents. Albert Kent sent his wife and son William to California after the terrible fire in Chicago in 1871. Mrs. Kent saw some land while out for a drive and told her husband she "had been looking into Paradise". It was Annie Ross Worn's property. Mr. Kent bought five hundred acres from her. Much later, Mrs. Kent described the creation of the garden for Margaret Kittle Boyd.

She told Mrs. Boyd that both house and garden had undergone many changes. At first they had a formal garden with a fountain in the centre and many flower beds edged with box. It had been designed by a landscape architect whose name she did not know. After the Chicago experience, one of Albert Kent's great concerns was fire. He planted three vineyards and a large orchard to act as baffles against a fire consuming this property, but in addition the fruit was itself worth having.

Like his neighbour Dibblee, Kent supervised the disposition of the trees and shrubs in his garden very closely. He chose specimens of each of the true cedars, Lebanon, Atlantica and deodar, and put them in about 1873. They all grew to majestic proportions.

William Kent was concerned about conservation and the environment before those became household words. He donated the part of his land with Mount Tamalpais on it to the state of California, to be maintained as a park *in perpetuo*. (28) Much of the rest of his land became the town of Kentfield, named for him by his wife after his death.

Captain William A. Richardson and Sausalito

Here is more from Butterfield: 'Many gardens are in the making at Sausalito. In the cemetery is a specimen of *Cunninghamia*, large and old, about forty feet high, which must have been planted many years ago.' Butterfield said very little more about Sausalito.

Margaret Kittle Boyd fills this gap in Butterfield's narrative. She goes back as far as 1826, when John J. Reed moved to Marin. He had wanted the Rancho Sausalito, but had to settle for the Rancho Corte Madera del Presidio.

Reed planted an orchard at the head of Richardson's bay on the road to Belvedere. ("Richardson's Bay "is an anachronistic term, since Richardson did not reach Marin until ten years after Reed.) Mrs. Boyd said the orchard was still in existence a hundred years later. John Reed married Senorita Hilarita Sanchez, youngest daughter of the commander of the presidio, Jose Antonio Sanchez in 1836. More than forty years later, when a railroad was built from Tiburon to San Rafael, the first station on the new line was called Hilarita.

William Richardson

William Antonio Richardson, an English naval officer who decided to stay in California in 1822, moved to Sausalito in 1836. He had married a daughter of the commandant of the presidio, Maria Antonia Martinez, in 1825. When he settled in Yerba Buena (San Francisco), he was the first non-Spanish person to do that. Eight other "Anglo" seamen from the United States, England and Ireland, including John Gilroy, were in different parts of the province at that time.

At first he could only afford a small bare shanty in Sausalito, but later built an adobe with a few fruit trees and shrubs around it. Mrs. Boyd quoted William Heath Davis on the topic of early rancheros: 'The houses of the rancheros were usually built against entirely open ground—having in view always security against the Indians". The shortage of water was a much more likely reason for the absence of ornamental planting but security cannot be completely discounted.

Many sad changes overtook the Richardson family as a direct result of the gold rush. The captain was not immune to the desire to get rich very quickly. He mortgaged his property unwisely and eventually lost it. His heirs had a few remnants left but a somewhat unscrupulous lawyer named Throckmorton swindled them out of even that. It is a bitter irony that such a man as Throckmorton should be immortalized by a street with his name in Mill Valley.

Captain Henry Harrrison

Another English naval officer settled in Sausalito some years after Richardson, Captain Henry Harrison. He planted a garden in the "English" style, according to Mrs. Charles Mason, a friend of Margaret Boyd's, though it is not quite clear what she meant. Native oak trees and hazelnut bushes were prominent. The garden was crossed by well-kept paths leading up the hillside to enjoy the view. He provided benches covered with ivy at the top of the paths. Harrison also liked box hedges, and some of the ones he planted continued to exist for many years after he died.

Nurseries

It is not surprising that nurseries began business in Marin at about the same time as all these estates were being developed. The first one was owned by William Collie, a Scotsman who had started with a flower shop and nursery in San Francisco. His successor at the Marin county location was Thomas Plant (appropriate name). All trace of these businesses and their plants have disappeared.

By 1939 there weretwenty two nurseries in Marin County, several of them very specialized such as Elizabeth Hardee's Iris Gardens and the Bolsa Dahlia Garden. Harold Growcott had a nursery on the appropiately named Butterfield Road in San Anselmo. There was also a Butterfield Nursery on Butterfield Road in San Rafael. Thomas Kirkwood specialized in orchids. Two of the names, A. Arata and C. Hattori, sound Japanese.

Belvedere

Belvedere remained rural until late in the nineteenth century, but then was discovered by rich San Francisco families looking for a sunnier place to spend the summers. William Ralston, the doomed banker, led the way, spending thirty summers there. One of his granddaughters, Dorothy Page Buckingham, left a brief memoir in 1968 about vacations in Belvedere and some of the other early gardens. Her mother, Ralston's daughter, lived to be almost a hundred years old, dying in November 1964.

Israel Kashow

Belvedere island belonged to John Reed, but Israel Kashow, a burly farmer from Ohio, had squatted on it from 1855, running herds of sheep and cattle. He built a house and garden, and laid out an orchard. In spite of his unorthodox views on land rights, he was a good citizen, serving on the Marin grand jury in 1866. Reed kept trying to get him off his land. It took several lawsuits, but in 1885 Kashow had to go. He still kept waterfront property he had secured at an auction which would later be downtown Belvedere and Tiburon. It remained in his family until 1950.

One lone pitiful looking pear tree survives from Kashow's orchard. It is next to the Belvedere Town Hall. In spite of its dilapidated state, leaves and buds faithfully appear each spring. The City of Belvedere has put a commemorative plaque on the tree.

William Ralston and his family

Ralston planted groves of eucalyptus around Belvedere. Mrs. Buckingham thought he was the first person to plant eucalyptus in California but that tree has a very tangled history in the state. He might well have been the first to plant it in Marin. She said nothing much else about the garden at his house on Beach Road except for recalling the fragrance of vines climbing outside her window.

The Pages were related to the Maillard family in San Rafael, whose garden was described previously. Dorothy Page Buckingham commented on its beauty, particularly the ferns. By the time she was old enough to notice such things, the gardeners were all Italian, no longer Chinese.

In 1946, the Belvedere Mothers' Club held a garden tour to raise money for charity. Three historic premises were to be open to the public for the first time. Mary Huntington's garden had two ancient vines, a wisteria planted in 1895 and a gigantic double cream-colored Cherokee rose. Harry Allen 's garden contained subtropical trees, ferns and shrubs, including a Chinese magnolia. The attraction at Jack Heidelberg's garden was the antique greenhouse, built many years before. Nine other families allowed people to visit their gardens that day, but the gardens were not as old as the ones singled out here.

Rey Estate

The archives of the Belvedere Tiburon Landmarks Society contains another memoir which focused on an early garden, the Rey Estate in Belvedere. The property was extensive, taking up both sides of Golden Gate Avenue at the south end. The house was designed by Willis Polk.

Helen Lavery Rey was an avid gardener. She planted violets beside all the paths. She had a special fondness for begonias, growing many varieties of them. At one point she visited Luther Burbank in Santa Rosa. Although the land at that end of the island was sloping, she had a sufficiently flat piece of ground for her main flower beds. The sloping sections were planted with nasturtiums which scramble up hillsides very well. Roses and japonica grew on the west side of the house. The author of this essay, Nan Reardon, lived in Belvedere from 1907 to 1921. During that time there were no other houses near the Reys. Their orchard with its cherry trees, loquats, apricots, citrus and almonds occupied another large section of the site. A public park now stands on some of this land.

Tiburon

Belvedere had more sunshine than Tiburon and became a summer resort very early. Tiburon was the "poor relation". It was cool and foggy like San Francisco and home to noisy railroad yards.

Small houses for the railroad workers were perched atop the sharp hills. The fashionable families from San Franscisco did not pass very much time there. It was only late in the twentieth century that Tiburon began to be taken over by the wealthy.

Lands of Keil

One landowning family did live there from quite early on, the Keils. Their thirty eight acre holding sloped down to the edge of the water, making it a challenge to create a garden. The grandmother of the present owner, Mrs. Hugo Keil, was very interested in horticulture. She laid out a hillside garden in 1900 with the assistance of John McLaren, using European beeches *(Fagus sylvatica)*, buckeye *(Aesculus californica)*, camphor trees *(Cinnamomum camphore)*, strawberry trees *(Arbutus unedo)*, bottlebrush *(Melaleuca leucadendra)* and various shrubs to give the impression of an English woodland.

According to myth, Mrs. Keil was in charge and gave McLaren instructions but it seems more likely that he imposed his style and taste on her. This garden is still extant. One of his landscaping techniques was to "layer" the trees, with smaller shrubs and trees in the foreground and larger ones in the background, going up the slope.

There are a Japanese garden, an artificial lake constructed as the backdrop to a movie, an orchard and many rich stands of rhododendron and camellia. The Keil property also has two enormous sequoia, tulip trees, jacaranda trees, buckeyes and hawthorn bordering the drive. At a later date, the landscape was revised by Thomas Church.

Sonoma County

'Sonoma County has the last Spanish mission established in California and the one farthest north. Mission San Francisco Solano was built on a site selected on July 4, 1823, at which time Butterfield's paternal grandfather was thirteen years old. The Town of Sonoma was started in 1848 and was incorporated in 1850. Most people nowadays associate Sonoma with wine and agriculture but to Butterfield it was the scene of the Bear Flag incident, an affair without honor in his opinion.

Mariano Vallejo

At the time, General Vallejo was living in his old house. It was on the 14th June, about 6 o'clock in the morning. Butterfield quoted from Vallejo's record: "and a very nice morning. I heard halooing and I didn't know who it could be. There were gates at my place with big locks and they were so high that I could not see what was going on and about the first I felt was a big rifle at my breast and another and another, and another came at me with a knife and so I was forced to surrender . . . . So I surrendered myself and we began to talk. And I saw from the window a piece of cloth, representing a flag, the colors were white and red and in the center was the picture of a bear. This was the bear flag." (Note 64)

Even before Vallejo came to Sonoma, he had an adobe at Petaluma with two stories and a "piazza" and courtyard. After moving to the adobe in Sonoma he lived quite comfortably. At the time of the Bear Flat incident, the Vallejo family had mirrors, tables, chairs, and a piano, to which only families of great refinement were accustomed. Dona Francisca Benicia Carillo, who married General Vallejo, had that grace, ease, and warmth of manner that melted the hearts of men and made all friends feel contented.

General Vallejo sought to improve the house and garden. In 1850-51 he built his "Lachryma Montis," a large Gothic structure costing nearly $60,000. The pavilion had an iron gate, and there were glass and bamboo from China. He had an orangery, lemon groves, olive orchard, and nopal cactus hedges. Vallejo planted pear trees as early as 1838, and grew grapes for wine.

Santa Rosa and Luther Burbank

'Ygnacio Carillo owned Rancho Santa Rosa. The first house was built in 1839 and Santa Rosa was laid out in 1853. The old rancho building about a mile away was built in 1852. In 1875 a frail young man, Luther Burbank, arrived without any money or much knowledge of plants. He had developed the Burbank potato and advertised for buyers. He visited many people and gardens to learn about plants and methods of plant breeding. These first years were hard for Luther Burbank. Every step ahead meant great effort.

His work with ornamental plants began in the early 1880's and continued until his death in 1926. We think of his Shasta daisies, "Alaska" and "Chiffon," and his tritomas, "Tower of Gold" and "Red Towers," all of which are still listed by some nurserymen. Burbank's delphiniums were stepping stones to something better. He worked with the Oriental poppy and various other flowers but those just listed are best known today. '

He is buried beneath the spreading deodar cedar boughs near his old home. Luther Burbank had purchased land at the edge of Santa Rosa in 1878. Since then the city grew up around his home. After Luther Burbank's death his widow gave the gardens to the City of Santa Rose. She is buried in the garden of the adjoining house (1958).

James and Frances McLaughlin

There are many old homes in Sonoma County but we might select one to illustrate the early appeal that brought in settlers. Frank Briggs came across the plains with Kit Carson and was among those who helped hoist the Bear Flat at Sonoma. Frank Briggs no doubt exerted his influence to have his nephew James and wife Frances McLaughlin settle near Santa Rosa in 1867.

At first they built a small house but later they replaced it with a larger one shown in the Figure 40. This was some time in the 1880's. Soon they had a fine garden. Like some other early settlers they had a deer or other animal made from metal and placed at the edge of the lawn with shade trees in the background.

Figure 40 James and Frances McLaughlin's residence in Santa Rosa about 1885. The house was built in the eighteen seventies. (Reproduced by permission of the Regents of the University of California)

Petaluma

Petaluma is a few miles south of Santa Rosa. It is the old native name for this spot, just as "Sonoma" is a native word. They sound superficially Hispanic but are not Spanish. Mariano Vallejo built an adobe there in 1850. W. H. Pepper established his nursery in Petaluma in 1858 (Pepper's Nursery) Two years later William Sexton founded the Petaluma Nurseries. W. A. T. Stratton was a third nurseryman who came later and specialized in eucalyptus trees. In 1877 he advertised camellias, pond lilies, begonias, dahlias, ferns, and roses. We still see trees that must have come from one of these early nurseries (circa 1940).

Cloverdale

Cloverdale was started in 1856. Butterfield wrote 'The Citrus Fair held there each year is a great credit to the community. H. G. Heald helped found Healdsburg on Fitch's grant in 1852. I recall the beautiful second growth coast redwoods on the highway leading along the Navarro River to the ocean, trees that would please even the redwood specialists.' One of the leading nurserymen of the next generation , Leonard Coates from England, trained with Heald in Healdsburg.

Town of Sonoma

One garden which must be mentioned even though Harry Butterfield may not have been aware of it is the landmark Donnell property in the outskirts of Sonoma. This was designed soon after World War II by Thomas Church and has attained almost iconic status. It was the first time anyone created a swimming pool based on Cubist principles, the so-called "kidney" pool. This now classic shape is almost a cliché today.

The rest of the garden was also laid out with great skill and subtlety, leading the eye onward as one follows the curving paths around the natural slopes. Oak trees which were old when Church was working were maintained and highlighted in his plan. One was surrounded by a dark red brick terrace to create an outdoor "room". Church kept the plant materials very simple and rather subdued. This garden was not about horticulture but about space and distance. From the terrace one can see right across the Bay to San Francisco. The Donnell estate is a working ranch and the garden is not open to the public.

Lake County

The principal town in Lake County, Ukiah, had its beginning about 1856. The Fetzer winery in Hopland supports an outstanding modern garden which should be noted in this book. The underlying principle is fidelity to California's natural resources. Edible fruit and vegetables mingle with ornamental plants very effectively. Everything is grown on organic principles. All the fruit may be picked by the public. No one who has visited it and eaten the sweet ripe plums, or heirloom tomatoes imaginatively grown as hedges on vineyard props, is likely to forget the joy and beauty of this place.

One large, deliberately overgrown bed contains all the tubular-blossomed, brightly colored flowers that buttterflies and humming birds enjoy: penstemons, buddleias, hollyhocks and many varieties of verbena ranging from fire engine red to deep rich crimson. This profusion in itself would make the garden memorable, but it is only one among several notable features to be savored.

The day we went there, some former rose trellises supported squash plants. Hugh white, green and yellow globes hung from the trellises like so many lanterns. It takes a special sort of vision to come up with the idea and then make it work.

Clumps of glorious ornamental grasses cover a field with exquisite shadings of green, grey, dull gold and all the colors in between. Roses abound, both climbing and standard. Allees of espaliered fruit trees are part of the formal garden. Olive trees supply shade along the entry paths, together with towering ancient oaks. The herb garden rambles happily over a large space. Mexican fennel, tansy, lemon verbena and many others provide intense aromas in the hot sun.

The estate was once the property of the Haas firm, the largest hop brokers in the world. Fetzer bought it in 1984 and has extended its life. Fetzer is in the process of making memories of its own. Even allowing for the necessity of marketing and brand differentiation in a most competitive business, this garden can count quite legitimately as one to remember in Butterfield's sense.

Mendocino County

Mendocino county was named for Don Ricardo Mendoza, a Spanish nobleman who visited Alta California in the early eighteenth century. According to Butterfield, 'Mendocino City is near the wonderful stands of native rhododendrons which may be in full bloom in June.'

Carl Purdy

From Butterfield's manuscript: 'At this point we should pay homage to Carl Purdy (Figure 41), pioneer and friend of all who met him, whether high or low in position, a man who knew Burbank's failures and successes perhaps best of all, a man who at eighty retained interest in the future. Carl Purdy was always a little ahead of the ordinary gardener's interest in planning his nursery work.

As he sat in my office for more than an hour in 1941, I did not realize that his years were soon to be numbered, yet he chatted about his life's highlights, his contacts with men and women. There was an inner glow about him which showed that he looked for the good in people with whom he dealt and forgot the meanness of those of less ability.'

'Carl Purdy moved to Nevada at the close of the Civil War with his parents when he was four years old, and then later to El Robles, a few miles south of Santa Rosa in 1870. His parents bought a hop ranch there. As a young man he was very anxious to learn. One of his neighbors, Alexander McNab, a Scotsman and good gardener, encouraged him to continue his education. Mr. McNab put Purdy in touch with the Director of Central Park in New York City to supply seeds of wild flower for the park.

For a short time Purdy was a school teacher. He married Vesta Moore, daughter of a West Virginia doctor in 1888. By then he had decided to concentrate on nursery work. A year before John Lewis Childs had ordered 5,000 mixed Calochortus bulbs and increased the order to 25,000 in 1889. A year later he ordered 75,000. This was the beginning of Purdy's specialty in native California bulbs. After Burbank had been to see Purdy's bulb beds he established a joint account with him to grow Burbank's hybrid lilies.

Carl Purdy began retailing in 1893. He issued his first nursery catalog in 1895. Butterfield owned a later copy. During the last forty years of his life, Carl Purdy wrote extensively about California native bulbs and wild flowers. For a time he grew large daf-

Figure 41 Carl Purdy (1861-1942) famous for his introduction of

Western native plants.
(Reproduced by permission of the Regents of the University of California)

fodils for the San Francisco market around 1915. As early as 1904 he had introduced large Darwin tulips and sold the flowers to San Francisco florists.

Before 1915 he also did some landscape gardening, for such clients as A. W. Foster of San Rafael, Mrs. Phoebe Hearst of Pleasanton, (William Randolph Hearst's mother), Mrs. Diamond of Woodside, and the Awahnee Hotel in Yosemite. At the 1915 International Exposition in San Francisco he put in several gardens, including one for a B. Farr of England. This latter activity piqued his interest in irises. Subsequently Henry Correvon of Geneva, Switzerland, visited "The Terraces" and sent Purdy a complete collection of Sempervirens. He also sent him a large number of rock plants which helped Carl to supply the demand that soon developed.

Carl Purdy was an honorary member of the California Horticultural Society and a member of the Royal Horticultural Society of England. At the age of eighty he did more work and had a keener mind that many men half his age. His philosophy was one of continued activity. I recall hearing him say, "When all improvements have been made that you can think of it will be time to sell out and start over again." Carl Purdy did more to put native plants into our gardens than any man of his day. We need more fine men like Carl Purdy of "The Terraces." '

Those who have traveled over the Redwood Highway (Route 101) leading northward from Marin County to Humboldt and Del Norte Counties know how beautiful scenery can be in the North Coast Counties. A very heavy rainfall makes the growth of giant Coast Redwoods possible. They are probably the tallest trees in the world, judging from reliable records. Other native trees also grow to enormous size in this part of California.'

Albert F. Etter and strawberries

We often see the Madrone tree (*Arbutus menziesii*) grown as a medium sized ornamental plant but a specimen growing on the old Etter's ranch at Ettersburg in lower Humboldt County is enormous. This tree is about seventy five feet high, with a crown spread of ninety feet, and a trunk diameter at the smallest diameter a few feet from the ground of nine feet, one and a half inches.

It was here that Albert F. Etter produced Ettersburg 121, one of his lasting strawberry varieties. Federal plant breeders have used some of his strawberry plants in breeding such modern varieties as Redheart, Southland, and Corvallis. Etter worked also with plums, gooseberries, and apples.

Hoak family

'One of the show places in northern Mendocino County was that of the Hoak family. The land was known to the Pomo Indians as the "Place of Many Waters." Pioneer horticulturists such as Mr. Hoak loved flowers and trees better than silver or gold. In the early days he would make a winter trip to different sections of the state, collecting bulbs, plants, and seeds of all sorts. In 1874 he went as far south as Cucamonga to visit Daniel Miliken. He also purchased bulbs from Stephen Nolan of Oakland.

Hoak travelled south by the old inland stage and returned to Mendocino City by steamer. Butterfield pictured that trip with its varied scenery. Just a few years before he had gone to Mendocino City with his wife to see the wild rhododendrons. At that time they made up perhaps fifty percent of the native shrubs and trees.

In his travels as an avid horticulturist and home owner Hoak bought his fruit trees from nurseries in Sacramento and in the San Francisco area. He planted the first eucalyptus tree in Mendocino County, according to his daughter, Charlotte M. Hoak of South Pasadena. He paid $5 for a little nine-inch tree.

Mrs. Hoak had the first double white geranium in the area. It came from San Francisco, possibly the "Aline Sisley" brought in from France before 1875. She paid $1.50 for it. When she arrived as a pioneer bride in 1869 she received the new Hybrid Tea rose, La France, and a camellia as wedding gifts. Seed and bulbs were ordered from England, Germany and France. Lemoine of France was among the European dealers. Charlotte, their daughter, got her first gladiolus bulbs from Lemoine.

No wonder this daughter inherited a love for flowers and native plants. At the age of eighty three in January 1958 she was planning to tell this story in print "*A Child in the Gardens of Yesteryear.* " Imagine the impressions of the "living giants," the coast redwoods that all of us appreciate so much. Her "gardens of beauty without lawns," the "roses in the gardens of yesterday," "pioneer herb gardens," "the enchanted woodlands," and "through the pygmy forest to the old gardens of Mendocino" tell her story in a way that all of us can admire.'

Charlotte M. Hoak influenced the lives of many school children in her work as a teacher, because of her interest in horticulture and the native flora. She also suggested a significant project to the National Council of State Garden Clubs: preserving the story of America's gardens. The resulting book compiled in 1951 by Elvenia Slosson, the president of the council, is very evocative: "*Pioneering American Gardening*". (29)

Redwood Highway

'The Redwood Highway north leads on through the wonderful memorial redwood groves. What better memorial could have been devised. Stop at the Richardson Grove and see what the tree rings on an old redwood stump can tell during so many years of history.

The highway leads past the redwoods into Eureka where a few fine old houses may still be found, showing their particular form of beauty and the plants the gardens contained. The road continues past Arcata and north through more of the largest coast redwoods in the world.

If possible, travel while the rhododendrons are in bloom in

about June., but the glory of the redwood forest is not diminished even in the heavy rains of winter with the rivulets pouring down from a sylvan height along the highway.'

Mendocino Coast Botanical Gardens

In the late 1960s, some citizens of Mendocino planted a small but exquisite botanical garden near the coast. It contains native plants from the area but also many other beautiful varieties of shrub, perennial and annual flowers. As one moves toward the shoreline from the entry, the gardens become increasingly wild. The slightly formal heritage rose garden and Mediterranean garden give way to fern, rhododendron, tanbark oaks, Monterey pines, redwood trees and other wild plants. The gardens offer a haven to an endangered wild flower found only in Mendocino, the Mendocino coast paintbrush. Harry Butterfield most probably did not know of its existence. It certainly was not included in his book.

CHAPTER 17

Old Gardens of Santa Barbara County

Butterfield noted: 'On an October day in 1542, a group of sea-weary sailors under the command of Juan Rodrigues came to anchor briefly in the quiet waters of Santa Barbara. California was then almost forgotten for sixty years until Sebastian Viscaino entered the same waters on December 4, 1602. That date marked the death of Santa Barbara and so he named the place Santa Barbara.

The Santa Barbara Presidio was founded in 1782. Father Serra was deeply distressed at not being permitted to found a mission. Grieving, he walked north to his beloved Carmel. He died there in 1784. There was no mission at Santa Barbara in his lifetime.

Butterfield continued: ' Santa Barbara County offers an enchanting mixture of landscape vignettes, both natural and man-made. The old native sycamore at the northwest corner of Milpas Street and Quienientos in Santa Barbara is a link between the unspoiled past, when Spanish sailors looked for a light in its branches, and the gardens which we call modern. Gardens have come and gone, and the Missions were neglected for a long time and almost forgotten.'

Then the Americans appeared. Some married into Spanish families, others helped change a presidio village of a few hundred souls to a thriving and beautiful city. Kevin Starr has traced the way in which the City of Santa Barbara self-consciously and intentionally became a "Spanish" city. (30) From the time it was founded as a mission and presidio the actual town which grew up was quite non-descript and uninteresting. The Spanish influence seen in the names of the streets, in the gardens, in the buildings is utimately because of the efforts of Thomas Storke, Bernhard Hoffmann and Pearl Chase, three imaginative and civic-minded citizens.

This vision of the city also limited growth. Santa Barbara did not have a lot of space in which to expand, but it has maintained its coherent small town character and avoided becoming like Los Angeles or San Diego.

Lompoc

Butterfield wrote 'As the early Spanish explorers travelled through the peaceful Lompoc Valley they recognized that here was a place where crops and other plants would grow. Near the northern rim, east of the present Lompoc, the padres decided to built a mission. They drew up plans for Mission La Conception Purisima de Maria Santissima and founded it in December, 1787. An earthquake and rains in 1812 destroyed the first buildings but because there was a fine spring three miles to the east, they chose to build anew.'

At the new location the Franciscans built a monastery, small chapel, and workshop. They held religious services in the large church at the west end. Several large fountains in the southern foreground carried the water from the spring on the slope behind the mission. The mission prospered and souls were saved.

From 1815 to 1825 La Purisima was the seat of all California missions, but the Mexican revolt of 1821 and the subsequent secularization spelled a doom that was unmerited. Indian followers needed financial assistance to maintain the mission.

Without such aid the adobe walls finally crumbled. From dust to dust was the story of the man-made buildings. Sagging walls clogged the spring. Gray ground squirrels dug their holes in a copper-bottomed tallow vat. Birds perched in the old pepper tree near the edge of a dry-walled fountain. Cattle roamed on the Julian Rancho to the eastward. American settlers planted lima beans unmindful of the mission history.

By 1894 the sun, time, weather and vandals had completed

Figure 42 Mission La Purisima at Lompoc before restoration
(Reproduced by permission of the Regents of the University of California)

the destruction of this old landmark. Golden fields of mustard did so well near the flowering hillsides that growers began to plant other flowers for seed. Fields of larkspur, sweet peas, nasturtiums, and many other flowers soon dotted the landscape, like patches in a giant quilt or a design on some Persian carpet. Now thousands of acres supply tons of seeds for the rest of the world.

One day in the 1930s a group of men visited the old mission and its gardens. They hoped to restore the pitiful remnants of a once prosperous, vibrant community, where the adobe walls had patterns in the plaster and water flowed from the fountains. The hand hewn beams now gnawed by termites were still there, strewn over the old floors. Sketchy pieces of tile were still visible, scattered around the ruins. There was no hint of the tallow vat and little of the floor plan of the building. (Figure 42)

Restoration of the mission

Butterfield said that the restorers 'visualized a Spanish garden, not exactly the old scattered garden but rather a Spanish style of garden to be filled with Spanish flowers, herbs, and fruit trees as well as some native plants. In order to carry this work forward, the restoration group obtained a five hundred and seven acre tract of land in 1933, partly from gifts and partly by purchase.

The National Park Service aided by the Civilian Conservation Corps undertook restoration. Soon the monastery building re-emerged and at the west end a large church came into being. Old fountains were cleared and patched, ditches cleared or rebuilt.

They found the tallow vat by digging for it. They found the old spring on the hillside and made it flow again into the fountains. It was once again possible to do the laundry as in Spanish days. Craftsmen made copies of Spanish furniture and built benches, chairs, chests and doors in the right places. They too worked with hand hewn beams. Flat tiles were burned to match the old ones. Doorways again opened for visitors. Locksmiths studied ancient design. Decorators tinted the walls to resemble the original plaster.'

During the course of the restoration, a careful archaeological study was carried out. Many artefacts from the beginning of the mission were recovered. This study has been repeated more recently, in the 1980s.

Part of the work in the 1930s led to a better understanding of which plants grew at the mission. Professor George Hendry of the University of California at Berkeley had the inspiration of examining the adobe bricks for the plant matter embedded in their structure. (31) Old seeds, desiccated for almost two centuries, were coaxed into germinating. As the plants were indentified, Professor Hendry searched the old Spanish literature for references to when they were first sent out to the New World. The article he wrote on this topic in 1934 is an enduring classic.

Outside in the garden, the late E. Denys Rowe, who had planted the garden at Santa Barbara Mission years before, applied his skill and art. Scions of Spanish pear varieties were gathered from other mission sites and grafted onto rootstock. Olive trees grow again as in mission days. Mission figs from Santa Clara are again fruiting, perhaps fewer in numbers than before the 1830's. The pomegranate has its place, also the Mission grape vine and red Indian peaches. Patriarch Capolin trees (*Prunus capolin*) at one of the Ortega farms near Arroyo Hondo furnished scions for young Mexican cherry trees which are now fruiting as in pre-American days.

A pleasing blending of ornamental plants was planned and executed. The restorers brought ceanothus, penstemon, wild buckwheat, and other plants from the Mesa wilderness. Giant reeds (*Arundo donax*) sprout canes ready to thatch a roof or build a fence. The umbrella tree (*Melia azederach*) has a crop of berries for making a rosary. Four-o-clocks bloom and scatter their black seeds. *Acacia farneshiana*, as well as the lemon verbena, again supply fragrance. The Castilian rose scents the air. Rue and other mint-scented herbs again carpet the ground. Mocking birds sing in the aged pepper trees or feed on the red berries.

This Spanish garden is in excellent hands. The cross stands high on the mission tower looking down on red tile roofs and a garden dedicated to Spanish memories. Now a State Historical Monument, La Purisima and its garden await enthusiastic visitors. Unlike missions which are now in the heart of modern cities, La Purisima is still reached through open meadows in a completely rural region. There is a loneliness to it, and a feeling of austerity probably more the way it felt at the beginning.

Before leaving the Lompoc Valley, the visitor should see the flower fields, the largest in the world. Local gardens and nurseries also very interesting. A broad-topped *Pittosporum tobira* on the Guy Tibbits Ranch near Lompoc had a crown spread of twenty four feet in 1929 and measured twelve feet in height at that time.

Ranchos and "Californios"

'In 1817 the hills to the southeast of Lompoc served as a cattle range for the Presidio of Santa Barbara. In 1837 Don Jose Antonio Julian de la Guerra y Noriega was granted eleven leagues, in all 48,000 acres, of this range land. Don Jose built a low rambling house, with verandas, to the north of the present San Julian Highway.

T. B. Dibble bought the property later and employed T. Wilson to be the manager. An old garden is hemmed in by a picket fence in the foreground. Oaks and pines border the house. Near the west wing a Japanese privet (*Ligustrum lucidum*) is still growing, reaching to the gable. It may date back to the 1870's.'

Benjamin Foxen

'A side trip through Foxen Canyon, Garey, Los Olivos, Ballard, and Solvang to Santa Inez Mission brings up old memories. Benjamin Foxen, an English sailor, came to California in 1826 and married Eduarda Osuna. He settled in 1827 in the present Foxen Valley. All went well until 1846 when the American soldiers pushed southward on their way to Santa Barbara and Los Angeles.

The Foxen home was surrounded by a fruit orchard and small garden, a pioneer effort in those days. Word came that the Mexicans were lying in ambush at Gaviota Pass near the ocean so with the advice of Foxen, the Americans veered to the east through the Santa Inez Valley, then on over the summit leaving the Mexicans waiting. When they found out about this diversion they were so angry they cut down Foxen's fruit trees.'

Ballard

Ballard lies a few miles northwest of Santa Inez Mission. The Alamo Pintado (Painted Cottonwood) flows through this land. This stream is named after the Black Cottonwood, *Populus trichocarpa*, whose leaves supply rich yellow hues in the autumn.

A large Eastern Black Walnut (*Juglans nigra*) planted from seed by Mrs. Rebecca West in 1886 is still growing at Mr. and Mrs. Carroll Nelson's estate in Ballard. The tree has a spread of about seventy seven feet. (1940s)

Santa Inez Valley

The Juan y Lolita Sycamore (*Platanus occidentalis*), perhaps the largest sycamore tree known , is in the Santa Inez Valley. The smooth spotted trunk, often reclining, makes this tree outstanding in California. The wonderful specimen referred to is a hundred and sixteen feet high, and the spread is a hundred and fifty eight feet.

"Conservation Oak", a Coast Liveoak fifty two feet tall, (*Quercus agrifolia*), has a spread of a hundred and seven feet (1940). It was dedicated in 1933 to the Los Prietos Conservation Corps.

The central point of interest in the Santa Inez Valley is Mission Santa Inez, founded in 1804, the nineteenth of twenty one missions in California. It is near Solvang, about forty three miles northwest of Santa Barbara by Highway 150. The mission building has had its tribulations. In 1911 the bell tower fell down but has since been restored. The modern garden is lovingly tended by local gardeners.

Capuchin Franciscans "restored" the grounds in the 1920s, actually creating a whole new garden where none ever existed before. Brilliantly colored beds of cannas, roses, hollyhocks and other flowers grow near tall palms, olive trees, eucalyptus and pepper trees.

Refugio

Rancho de los Ortegas included Refugio in early days. (Refugio is now a state beach.) One day in 1822 a young Spanish Californian rode into the Ortega Rancho headquarters and was welcomed in true Spanish fashion. There were no highway, no railroad, and no horses and buggies in those days. Mariano Vallejo noticed the garden at El Refugio, perhaps less than four acres, with Mission grape vines and a dozen or so fine orange trees. (Note 65)

More ranchos

There are several fine old ranchos along Highway 101 east of El Refugio. Dos Pueblo Rancho at Naples consists of 4,500 acres

302 ~ JUDITH M. TAYLOR MD AND HARRY M. BUTTERFIELD

on both sides of the highway for miles, with a long ocean frontage. (1940s) These directions are out of date: there is no Naples on a modern map, no route 150. The first Spanish explorers found two Indian *rancherias* or villages at the site, hence the name. The old Don ranch house is on the west side. There are a number of buildings, a delightful garden, broad vistas, and a collection of evergreens.

Colonel Hollister

Colonel W. E. Hollister settled west of Santa Barbara before 1870. Historians associate him with early San Benito County. A date palm which he planted in about 1872 bore fruit in 1889. Colonel Hollister planted a coffee tree and other tropical plants, such as three kinds of bananas, including *Musa enseta* and *M. cavendishi*, also the tuna or prickly pear. So enthusiastic was he about the future of his district that he got other friends to settle near his ranch, including Ellwood Cooper and Joseph Sexton.

The 4500 acre Rancho Goleta was granted to Daniel Hill in 1846. The land west of Goleta was excellent for farming. Ellwood Cooper visited California in 1868 and while at General Naglee's estate in San Jose admired the eucalyptus trees. This must have influenced him in planting many eucalyptus on his property when he settled in Santa Barbara County. He made arrangements with Colonel Hollister to select a farm site for himself and his wife, Sarah.

Ellwood Cooper

A youthful forty one year old man, Cooper settled in California in 1870 and at once proceeded to plant eucalyptus trees around his farm. His wife, the former Sarah Moore, was an amateur botanist and horticulturist of some standing, with a particular interest in ferns. She was also the gardener of the family while Ellwood Cooper was interested in forestry and fruit growing.'

He grew olives and citrus to make a living. Initially, growing olive trees was an extraordinary step into unknown territory. Together with Frank Kimball in San Diego, he founded the modern commercial olive industry. Cooper took large numbers of cuttings of the rather pitiful surviving olive trees in the Santa Barbara mission orchard, while Kimball did the same thing at the San Diego mission at about the same time, probably in 1870. Each man planted extensive orchards from the cuttings, Cooper in Goleta and Kimball at National City. (Figure 43)

Figure 43 Ellwood Cooper
(Reproduced by permission of the Santa Barbara Historical Society)

They both had a lot of courage and used common sense to guide them. The trees flourished and both men made olive oil for many years after that. Other people admired and emulated them.

The olive tree is very special because of its romantic and historic past, not just as a source of a prosaic food. It is central both to Judaism and Christianity, and the symbol both of peace and strength. Making olive oil could be equated with aspirations to godliness.

For about thiry years, numerous varieties of olive tree were imported and planted all over California, until the supply of olive oil outran the available market. Imported oil from Spain and Italy was far cheaper, and the Californians could not compete.

'In time Cooper became a leader in the California State Board of Horticulture. He still found time to grow eucalyptus trees and he wrote a book on this subject, *Forest Culture and Eucalyptus Trees*, 1876. The permanence of his efforts is reflected in the trees that still remain on the old Cooper property at Ellwood.

Trees to be seen in Ellwood Garden include *Celtis australis* (Australian Hackberry), *Ficus elastica, Pittosporum tobira, Eugenia paniculata* towering to seventy two feet, an English yew (*Taxus baccata*) that is twenty four feet high and has a crown spread of thirty six feet.

Among the eucalyptus trees at Ellwood are *Eucalyptus gomphocephala* (Togart tree), *E. hemiphloa* (Gray Box), *E. occidentalis* (Flat-Topped Yate Tree), *E. rostrata* (Red Gum), *E. rostrata* var. *acuminata* (Yarrow), *E. blakleyi, E. elaephora,* and "Ellwood Queen", a grand old specimen of Lemon-Scented Gum (*E. citridora*) planted in 1887. It stood a hundred and thirty feet in height. There are no branches for the first thirty seven feet. This beautiful tree inspired the poem by Samuel Marshall Illsey in 1919, "In Ellwood Garden."

Sarah Cooper studied native ferns in her locality and asked Asa Gray to help her name some of them. She was a strong advocate of herbaceous perennials and in an address before the California State Board of Horticulture in 1892 mentioned the Iceland poppy, *Leonotis leonurus, Linum flavum,* and many others in particular colors for flower beds. She called attention to the proper placement of these ornamental plants, suggesting that small plants might find safety in a rockery.

Mrs. Cooper had already learned that many succulent plants are a little hard to manage in the garden if one is seeking the best landscape effect. She was familiar with echeverias, cotyledons, sedums, sempervirens, and crassulas. These succulents still reach perfection in the Santa Barbara County area.

The Coopers sold their ranch to C. J. M. Crichton, a Scotsman, when Mr. Cooper was eighty three years of age. In 1921 the Doty Brothers bought the property. More recently it has been owned by Frank Russell and Lawrence Doty. Goleta is now the campus of the university of California at Santa Barbara.

Butterfield thought about the days of Daniel Hill as he traveled through Santa Barbara county. There was the Modoc Indian, Pedro Ygnacio, tending the seedling orange trees at the Old Indian Orchard, seven miles northwest of Santa Barbara. These orange trees were planted about 1860 or earlier. Fred G. Stevens uprooted all the trees except for nine in 1933 but two of these were still in good condition at last report. Joseph Sexton visited the property as far back as 1872 and bought oranges at twenty five cents a gunny sack.

Nurseries

Joseph Sexton

The name of Joseph Sexton brings up pleasant garden memories. Many people think of him in connection with the Santa Barbara Soft Shell walnut which he helped develop. Russell Heath of Carpinteria told a story about this which will be related elsewhere. Sexton made lasting contributions to California horticulture.

Joseph Sexton, when not quite eleven years old, arrived in California with his parents, on January 4, 1853, coming by way of Nicaragua. For a while the family lived in Petaluma in Sonoma County where they ran a nursery. This gave him valuable early experience.

His family later moved to Santa Barbara in 1857. In 1866

Joseph married Lucy Foster of Goleta. He eventually took over the family nursery. Victoria Padilla, in *Southern California Gardens*, commented that the Sexton nursery was a veritable botanical garden in the breadth of its stock. (32)

The public admired the handsome plantings of *Strelitzia*, the avenue of Lombardy poplars, a cork oak and a dragon tree, as well as the thousands of fruit trees, shubs and exotica on display. It was probably a destination for an afternoon walk, even if one had no intention of buying anything, especially in a quiet seaside town with very few diversions.

Sexton issued a sixty two page catalogue in 1877, with illustrations. He imported so many plants from the Orient, Australia and Southern Europe, that he maintained his own depot at the docks.

Two hundred varieties of pinks and carnations and two hundred varieties of rose were only part of the treasures one could obtain from Sexton. Because the town was still so young there were no driven amateur horticulturists to try out new varieties and make the public aware of what could be done. Sexton filled that role in addition to running his business.

With the aid of Sarah Cooper, he got seeds of fruit trees and walnuts from San Francisco. The seedling walnuts he started in 1867 developed into the Santa Barbara Soft Shell type from which later developed the leading varieties planted in southern California.

Sexton's "Santa Barbara Nursery" was at the corner of Montecito and Castillo Street. In 1877 his brother L. C. Sexton remained at the nursery while Joseph Sexton worked at his home near Goleta most of the time. Later a sales yard was established at 708 State Street. Remnants of his old nursery still remain but let's visit the Sexton property east of Goleta on the north side of the old highway and there view the garden.

One of the notable trees to be seen in the old Sexton garden is *Albizzia julibrissin,* the tree known as mimosa in many southern states, and referred to locally in Santa Barbara as the Sexton Silk Tree. It has measured a spread of over eighty one feet and the branches are stepped up to thirty five feet. All this growth was made after about 1895. The silky pink flowers are beautiful in the springtime.

An evergreen tree from New Zealand rarely seen in California is *Alectryon excelsum*, the Totoki or New Zealand ash. One of the trees planted by Joseph Sexton develops jet black seeds in a red setting. A fine specimen of *Araucaria excelsa* may be seen from the highway, about a hundred feet tall. Hummingbirds like to nest in its lower branches.

The specimen of *Escallonia montevidensis* on the Sexton property several years ago had a crown spread of thirty eight feet, and a height of about twenty three feet. It is probably one of the best specimens in California. (1940s)

A list of other ornamental plants to be seen at the old Sexton property includes *Abies nordmanniana* (Nordmann fir), *Castanea sativa* (Spanish Chestnut), *Datura arbores* or Angel's Trumpet, *Hymenosporum flavum, Iagunaria patesoni, Jubaea chilensis* (Syrup Palm or Coquita), *Magnolia grandiflora, Melaleuca leucadendron* (Cajeput Tree) with spongy bark, and a fine specimen of Monterey Pine which is nearly at its life span.

Pittosporum phillyraeoides with its weeping branches and slender leaves should be planted more, since it is able to squeeze in a narrow place. *Podocarpus latifolius* is a rare species about twenty five feet in height at the Sexton property. *Psidium cattleianum* or Strawberry Guava is well named for its flavor. *Rhapis excelsa* near a small greenhouse is a reed-like fan palm sometimes known as Bamboo palm.

There is also a hybrid tree, the Sexton Flame Tree (*Brachychiton populneum* x *B. acerifolia*). This specimen was planted in about 1898. Near the east side of the old Sexton home is a tall specimen of *Strelitzia nicolae*, thirty two feet high many years ago, and noted for its cockatoo flowers while the leaves resemble those of a banana plant.

Joseph Sexton died in 1917, leaving a remarkable horticultural legacy. Even quite late in his life, he was always seeking better varieties of established fruit. He went to Hawaii several times and returned with improved avocados. Quite possibly William Hertrich at the Huntington orchards bought avocados from his nursery after Mr. Huntington's avocado epiphany at a club luncheon in Los Angeles. (v.i)

Sexton's old garden was sold in the 1940s, but his children and their descendants must have considered the garden priceless. This is the inheritance which Joseph and Lucy Sexton left for the present generation. When Dr Fenzi (Franceschi) came to Santa Barbara, his initial inventory consisted almost entirely of Sexton's introductions.

Senator W. W. Stow

In 1873, Senator W. W. Stow bought thirty five acres of orchard land. He purchased walnut trees from Russel Heath of Carpinteria and lemon buds from an old lemon tree in Alameda, doubtless the same strain sold by Colonel Warren of Sacramento in 1853. Senator Stow was the first to grow commercial lemons in his district.

Today La Patera, the Duck Pond, northwest of Goleta, consists of a thousand acres, two hundred of them in lemons. Edgar Stow, the son and his wife were in charge of the property more recently. Here is a garden to match that of the Coopers' and Sextons'. The Stow Soft Shell Walnuts probably served as foundation stock for the Santa Barbara Soft Shell walnuts developed by Joseph Sexton. Butterfield catalogued the ornamental plants in the 1940s.

A Spanish fir (*Abies pinsapo*) was about thirty feet high. The specimen of *Castanospermum australe* (Moreton Bay Chestnut) was forty feet high in 1940, and is famous for its flowers of orange to yellow with some red. *Cryptomeria japonica,* a forest tree from Japan, stood sixty three feet high. There was also a fine old specimen of *Eugenia australis (E. myrtifolia).* The Evergreen dogwood (*Cornus capitata*) is found in this garden. *Metrosideros tomentosa,* the New Zealand Christmas tree, produces dark red flowers in terminal racemes. A *Sequoia sempervirens* (Coast redwood) towered to ninety three feet.

The old Ringleaf or Corkscrew willow (*Salix babylonica* var. *crispa*) is a reminder of some eastern gardens. Where but in California could such plant associations exist—Spain, Australia, New

Zealand, Japan, India, China, and California all represented in one garden.

Driving north on the old San Marcus Road to see the "Laurel of San Marcus" in front of Marble Ranch, east side of the highway. It is over ninety feet high and has a branch spread of about a hundred feet. This is a fine natural specimen, growing wild.

Leucadendron grove

Returning to Highway 101 and continuing east one reaches a turnoff to Hope Ranch Park, a ranch with 2000 acres. This represents another of the old Santa Barbara Mission holdings, later of Las Positas y La Galera Rancho. Butterfield thought that there were more than a hundred and fifty houses in this area at the time he visited. *Eucalyptus polyanthemos*, which furnishes circular leaves valued by florists, lines some of the roadways, but of even greater interest is a grand colony of Silver Trees (*Leucadendron argentum*), perhaps the best in all California.

This has been listed as Santa Barbara's most spectacular tree. The silvered leaves and interesting cones rightly give it high standing, however it is not a happy tree in cooler regions. This native from Table Mountain in South Africa was first grown in San Francisco but was unable to survive in that area. H. J. Rhodes of Santa Barbara sent seeds of this tree to the University of California as early as 1883 so Santa Barbara gardeners have been interested in the Silver Tree for perhaps seventy five years.

The present gardeners at the Strybing Arboretum are optimists. They have planted two young *Leucadendron* trees in the eclectic entry garden, close to a sheltering wall. It wil be interesting to see how they do.

Edward Owen Orpet

Butterfield wrote: 'Older gardeners may remember the garden and nursery of Edward Owen Orpet (Figure 44). He died on November 12, 1956. Some years before his death a nursery salesyard was established in front of his old home by McKenzie, from the Santa Barbara Park Department.'

Figure 44 Edward O. Orpet, 1863-1956
(Reproduced by permission of the Regents of the University of California)

Orpet arrived in Santa Barbara in 1920 at the age of fifty seven and for a time was in charge of Santa Barbara parks. He used this position to encourage the planting of street trees. The son of an English gardener, he had been apprencticed very early to the gardener's trade. After leaving England he had worked in Massachusetts and Illinois, where among other things he experimented with hybridizing Cattleya orchids for his employers. In 1888 E. O. Orpet became an American citizen.

He imported many ornamental plants, such as *Thunbergia gibsoni* from Africa, *Puya alpestris* from South America, and various succulents from abroad. His seedling *Echeveria s* are known to the present generation under such names as Orpet's Chocolate.

Edward Orpet believed he had originated *E.hoffmannii*. He had a part in developing different leaf forms of *Kalanchos beharensis*. *Strophanthus speciosus* with its star-like flowers, *Oxera pulchella*, a vine from New Zealand that has beautiful tubular white flowers in winter and some of the shrubby species of *Eucalyptus*, such as *Eucalyptus macrocarpa* were all to be found at his nursery.

Orpet contributed several articles to L. H. Bailey's *Cyclopedia of American Horticulture* in 1914. He spent three years with the U.S. Department of Agriculture at Chico. Few men have had such an opportunity to contribute to California horticulture. The second Mrs. Orpet looked after him very devotedly in his last years. She is an expert in ice plants and other succulents and bulbs.

Orpet died in 1956 at the age of ninety three. He was clear and active until the very end.

Mission Santa Barbara

Mission Santa Barbara was founded in 1786. The first mission building was started the following year. The Franciscans attracted nearly two hundred natives who worked very hard. Construction of a larger church began in 1789 and by that time four hundred and twenty five native neophytes were reported to be there. Still a third church building was begun in 1793 and the foundation of the present mission building was laid in 1815.

Santa Barbara Mission was secularized in 1834 and its lands confiscated by the governor. Unlike the situation at other missions, the governor did allow the Franciscans to conduct services in the mission church throughout that bleak period. The mission property, with the exception of the church and cloister, was leased on June 10, 1846 by Dr. Nicholas Den and Daniel Hill for $1,200.

American soldiers took charge in that same year. The American flag was raised over Captain A. B. Thompson's residence, later the site of the St. Charles Hotel, on December 27, 1846. Gradually civil authorities took over until in 1850 the City of Santa Barbara was incorporated. In 1865, Abraham Lincoln restored the mission to the Catholic church.

Santa Barbara changed slowly in becoming a city. Streets were cut through or widened, houses were built and gardens laid out. Sometimes the old Spanish buildings fitted into the new plans and many times they did not. Like Procrustes of old, the new builders lopped off a little here and a little there so today Santa Barbara's old buildings are not all in their original locations.

Many streets have Spanish names suggesting their rich historical background. Indian lore is preserved in Anapamu, Rancheria, Cacique, Dos Pueblos, Islay, Pitos, and Valerio. The Spanish days are recalled by such names as Arellaga, Carrillo, Castillo, De la Guerra, Figuero, Gutierrez, Laguna, Salsipuedas, Sola, and Victoria. History is reflected in Canon Perdido, Quinientos, San Pascual, and Voluntario. The history of the Mission is reflected in Los Olivos, Junipero, Mission Road, and Padre.

The Franciscans of Santa Barbara Mission set a good example in growing ornamental plants long before the Americans came. Nowhere in California is the Spanish and Mexican influence more noticeable than in the City of Santa Barbara. There is also an American touch to the gardens, but utility was originally uppermost in the minds of the Spanish settlers. They planted grape vines and orchard trees.

Mariano Vallejo visited Santa Barbara in 1886. The change from the time he rode down as a young man in 1822 must have been striking. His many relatives and friends met him, including

Don Carlos Carrillo, a first cousin. (Note 66) He visited Mr. T. B. Dibble's home, to get a better view of the city and gardens. Dibble had married Don Pablo de la Guerra's daughter. Ellwood Cooper came with a carriage and took the General for a ride.

Vallejo had an almost biblical tone when he wrote "And as I saw the whole thing and it was so familiar to me that sometimes my tears came out . . . . So I went to Santa Barbara to study old times and I cried." after his visit.

A Tour of Santa Barbara's Gardens

Butterfield provided fairly elaborate directions for seeing all the historic garden sites in old Santa Barbara. They resemble the Monterey "Path of History". The interested reader should refer to Appendix G to find out more about them.

Santa Barbara Botanical Garden

No visitor to Santa Barbara should miss seeing the Santa Barbara Botanical Garden in Mission Canyon. It is nestled in an area where many native workers built the old concrete dam in 1807. The dam is still there on the creek. The natives worked under the guidance of practical mission fathers. We marvel at the dam's survival, since it was built with locally prepared materials.

In 1926 Mrs. William H. Bliss bought enough of the Mission Canyon land to create a park. Dr. Elmer J. Bissell served as director until 1936. More land to the west of the park was added in 1940. A board of trustees, advisory council, and staff workers made plans to insure proper grouping of California native plants. This garden is a treasure trove of native plants.

Ten sections have been laid out. The Arroyo Section south of the Administration Building contains water-loving plants and stream-side plants. The Canyon Section on the west bank of the creek is devoted to plants indigenous to Mission Canyon. The Ceanothus Section just south of the Administration Building has specimens of the genus *Ceanothus* and may be reached by the Ceanothus Trail and Island View Trail. The Chaparral Section lies to the north of the entrance with plants indicative of the chaparral. The Desert Section is opposite the entrance. The Foothill Section to the north of the Garden entrance by Mission Canyon Road contains shrubs and trees native to the California foothills.

The Forest section lies east of Mission Canyon Road and has broad-leaved and cone-bearing trees. The Island Section, just south of the entrance, along Mission Canyon Road, contains plants from the Channel Islands. The Meadow Section north of the Administration Building has small colorful shrubs, perennials, and ground covers. The Woodland Section north of the old Mission Dam and Foothill Section may be reached by the Indian Trail. It has plants from shady canyons and woodlands, such as live oaks, cypress, and sycamores. The new addition west of the creek protects the Garden against future subdivisions to the west.

Picking the most outstanding native plants grown in the Botanical Garden is a matter of personal preference. Butterfield gave special mention to the Santa Cruz Island ironwood (*Lyonothamnus asplenifolius*), since it is the official tree of Santa Barbara County, adopted by the County Board of Supervisors in 1935. At first glance this tree looks like a Coast redwood but the leaves are different and in season there are large trusses of white flowers, showing it is not a conifer.

Abies venusta , a pine tree from which the Indians gathered resin to burn on special occasions at the request of the padres, is also unusual. Its native habitat is restricted to San Luis Obispo and Monterey Counties. Orginally discovered by T. Coulter in 1831, William Lobb introduced it into England in the early 1850s, at the time the gold rush was in full swing.

The liveoaks, the pines, redwoods, *Torreya californica*, several species of cypress trees, the California Incense cedar (*Libocedrus decurrens*), California Black walnut, and California Fan palm (*Washingtonia filifera*) are other natives of great interest.

California flora is rich in beautiful ornamental shrubs, such as the many species of *Ceanothus*. *Ceanothus arboreus, C. cyaneus, C.*

dentatus, C. grisseus, C. impressus from Santa Barbara County, *C. purpureus* from Napa County, *C. roweanus* from Mt. Tranquillon, and *C. verrucosus* are among the most popular. The Giant Coreopsis (*Coreopsis giganteus*) bears large yellow daily-like flowers. *Dendromecon rigida* is the shrubby Bush Poppy. *Eriogonum arborescens* from Santa Cruz Island is a giant among the buckwheats. *Fremontia mexicana, Rhus ovata, Romneya coulteri* (Matilija Poppy), *Ribes speciosus, Simmondsii californica,* and the popular Toyon or Christmas Berry are worth searching for among the native plantings.

Hillside Park

Hillside Park is a short distance to the east below the site of the old Santa Barbara State Teachers College. It would be hard to find another place where so many rare trees and shrubs can be found in a single planting as in this small park. For the benefit of future visitors and students it makes sense to name some of the more outstanding specimens of the approximately five hundred trees and shrubs that are labeled. Here again, the choice is a personal one.

(A fuller list of these plants is found in Appendix D)

Dr Emanuele Fenzi ("Dr Franceschi")

Franceschi Park at Mission Ridge provides a fitting setting for many scenes to follow. Dr. Emanuele O. Fenzi (1843-1926) who is best remembered in California as "Dr. F. Franceschi" (Figure 45) came to California in 1893 and finally settled in Santa Barbara at the site of what is now Franceschi Park.

Dr Fenzi came from a distinguished and wealthy banking family. He had diverged from the family calling to go into horticulture. His older relatives were shocked, but after his grandfather died, he dutifully went back into the family business. When financial ruin came, during an unstable period in Italian affairs, he was not able to rescue the bank and had to flee the country.

Figure 45 Dr.Emanuele Fenzi ("F. Franceschi") of Santa Barbara
(Reproduced by permission of the Regents of the University of California)

He tried to settle in other parts of the United States, but found Santa Barbara like a fish finding water. Here he could be at home. He assumed a new name because he thought people would be put off if they knew about his business failures in Italy.'

He is remembered as the outstanding plant importer of his day, but before we get to his imports it is valuable to recall what he did when he first arrived. Having had a good education, he was systematic and methodical in his ways. Dr Fenzi made the first scientific list of the plants he found already growing in his adopted territory, something no one else had done previously. With that behind him he could go forward and add more plants to the list, filling gaps if possible. Joseph Sexton had assembled the lion's share of the flora Fenzi listed.

Fenzi then imported many plants into California for the first time, such as the Evergreen grape, (*Cissus capensi)s*, *Conzattia arborea*, various species of bamboo and palms, probably *Aberia* or *Dovevalis caffra*, the Natal Palm (*Carissa grandiflora), Pittosporum hawaiiense* (1907), *P. heterophyllum* (1908), *P. tetrasperum* (1897), species of *Schotia*, and many credit him with *Lippia canescens*, although this plant was probably here many years before. Even with his list, he may not have known that some plants had been imported previously in other places. Let us look at some of specimens that have been grown in Franceschi Park, Santa Barbara.

Some Plants in Franceschi Park

Acacia cyclops	*Eugenia jambolana*
Acer oblongum	*Garrya laurifolia*
Alstonia scholaris (Devil Tree)	*Homolanthus populifolius* (Queensland Poplar)
Catha edulis (Khat)	*Inga affinis*
Cissus capensis (by doorway)	*Koelreuteria bipinnata* (Chinese Lantern tree)
Conzattia arborea	*Phyllanthus ferdinandi* (Rivulet Tree)
Cryptomaria miersii	*Pinus longifolia* (Longleaf Pine)
Cryptocarya rubra	*Sterculia platanifolia* (more properly called *Firmiana simplex*)

A specimen of the last named tree, *Firmiana simplex*, the Bottle Tree, had been found growing at Sutter's Hock Farm above Sacramento in 1858. The old sometimes becomes new in California.

Dr. Fenzi was active in Santa Barbara between 1893 and 1913.

At first he worked with an established nurseryman, C. F. Eaton. In 1895 he took over the nursery by himself and re-named it the Southern California Acclimatization Association. The name explains the purpose, to bring this great wealth of plant material to California. The results may be seen in many Santa Barbara gardens. He imported plants from all over the world. His 1897 catalogue listed ninety palms and cycads, twenty four bamboos, a hundred and thirty ornamental fruit trees, over a hundred economic fruit trees as well as numerous ornamental shrubs, trailing plants and bulbs.

Unfortunately, Fenzi was not business minded and never managed to make enough money with the nursery. David Fairchild, the famous plant explorer, visited him in 1898 and was extremely sceptical about the possibility of making a living from specialized horticulture in such a small town, although he did admire his skill and knowledge. Fairchild helped Fenzi by sending him seeds and plants to test in the California climate.

Fenzi concentrated on "woody and half-woody" plants, growing them from seed. He did not import annuals and was not interested in hybrids. Later he turned to California native plants such as the ironwood tree from Santa Cruz island offshore. Relying so heavily on seeds to germinate was risky because all too often there was no result. He succeeded with the ironwood tree because he took cuttings and rooted them safely.

In addition the public did not understand what he was trying to do and failed to buy his stock. He eked out a living with landscape projects and maintenance, but he never managed to narrow the gap between expensive imports and low demand. The partnership with Peter Riedel , in 1907, lasted less than a year, but Riedel continued to work in the Association for more than ten years while Dr Fenzi worked from home.

During his time in Santa Barbara, Fenzi wrote many articles for the California scientific literature as well as articles in the Italian literature which spread the story of his work all over Europe. He was supremely generous with his time and knowledge.

When twenty years had passed he accepted an offer from the Italian government to supervise the introduction of new plants into the then Italian colony of Libya in North Africa. The struggle had become too much for him. At the age of seventy two, he started a new life when most men are retiring. He died in Libya in 1926.

Peter Riedel

Johannus Petrus Bruinwold ("Peter") Riedel, born in 1873, was the son of a Protestant pastor in Holland. Like Fenzi, he was supposed to go into the family business, religion in this case, but also was passionate about plants. His father very reluctantly allowed him to obtain a certificate in horticulture. In 1892, when he was nineteen, Riedel decided to leave Holland and emigrate to the United States.

He met Kate Sessions in San Diego and through her found his way to Santa Barbara where he worked for fifty years. Riedel was indispensable to Santa Barbara horticulture because he carefully maintained the new plants which poured in and made sure they were properly handled over the succeeding years. Many plants had simply withered and disappeared until he started to do this.

Peter Riedel thought that the beauty and tone of a city like Santa Barbara depended more on the collective impact of numerous small private gardens than on large public parks or grand estates, a view which Butterfield also held.

Residential gardens

Here is Butterfield on the subject: He wants the reader to see what he saw, the gradual building up and accretion of impressions culminating in a feeling for the city as a whole. 'Returning from Franceschi Park by way of Grande Avenue, stop at 1630 Grande Avenue to see a fine specimen of the Dragon tree (*Draecaena draco*), from the Canary Islands.

A block further on at 1754 Grande Avenue is a garden specimen of the Crape Myrtle(*Lagerstroemia indica)*. Continue west to

2227 Garden Street where there is a fine specimen of the Coast redwood (*Sequoia sempervirens*). It was ninety five feet tall in 1940.

At 2044 Garden Street there are two outstandingly beautiful and interesting types of palm. The Syrup Palm (*Jubaea chilensis*) is represented by two specimens just inside the hedge, the largest being fifty four feet tall in 1939. In contrast notice two slender King Palms (*Arachontopanax cuninghamiana*) which bear lavender flowers on the trunk below the fronts. The Cocos Palms (*Arecastrum romanzoffianum*) are similar.' This is micro-history at its most "micro". More of these observations are in appendix G.

East and West Alameda Plazas

Santa Barbara is famous for its fine parks. The most famous are known as East Alameda Plaza and West Alameda Plaza, lying on either side of Santa Barbara Street between Garden and Anacarpa. Nearby are the El Mirosol Hotel grounds. 'First take a look at the old Australian Tea Tree (*Leptospermum laevigatum*) at the corner of the hotel grounds. It was planted by E. Denys Rowe in 1907 and years ago had a spread of at least thirty six feet. Next go on to the East Alameda Plaza. For the benefit of the visitor looking at trees in this plaza, the following notes are appended.

The Australian willow (*Agonis flexuosa)* has pendulous branches and white blossoms in early summer. *Agathis robusta* is known as the Australian Dammar-Pine, a tall tree with lance-shaped, deep-green leaves, a rather uncommon conifer. Lawson cypress or Port Orford cedar (*Chamaecyparis lawsoniana*) is a hardy native cypress-like tree that comes in many forms. *Erythea armata* from Mexico is commonly known as the Blue Palm and grows to a height of forty feet. Old leaves hide the trunk, in the same way as the Washington fan palm.

A specimen of *Eucalyptus botryoides* is sixty feet tall. It has rough bark. *E. tereticornis* or Forest Gray Gum, is a hundred and twenty two feet tall. The Rose Apple tree, (*Eugenia jambos or Syzygium jambos)* first listed by Colonel Warren of Sacramento in 1853, has fruit about two inches in diameter. *Libocedrus decurrens* or Incense Cedar is another native tree.

Picea sitchensis or Sitka spruce comes from Alaska and likes dry summers. *Pittosporum buchanani* from New Zealand has solitary dark purple flowers, and leaves about five inches long. Also in this park is a *Pittosporum undulatum* , very large with a crown spread of about fifty two feet and a height of fifty six feet. Few specimens are its equal. *Quercus ilex* is an evergreen oak known as the Holly oak or Holm oak. *Rhus lanceolata* (Karree Broom) is a spreading evergreen with seed clusters like those of the pepper tree. This is perhaps the finest specimen in California.

An Australian Flame Tree (*Brachychiton discolor*, previously called *Sterculia discolor)* is a deciduous species with maple-like leaves and pink bell-shaped flowers. Many have heard of the Montezuma Bald-Cypress in Mexico City . The specimens in East Plaza were planted in 1907 by Arthur Longmire under the direction of Dr. A. B. Doremus using seed sent from Mexico.

Finally, there is Brisbane Box (*Tristanea conferta*), related to the eucalyptus. The leaves are more like those of the madrone.

Over in the adjoining West Plaza are ten trees of interest. *Chamaerops humilis* is a fan palm that supplies a hair substitute for mattresses. *Dracaena draco* (Dragon tree) may be found near the Canary Island Date palm. *Pinus halepensis* (Aleppo Pine) is a valuable street tree. *Pinus radiata* is the fast-growing Monterey Pine of California. *Pittosporum eriocarpum* from the Himalayas is occasionally found in Santa Barbara gardens.

Podocarpus elongatus (African Fern pine) is represented in this park and comes from seed supplied in 1910 by Mrs. Stewart Edward White. She brought it back herself from Africa. It is reported that on travels in Africa the natives knew her as "The lady who says go get that." The largest specimen is about fity feet tall. *Populus nigra* var. *Italica* is the well known Lombardy poplar. A specimen in this park is located opposite 116 East Sola Street. French nurserymen listed this poplar at San Jose in 1858.

Prunus integrifolia (P. lyoni) (Catalina cherry) has entire leaves. The fruit may be eaten but is very laxative. *Quillaja saponaria* is a

Chilean tree used for making a soap or shampoo, hence the name of Soapbark tree. It should be more widely planted, being long lived and reasonably hardy and drought-tolerant. *Toddalaria lanceolata* (White Ironwood) sometimes known as *Vepris lanceolata* comes from South Africa and bears white flowers in terminal panicles.'

Santa Barbara horticulturists

The early horticulturists of Santa Barbara and Montecito should be remembered. Many of them have now become quite obscure but they were important in their day and each made a contribution., R. J. Rhodes, E. Denys Rowe, Charles Reed and John Spence are practically only names now. This is a pity as Rowe, for example, was very important in the restoration of the missions.

Dana B. Clark and Dr D. M. Dimmick

Dana B. Clark lived in Montecito. He planted ten acres of olives in 1871. In 1874 he issued a catalog and advertised bananas, the strawberry guava, date palm, and cherimoya.

Dr. D. M. Dimmick grew *Lapeirousia cruenta (Anomotheca cruenta)* in 1884. Theodosia Shepherd of Ventura secured specimens of tuberous begonias from him when she first began to grow begonias. He produced flowers of *Dorvanthes palmeri* in 1887 and this may have furnished the seed distributed by Henry Chapman Ford.

A. B. Doremus

Dr. A. B. Doremus has been called the "Father of Santa Barbara Parks." He came to California in 1882 at the age of 40 "to die" but lived to introduce plants and to experiment. Not only did he not die prematurely, but he helped with Santa Barbara Parks when he was ninety years old. His death was mourned in

1927. The Stone pines on East Anapamu between Olive and Milpas may be credited to him. Ralph Stevens extended this planting to Garden Street in 1929.

Henry Chapman Ford

Henry Chapman Ford, a noted landscape artist, was interested in plants. In 1880 he had species of *Brachychiton* and *Mackaya bella*. His article in the *California Florist* in 1889 predicted the coming of many fine ornamental plants which we have in gardens today. (Note 67) In 1889 he advertised seeds of *Dorvanthus palmeri* which had been previously offered by William C. Walker and others in earlier days. Ford is important in the series of events which led to the restoration of the missions, through his paintings and sketches.

Frances Oliver

Francis Oliver is said to have introduced *Carpobrotus edule*, the ice plant, which has run wild along California beaches for good or ill. Charles A. Reed owned the "Tropical Nursery" in Santa Barbara. In 1877 he had banana, weeping juniper, and various rare plants. He was very interested in landscape gardening. John Spence, working from 2114 Modoc Road, specialized in palms before 1890. There was a handsome old horse chestnut on his property.

Ralph Kinton Stevens

Ralph Kinton Stevens (Figure 46) was the father of the well known landscape architect, Ralph Stevens. Stevens senior ran the "Palm and Citrus Nursery" in Montecito and issued a nursery catalog in 1894. At one time he advertised six kinds of bananas and grew caper plants.

*Figure 46 Ralph Kinton Stevens of Santa Barbara (This photograph
was obtained from Stevens' granddaughter by Butterfield)
(Reproduced by permisssion of the Regents of the University of
California)*

Dr Lorenzo Gordon Yates

Dr. Lorenzo Gordon Yates of Montecito was a Fellow of the
Royal Horticultural Society in England and of the Royal Herbarium (at the Royal Botanical Gardens), Kew, before 1890. This

gave him an opportunity to become acquainted with many rare plants. After settling in Montecito several years later he proceeded to plant some of these.rarities There is evidence he imported trees directly from England.'

Dr. Yates was born in England on January 12, 1837, and moved to America with his parents in 1851. In 1864 he went to California by sea. After living for a time in Centerville, Alameda County, he settled in Santa Barbara in 1882. He was a dentist by profession, but other interests seemed to be dominant. He belonged to numerous scientific organizations, such as the Linnean Society of London. For a time he belonged to the Royal Horticultural Society of England and Royal Botanical Gardens at Kew. He was also known for his knowledge of shells and geology, as well as Indian lore.

Dr. Yates may be best remembered for his many articles on ferns. His book, *All Known Ferns* was perhaps his greatest contribution but he also wrote *Ferns of Hawaii, Ferns of New Zealand,* and had other manuscripts in preparation at the time of his death, January 31, 1909. He was County Horticultural Commissioner in Santa Barbara County for six years.

Dr. Yates's rambling old garden contained such trees as *Calodendron capensis* (Cape Chestnut), *Cupania anacarioides, Acacia capensis,* carob, and *Kigelia pinnata.*

Montecito

Butterfield loved Montecito: 'Montecito lying adjacent to Santa Barbara on the east is famous for its beautiful houses and gardens. Originally the land in this area formed a part of the Presidio. Wilbur Curtis settled there in 1858. Montecito Hot Springs was known to early vacationers but most of the area was devoted to farms and orchards in those days. Tropical fruit trees were planted in some early gardens. Silas Fox planted an avocado tree in the garden of Mrs. F. Sawyer about 1872. Dana B. Clark's ten acres of olives planted in 1871 have been mentioned.

A short tour of Montecito gardens might start south of Highway 101, at the southwest corner of Cuesta and Montecito Avenue where Mr. and Mrs. Percival Jefferson have lived in recent years. This garden is formal and with beautiful reflections. "Miraflores" has pleased many visitors.'

Montecito's gardens provide the one exception to Butterfield's apparenet indifference to expensive modern gardens designed by landscape architects. All the gardens to be described below were recent by his standards and not in the same category as his other "gardens of memory". It is not clear why he decided to include them in his inventory. One possibility is that their owners respected him and he was invited to visit the gardens and comment on them.

"Solano," Mrs. Frederick Forest Peabody's estate, lies at the east edge of Santa Barbara, at the junction of El Camino Viejo with Alston Road. (Note 68) Beautiful paths lead through a formal garden.

"Arcady" is just to the north of "Solano," at the southwest corner of Eucalyptus Road and Sycamore Canyon Road. (Note 69) It belonged to George Owen Knapp. Tall Blue gums, terraces, and a formal garden are some of its highlights.

"Pepper Hill," Miss Gwenthelyn Jones's house, is at the southwest corner of El Camino Viejo and Sycamore Canyon Road. Terraces, flagstone walks, formal hedges, Italian cypress, and *Eucalyptus amygdalina* are a few of the many points of interest.

"Grayholm," David Gray's estate, comes next. Native oaks and natural rocks make this a truly gray home. Mrs. DeWitt Paschall's property is at the southwest corner of Alston Road and Olive Hill Road. The large Cocos palms there are distinctive.

Driving east on School House Avenue one reaches Ralph Isham's property. It is famous for its Pompeian Court.

Mrs. F. S. Gould of 403 San Leandro Lane had an estate filled with rare plants. They included *Acacia pendula, Aleurites moluccana, Alphitonia excelsa* (Australian Cooper's Wood), *Cupania anacardioides* (Carrot Wood), *Diospyros cargilla* (persimmon*), Eucalyptus punctata, Ficus ovata, Grevillia hilliana, Markhamia* *platycalyx* in the *Bignonia* family, *Melaleuca leucadendra, Pittosporum phillyraeoides, Schotia latifolia, Schotia speciosa,* and *Brachychiton discolor.*

'W. R. Hall lived at "Glenoaks" on the south side of East Valley Road. Its formal rose arches are outstanding. George C. Kendall. had an informal garden at his property "Illahee" on the north side of Buena Vista. It is nestled in the foothills where shady live oaks welcome the visitor. Close to this is "El Habar," Craig Herberton's Spanish style house, bordered with trim formal hedges.'

'Mrs. Oakley Thorne owned "Las Tejas," a fifteen-acre estate on the south side of McIntosh Lane. She loved her garden reflections, shady oaks, statues and many ornamental plants that kept a large crew of gardeners busy. On several occasions I have enjoyed visiting this garden. Mrs. Thorne was always as gracious as the garden was beautiful.'

The next house to the south belongs to C. H. Ludington. There are a pool and native trees to give a beautiful setting.

The Riven Rock Estate with its "El Reposa Pine" belonged to Mrs. George G. Hunter. This Monterey pine had a spread of a hundred and one feet.

The "Riven Rock Tree" is a Blue gum (*Eucalyptus globulus*) opposite the Riven Rock Estate beside the road, growing in a crevice in a sandstone boulder. It is supposed to have been planted there in 1893 by Owen Stafford and his brother.

F. T. Underhill's estate is close to the late Dr Lorenzo Yates' garden. Open lawns, bordered by Giant Bamboo, add a new note to many of the Montecito estates.

At the northeast corner of Palm Avenue, almost in Sycamore Canyon Road, is "Questa Linda", E. Palmer Gavit's property. This estate must once have been an old olive orchard. The olive *allée* or lane seen there today makes one of think of a mission planting.

Driving south from the Sycamore Canyon Road one comes to the W. H. Coles estate. It has a fine specimen of *Acacia pendula*, about halfway up the slope. This is not a common species, although it is not new either. The pendant branches resemble those of *Pittosporum phillyraeoides* somewhat.'

Lotusland

Butterfield may not have known about the following, most unusual, estate since it was not yet mature in his period and was not open to the public. In 1941, an exiled Polish singer, Hanna Puacz, better known as Madame Ganna Walska, bought property in Montecito she named "Lotusland".

Mme. Walska was married six times but always sought more experience in this world and other –worldly matters than could be found in mere marriage. She developed the estate in concert with several well known landscape architects, to reflect her deep sense of the theatrical and the fantastic expressed through plants.

The garden contains the most unorthodox groupings of plants in which seeming excess creates deeply dramatic tableaux. Mme. Walska was passionately interested in this garden all the rest of her life, inspecting it carefully twice a day. She established the Ganna Walska Foundation in 1958. The garden recently became open to the public. It is still not freely accessible but can be seen by appointment.

Carpinteria and Its Gardens

Butterfield tells us the following: 'Carpinteria takes its name from an episode back in 1769 when the first Spanish expedition northward was made to re-discover Monterey Bay. This expedition came upon a group of Indians making a boat in this area, hence the choice of name. The earliest plantings date back to the Mexican period.

An unknown Mexican woman planted a grape vine in about 1842 that ultimately bore about ten tons of grapes each year. Its trunk was said to be almost nine feet in circumference and was on the Jacob Wilson property in 1904.

By 1939 the vine was dead but the stump was on display at the Fish Auto Camp. The very mild climate and fertile soil about Carpinteria probably account for the phenomenal growth of this vine.

Colonel Russell Heath

'Colonel Russell Heath settled in Carpinteria in 1858 and Henry Lewis in 1860. Colonel Heath obtained Spanish walnuts from William Wolfskill in Los Angeles and became widely known as a walnut grower. (Note 70) Years later, in 1873, Senator W. W. Stow of Goleta bought walnuts from the Heath orchard and was surprised to find a few softshell seedlings in the lot. Checking back, he learned that one of the Heath trees also had soft shells.

Colonel Heath sold his walnuts in the San Francisco market and believed that the nuts purchased by Joseph Sexton may have come originally from the orchard at Carpinteria.

Today the old grape vine is gone and the new highway by-passes Carpinteria, but visitors may wish to reserve a little time to visit a large Torrey Pine (*Pinus torreyana*). It is in the garden of Wendholme, easily seen on the north side of the main street in Carpinteria. Thomas W. Ward planted a seedling Torrey Pine, in 1890, supposedly collected on Santa Rosa Island. After thriving for many years, this Ward Torrey Pine is probably the grandest specimen of this species in California.

There are several fine old ornamental plants at the Russell Ranch near Carpinteria. One of the largest Candlenut trees (*Aleurites moluccana*) grows there. A Silk Oak (*Grevillea robusta*) with its fern-like leaves and billowing orange-yellow flowers in late spring and summer, was ninety four feet tall in 1939. There are also very tall specimens of *Pittosporum tobira* and the Brazilian Pepper tree (*Schinus terebinthifolius*).'

Carpinteria's "Giant Eugenia"

'One of the outstanding trees in Carpinteria is an Australian Brush cherry (*Eugenia paniculata*. var. *australis*), known locally as "Carpinteria's Giant Eugenia." It stands on the edge of the Fish Ranch west of Palm Avenue and the High School, south of the old highway through town. It is not far from the famous Torrey Pine already mentioned.

Other beautiful ornamental plants are to be found in Carpinteria. A Sweet Pittosporum tree (*Pittosporum undulatum*) is at the corner of the old highway through town and Maple Street. There is a grove of Silver Trees (*Leucadendron argenteum*) in front of the Carpinteria Women's Club.'

CHAPTER 18

Ventura County

Butterfield established the early history of Ventura County: 'El Camino Real de San Buenaventura led past the ninth mission to be founded in California, Mission San Buenaventura. Father Serra took possession of the ground on March 31, 1782 and erected a rough-hewn cross on the nearby hill to the north. By 1800 this mission had the largest crops of any of the California missions. The present church building was dedicated on September 10, 1809. When Sir George Simpson visited the mission in 1821 he saw the plantain, coconut, indigo plant, and tobacco. It was probably some time before this that the old palm and olive trees were planted. Two of the old mission palms once grew half a block south of Main Street. One blew down in 1876.

Today old *Araucaria excelsa* trees tower well above the mission to the east side on Main Street but the mission plantings do not hold first place in Ventura's gardens of memory. Instead a woman's garden rates that honor.

Theodosia Burr Shepherd

A frail woman of twenty eight arrived in Ventura-by-the-sea with her husband and children in 1873. (Note 71) She ultimately found her true calling in Ventura after a tempestuous life. Her husband, a lawyer by training, became editor of the *Ventura Signal*. Edith, her fourth child, was born there on August 5, 1876.

The next year, 1877, was very dry. Life was even harder than usual. The family had no money except for the pittance from the newspaper. Children needed clothes and some amusements, even if only very meager ones. They also needed books for their education .Feeling rather desperate,their mother inserted a notice in the "exchange column" of *Harper's Young People* offering to exchange pepper tree berries, sea mosses, shells, and pressed California wild flowers in return for fancy work for her children. She went on to add pampas grass plumes, wild flower and garden seeds but lacked money to grow these plants properly.

It is worth a brief digression to understand Mrs Shepherd's experience better. She was born in Keosauqua, Iowa, a raw frontier town, in 1845 to a family named Hall. The first tragedy of her life was the loss of her mother when she was a little girl of seven, leaving her father a widower with two young children. Her grandparents did their very best to help him bring up the children, but they were elderly and fixed in their ways. She was a free spirit and unused to dull routine. Her father, an attorney, very frequently took the bright little girl with him on his legal circuit, to cheer himself up.

Mr Hall had a passion for flowers and gardens. Theodosia learned the correct names of plants while still very young and learned too that they provided a solace all their own.

When Mr Hall remarried, it was a catastrophe. Theodosia never really recovered from this. Her stepmother comes through as a classic example of that species, intolerant, jealous of the child's hold on the father and determined to eradicate all trace of his affection. Theodosia never yielded to the stepmother's demands and as a result, was continually punished.

After the father also died fairly young, Theodosia was pushed out to live with distant relatives as a true "charity" child. Her disobedience was notorious, causing even those who wanted to help her to turn away. It is almost a true life re-enactment of Jane Eyre's arrival at Lowood School. Her need to get away from this humiliating situation drove her into an early marriage with a good but impractical man,Will Shepherd.

It became essential for her to earn some money herself. Will

Shepherd frequently managed to ruin his chances of prosperity through quixotic adherence to unpopular principles. Only many years later would he make some money in real estate, taking advantage of the arrival of the railroad.

Mrs. Shepherd always managed to have some sort of flower garden wherever they lived, and even in fly-blown Ventura, achieved considerable renown for her skill. The response to her exchange activities gradually became overwhelming. She pressed all her children into service, making the floral ornaments, and working extremely hard to grow the seeds.

In 1882 Mrs. Shepherd (Figure 47) sent a package of California curiosities and several varieties of flower seeds to Peter Henderson of New York. He wrote to her in return, "I am certain that California before fifty years will be the great seed and bulb-growing country of the world. You have the exact conditions of climate necessary to grow seeds, and I would advise you to at once begin systematically."

Novelties and choice things cost money so at first she had to be content with exchanging flowers and bulbs with neighbors. After two years of exchanging, her collection outgrew her grounds. She coaxed her husband into buying an adjoining two acres. By 1886 she issued her first catalog and then a wholesale catalog the year following. Between then and 1892 she issued three more. Lack of capital and experience were her chief enemies, but she was never easily discouraged.

In 1892, before the Sixteenth Fruit Growers Convention, Mrs Shepherd predicted "California will, in the very near future, be the seed and bulb-producing country of the world, and be the great nursery of the world as well." She added "Immense nurseries for growing choice and rare palm trees, shrubs and bulbs for export . . . . No state has so great a future; no state can supply so great a demand, as this our California . . . . All the gold, and more than has ever been taken from her bosom will be poured into her lap again, in exchange for the valuable products that grow in her rich soil." Mrs. Shepherd had taken the advice of Peter Henderson. She had foresight.

Figure 47 Mrs. Theodosia Burr Shepherd Picture taken before 1900.
Photocopied from her 1900 catalog.
(Reproduced by permission of the Regents of the University of California)

In 1890 Mrs. Shepherd planted named varieties of *Petunia hybrida grandiflora*, such as Prince and Princess of Wurtenburg, and spent much time crossing flowers. One morning she showed her neighbor, Mrs. Gould, how to do this work and proposed that she specialize in this flower. The next year Mrs. Gould delivered about twenty flowers to Mrs. Shepherd, no two alike, "all perfect in form and color and giants in size."

Pictures of these new flowers were taken and sent east, followed by introductory matter, descriptions and letters of recommendation. After they reached Peter Henderson in New York they were christened "The Giants of California." Such was the humble beginning of this fine strain of petunias.

Harry Butterfield was once asked to accompany a garden club on a tour of San Mateo and Santa Clara Counties. The driver of their chartered bus heard him talking about earlier days. He asked Butterfield if he had ever heard of Mrs. Gould of Ventura. Butterfield replied that he had and mentioned some of her work with petunias. The young man smiled in modest pride and said he was her grandson. He had good reason to be proud. "Theodosia,", a more modern version of one of these petunias, is still grown.

A neighbor, Mrs. M. E. Dudley, described Mrs. Shepherd's effort this way, "It is a living, blooming exhibition of what an enthusiastic, energetic woman can accomplish." (Note 69) At that time Mrs. Shepherd had two acres at her home nursery which faced on Main Street and five acres a mile to the east. She sold callas, cannas, and smilax for seed and decoration wholesale.

A night-blooming cereus (probably *Nyctocereus serpentinum*) was thirty five feet high, and the tree begonias were ten feet tall. There were papyrus cyclamens, bouvardias, and costly novelties. She grew heliotrope along her two hundred foot frontage on Main Street. One can only imagine the enticing fragrance which came from a two hundred foot drift of heliotrope.

Any appraisal of Mrs. Shepherd 's introductions should mention her begonias, cosmos, California poppies, small geraniums, petunias, heliotrope, and rare succulents. Her catalogs dealt in superlatives, such as "grand, giant cosmos, showy geraniums, gigantic petunias, festive poppies, grand new climbing begonia, and magnificent coleus" but she was probably justified. No one else had anything close to her cultivars. In 1900 she listed a double poinsettia but not the variety grown today.

Begonias such as Marjorie Daw were probably among her favorites. Among the tall cane begonias she had Sylvia and Dearest

Mae, also Pink Rubra and Rubra Bamboo. Her single semperflorens were listed as Sea Shell, Couldlet, and Brilliant. In the Rex group she grew Silver Cloud, Amethyst, and others. Dr. Dimmick of Santa Barbara supplied her with Odorata alba, Edmondsi, and Evansiana, forerunners of some tuberous begonias.

Mrs. Shepherd died on September 6, 1906. She will always be remembered for her Ventura gardens. Harry Butterfield's first recollection of a nursery catalog was one of hers. His father received it from her in about 1900. Her influence on others has been immense.'

Residential gardens

T.R. Bard Estate

The T. R. Bard Estate in Port Hueneme in Ventura County is probably not as old as many gardens of memory and yet it contains so many rare plants that should be listed. Thomas Robert Bard was a US senator early in the twentieth century. His house, built in 1913, was designed by Myron Hunt, the architect of the Huntington Library, but Bard laid out the grounds and garden himself. Today this mansion, known as "Berylwood", is an officers' club. The grounds have been well maintained and are still in good condition.

'Sometimes it is hard to say who first imported certain species, such as *Bomaria caldishiana*. Charles Abraham of San Francisco listed it early but may have obtained it from the Bard Estate. It is hoped that a simple listing will interest the plant lover and serve as a record for future comparison. (See Appendix E, p 449) (Note 72)

Olivas Adobe

'The Olivas adobe stands on Rancho San Miguel about one and a half miles south of the highway or three miles from Ventura and from the Santa Clara River bridge. This old rancho has a walled garden, and a courtyard with a fountain. It is close to the Santa Clara river, one of the few rivers which still flows freely. An off-shoot of this is the creek at Rancho Camulos, forty miles away. The Olivas adobe is now under the supervision of the City of San Buenaventura'.

Rancho Camulos

Thirty miles east of Ventura by way of Santa Paula and close to Camulos Railroad Station on the Southern Pacific, (three miles east of Piru), is the Camulos Rancho. Ignacio Del Valle went there in 1861 from his Los Angeles home. This estate has not been open to visitors until very recently, after one of the more recent owners died. The earthquake in 1994 caused considerable damage to the building.

'The large Paradox Hybrid walnut tree growing there is a fine specimen. It is believed to have been planted by members of the Del Valle family in about 1870. In 1940 the tree had a spread of a hundred and twenty nine feet. This old garden also contains an enormous lemon verbena.

Helen Hunt Jackson visited the ranch and used part of it as a background for *Ramona*. (35) Mrs Jackson recorded some notes about her visit. Dona Ysabel, Mrs Del Valle, was not at home. A servant showed her over the house and she responded to the atmosphere, though she was not totally uncritical about the absence of the lady of the house.

Another important landmark event also took place at Camulos. In 1871, the owners prepared the first commercial olive oil for sale in California since the time of the missions. They used the grindstone and weighted beam from the Ventura mission to make the oil just as the old missionaries had done about seventy five years before.

Del Valle family

Unlike many old "Californio" families, the Del Valles managed to stay ahead of the legal challenges to their title and not only kept their property, but increased its value. Ignacio Del Valle rode the various cycles of prosperity skilfully, planting citrus orchards after the wheat and cattle failures led to large losses. Later he grew grapes very successfully. The olive oil factory was an additional sideline.

One of his sons practiced law in Los Angeles. That helped the family a great deal. Another relative later became a state senator, and played a minor role in settling one of the early olive oil controversies in about 1918.

'Not far from Santa Paula on the Anderson Ranch is a fine specimen of the Chilean tree, *Cryptocarya miersii*. This may have come from a promotion run by the *San Francisco Bulletin*, distributing seed in the late 1870's. Although *Cryptocarya* is handsome, it is not widely grown.

Ventura County was a part of Santa Barbara County in the 1860's when George Briggs left Marysville. He lived in the Santa Paula area. There is a Briggs School district in Santa Paula. He returned north to Oakland and finally settled in Davis where he died in 1885.

Women in Ventura played an important role in pioneering the seed business. The names of Mrs. Theodosia B. Shepherd, her neighbor Mrs. Gould, and Mrs. R. Richard Bard will long be remembered.' Mrs Richard Bard was the daughter in law of the senator, Thomas Bard. Her maiden name was Joanna March Boyd, and she was active at a much later date than the other two women.

CHAPTER 19

Los Angeles

B utterfield wrote: 'It was a summer day, August 2, 1769, when Gaspar de Portola and his party reached the vicinity of Los Angeles. A little over ten years later, on September 4, 1781, the Pueblo of Los Angeles was started by Governor Felipe Nieve. El Pueblo de Nuestra Senora de los Angeles de Porciuncula is the full name of the second Spanish city to be established in California outside the presidios. In time a plaza took shape, just to the north of the present Plaza in Los Angeles. A chapel was started in 1784 but the present church, Nuesta Senora la Reina de Los Angeles (Our Lady, Queen of the Angels) was not begun until 1814. The church was dedicated in 1825. The early settlers named the small river that ran through the pueblo the Reina de Los Angeles too.

Pepper trees arrive

Heavy rains in 1861 caused the church's roof to fall in and the historical structure had to be rebuilt almost completely. There was an old pepper tree north of the church in 1850, possibly grown from seed from Mission San Luis Rey's trees.

The Chilean "pepper" tree , *Schinus molle* , was said to have been brought to California by a sailor *en route* from Chile in the late 1830s. The name was chosen because the attractive pannicles of blossom turned into small black fruit very much resembling peppercorns. John Temple , later "Don Juan Temple" planted a row of pepper trees on Main Street in front of his store on January

31, 1861. It was also at this time that shrubs and trees were set out about the church when it was reconstructed.'

"Anglo" families in old Los Angeles

Los Angeles is referred to as a Spanish city. As late as 1850 there were only forty people in Los Angeles not of Spanish descent. These included Harris Newmark and his family, from Germany, and the Wolfskill clan, originally from Ohio. (33) Other significant non-Hispanic residents were the Vignes family, proto-vintners, producing quite good wine from Mission grapes long before Agoston Haraszthy started his work. The rise of horticulture in California and much of its commerce may be traced to the activities of these pioneers.

Hugo Reid, the "Scotch paisano" of Los Angeles, was an interesting and complex man who married a half-native woman, Victoria. (34) Reid had left Scotland and wandered around the world rather restlessly when he arrived in California in the 1820s. Victoria was illiterate and proudly so, refusing to learn to read, and attributing the problems of her children to this unnatural activity.

Many scholars believe that Ramona, the title character in Mrs Jackson's novel "Ramona", reflects much of Dona Victoria's behaviour. (35) She was still alive when Mrs. Jackson visited old Los Angeles and an object of considerable interest. The Reids had owned Rancho Santa Anita but Victoria was very poor at the end of her life.

William Wolfskill

William Wolfskill had been a trapper at one time and had come into California by the southern route, the "Mormon Trail", in the late 1820s, pursuing otter skins. (36)The place attracted him enough to stay. He took Mexican citizenship, adopted the Roman Catholic faith and married Maria Magdalena, the daughter of Don Jose Ignacio Lugo. This entitled him in his new guise as

"Don Guillermo" to own land and property under Spanish-Mexican law.

He bought the Santa Anita Rancho after the death of Hugo Reid. Wolfskill planted the first commercial orange orchard between Alameda Street and the Los Angeles River north of 7th Street where the old Arcade Depot was later erected. The Reid-Wolfskill property passed into the hands of E. J. ("Lucky") Baldwin in 1875. Eventually a residual hundred and fifteen acres of the original 13,500 ranch became the Los Angeles County Arboretum. The county has preserved Reid's adobe and much of the planting.

The story of how Wolfskill started his orange groves is very interesting. He was walking along the wharf one day when a ship from Hawaii discharged a cargo of rotting oranges. Instead of watching them throw the fruit out, he bought all the oranges for a very low price from the captain. He instructed his workers to extract all the seeds and planted them in his orchard. At one fell swoop he started thousands of seedling orange trees.

Wolfskill had about a hundred and forty acres in 1860. His house and grounds were unusually neat and well kept. "Don Guillermo" prospered mightily, and eventually settled many of his twelve siblings in California. The first soft-shell walnuts in California may have developed from nuts taken from his orchard to Carpinteria by Russell Heath.

He also had a son out of wedlock, Timothy, whom he cared for with the rest of his family, without any discrimination. When Wolfskill first settled in Los Angeles, the missions were still active and successful. He always said that he enjoyed the peace and quiet beauty at Mission San Gabriel above all things.

Fruit growing in Los Angeles and the coming of the trans-continental ralroads

The gold rush energized the fruit growers of Los Angeles. By the late 1850s, grapes, pears and oranges were being shipped regularly to San Francisco where they fetched excellent prices. With the completion of the trans-continental railroads, and the capacity to refrigerate perishable fruit, their market extended across the continent to the East coast. California horticulture was on its way.

The legend that William Wolfskill shipped the first carload of oranges east alas is only a legend. He died on October 3, 1866. The railroad was not completed until several years later. It was his son, Joseph, who managed the old orange orchard with one of his sisters after their father died, who dispatched that first cargo.

Butterfield: 'In 1845 when John Bidwell made his visit, the Los Angeles population was estimated at about two hundred and fifty. By 1850 the town had grown to six hundred and ten. Even when the Butterfield Stage was started in 1858, there were so few people in Los Angeles that the stage sometimes dropped off the mail bag several miles away on the main route. Fortunately the City of Los Angeles has retained much of the Spanish influence. It is now said that Los Angeles has more persons of Mexican ancestry than any city in the world outside of Mexico City.

First gardens

Others have told the history of early Los Angeles but without the story of her early gardens and gardeners. Manuel Requena, first alcalde, Jean Louis Vignes, ("Don Louis"), and John Temple, ("Don Juan Temple"), in whose house the vigilante committee assembled on April 7, 1836 and who later planted the garden at El Cerrito Rancho north of Long Beach, were important in shaping the nascent city. They had followed the same path of conversion (if necessary) and marriage to a local woman as Wolfskill and Reid, in order to benefit from the otherwise lax Mexican rule.

Upper Main Street was initially called *Calle de la Virgenes* , and later changed to San Fernando Boulevard. This led to Mission San Fernando. The lower part was referred to as *Calle de Eternidad* because it led to the cemetery in the Plaza.

Spanish and Mexican settlers such as Don Pio Pico, and Don Juan Bandini were very important. Their homes were friendly, offering generous hospitality for all even though their gardens were sparse. Such gardens might only contain a Mission grape vine or be sheltered by a pepper tree. Water was scarce, therefore so were ornamental plants.

Jean Louis Vignes

Jean Louis Vignes had reached Los Angeles in 1829 and settled on what became Aliso Street west of the Los Angeles River. The large sycamore (*Platanus racemosa*) near the gateway leading to his adobe is said to have suggested the name for the street. *Aliso* refers to the alder and not the sycamore in Spanish, nevertheless, Aliso Street and Don Louis "de Aliso" became associated.

Part of Vignes' hundred and four acre property was surrounded by a high adobe wall. Early settlers remembered the immense gate by the old sycamore tree. When the Philadelphia Brew House was built in later years this old sycamore was cut down.

Out at Mission San Gabriel the padres had installed an iron fence from Mexico to surround the mission orchard. After the fence rusted unused over several years, Don Louis purchased it and moved it to his home on Aliso where it was set up around his small garden and orangery.

Don Louis has been credited with the planting of the first orange orchard outside the San Gabriel Mission orchard, the trees being planted about 1834, but it seems probable that William Wolfskill preceded him by a short amount of time. Vignes even introduced quail in his garden. He covered over the top of the enclosure with wire netting to hold them, although this expensive luxury was abandoned in later years as the orange trees grew in numbers.

The Vignes' adobe faced Aliso Street on the south side, about a quarter of a mile west of the Los Angeles River. Jean Louis Sansevain, a nephew, came in 1849 and bought his uncle's vineyard for $42,000. In those days Aliso Street stopped at the Sansevain vineyard but an old grape arbor covered the path that continued eastward to the river. Many early celebrations were held in this old Vignes garden.

To reach it one travelled by the Aliso Road, then over a turn by the little old Aliso mill and along past Dr. Leonce Hoover's property (on present Macy Street) to the river. Pierre Sansevain came to the United States in 1839 but did not join his brother until 1857. Don Louis de Aliso, died on January 17, 1863, at the ripe old age of ninety one. The Sansevain brothers continued their work and became famous for their sparkling California champagne but that is another story. Don Louis was perhaps the first notable gardener in Los Angeles.

Manuel Requena

Manuel Requena, who came from Yucatan, lived on the east side of Los Angeles Street, not far from the Vignes property. Subsequently Requena Street extended through his land. In 1858 he had seventy two bearing orange trees which had been planted in 1853. A large Mission fig was noted. Old peaches, pears, almonds, lemons, citrons, shaddock, and English walnuts completed his fruit garden.' (Note: shaddock is a variety of grapefruit, *Citrus decumana*, named for a Captain Shaddock who flourished in the late seveneenth century.)

Manuel must have been an upright citizen. As alcalde he informed the vigilante committee that they could not take the law into their own hands. A prisoner had to be dealt with solely by the legal authorities. In 1852 he was a county supervisor. He died on June 27, 1876, at the age of seventy four.'

Report of the California State Agriculture Society

'The present City of Los Angeles gives little indication of what the first American gardeners saw. A committee from the California State Agricultural Society gave their impression in 1858 in these words, "At the north the ragged mountain range marks the outline on a cloudless day—at the east the broad valley leading to San Bernardino, and the San Gorgona pass of the Sierras, walled on the left with a range of gray rocky mountains and on the right by the less high but more broken hills—on the south by a vast plain, into which the stream (Los Angeles River) sinks, and which seems as level as the sea is calm; while at the southwest and west the Pacific, at a distance of fifteen miles, rolls on the beach such large breakers as not infrequently to fill the air at twilight as with deep murmurings of distant thunder—while before you (looking east and southeast), within two and a half miles, there is a city of several thousand inhabitants cultivating all the fruits of the temperate zone and many of those from the torrid, together with the floral and arboreal productions of every clime, and three fourths of a million vines, producing an endless variety of the most delicious grapes." That writer must have run out of breath before running out of words when he tried to describe Los Angeles in 1858.'

Thomas J. White

'Dr. Thomas J. White, born in St. Louis, and Speaker of the first California Assembly at San Jose in December, 1849, bought fifty acres north of Dr. Leonce Hoover along the Los Angeles River above the present Macy Street. He was vice-president of the California State Agricultural Society in 1857 and justly so for as early as 1856 he imported forty seven varieties of grapes from France. In 1858 he was growing nine varieties of figs, the white sapote, avocado, mango, tamarind, lemon, lime, and orange. At the State Fair that year he received the first prize for his apricots. The "native" apples on his property were an inheritance from an earlier Spanish garden.'

'Picture Dr White's old garden: "The dwelling is situated about five hundred yards from the street and approached by a drive bordered by noble English walnuts and luxurious pomegranates to within a hundred feet of the house where it branches and encloses an oval containing a large fountain, ornamented with sea shells, coral, evergreens and flowers. On the other side of the fountain, in a triangular form, there is another fountain embowered as the central one. The whole plot between the house and the street, is laid out with serpentine walks and set with ornamental trees and shrubbery representing a view from the elevated porch of the dwelling that is both picturesque and beautiful." (Note 73) The trees included the maple, locust, mulberry, catalpa, filbert, arbor vitae, and Pawlownia. The house was of brick, thirty six by forty feet and had a veranda as did most of the Spanish houses of that day.

Judge Isaac Stockton Keith Ogier

Judge Isaac Stockton Keith Ogier arrived in California in 1849 and moved to Los Angeles two years later. (Note 74) He was assistant district attorney in 1851 and served with the volunteer police in 1853. His approximately six acre property was near the present Macy and Date Street, east of Main Street. The Ogier home was a large two-story adobe, finished outside to represent blue stone in a fashion quite similar to that used by William Workman near Puente. The front yard had a fountain in the center surrounded by a great variety of well-displayed shrubbery.

The visiting committee of the State Agricultural Society liked the Ogier property. They reported in 1858, "The lady of the mansion appears as much at home in her garden as His Honor on the bench of the United States District Court." Judge Ogier received William C. Walker's Golden Gate Nursery catalogs and probably ordered ornamental plants for his garden from them. He died in Holcomb Valley in May, 1861.

Matthew Keller

Matthew Keller, who died in 1881, was known in early Los Angeles as Don Mateo Keller. He had a shop on the corner of Los Angeles and Commercial Street. His vineyard faced Aliso, on the sunny side. Keller raised many interesting ornamental plants before 1860. In 1858 he had 1,000 pepper trees, castor beans, aloes, and indigo. Don Mateo may have helped to establish many gardens in Los Angeles.

His orchards contained two hundred "native" oranges, three hundred and fifty orange trees from Central America, fifty limes, and twenty five citrons in in 1858. Others have told about his interest in property in early Los Angeles County, but he was also a significant gardener. He was also very much interested in the current grape industry, as indicated by his writings. (Note 75)

John Semple of Los Angeles was the first to plant shade trees facing his building, on January 31, 1861. Charley Ducommon also planted trees at that time. Several spreading trees in front of the Bella Union Hotel had been planted previously. Within five years many pepper trees could be seen along streets in Los Angeles. Don Matthew Keller and others may have supplied these trees.

The scarcity of ornamental plants in early Los Angeles gardens was partly due to a scarcity of water for irrigation. Water was not piped for fighting fires until several years later in 1858. People stored drinking water in *ollas* suspended from a cool veranda roof. Unlike ornamental flowers, grape vines could be started with very little water. These were all that most people had in their gardens. Here and there were a few Spanish flowers. No doubt some ornamental plants were brought in from the Golden Gate Nursery in San Francisco, since we know that at least Judge Ogier had received William C. Walker's 1858 catalog.

Harris Newmark described an old Mexican lady who lived at the corner of San Pedro and First Street. Behind her adobe was an attractive vineyard. Neighbors were always welcome in her garden because it served as a quiet and restful retreat. It was there that Harris Newmark proposed to his future wife and was accepted. The wonderful and unlikely story of a German Jewish family finding Los Angeles so early, and prospering there is fascinating. In order to find Jewish brides, both the Newmark brothers had to go to New York.

Leonce Hoover

'Dr. Leonce Hoover's property was on Macy Street between old Aliso Mill and the Los Angeles River, or about a quarter of a mile from the Sansevains. Dr. Hoover had been a surgeon in Napoleon's army, and came to Los Angeles by ox team. His ten-acre home is now occupied by the Cudahy Packing Company at

103 Macy Street. (1950s) Dr. Hoover spent a considerable amount of time in the drug store at the Temple Block on Main Street. His family included a son, Vincent, and two daughters. Dr. Hoover died on October 8, 1862.'

John Frohling

John Fröhling and Charles Kohler are best remembered for their grapes and wine and for their connection with the German colony that founded Anaheim. They had a well-planted garden on their twenty-acre property near 7th and Alameda south of William Wolfskill. An avenue of oranges ran from the gates to the house. Their two hundred foot arbor had a summer house in the center. Trees, clematis, and a willow fence formed part of the old garden.

Important Citizens and their gardens

John Gately Downey, governor of California in 1860, had a country home as well as a house in Los Angeles. In front of the latter were large Monterey pines and Banksia roses. Governor Downey's country house was on the Norwal and Puente Hills Road three miles north of Los Nietos. The city of Downey, established in 1875, was named in his honor.

Judge Robert Widney and his wife came to California in 1868. After living for a while in the Sacramento Valley they moved to Los Angeles. There the Judge helped found the University of Southern California. He was president of a company that planted a hundred and forty acres of eucalyptus trees between Los Angeles and Anaheim. The University of Southern California was established on a three hundred and eight acre site in 1880. Some trees were set out in 1881 and others added later.

The Widneys lived at 310 South Olive Street in Los Angeles. In 1890 all the space in his back yard was set aside to grow chrysanthemums. Jana Shigeta was hired to grow the plants. Between 700 and 1,000 varieties and a total of 4,000 plants were set out. Over 20,000 stakes were used to support the flowers. Some varieties were trained like a parasol (fountain cascade). The best of the collection was exhibited at the fair in Los Angeles on October 29, 1890.

'This is one of the earliest cases where a Japanese person was hired to grow ornamental plants in California. A little later, in 1894, a Japanese nurseryman in Oakland, H. Yoshike, issued a catalog devoted almost entirely to chrysanthemums. (Note 76) The senior Domoto brother is another example of a Japanese nurseryman coming to California. These migrations began quite soon after Japan became accessible to the West.'

'Judge H. C. Hubbel's home at the east end of Aliso Street was known as "Mt. Pleasant." His *Araucaria columnaris (A. cookii)* and *A. cunninghamii* may be classed as rarities. The present Orthopedic Hospital at 2400 South Flower Street is the site of a former house and garden where six species of Araucarias and an old rubber tree once grew.' (1940s)

I. W. Hellman's home was on land owned in part by the Farmers and Merchants Bank with which he was connected. The *Araucaria bidwillii* tree which grew there was infested with one of the araucaria scales. The precise nature of the pest was not discovered until 1897, years after it made its appearance. Mr. Hellman grew many kinds of rare shrubs. He was an important Figure in the wheat exporting business, and also important in his own person. He was not far short of seven feet tall and broad to match.

W. Van Nuys lived at 7th and Spring Streets in 1890. He had a large lawn and rare plants in his garden. As we walk along these streets today it is hard to imagine this area was once a residential district.

Southern California Floral Society

It was also in 1890 that the Southern California Floral Society was formed. Seventy five people were present at the opening meeting. The organization held a flower show in Hazzard's Pavilion on November 11, 1890. The name, "Southern California Floral Soci-

ety" was written over the stage in white and yellow chrysanthemums. Prizes worth $1100 were offered.

Nurserymen, horticulturists and orchardists

American gardeners, nurserymen, and fruit growers came to
change the whole picture of gardens in the old town. Men like Dr.
William B. Osburn, Dr. Thomas White, Judge I. K. Ogier, Ozro
W. Childs, are some of them. There were also men from other
lands, such as the Germans Mathew Keller, Dr. Leonce Hoover,
and Fröhling. Eugene Germain was French.

Victoria Padilla, in her comprehensive *Southern California
Gardens*, traced the increase in nursery activity throughout Cali-
fornia partly to the extraordinary influence of two books by Peter
Henderson. Henderson was the leading horticulturist in the United
States in the 1860s. He was the man who encouraged Mrs. Shep-
herd in her endeavors many years later.

In 1865 he wrote *Gardening For Profit*, followed by *Practical
Floriculture* in 1868. These books came as a revelation. Up until
then, the secrets of a successful nursery were a mystery to most people.
Amateurs could not compete. Now any intelligent person who could
read and who was prepared to work hard, knew what to do.

Victoria Padilla credited several men as being among the very
first to open commercial nurseries in Los Angeles.

Thomas A. Garey

Thomas A. Garey started his business in 1865 on South San
Pedro Street. Garey particularly prized fine tropical and semi-tropical fruit trees, developing a seedling lemon he had found on C. R.
Workman's property for widespread commercial use. This was the
"Eureka"lemon. Other than this one tree, Garey recognezed that
budded fruit trees were more viable commercially than seedling
trees. Possibly his name was given to the boulevard in Pomona
noted by Butterfield.

Dr H. Shaw

Dr Shaw mainly grew citrus on his forty five acre ranch. Mrs Shaw liked to welcome visitors, visitors who presumably became customers later on, with cake and wine. Shaw's stock came from Nicaragua. He had visited that country and brought orange seeds back with him.

Fisher and Richardson

This firm had a large stock of semi-tropical fruit trees at its large and very well-kept nursery.

Joseph Dieterich

Joseph Dieterich opened a nursery primarily devoted to indoor plants. He had extensive greenhouses and was a pioneer in popularizing these flowers. Victoria Padilla considered him, with Louis Stengel and Eugene Germain, to be the three most influential of the early nurserymen because of their vision and imagination.

Butterfield considered the men noted in this next section to be important pioneer nurserymen.

William B. Osburn

Among the first settlers who organized a truly commercial nursery was Dr. William B. Osburn, once superintendent of schools. He came with Stevenson's Regiment in 1847. By 1850 he had a drug store. He was also postmaster in an old adobe building on Los Angeles Street. In October, 1854, he first shipped grapes to the East, long before the railway system was built.

Osburn inserted this announcement in The *Southern Californian* on March 14, 1855: "The subscriber has just received from the garden of J. J. Thomas the celebrated horticulturist of Macedon, New York, 1000 rosebushes including a hundred varieties, among which are summer blooming roses fifty kinds, hybrid perpetuals, hybrid China, hybrid Damasks, climbing roses, Teas, Noisettes and Dailies: also a small but select variety of flowering shrubs all in good order. Still on hand and for sale a few choice fruit trees. Wm. B. Osburn." (Note 77) In time he had 20,000 roses and a hundred and eighteen varieties. This man of many activities has rarely been thought of as an early Los Angeles nurseryman but here is the record. He died on July 31, 1867.

Ozro W. Childs

Ozro W. Childs arrived with his family in Los Angeles in 1850, from Vermont. Childs had worked at various trades, including tinsmithing. He worked as a tinsmith when he first arrived in Los Angeles, but soon branched out into other occupations. Whatever Childs did turned out to be successful and make money.

Childs started his orchard in the heart of present downtown Los Angeles in 1856 and in 1857 began a nursery with W. Huber. In 1858 he reported he had forty four acres in grapes and vegetables. His house stood near Main and 11th Street. Part of his property occupied the present 1151 South Broadway. (Note 78)

He owned land extending from 6th to 12th and Main to Figueroa. Mrs. Childs, no mean horticulturist herself, set her heart on certain street names at the time the property was subdivided, calling one Faith (now Flower), the next Hope, and the third Charity (now Grand). She used the Spanish term, "Calle de los Chapulsas" (Street of the Maids) to name Figueroa. Only Hope retains its original name today. Mrs Childs was deeply interested in fuchsia, a rare plant in Los Angeles at that time.

Childs is also remembered as a man who cared deeply about the city itself, not just as a vehicle for him to make money. He believed in giving a great deal back. Childs built an opera house, helped to organize a farmers and merchants bank and donated land for the future University of Southern California. Mr. Childs had received his South Broadway property as part payment for digging a long irrigation ditch for the city many years before.

The O. W. Childs Nursery issued a catalog and specialized in exotic plants. He claimed to be the pioneer florist in Los Angeles. It is said he had the rarest exotic plants of any garden in Los Angeles. The *Livistonia chinensis* palm on his property was transplanted to Huntington Gardens at San Marino after H. E. Huntington purchased Child's Main Street property. Thomas A. Garey, who introduced the Eureka Lemon, succeeded the previous manager, Mr. White, in the nursery.

John Gralck

John Gralck came to Los Angeles after spending several years in Central America. The ornamental plants grown at his nursery in 1877-78 were rare for his time. (Note 79)These included *Testudinaria elephantipes* (Elephant's foot), a succulent vining plant that is still rare in collections. He had *Cornus capitata (Benthamia fragifera)*, the Himalayan Evergreen dogwood, the lotus persimmon, *Pawlownia impialis, Beoussonetia papyrifera* or Paper Mulberry, and the edible passion fruits. Mr. Gralck was among the first to grow avocados commercially.

C. G. Packard

The Ravenwood Nurseries of Highland Park (C. G. Packard, Proprietor) exhibited *Chrysalidocarpus (Areca) lutescens, Adiantum trapeziforme, A. cuneatum,* Le Grandii, a form of *A. cuneatum* var. *gracillimum, A. moorei (A. amabile), Hypolepsis repens, Asplenium viviperum, Microlepia hirta cristata, Setalobium cicutarium, Dicksonia antartica,* and *Ficus parcelli.* This list illustrates the range of plants that southern California nurserymen had imported and were displaying in 1890. (Note 80)

C. H. Hovey

C. H. Hovey of the Raymond Nurseries near Pasadena won first place for decorative plants, ferns, and carnations. Byron O. Clark of the Park Nursery, Pasadena, won the first prize in chrysanthemums and conifers. The variety, "Lillian Bird", was considered to be the best light pink chrysanthemum in the show. Butterfield notes he grew this chrysanthemum as late as 1917.

E. D. Sturtevant

E. D. Sturtevant, who had come to California from Bordentown, New Jersey, exhibited aquatics, such as *Nymphaea lotus* var. *dentata*, *N. capensis* var. *zanzabarensis*, and *N. devoniensis*. (Note 81) Mr. Sturtevant also showed what could be done in a "lawn vase," using *Ceroxylon niveum*, *C. andicola* (Wax Palm), *Livistona rotundifolia*, *Strelitzia augusta*, and *Gleichenia fabellata* (an Australian fern).

Sturtevant's nursery was in what is now Hollywood, at the corner of Western Avenue and Los Feliz Boulevard, according to the late Ernest Braunton. After Sturtevant sold his aquatic garden to his assistant, Harry Johnson, he secured the property on Western Avenue at Franklin. Ernest Braunton planned the grounds. It is possible that the beautiful water lilies at Harry Johnson's Paramount Avenue house are descendants of the plants grown by Mr. Sturtevant.

Louis J. Stengel

Louis J. Stengel was an early Los Angeles nurseryman who owned the "Exotic Gardens and Nurseries" in 1882. He advertised "all sorts of arbor vitae, cypress, palm, magnolias, grevilleas, Japanese plants, bamboos, gardenias, roses, bulbs, lilies, amaryllis, tuberoses, gladiolus, hothouse and bedding plants—plumes of pampas grass shipped and grown for eastern and European market."

Eugene Germain

Eugene Germain reached Los Angeles in about 1870 and started his business a year later. The firm exported callas, freesias, and other bulbs. The seed house was opened in 1884 and remained in the Baker Block until 1892 when it was moved to South Main Street. In time the Germain Seed and Plant Company added many kinds of succulent plants, listed in the firm's catalog for 1900. Ernest Braunton worked for the firm from 1889 to about 1891.

Ernest Braunton

Ernest Braunton came to California in 1887 and moved to Los Angeles in March, 1888. He was the editor of the garden section of the *Los Angeles Times*. He also served as a member of the County Board of Forestry, the Los Angeles Park Commission, and in various other capacities. Braunton's *Garden Beautiful in California*, published in 1915, was based on his wide experience as a landscape gardener.

He started some of the work for H. E. Huntington at San Marino, such as the water garden, "seven ponds on seven levels, always a delight to H. E. Huntington.", but it was William Hertrich who completed it. These structures are still in existence. (Circa 1950). Braunton reported that a specimen of *Livistonia chinensis* taken from the O. W. Childs' garden in Los Angeles by Mr. Huntington did not survive. (Note 82) Mr. Braunton continued as a popular writer and editor until his death, a man with a great wealth of information on early gardens in southern California.

William Hertrich

William Hertrich, followed Braunton. He served Huntington faithfully for many years, first simply as a landscaper, but eventually as full manager of the entire estate. The Huntington Library printed Hertrich's recollections of almost fifty years of service as a retirement gift. (37) (Figure 48) In this otherwise rather dispassionate book, Hertrich indicates he did not care for Braunton. It is not clear whether it was professional jealousy or for some other reason, but he accused Braunton of dishonesty.

figure 48 William Hertrich
(Reproduced by permission of the Regents of the University of California)

Hertrich had learned landscape gardening in New England, but left for California in 1903 and never returned east. As soon as he succeeded Braunton, he persuaded Huntington to set up a nursery very quickly. There he raised many of the handsome trees which still stand today.

Huntington felt very strongly about the old oak trees on his new estate. No one was allowed even to think of cutting them down. When a surveyor drilled his pin into the bark of such a tree, to use as a rangefinder, Huntington was enraged. The hapless employee felt as if this might be his last day on earth.

It was Hertrich who had the idea for a cactus garden and convinced Henry Huntington that it would be both beautiful and of botanical benefit. Mr Huntington was at first extremely doubtful because he had been badly scratched by cacti when working in the Arizona desert, and disliked the the entire tribe intensely. The offending plants were probably chollas, the "teddy bear cactus". Hertrich persisted, telling him how an arid hillside could be improved with succulents, if nothing else.

Cacti and succulent plants were becoming very fashionable at that epoch. Nathaniel Lord Britton and Joseph Nelson Rose began their groundbreaking work on the classification of cacti in 1904 and published the four volumes of their definitive text from 1919 to 1923.

In the end Huntington adopted the suggestion and Hertrich found many extraordinary specimens of aloe, crassula, euphorbia, mesembryanthemum, and saguaro (*Carnegia gigantea*) on his trips to the Arizona desert and Sonora in Mexico. There was an element of competition in this pursuit, and Huntington may have enjoyed that aspect of it. Arthur Letts, a neighbouring property owner also collected succulents, and they occasionally bid for the same plants.

Hertrich refined the process of growing oranges successfully on the Huntington ranch, and he also made the owner's dream of an extensive and unique collection of palm trees a reality. His conscientousness and reliability, and evident imagination endeared him to Huntington. Between them they created the Japanese garden, the cycad section, the rose garden, the lath house, the aviary, the citrus nursery, a collection of oriental persimmons, the avocado orchard (started by seeds Huntington brought back from the cook at his club) and a few others.

William Hertrich did have a few faults. Beatrix Jones Farrand, a noted landscape architect from Boston, and one of the very first women in the field, moved to San Marino when her husband, Max Farrand, became director of the Huntington manuscript collection. Hertrich could not abide her, and disliked even seeing her in the garden. She was extremely cautious about making any professional observations, but he was obviously terribly threatened by her knowledge and skill. They were about quits, because she referred to him slightingly as "that Prussian". Mrs Farrand was Edith Wharton's niece.

Hertrich's employer rewarded him by continually increasing his responsibilities. Without the significant horticultural groundwork done on the estate during its period as a private dwelling, there would not have been the same impetus to change it to a botanical garden after the Huntingtons' deaths in 1927 and 1928 respectively.

Washington Gardens

Washington Gardens at the southwest corner of Main and Washington in Los Angeles were started on thirty five acres bought by D. W. Waldron in 1874. Butterfield remembered visiting this old park when a freshman in high school. The park's name was changed to Chutes Park.

Charles F. Lummis

Charles F. Lummis' house, known as "El Alisal," was built around a large sycamore tree. The tree had become famous when "Greek George" stopped his camels there. Lummis was an articulate spokesman for many artistic and social causes. In many ways, Lumis was the prototypical hippy. He seldom bathed and wore southwestern clothing rather than the expected suit and tie. In spite of this unconventional behavior, Theodore Roosevelt had enormous respect for him and his knowledge of the west. Lummis was a consultant and advisor to "T.R." for many years.

Today's visitors will probably find a large Moreton Bay fig

(*Ficus macrophylla*) at 20th Street and Compton Avenue, unless it has been removed in the past few years. (Circa 1950) This tree had a diameter of about eighty six inches and was seventy five feet tall in 1938. The crown spread was over a hundred feet, almost, but not quite as large as the fine specimen in Santa Barbara west of the Southern Pacific depot.

Parks in Los Angeles

Los Angeles parks have many interesting ornamental plants, some important historically. The seven hundred and forty eight acre Elysian Park was dedicated in March, 1886. Exposition Park was first leased in 1911 and purchased in 1912. It occupies about a hundred and fourteen acres. Griffith Park was donated to the city on March 5, 1892. It was originally about 3,000 acres, but several hundred more acres have been added.

Hollenbeck Park, a little more than twenty acres, was given to the city on January 16, 1892. The eleven acre Lafayette Park was donated on December 4, 1899. Lincoln Park was purchased on March 11, 1881, and dedicated as a park on August 18, 1883. Pershing Square, as it is now known, extended for four acres from Fifth to Sixth and Hill to Olive Streets. It was dedicated as a park in 1866.

The thirty two acre Westlake Park was received by exchange in 1866. Aside from the Plaza, Pershing Square, and Westlake Park are the two oldest parks in Los Angeles. Unfortunately, Westlake Park has been taken over by gangs, and is not too safe for ordinary people any more. (Circa 1950)

Pleasure resorts, such as the Tivoli Gardens on Wolfskill Road, dating from 1860 may be of historical interest. The adobe in Hancock Park was built about 1810. The Hancocks were important in the excavation and scientfic study of the La Brea tar pits.

Remnants of early rancho gardens are widely scattered over Los Angeles County. In addition to those mentioned elsewhere, the old pepper trees on the Jose M. Ramirez Tract on a portion of

Rancho Santa Gertrudes near Santa Fe Springs may be listed. Lemuel Carpenter once lived on this ranch.

Centinelo Rancho

The Centinelo Rancho House on the Old Rancho Ahuaje de la Centinela where Inglewood is now located has its vine-clad *corredores*. Butterfield's father worked at Inglewood in 1888. Still other rancho gardens have come and gone. Occasionally some pioneer tree remains, such as the Robertson eucalyptus tree out on Robertson Avenue near Pico. One hopes that groups interested in pioneer horticulture will see that worthy old trees or gardens get appropriately marked.'

Great landscape architects

In the 1920s, as film and oil wealth began to accumulate, many large estates were built in Los Angeles. Architects and landscape architects were stimulated by the Spanish history of the region and, given unlimited resources, designed truly remarkable places. These are not Butterfield's gardens of memory, but one cannot omit the names of Elizabeth and Lockwood de Forrest, A.E. Hanson, Paul Thiene, Florence Yoch and so many others from the record.

Descanso Gardens

Descanso Gardens are a more recent source of memories for Angelenos. Abundant camellias almost forming a forest are only one of its beauties. The property was originally a nursery started in the 1930s, but about forty years ago became a public institution. Descanso offers several superlatives: the largest number of iris varieties in the United States, the camellias, a Japanese Tea House, and lilacs and roses on a heroic scale. All this is in a woodland setting very near downtown Los Angeles.

CHAPTER 20

Pasadena

Butterfield once again set the scene: 'On Easter morning in 1770 Gaspar de Portola and his party of sixty six soldiers, priests, musketeers, and Indians saw an oak tree while riding along the rustic Arroyo Seco at South Pasadena. They camped under the tree. For many years "Cathedral Oak" served as an overnight shelter for padres and other travelers on their journey between San Gabriel and San Fernando.

El Molino Viejo

In 1810-12 Claudio Lopez built a grist mill on the old Hill Road west of San Marino, often referred to as El Molino Viejo. It is a private residence now. Colonel A. L. Kewen called his estate "El Molino" because it included the old mill where the Huntington Hotel now stands.

Rancho San Pascual

Rancho San Pascual was granted to Dona Eulalia Perez de Guillen in about 1826. Jose Perez started to build an adobe at the foot of Raymond Hill in 1839 but he died in 1840. General Jose Laria Flores, while provisional governor of California, was wounded and took refuge in this old adobe after the Battle of La Mesa. Much later, Marshall Neal lived at the adobe until the 1950s.

When George Whitefield Hathaway, an employee of the Bixbys, arrived with his sheep in 1854 he rented part of Rancho

San Pascual from Manual Garfias. (Note 82) The rancho was enormous. It once covered the present Pasadena and South Pasadena, over to the Santa Anita Rancho on the east and the Arroyo Seco on the west.

No one knows what Manual Garfias planted around his first house on the ranch. Many years later the Indiana Colony promoters bought 4,000 acres of this old San Pascual Rancho. Contemporary maps showed Indiana Colony where Pasadena now stands. Mt. Wilson is always in the northern background.

The San Gabriel Orange Grove Association sought to develop 4,000 acres of the old San Pascual Rancho after purchasing the property in 1874. This title was occasionally seen on maps as late as 1879 though it officially ceased to exist on April 22, 1875, in favor of Pasadena.

Nurseries

Raymond Nurseries

The Raymond Nurseries, situated near Raymond, had a very good collection of decorative plants, such as ferns, chrysanthemums, and succulents. In addition to a long list of *Sempervivum* species and Aeoniums, this firm also listed Dudleyas and Echeverias, all labelled as *Echeveria* species. (Note 83) Some of the species offered in 1890 were *Dudleya farinacea, Echeveria agavoides, E. pumila, E. scapophylla* (one of the hybrids), and *E. atropurpurea.*

Monrovia

'Monrovia was founded in 1886 by William N. Munrow. The old Pioneer Nursery in that city planted many ornamentals in early gardens (see "Sierra Madre Wisteria" below). This nursery has been owned by a succession of people and is still well known over all California.'

Park Nursery

'Byron O. Clark was manager of the Park Nursery Company in Pasadena. He was important in horticultural circles, through his writings and lectures. One of his contributions was to introduce Hawaiian pineapples as a commercial crop. In addition to his prize chrysanthemums, he grew various conifers, such as the golden form of the Monterey cypress. He was also responsible for germinating the seeds of the deodar cedars in the "mile of Christmas trees" in Altadena.'

' Captain Woodbury had returned from India with seeds of the deodar cedar, probably in 1882. Deodar cedar had been grown in California since the 1850's. T. L. Hoag, Woodbury's foreman, planted some of the deodars along the driveway leading to the Woodbury home, entering from Sacramento Street. Recently the driveway has been connected with the Foothill Boulevard to the north. (1950s)'

'After Mariposa was extended north to the Woodbury property, more deodar cedars were planted so that now that the avenue is about a mile long. Claims that these trees were the first deodars to be planted in California should be ignored.'

Thomas Chisholm

'Chisholm opened his nursery in 1876, one of the very first in the town. He specialized in dwarf Japanese trees, a rather exotic choice in those days.'

J. C. Wallace

'Wallace had been Benito Wilson's foreman before going into business for himself. It was Wallace who made the loquat popular as a decorative tree. He also had an enormous rose bush on his property.'

Residential gardens

Jeanne Carr

From Butterfield in the 1950s: 'As one approaches Carmelita Park from the west across the Arroyo Seco bridge in Pasadena, a beautiful old garden appears, belonging to Mrs. Ezra Carr (Jeanne). It has a specimen of Guadalupe cypress and other trees. There were seventy five species of *Eucalyptus* from the University of California, including Blue Gum and *Eucalyptus rostrata* planted in 1873. They flowered in 1879. In 1880 Mrs. Carr planted pines, sequoias, larches, and tulip trees from seed.

By 1892 she had hakeas, *Metrosideros, Nandina, Daphne,* laurestinus, lilacs, and various deciduous flowering shrubs in her garden. She also claimed that the collections of sedums and sempervivums, which she secured from Professor Asa Gray, were widely distributed in California by 1890. The name *Sempervivum* in those days was used to include species now referred to as eoniums, as *Aeonium canariensis* and *A. tabulaeforme*. Mrs. Carr was also one of the earliest gardeners in southern California to be interested in succulents.'

Professor Ezra Carr had served as a professor of agriculture at the University of California shortly after the Berkeley campus opened for students in September 1873 but various factions made his position unsatisfactory. He resigned and moved with his wife to Pasadena. The story of Mrs. Jeanne Carr of "Carmelita" shows a pioneer spirit in gardening. (In her monograph on the history of the university, Anne Foley Scheuring details Carr's unsuitability for the position. It was not a purely political ouster.) (16)

Benjamin Davis Wilson

Long before there was a Pasadena, Benjamin Davis Wilson ("Don Benito" Wilson) bought a hundred and fifty acres of land to establish his Lake Vineyard. The old fruit garden had been known as La Huerte del Cuate roughly meaning "a garden beyond compare."

Don Benito acquired this garden through his first wife, Ramona Yorba, after it had passed through several other people's hands, according to Governor John Gately Downey. Wilson carefully nurtured the original planting and extended the garden by adding new material.

Much of the time Don Benito lived in Los Angeles at the corner of Macy and Alameda. This house was later sold to the Sisters of Charity. The old Lake Vineyard property had a remnant of the Mission San Gabriel planting of seedling orange trees. It could be reached through 1540 Oak Grove Street, San Marino, to the west of Huntington Gardens. (Note 84) Some of these old orange trees are probably still growing, on Oak Knoll.

Wilson laid out the trail to Mt. Wilson. He was extremely important in the history of Southern California. His work in the State senate in the early 1870s ensured that Los Angeles had railroads. He also had legislation passed which paid for the dredging of Los Angeles Harbor. Without these essential underpinnings, Los Angeles would have taken much longer to become a major commercial center. The townspeople carried Wilson on their shoulders when he came home after these achievements.

In 1858 he had 10,000 young orange trees in his nursery, 16,000 vines in bearing and 22,000 young vines just started. His property extended down to the Alhambra Road after he bought more land. His daughter "Sue", a contraction of her name Maria de Jesus, married James de Barth Shorb. As he grew older Don Benito lived with the Shorbs at Shorb Station.

Colonel A. L. Kewen

Colonel A. L. Kewen bought the old grist mill of the San Gabriel Mission in 1859. This was the reason for the name of his estate, "El Molino". He had four hundred and fifty acres which later became the site of the Hotel Huntington. The Wentworth Hotel had stood on the site before Huntington bought the property in

1912. The Colonel was a veteran of the Mexican War and came to Los Angeles in 1858. He served as California's first Attorney General and was superintendent of Schools at one time. One of his daughters married Dr. Thomas White of Los Angeles.

While oranges were an important crop on the El Molino Estate, the family also had a fine private garden which early settlers knew quite well. Each year Mrs. Kewen sent five hundred calla lilies for the Easter service at the church, according to Mrs. Sarah Smith in her book, *Adobe Days*. Unfortunately the estate did not survive Kewen's death in 1879. It rapidly fell into disrepair.

General Stoneman

General George Stoneman, a retired army officer, lived about two miles southwest of Wilson's Lake Vineyard, just beyond the Kewen property. Early settlers remembered the old Stoneman home, "Los Robles," also the grapes and winery on his property and a few old rare trees. Major General Stoneman was active in politics and became governor in 1883. Wilson and Stoneman were old friends from before the Civil War. Nothing remains of his estate, but the state has placed a landmark plaque at the site.

J. A. Graves, an early settler who wrote about southern California, lived near General Stoneman, and planted Araucarias at his home about 1876.

James de Barth Shorb

James de Barth Shorb lived in a large house on the site of the present Huntington Art Gallery. His estate was called "Mountain Vineyard." The original land grant was the San Marino Ranch, named for a town in Italy. That is why the city so secretly put together in 1913 by Huntington and his cronies was called San Marino.

Shorb had ten acres of acacias in 1875, indicating an interest in beautiful trees. Ernest Braunton once wrote to Butterfield that J. de Barth Shorb "had some rare plants not owned by others, a rare horticulturist.". His principal concern was irrigation, a topic he promoted tirelessly. He laid down three hundred and eighty miles of pipe for his vineyards and citrus groves.

Henry Edwards Huntington

In 1903, Henry Edwards Huntington bought Shorb's former land from the Farmers and Merchants Bank of Los Angeles, initially as an investment. It rapidly became clear that what he really wanted to do was to establish a handsome country estate on this land, even though his wife was rather lukewarm about the idea. She preferred to live in Paris or New York.

Huntington tore down the old Victorian house built by Shorb and created the great palace now housing his art collection thinking it would please his wife. It seems as though she accepted the homage but shrugged anyway. The importance (and difficulty) of pleasing Mrs. Huntington is a persistent thread throughout William Hertrich's memoir. The enormous house was later supplemented by a separate library to hold the collection of rare books.

Several neighbors lived to the east of the Shorb ranch. Luther H. Titus owned the "Dewdrop Vineyard" and was a breeder of fast horses.Titus had been successful in the gold rush in 1849 but went home to Erie, New York instead of staying on in California. He returned to California in 1869, and bought his ranch near San Gabriel. Titus was one of the first to use iron water pipes for irrigation, possibly because of Shorb's influence. After his first wife died, he married Ella Crary, and bought the Horseshoe Ranch on San Pasquel Avenue in East Pasadena as her wedding gift.

Henry Huntington ultimately bought up all the properties in the area, and this led to the incorporation of the City of San Marino in April 1913.

A. B. Chapman

A. B. Chapman, who introduced the Valencia orange, lived to the east of Titus between L. J. Rose and E. J. ("Lucky") Baldwin.

E. J. ("Lucky") Baldwin

Baldwin had made a huge fortune in mining and property, hence his nickname. He used his riches to make the Rancho Santa Anita property outstanding if a little ostentatious. The lagoon was restored and surrounded by *faux* "mountains", little canals and winding drives. Wolfskill had planted eucalyptus trees and there was a fine stand of native oak trees there pre-dating them all. Baldwin added exotic trees from China and Australia such as gingko, tea trees, pepper trees and palms.

Leonard Rose

Leonard J. Rose, born in Germany, was famous for his "Sunnyslope Vineyard". He was primarily interested in grapes and wine making but he also had an ornamental garden. He loved race horses yet found time to plant a eucalyptus tree on his property in about 1864. This tree was seventy five feet high in 1872 when Charles Nordhoff visited Sunnyslope. Titus' son said that the San Gabriel Valley attracted his father because water was relatively accessible.

Leonard Rose had bought a hundred and sixty acres from William Wolfskill in 1860. In time he increased his estate to 2,000 acres and called it "Lamanda Park", named in honor of his wife Amanda, (with his first intial added to it). In 1930 Lamanda Park became East Pasadena. A part of the San Gabriel grape vine which will be mentioned later also belonged to him.

Earlier Angelenos in Pasadena

Hugo Reid, the "Scotch Paisano," was at Santa Anita in 1844 when James McKinlay visited him. Reid planted his orchard in about 1840. The old adobe and the lake nearby now belong to the State of California and form part of the Los Angeles County Arboretum in Arcadia, governed by a board of directors.

William Wolfskill once owned this old rancho but gave it to

his son, Lewis Wolfskill. Lewis sold the property to Harris Newmark and Newmark in turn sold Santa Anita to E. J. Baldwin.

Henry Dalton also had a section of the original rancho. Dalton's daughter married Lewis Wolfskill. The old Blue Gum trees growing near the old adobe, now at the Arboretum, may have been planted by William Wolfskill in the early 1860's. It is possible the young trees came from Australia, or from seed descended from Mrs Gillespie's original imports to San Francisco.

The eucalyptus trees were probably the first ones to have been planted in southern California, even older than the trees planted by L. J. Rose in 1864.

City of Sierra Madre

Nathaniel C. Carter bought 11,000 acres from E. J. Baldwin in 1881 to establish the City of Sierra Madre. Abbot Kinney heard of the colony and settled there. He named his estate "Kinneloa". Mr. Kinney was chairman of the State Board of Forestry in 1886 and wrote a book on eucalyptus in 1895. He was among the leading promoters of the City of Venice.

In 1893 Mrs. W. F. Brugman purchased a small potted wisteria from the Pioneer Nursery in Monrovia and planted this beside her front steps on Scenic Point, now 201 West Carter Street, Sierra Madre. It became enormous, as wisterias can do when well tended. By the time it was ten years old, it became a favorite with tourists.

Sierra Madre's Wisteria Fete became an annual affair in 1920. Another resident, Mrs. Estella Fennel, purchased Scenic Point with the wisteria vine but was troubled by unsolicited visitors from morning to night during the blooming season. She transferred title to a local civic organization.

Mrs. W. J. Lawless, a lover of plants and formerly president of the Woman's Club, purchased the property from her organization and removed the old house. (Note 86) In its place she built a beautiful white pergola. The vine was carefully untangled and twined about the new support. Landscape architects built pleasing walks, a Memory Garden, a Garden of Repose, and a Mediterranean Rose Garden as a setting for the wisteria vine.

Mrs. Brugman never dreamed that people would come from all over the world to visit the wisteria vine she had planted. Fortunately civic pride and the efforts of Mrs. Lawless made the preservation of the vine possible, otherwise it would have gone the same way as most old wisteria vines. More cities should aid in the preservation of such historic plants because they can be a great civic asset.

Coolidge Rare Plant Gardens

The Coolidge Rare Plant Gardens were on Foothill Boulevard north of Colorado Street. D. W. Coolidge died many years ago, but his daughter, Mrs. Mulvehill, took charge and carried on her father's work. He had secured seeds and plants from the Arnold Arboretum, Bureau of Plant Industry, and from foreign countries. Among other things, he grew a seedling from an old Vielchenblau rose and named it IXL. 'Today some nurserymen use this rose as a vigorous understock for making standard or tree roses.' (Butterfield)

CHAPTER 21

San Gabriel Valley

B utterfield wrote: 'The Spanish overland expedition from
San Diego in 1769 passed by land which later became
the site of Mission San Gabriel. The Mission was founded two
years later. Anza's Expedition reached the Mission on March 22,
1774. The Mission attracted most of the early travelers.

Mission San Gabriel

Later on when the pioneers began to arrive, nearly all of them
came by way of the Mission. The Mission had about three and a
half leagues of land on which the Franciscans supported themselves by growing wheat and running cattle.

By 1774, when Mission San Gabriel had its first really abun
dant harvest, Father Serra corresponded with Viceroy Bucareli in
Mexico City. He noted they had reached the point at which some
improvements were appropriate and wanted to start fruit orchards
and vineyards. Bucareli agreed. When did he not agree with the
charismatic and insistent Father Serra?

Father Zalvidea, the superior, sent a pack train to Mexico to
obtain cuttings and seeds for the Mission orchard. The only
remannts of this old mission planting were to be found at 328
West Mission Drive, formerly the home of Colonel L. M. Purcell
(Figure 49). JudgeVolney Howard lived there briefly in 1852. The
original mission orchard was protected by a cactus hedge, Las Tunas, (or cactus) and this became the name of the property. Nothing is left now.

Figure 49 Entrance to Purcell house, San Gabriel, next to remnants of Mission San Gabriel orchard.
(Reproduced by permission of the Regents of the University of California)

Originally Father Zalvidea's garden or orchard contained oranges, citrons, limes, pears, apples, and olives as well as the vineyard, planted in about 1780. (Note 87) There were pomegranates and a cactus hedge. The mother vineyard (*vina madra*) was started at the Mission. The first orange trees in Alta California were brought up from Lower California and planted in about 1804, possibly earlier. Two old orange trees, four olives, two pecans, coconut palms, a lemon verbena, and remnants of a Nopal cactus hedge survived until 1950.

Practically nothing is known about the ornamental plants at San Gabriel Mission, though they probably had some, similar to those reported at Santa Barbara. The first mission site was north of Montebello, not far from Temple's Corners. An old fan palm marks the site of Temple's adobe near where the first mission was started. The present Mission San Gabriel is several miles to the north.

Grapevine Adobe

The "Grapevine Adobe," a block west of the Mission at the corner of Mission Boulevard and Santa Anita, should be mentioned because false claims have been made for the old grape vine there. This vine has nothing to do with the early mission garden, regardless of various claims to that effect. It is a native grape vine and not a Mission grape.

This particular vine came from a canyon near Don Benito Wilson's home. It was transplanted to L. J. Rose's Sunnyslope Vineyard but Mr. Rose did not care for the native grape. It was transplanted again in about 1861 to its present location near the Grapevine Adobe. The late Charles Adams landscaped the adobe's grounds in 1927 and could vouch for the facts. He was a noted expert in Southern California garden history. (Note 88)

Workman-Rowland Party

Another important event in the early history of southern California was the arrival of the Workman-Rowland Party of 1841. William Workman, John Rowland, John Reed, and others reached the region on November 5, 1841.

William Workman went to New Mexico in early life. He married and remained there for about sixteen years. John Reed, one of Workman's sons-in-law, joined the Workman-Rowland Party in New Mexico. Workman, Rowland and Reed all lived very near each other.

No one would have expected these men to have well-landscaped property, considering the diifculties and unsettled conditions they endured for many years, yet William Workman, an Englishman, did make an effort to lay out a garden at his house.

In 1858 the adobe buildings were colored and penciled to represent stone, forming a patio court, seventy five feet by a hundred feet. (Note 89) Tropical fruits grew well in this court. The grounds showed taste and intelligence. The vineyard nearby had 10,000 vines. No doubt the garden design was similar to that around many early Spanish homes in California.

Captain John Rowland had the same amount of land as William Workman, many thousands of acres, but he only cultivated two hundred acres in 1858. He had ornamental trees, osage oranges, and a brick house (it might possibly have been adobe).

Workman had the northern portion of Rancho Puente and Rowland the southern half.

John Reed laid out his grounds much like those of Rowland's. These men pioneered the way for later generations in their territory. It is remarkable that they should have advanced so far in just a few years. Well designed adobes, the finest brick farm house seen in the low country, large vineyards, bees on Captain Rowland's farm, and ornamental shade trees, could be seen on Rancho Puente during the 1850's, together with many thousands of acres of range land.

William Workman and John Rowland are both buried in a little chapel near Puente. The road through the hills to the south toward Whittier leads past an old mill site and was a familiar route for early settlers. The stage coach went via Valley Boulevard through Puente between San Gabriel and San Bernardino.

CHAPTER 22

Glendale and San Fernando Gardens

Modern Glendale occupies the old rancho once owned by Don Jose Maria Verdugo, and granted to him by Governor Pedro Fages in 1784. This is often referred to as the Rancho San Rafael grant and includes the territory between Arroyo Seco and Mission San Fernando. Glendale, Eagle Rock and Verdugo City are now within its former borders.

Don Jose Maria Verdugo

Verdugo left his property to his son, Julio, and a daughter, Catalina. Julio took the southern portion and the daughter, who was blind, took the mountainous part of San Rafael Rancho to the north.

The whole Verdugo property finally came into the possession of Fernando Sepulveda after he married another one of the daughters. Julio Verdugo's property extended north from Los Feliz, and east of San Fernando Boulevard to the Arroyo Seco. Jose Maria Verdugo had the largest grant in all California under the original Spanish rule, more than 36000 acres. General Castro and Governor Micheltorena met on this old rancho.

Casa Adobe de San Rafael

There are two old Spanish gardens in Glendale which deserve special mention. Many stories have been told, about them but some of these are questionable. Verdugo Inn, or Casa Adobe de

San Rafael at 1330 Dorothy Drive between Stocker and Spencer is now a Glendale park.

Maria Sepulveda is reported to have had fifty acres of Rancho San Rafael when she married Don Tomas Sanchez. She moved to Casa Verdugo Inn in 1875. This garden has eucalyptus trees, orange trees, olives, pomegranates, oleander and ailanthus, the sort of planting one might expect to see in old Spanish gardens in southern California.

Teodora Verdugo, one of Catalina Verdugo's nieces, supposedly built her adobe off Canada Boulevard on Capistrano. Governor Pico signed a treaty with Fremont under a large oak close to this house. Maybe an adobe was built there about 1834 but the one there now was built many years later. This could be the house at 2211 Bonita Drive, off Canada Boulevard. It is still in private hands, with a well stocked garden..

One of the former owner's sons told Butterfield that he helped build the present adobe in 1890. An old climbing rose, a wisteria, olive, black locust, orange, and eucalyptus trees are in the garden, as well as oleander, bracken ferns, and a variegated periwinkle vine. The old oak tree not far away could in fact be the tree beneath which Pico signed a treaty.

Mission San Fernando

Mission San Fernando was started in 1797 by Father Lasuen. It also had a garden. Early visitors reported the agave (*Agave americana*), olives, figs, lemons, oranges, and the prickly pear or tuna. Edwin Bryant in 1846 saw a rose bush in the cemetery. With the restoration of the mission, present and future generations have a better opportunity to visualize the early setting for this garden, even though a number of details may have been changed. Other old garden sites in the area may be marked by Blue Gum trees.

For many years Don Andres Pico owned and occupiedthe Mission.There were immense aqueducts and reservoirs for irrigation. Pico used Indians to work the land and dry pears from the old orchard. To prepare for drying the fruit, the Indians would spread corn stalks and weeds on the ground, then lay the pears over this surface to dry.

They also aided in making olive oil. The proprietor pressed eight hundred gallons of olive oil in a single year from the five hundred old olive trees. It is probable that a few fan palms were also grown on the mission lands.'

CHAPTER 23

Long Beach

Three principal families dominate early Long Beach history: the descendants of Abel Stearns, those of John Temple and those of the Bixbys. Butterfield wrote: 'Don Abel Stearns, who came to California in 1829, acquired Rancho Los Alamitos through his marriage to Arcadia Bandini, one of Juan Bandini's daughters. She was also related to Manuel Nieto. Dona Arcadia was only fourteen years old when she married the forty year old Stearns, but already a noted beauty.'

Rancho Los Alamitos

Stearns era

Part of the time Abel Stearns lived in his "El Palacio" at the Barker block near the Plaza in Los Angeles but he built the adobe hacienda on the bluff. The Bixbys lived there east of Long Beach for many years. This adobe built in 1844 still stands, but the old Anaheim Road that used to pass on the north side is now closed to through traffic.

Little was planted there until after Abel Stearns' death on August 23, 1871. Mr. Stearns' business had suffered severely from the drought of 1864, when he lost thousands of animals. He ultimately lost the whole ranch to Michael Reese who foreclosed on the mortgage. Stearns owned land as far as Westminster, founded on part of this old rancho. Los Alamitos is also on this ranch.

Bixby era

Following Reese's foreclosure Los Alamitos Ranch was divided three ways. Flint, Bixby and Company , John Bixby and Hellman all had a third each. John Bixby, cousin of Jotham, came to California from Maine in about 1869. He lived at Wilmington until about 1875 when he went to the Alamitos Rancho.

His nephew Fred Bixby took over the management of this ranch. Fred Bixby was later associated with the State Fair in Sacramento and many other worthy causes. "Tall Uncle John" Bixby busied himself with rancho business while his wife saw to the planting of the garden. John Bixby died on May 16, 1877 but the family continued to hold the property.

The eucalyptus tree, pepper tree, a fine expanse of lawn, two fuchsias, and a rare yellow calla were among her prized possessions. Mrs. Bixby Smith pictures the Bixby home for us in her book *Adobe Days* , "The vision and industry of one little woman made from the dilapidated pile of mud bricks one of California's most charming homes; whose generous hospitality continued by her son (Fred) and wife, have made the old place widely known."

John Bixby planted the trees in the oldest Long Beach parks and also the pepper trees along Anaheim Road. All through the 1880's and 1890's the long row of pepper trees greeted travelers along this road. Present generations are enjoying the foresight of "Tall Uncle John"[2].

Rancho Los Cerritos

Another Southern California property came into the hands of an "Anglo", John Temple, ("Don Juan"). The territory about Long Beach and northward was originally granted to Manuel Nieto in 1784, a retired soldier in the Spanish army. Don Juan Temple married Rafaela Cota, a descendant of Manuel Nieto. He proceeded to buy out the rest of the heirs to Rancho El Cerrito, paying each of the other heirs $275.75, according to Mrs. Bixby Smith.

In 1844 he built the adobe, Rancho Los Cerritos, which still stands to the west of Signal Hill and north of Long Beach. The hacienda had its *correodores* and brea roof. Juan Temple laid out an Italian garden, importing bricks from the East by way of the Horn to mark the borders in herringbone fashion.

The garden had a few black locust trees, an oleander, oranges, lemons, figs, apples, pears, and Italian cypress trees. Juan Temple died on May 31, 1866 and then Flint, Bixby and Company bought the old rancho. Jotham Bixby became manager and bought a half interest in 1869. In 1880 the owners of El Cerrito sold 4,000 acres to the American Colony under W. E. Willmore. This was the beginning of the city of Long Beach.

Butterfield's memories

Butterfield remembered Long Beach when it was just a small village. He graduated from the old Long Beach High School in 1909 and had fond memories of the area. He wa also familiar with the Temple property.

In *Adobe Days* Mrs Bixby Smith, one of the Bixby daughters, pictured life at the ranch in the old days. There was a wide porch where the sun shone through the rose vines and flecked the floor with shadows. The Madeira Vine showered the summer house with its fragrant white blossoms. The black locust trees which Juan Temple planted flowered in season and the Castilian rose blossomed beneath them.

As if the rose fragrance were not enough, anise added its touch to the old garden. The old pepper tree shaded the small gate that led to the wool barn. The Italian cypress trees grew in "islands' between the brick walks

With Mrs. Bixby Smith we see again the curious green rose and prickly Scotch roses as well as "Ragged Robin" and "Chromatella". Blue agapanthus, purple iris and white-plumed pampas grass with its saw-like grass blades were important plantings. There were two century plants. Honeysuckle, lilacs, lemon verbena, and heliotrope gave additional fragrance. Pomegranates lent an air of Spanish beauty and the boggy mint bed was just as fitting. Today the old grounds are well preserved, though slightly remodeled.' (1950s)

Public parks

Both Rancho Los Alamitos and Rancho Los Cerritos are now owned by the City of Long Beach. The noted landscape architect Ralph Cornell was employed to restore the gardens at Los Cerritos. More recently, Marie Barnidge McIntyre, the horticulturist at the Long Beach Parks Department, has begun to catalogue the plants which were used originally. She is recreating a more authentic site. The remnants of an olive tree planted by John Temple, the first American owner, can still be seen in the grounds but it is dead. Two pomegranate trees also date from the original period. Cornell left the brick lined walks intact, but planted a few things which were anachronistic.

Some of the early structural features are still to be seen in the grounds. There are a well and the old adobe oven, with the water tower. These remind us that cooking was an outdoor activity in those days. A formal herb garden still has its old sundial, among the lavender, teazles, germander, roses and lemon grass.

At Rancho Los Alamitos, two gigantic Moreton Bay fig trees remain very impressive. The grounds are more extensive than at Los Cerritos, divided into a number of smaller subsidiary gardens or "rooms". Florence Yoch, the noted Southern Califonia landscape architect, created a formal rose garden near the perimeter of the property. One section of the grounds contains a large and varied collection of succulents. The elder Mrs Bixby created a small private or "secret" garden across from the main patio in which she liked to sit and watch her children, and later, grandchildren play.

Juan Jose Dominguez' rancho

There were three grants of land to Juan Jose Dominguez in 1784. Sargento Cristobol Dominguez was the first owner of one section followed by his son Manuel in about 1825. Manuel lived on the old Dominguez Rancho until his death in 1882.

The adobe hacienda stands on the hillside west of the Truck road about ten miles north of San Pedro. It has been remodeled and given to the Claretian Order as a seminary to train priests. Once the old gardens contained historic trees but now there is little of the original left. The remodeling did give the adobe an air of respectability.

CHAPTER 24

Santa Monica

Hancock Park

The old adobe in Hancock Park, on the way to Santa Monica via Wilshire Boulevard, was built in about 1830. That is a short time compared with the saber-toothed tiger, the mammoth, and other creatures that were caught in the quagmire of sand and oil, referred to as the brea pits. Charles Gibbs Adams replanted the grounds about the adobe so visitors could more fully appreciate the grounds.

San Vicente and Boca de Santa Monica had a long history as ranchos before Senator John P. Jones and Colonel R. S. Baker translated their dream of a beautiful city into action. Senator Baker must have loved trees and rare ornamental plants. He planted the Silver Tree (*Leucadendron argenteum*) at his summer home. Palisades Park in Santa Monica today is a monument to public foresight.

Soldiers Home

The Soldier's Home in Sawtell, now a part of Los Angeles, has many fine ornamental plants. Through a trust made in 1887, three hundred acres of land were set aside for the welfare of old soldiers. *Melaleuca lateritia, M. huegelii, Agonis flexuosa*, and similar plants were thriving there before 1910.

Ernest Robert pioneered in the growing of garden geraniums at his West Los Angeles Nursery. He remarried in his eighties and looked ahead to superior varieties with the help of his daughter. "Marie Robert" is a variety still grown.

Hugh Evans

Evans lived and worked in Santa Monica. He re-imported desirable ornamental plants that had been neglected. No one but a true lover of plants could have persisted in this attempt because in so many cases the work is not profitable. (Figure 50)

Figure 50 Hugh Evans Original partner in Evans and Reeves, West Los Angeles in 1939. Photo courtesy of Norvelle Gillespie. (Reproduced by permission of the Regents of the University of California)

Hugh Evans was born in Great Britain. He arrived in San Diego in 1892, before he was twenty years old. He planted his first garden in 1894 and learned that fighting rabbits and other pests is a price that may have to be paid for success. For a time he was in the nursery business and helped appraise real estate. Later he moved to Santa Monica where he continued his garden activities. His interest in gardens is hardly surprising as both his father and mother were keen amateur gardeners in England.

In about 1923 Evans began to import plants from abroad, seeking to find those best adapted to California conditions. Through reading and experience he laid out a trail that others may well follow. Perhaps a brief listing of his importations by year may be of general interest. (See Appendix H) (Note 90)

Still other plants grown by Hugh Evans at his nursery include *Euyrops athanasiae, E. spathaceus, E. pectinatus, Chamaelaucium uncinatum, C. gracilis, C. rubrum, Thenarda floribunda, Brittonastrum mexacanus (Gardoquia mexicana), Schizocentron elegans* and *Angelonia grandiflora* (possibly a form of *A. saticariaefolis*).

Evans brought in a number of hibiscus varieties from Hawaii, Bermuda, and Trinidad between 1923 and 1939. The various *Chamaelaucium*s are among the finest flowering shrubs in southern California and will likely become highly popular when better known. Some of the plant species listed above had been imported previously but Hugh Evans brought many for the first time.

Hugh Evans later moved his nursery from Santa Monica to 255 South Barrington Avenue, West Los Angeles. He and his two sons, Jack and Morgan (Bill), ran the nursery until it was discontinued. Hugh Evans retired in 1957.

Jack Evans started a landscape firm of his own. In 1958 Morgan Evans engaged in his own landscape business and disposed of the nursery. The Evans brothers helped landscape the Disneyland grounds at Anaheim and many fine properties in the Hollywood area. The wonderful group of imports, together with a few developments of their own, such as *Philodendron evansi*, ensures that the fame of the Evans family will continue. Hugh Evans' epitaph is in the wonderful plants still grown by Californians.

Santa Monica Forestry Experiment Station

'In 1885 the Forestry Experiment Station was founded near Santa Monica, between Rustic Canyon and Santa Monica Canyon. The old plantation of Eucalyptus, acacias, and other trees is now owned by the Uplifters Club of Los Angeles. It is fortunate that such an organization should be preserving what may be considered the greatest collection of eucalyptus trees in California. Many of the trees were set out before 1893 when the University of California took over this old plantation. Publications showing the kinds of eucalyptus and acacias planted were issued in early years.'

CHAPTER 25

Whittier

'The original Mission San Gabriel was a short distance northeast of Montebello near the river but this site was unfavorable because the river sometimes overflowed. The mission was moved about five miles up to its present location. Francisco P. F. Temple had an adobe on Rancho La Merced near the original site of the Mission. This area became known as Temple Corners. An old palm tree still grows in the area but none of the original plantings is left. Temple died in 1877.'

San Gabriel

'Juan Mathias Sanchez built an adobe quite far back from the present Lincoln Boulevard, about two miles southeast of Francisco Temple's adobe. Sanchez signed William Workman's note as demanded by E. J. Baldwin, then finally lost his property when Workman did not repay the note. A visitor to such adobe sites will probably find nothing more than an ailanthus surviving from the original planting, although later plantings around houses may be of interest.

The present generation may wonder how some of the small towns and smaller cities got started. There are historical accounts that will give the answers. For example Rivera is located on the old Los Nietos Rancho once owned by Manuel Nieto.'

Downey

Downey is another city that lies on this same rancho. Antonio Maria Nieto obtained his rancho very early and received a patent in 1774. Its title was confirmed for his widow in 1834 and conveyed to Lemuel Carpenter, who built an adobe. Lemuel Carpenter came from Missouri in 1833 when he was twenty two years old, in the same party as Workman.

Former governor John Gately Downey, along with James P. McFarland, purchased the property in 1859 following the death of Lemuel Carpenter. Governor Downey's old residence stood on the road between Puente Hills and Norwalk, about three miles north of Los Nietos. The Jose M. Ramirez Tract was on a portion of Rancho Santa Gertrudes near Santa Fe Springs. Early settlers remembered old pepper trees there in the 1850's. The City of Downey was established in 1873.

Parley Johnson house

In 1926, Mr and Mrs Parley Johnson commissioned Roland A Coate to design and build them a house and garden in Downey, in the old Spanish style. Johnson had grown citrus for many years very successfully.

The architect fulfilled their request in all its particulars. Made of adobe, the house has two stories, with a wooden balcony running along the upper story. The windows are deeply recessed with iron bars and there is a red tiled roof. There are patios and courtyards harking back to the old days in Monterey.

Coate created a lane running along the rear of the house with brick walls and olive trees growing on both sides, underplanted with shrubbery. In one of the courtyards, a handsome pergola frames the entrance. The City of Downey preserves and maintains this fine example of 1920s style.

Whittier

Micajah D. Johnson, who came to Los Angeles in 1876, was probably responsible for suggesting the name of Whittier. The neat little city has made a great effort to beautify the community. El Ranchito on the banks of the San Gabriel was leased in about 1906 to start an improvement.

Today the visitor is impressed by handsome trees in the streets. Holly Oak, (*Quercus ilex,*) grows on both sides of Oak Street, varying in trunk diameter from eight to ten inches and averaging close to twenty five feet in height.'

CHAPTER 26

Chino-Pomona-Ontario

R iverside and San Bernadino counties were richly settled
during the latter years of the nineteenth century. The
success of the San Gabriel mission showed how fertile the land
was. Many families built houses there and created gardens around
them.

Spadra and El Monte

'Spadra was once a small stop on the Valley Boulevard west of
Pomona, close to a hill, not far away on the south side of the old
road. There were a hotel and store, and of course a place for horses
to drink. During the past fifty years most of the old buildings have
gradually disappeared. A school and a few old houses still remain.
(Ca. 1950)

The first segment of the railroad ended here when it was being
built. The Butterfield stage also stopped here, just before veering
to the south to reach Chino Ranch on the south rim of the valley.

W. W. (Billie) Rubottom had moved to Los Angeles after the
breaking of the Yuba dam. A little later he took up a settler's claim
to a hundred and sixty acres at El Monte. The State Agricultural
Society's committee visited Rubottom's farm in 1858 and was struck
by the Indian corn ranging from fourteen to twenty two feet in
height. The committee also noticed that he had a assortment of
ornamental trees and vines.

Billie Rubottom left El Monte to build a tavern at Spadra in
the late 1860's. He planted a pepper tree, slippery elm, oranges

and two palm trees near the front entrance. The railroad from Los Angeles had been extended eastward as far as Spadra in 1875.

Rubottom had a good business. Originally there was an old adobe with two beautiful evergreen southern magnolias in the garden, and boxwood borders along the paths. The trees were planted about the same time that the brick house was built.

Pomona

Pomona's history has been told by others but the interesting story of early adobes and their gardens is not as widely known. The Historical Society of Pomona Valley has been working diligently to repair this deficiency. The society has restored and preserved seven residential sites. Butterfield prepared his book before this program began.

The Palomares family settled at the site of Pomona and had three different adobes. One was on South Kenoak Drive, a little distance south of the present Ganesha Park. An old oak tree marks the site of this early adobe. A tablet was placed on this tree, at the south side of Kenoak Drive, by the Daughters of the American Revolution in 1922. The present Palomares Adobe is at 491 East Arrow Avenue. It was the second one that Don Ignacio Palomares built.

Butterfield: 'Driving north on Garey Boulevard in Pomona, well to the north of Holt Avenue, the visitor may find an old house set back in a little orange orchard, at the corner of Walnut and North Park Avenue. This was 1569 Garey Boulevard.' (Ca. 1941) It is now 1569 North Park Avenue and the restored house is known as La Casa Primera de Rancho San Jose.

A small white adobe was still there in 1940. Large English walnut trees, black walnuts, oleander, cape jasmine, pears, and vines decorate the old grounds. This was one of the early adobes on Rancho San Jose, said to have been built in 1837. The City of Pomona purchased it in 1973.

Still further north, at Orange Avenue and Cucamonga, is the third Palomares Adobe site. (Note 91) Rubottom added to it and

Adolph Graffen lived in the old house later. There were two old palms in the grounds. Butterfield remembered camping by the eucalyptus grove across the road and also remembered the cotton-wood trees in horse and buggy days.

The old Holiday Ranch was sold to D. H. Collins. In about 1870 Mr. Collins planted pecan trees, the seeds coming from Texas. This old farm with its pecans may still be seen about a quarter of a mile from the bridge to the west of Spadra on Valley Boulevard, north side. (Ca. 1941)

Frank Hartness was another early settler in the area. He grafted native California walnut trees some time in the 1890's. Notice a few old Ailanthus trees that linger from some early planting.

Louis Phillips' house

Louis Phillips was born Louis Galefsky in Kempen. (38) This town was in Posen, a province of Prussia at that time, though it is really part of Poland.. He and his brother Fitel changed their surname to Phillips after emigrating to the United States. They went to California in 1850. Louis settled near San Gabriel. In 1852 he was one of the first people in Los Angeles to become an American citizen.

While they made no secret of being Jewish they also did not emphasize it. Some historians of Pomona county were not aware that Louis was a Jew. He had become expert at managing horse and cattle ranches while a youth in rural Prussia and used this to great advantage in California. It enabled him to become very wealthy indeed.

In 1863 he took over the management of the San Jose ranch to the east of Billie Rubottom's hotel. By 1866 he was the sole owner. An old adobe stood on the site, built by Ramon Vejar but Phillips decided to build a better house. The brick house was built in 1875, about a mile east of Spadra and on the south side of the old highway. It stayed in quite good condition until the mid-twenti-eth century. A grove of eucalyptus trees marked the site of an early school house that was moved to Spadra.

P. T. Boyle later bought the Phillips house. There were bamboos in the old garden and a fan palm planted by Don Ignacio Palomares in about 1850. A Mr. Lopez once had a store there and the adobe was used for fiestas, funerals, and church services. Roses, carnations, deciduous fruits, grapes and vines grew in the garden.

The wheels of the old *careta* used for guests were made of Blue Gum eucalyptus wood. Eucalyptus had not yet been imported when the Spanish held California, so the *careta* is probably much more recent. In time age made inroads so in 1939 the adobe was rebuilt by Charles Gibbs Adams The wisteria vine is again receiving attention and visitors may appreciate the old Palomares garden as reconstructed. It is open free of charge for all visitors. (1950s)

Eucalyptus and camphor trees

The eucalyptus trees lining the road to La Verne north of Pomona were planted by Captain Hutchison in about 1876. There was also an extremely large camphor tree on the north side of Holt Street at the Ebell Club House. This tree was planted in 1883 by John Packard . The label was placed on it on May 2, 1922. The tree had a spread of approximately a hundred and ten feet and the trunk is enormous. So far as known, this is the largest camphor tree in California, but not the oldest.

Palm trees

Driving south on Garey takes the visitor past the towering fan palms that line Garey a mile south, on the east side of the street. These palms must have been planted in the 1870's or 1880's, judging from the height of others of similar age.

Ontario

Ontario was subdivided in 1882 by George Chaffey, the land having been a part of the Garcia Ranch and a portion of Rancho Cucamonga. (Note 92) His brother, W. B. Chaffey, selected and planted the trees on Euclid Avenue. They named the avenue after the great geometer Euclid, a favorite of George Chaffey. The Chaffeys came from Canada, hence the name "Ontario". George Chaffey was an engineer with enormous vision, responsible for opening the Imperial Valley to irrigation by the Colorado River, among other achievements.

This long avenue is two hundred feet wide, with four rows of trees and a center strip through which the old car line ran in early days. Most of the trees were Australian, such as eucalyptus and grevilleas. Gum trees and grevilleas alternated. Palms and pepper trees were planted originally in the center strip but the palms were removed later.

Few avenues in all California are more scenic. A large banquet has been held each year in the central strip. People from many states congregated. Those from Iowa and Nebraska would sit at the same table to talk over old times while near them the old gnarled pepper trees served as decorations. (1950s)

Rancho Cucamonga

Rancho Cucamonga was granted to Tiburcio Tapia in 1839. He built an adobe, then left the rancho to the care of Maria Valdez who is said to have set out the mother vineyard. Tapia died in 1845. His daughter, Maria Tapia, married Leon V. Prudhomme and Mr. Prudhomme may be remembered as the man who was among the first to grow the fan palm. He took seeds from palms at Mission San Gabriel and planted them about his home in Los Angeles.

John Rains and his wife, Mercedes (Williams) bought this vineyard in 1858. He planted a hundred and sixty acres of grapes and built the adobe winery which is believed to be in good condition today. Rains may also have planted some of the old trees growing to the east of the adobe winery, such as walnut, eucalyptus, and sycamore. John Rains was murdered on Novmber 17, 1862. Two years later his widow married Jose C. Carillo. The old adobe was restored to its present condition by H. H. Thomas.

CHAPTER 27

Riverside to Redlands and San Bernardino

Riverside

'Riverside, the City of Beautiful Homes as well as the home of the Washington Navel orange, thrives by the Santa Ana River and by Mt. Rubidoux. Juan Bandini secured the grant of Jarupa, seven leagues or 31,000 acres of land. In 1846 he sold a part to Benjamin Davis Wilson.

Wilson lived at Jarupa for about three years. In 1846 he and Bandini disposed of their interest to Isaac Johnson and Colonel Isaac Williams of Chino Rancho. Johnson and Williams in turn sold a portion of this rancho to Louis Robidoux, a Frenchman who came from St. Louis. (Note 93) For some reason when they named the mountain they changed the spelling of his name. The Huntington Park Association acquired Mt. Rubidoux in 1906 and developed it as a public park. On April 26, 1907, the Easter Cross was erected. The first annual sunrise pilgrimage was made on Easter Sunday in 1909.

While on Mt. Rubidoux the visitor may wish to see a tablet placed on Loring Rock in 1923. It was unveiled on April 18, 1923, in honor of Charles M. Loring, a civic enthusiast who died early in 1922. Huntington Park, the ten miles of pepper trees lining the highway from Riverside to Marsh Field, and other street trees in Riverside were also planted in his honor.

Old adobes

It is hard for the visitor to imagine the broad sweep of land between San Bernardino and Los Angeles in the 1850s and 1860s with only just a very few buildings or settlements. On the north rim of the valley was the old Cucamonga adobe bought by John Rains and his wife, Mercedes. The other three places to stop along the north road were at George Dalton's, El Monte, and San Gabriel.

As late as 1870 there were no towns for many miles to break what many people then referred to as the "desert" west of Riverside and San Bernardino. It extended from the present Fontana to Cucamonga and south to the area east of Chino. There were drifting sand dunes and no water.

Robidoux built the Jarupa Rancho mill, about two miles west of Riverside and just to the south of the present highway. An American flag flew over the old burr stone set there as a monument

There were no gardens or houses to the south and east of Riverside. The land was devoted to pasturing herds, and growing grain, just as in the Mission period.

Mulberry trees

Louis Robidoux died in 1868. Louis Prévost of San Jose learned that the land might be purchased for growing mulberries and silk production so he bargained for the unsold portion of Jarupa Rancho, and also that of Don Abel Stearns, owner of Los Alamitos Rancho. This land extended eastward to where Evans park now stands near Santa Ana River.

Prévost's mulberry trees survived until fairly recently though he had died in 1869. (1950s) The silk venture came to an end because the state withdrew its support of tree planting. There was no one to continue his work.

Land companies

The Jarupa Rancho was sold to businessmen from the eastern United States in May 1870. The name of Riverside was adopted in December, 1870. Canals were completed in 1871, making it feasible to grow fruit.

Early fruit growers

George D. Carlton came from San Diego and started his nursery in partnership with Prior S. Russell. The apricot, "Woods Early," was originated in the garden of Mr. Wood. The first load of grape cuttings was taken to Riverside from George Dalton's rancho near Azusa by Scippio Craig. Carlton lived two miles north of town and a little west of Russell's "Semi-Tropical Nursery."

Tibbetts and the original Washington navel orange

By 1873, Riverside had three hundred people but there was little market for the produce. At that time there was a strip of land extending south of the village proper, about a mile wide, covering about 2,000 acres, of unsurveyed government land, and referred to collectively as Sunnyside. Still further south was the Hartshorne Tract referred to as Arlington. This land sold for $4 an acre in 1874.

Soon the government land was taken up by settlers in small lots, no more than thirty acres. Mr. and Mrs. Luther Tibbetts bought eighty acres. Their neighbor, Thomas W. Cover, had another eighty acres and his brother's property adjoined on the east.

In 1873 the Tibbets received two navel orange trees from William Saunders of the United States Department of Agriculture of Washington, D.C. Dr. Shamel has traced the complete history of importation of the Washington navel orange from Brazil into the United States in a federal publication. (Note 91) These trees were planted in the Tibbets' garden. Thomas Cover took buds from these trees to produce the first Washington Navel orange trees sold in southern California.

Originally the Tibbet's navel orange trees grew on Central Avenue near Palm Avenue but the one that survives may be found near the corner of Palm and Magnolia where it was transplanted. It is surrounded by an iron fence to protect it from the public.

Nurserymen

John Armstrong started a nursery in the Ontario –Riverside district which survived into the twentieth century. The Armstrongs specialized in fruit trees and had enormous fields of young olive trees for sale. Mr Armstrong also wrote small pamphlets detailing how to raise the olive trees and get the best crop possible.

Two other nurseries began very early: D. Turner and T. Brown, and W. J. Wilsey and O. Morris.

Magnolia Avenue

At about the same time a main avenue was laid out straight to the site of "Alvord," later to become known as Corona. All land tracts along this avenue were sold by 1876. New houses sprang up rapidly so it was decided to plant Magnolia Avenue. The first trees were set out late in March 1877.

This avenue was a hundred and thirty two feet wide. A row of eucalyptus trees was planted on either side. Pepper trees were set in the center with six magnolias at each street intersection, every half mile. Most of the 20,000 trees were planted on Magnolia Avenue by July 6, 1877.

Beautiful houses continued to be built for several years. Many of the gardens facing the street were lined with trimmed Monterey cypress hedges, broken here and there by open lawns and pleasing gardens, partly hiding the homes of the orange growers. One of these old houses at 7390 Magnolia was the home of Mr. and Mrs. E. T. Wall. Trees planted there in 1884 are now extremely large. An *Acacia melanoxylon* was ten feet, four inches in circumference in 1941. A coast redwood had a girth of fourteen feet six inches and is one of the most handsome of its species in the southland. The landscaping about this rural home is most attractive.

Victoria Avenue

Plantings on Victoria Avenue followed those on Magnolia, starting in 1892. The decision to create a long attractively planted avenue arose from the need to promote a new development with its subdivisions. The avenue was to provide access to a new development, "Arlington Heights", but it also stood on its own as a "linear arboretum".

Harold Snyder has written a definitive history of the origins of Victoria Avenue in "Pacific Horticulture". (39) The avenue was designed by Franz Hosp, a noted landscape architect of the day. Hops was born in Germany but had worked for many years in Cincinnati before settling in California in 1888.

The avenue is divided into quarter mile segments, with planted medians and borders on each side of the roadway. Hosp chose small flowering trees or deciduous shrubs for the medians. The segments were independent of each other, with a different series of plants appearing in each one. The medians are thirty feet wide, allowing room for considerable plant groups.

To accentuate the lateral borders, Hosp used Washington fan palms very effectively. One of the large specimens standing in the center at the head of Victoria was set in place in 1903 by Theodore Roosevelt . He presided over the ceremonies and the trees became known as the "Roosevelt Palm"

Most gardeners think of privets as small shrubs or hedge plants and yet some of those set out on Victoria Avenue have grown into trees. Specimens of *Ligustrum lucidum* on the south side of Victoria Avenue are among the largest in California. In 1941 one measured eight feet, nine inches in girth breast height.

The idea of a longitudinal arboretum has beeen used very successfully in Davis, at the University of California Arboretum, and in Beverly Hills along a stretch of Santa Monica Boulevard. John

McLaren's design for the development in San Mateo on Howard's land is a smaller but similar example of this approach.

The citizens of Riverside have banded together to save Victoria Avenue from being damaged or destroyed by modern encroachments. Every year they have a tree planting festival and they have also provided funds for other maintenance.

Other gardens

There are Silk Oak trees on both Victoria and Magnolia Avenues, *Grevillea robusta*. There is a fine row of Italian Cypress trees on Maude Avenue south of Victoria. *Acer rubrum* at 8133 Magnolia, E. F. Cole's residence , is over sixty feet. (1950s)

Palm trees

There is a fine collection of palm trees with sixy three varieties at 3502 Adams Street between Magnolia and Victoria, J. Harrison Wright's property. To the north, at 2700 Victoria Avenue, there is a specimen of *Bauhinia purpurea*. The Rumsey collection of palms is at 6700 Victoria Avenue. A specimen of *Pistacia chinensis* may be found at the junction of 14th and Victoria. The Alta Cresta grove of *Eucalyptus leucoxylon* on Victoria Avenue is worth seeing

The "Mother Tree" of *Magnolia grandiflora* grew at 6215 Palm Avenue, G. W. Murphy's home, for many years. It was in every respect a perfect specimen. (All these comments refer to the 1950s)

Fremont Park and Evans Lake

Fremont Park has many fine old shade trees. A few rare trees have been planted in this park in recent years but its greatest assets are its pleasing lake and shade trees.

White Park

There is an old specimen of the Climbing Cécile Brunner rose in White Park near the center of Riverside transplanted from the Hosp property at the end of Victoria Avenue where this climbing rose originated in 1895. There is a fine Australian Grass Tree (*Xanthorrea* sp.) in this park. The park also has imposing specimens of *Erythrine carcallodendrum* and *Lagenaria patersoni* . Carob trees grow near the street to the east.

The territory about San Bernardino was once used to support Mission San Gabriel. After the decline of the Mission, the land fell into the hands of Don Diego Sepulveda and the three Lugos, Jose de Carmen, Jose Maria, and Vicente. The Mormons tried to settle there and purchased 35,000 acres in 1851. At that time San Bernardino was three days travel from Los Angeles.

The town was laid out one mile square, with eight acres to a block. Irrigation ditches or *zanjas* were constructed and some of these are still in use after more than a hundred years. Until April, 1853, San Bernardino County was a part of Los Angeles County.

Mormon settlers

The Mormons had difficulty with the federal government in the late 1850's so an urgent appeal was made to those at San Bernardino to return to Salt Lake city. By 1858 many of the early settlers had departed. John Brown was one of the ones who stayed and continued to beautify his garden, planting trees and shrubbery. He sent seed of the "India Jelly Plant" to the California State Agricultural Society. We assume this was roselle (*Hibiscus sabdariffa*), an annual from the tropics of the Old World used to make jelly.

San Bernadino's "desert"

The "desert" west of San Bernardino in the 1850's and 1860's was covered by sagebrush, cacti, and wild flowers in season. Not until Cucamonga (Coco-Mongo) was reached on the north rim of the valley was this monotony relieved. Today there are hundreds of acres of grape vines growing in this sandy area. Windbreaks have aided in reclaiming the sand dunes. Water is pumped from deep wells.

The transformation of the sandy area was anticipated before 1860 when the California State Agricultural Society Report for 1858 stated, "this country must become immensely rich at a distant day. Its wine-growing capacities surpass the most extravagant anticipation of those who have seen it. " Fontana and nearby towns prove the truth of this prediction.'

CHAPTER 28

Orange County

Butterfield: 'The lower country near Santa Ana, Anaheim, and Tustin during the 1850s was rather dry and even barren, except near streams and moist ground. Portola and his party crossed this area in 1769 and Father Crespi with Portola named the territory, Santiago de Santa Ana. It was not until 1801 and 1802 that Governor Arillaga granted 60,000 acres of Parija de Santa Ana to Antonio Yorba. (Note 94)

In 1810 Antonio Yorba received the Santiago de Santa Ana. Rancho Lomas de Santiago was granted to Teodosio Yorba in 1841 and Rancho Trabuca went to Santiago Arguello in 1841. Mariquez was granted Laguna in 1844. These bare facts give us a hint of the situation when pioneer settlers began to think about building houses and making gardens. At the time there was no Orange County. All this territory was part of Los Angeles County.

The Yorbas held dominion near there. Two sons, Tomas and Teodora, moved their families to Burrel Point and planted olives near their adobe doorway. Later when the Americans came they knew this place as Olive Point and in time shortened the name to Olive.'

Placentia

'Daniel Kramer settled in the small town of Placentia in 1865. The first school came in 1874. William McFadden brought oranges from Mexico in 1869. Today this area is a modern Valencia orange district. Water from the Santa Ana River was brought in concrete ditches to irrigate the orchards. Very beautiful country houses were built soon afterwards.'

Butterfield remembered visiting this area as a boy well before 1900 but by that time much horticultural history had been made. Loquats had been found to thrive and new varieties were developed in this area. Until 1866, Flint, Bixby and Company had been farming near San Juan Bautista but in that year they moved south and took over various holdings, including the old Temple rancho north of Long Beach and some land in Orange County.

Bixby activities

Jotham W. Bixby obtained a large acreage of Rancho Canon de Santa Ana of Bernardino and Juan Yorba. Later when Don Abel Stearns was forced to sell some of his Los Alamitos Rancho the Bixby interests increased their holdings in what is now Orange County.

Today's visitor may not know these facts but they help to explain how Mrs. Bixby Bryant happened to provide land for a botanical garden in the Santa Ana River Canyon. Later the botanical garden was moved to the grounds of Claremont College.

Strong winds rush down through the broad sweep of the meandering river, fresh from the "desert" stretch in San Bernardino County and El Cajon. These are the dreaded "Santa Ana" winds. To protect their orchards from this onslaught, the fruit growers planted thousands of miles of windbreak trees, such as the Blue Gum and the Tecate or Forbe's Cypress. This weather pattern is not typical of the rest of Orange County.

Fullerton, Placentia, Tustin, Anaheim, Garden Grove, and Santa Ana were vivid parts of Butterfield's boyhood days. There were the Fourth of July celebrations in Fullerton where firemen had their competitions along with all the noise. This city with its Cocos palms, walnuts, citrus and fine homes was started on July 5, 1887. He recalled being there when the town was only ten years old. Just a few miles away is Anaheim.

Anaheim

'Camp Aleman of the Spanish became Anaheim in 1858 after the start of the Los Angeles Vineyard Colony in the previous year. Rancho San Juan Cajonde Santa Ana was granted to Juan Pacifico Ontiveras in 1837 and the ranch house was near Placentia. A. Langenberger, a German, married the daughter of Don Bernardino Yorba and was probably one of the originators of the colony plan.'

This group of men bought 1,000 acres from Juan Ontiveras and constructed an aggregate of four hundred miles of ditches. Eight feet lengths of willow were cut and planted around each of the German shareholders' places to serve as a barrier against roaming cattle. A fifty acre central area was set aside and fifty houses erected for the shareholders.

An old palm or ornamental tree still lingers from an early planting but most of what one now sees are modern gardens. A few years ago the city brought in some tall fan palms and planted them near the gore in the highway leading toward Anaheim from Fullerton. These palms may date back to 1900 or before. Today the public park in Anaheim attracts many summer visitors but the gardens we see are mostly modern.' (The Disney installation is the prime attraction in Anaheim now, in 2001)

Gustav Eisen

Gustav Eisen, (Figure 51) scientist and former manager of the Fancher Creek Nursery in Fresno, passed through Orange in 1890 on a trip to San Diego. He was a close observer of horticulture in early California. He had been born in Sweden, and became a master of many sciences and professions. Eisen was a colleague of Alice Eastwood at the California Academy of Sciences.

With him we see again "the shaded avenues with pepper and gum, cypress, pine or yellow flowering grevillea (*Grevillia robusta*) . . . . In the middle of the town there is a plaza with a beautiful fountain and an exquisite little garden well planned and bet-

Figure 51 Gustav Eisen (center)
(Reproduced by permission of the Koshland History Room, San
Francisco Public Library)

ter kept. The lawns are like the softest velvet, and bordered with blue and green flowers, with beds of sweet mignonette, while bananas and palms spread their stately foliage in the center." (Note 92) Today the plaza, the palms, and some grevilleas are still there. That young city of 1890 came of age long ago.

Santa Ana

Rancho Santiago de Santa Ana of the Yorbas had its sycamores and its mustard when the first Spanish adobes were erected. There were no material changes through the 1850's and late 1860's. In 1869 William Henry Spurgeon came to Santa Ana. To get a better view of the area he climbed one of the tall sycamores.

Santa Ana was founded before 1870 and its progress is recorded by Gustav Eisen in 1890 when he wrote, "Santa Ana, Orange and Tustin are like three precious stones in a ring of verdure. Only a few miles apart, they are like villas on the outskirts of a central imaginary city, from which wealthy and poor alike fled to a more retired country life, to enjoy both seclusion and society."

The city was incorporated on June 1, 1886. In addition to the few old sycamores that remain, a visitor of today may wish to see an old Moreton Bay Fig or rubber tree at 812 East First Street , known as the old Halladay Place. This tree was planted about 1874 and is one of the very large specimens in California. (1940s)

At the Bowers Memorial Museum on North Main Street there are some fan palms and *Araucaria bidwillii* trees, all about eighty five feet in height. An old Blue Gum planted around 1870 grows near the intersection of North Main with the highway near Orange.

Garden Grove

Garden Grove was started by C. Howe and A. J. Cook in 1877. Butterfield remembered the large weeping willows, the edible dates, strawberry guavas, and other fruits of 1892. The children would take the stems of callas and cut them in the same way a butcher cut soup bones. Many of the old palms and pepper trees are still thriving about Garden Grove, such as on the Nichol's estate just west of town.

Tustin

Butterfield attended grammar school in Tustin when he was six. The town was founded by Columbus Tustin in 1867 on the San Joaquin Rancho of Andres Sepulveda. It had the most beautiful gardens when Butterfield was a boy.

In 1890 Gustav Eisen wrote how the street car "winds its way under shady lanes on either side, bordered by large and graceful pepper trees covered with spice and fragrant blossoms . . . . On one side are old graceful trees with drooping limbs, on the other are well-kept cypress hedges trimmed square or even, or long natural barriers of ever-blooming geraniums in numerous varieties, of every favorite shade of color from crimson to palest pink. Over the hedges we look into bluegrass lawns, green and well-kept and exceedingly attractive."

Butterfield remembered the cypress tree from which switches were cut. He recalled the grevillea, flowers of golden silk and the seed pods which in a child's mind resembled the outline of an ostrich. There was also the old green rose from China which a San Francisco nurseryman exhibited in 1854. Tustin has its gardens of memory.'

Modern Tustin has taken good care of its horticultural heritage. In 1997, Carol H. Jordan, a staunch member of the historical society, published a small monograph on the landmark street trees of Tustin. (40) She assumed that many of them were probably supplied by local nurseries such as Theodore Schmidt and Timothy Carroll in Anaheim in the 1860s. There were also other nurseries in northern and central California, and a nursery in Sacramento sent out a lot of plants by mail. The "official " tree of Tustin is the Red-flowering Eucalyptus, *E. ficifolia.*

Butterfield continued: 'Once again my thoughts turn back to a boyhood garden on a farm not far from the Santa Ana River near the West End School. I can still picture the fancy-leaved border geranium, "Madame Salleron", and nearby *Salvia graggii* in the base planting, green foliage contrasted with scarlet flowers. On another farm was a Seven Sisters rose over the doorway. The swaying branches of a weeping willow tree made a soft sound which lulled me to sleep as a child.'

'While I was at Santa Ana High School, I liked to ride into the hills of Santiago Canyon, not far from the home of Mme. Mojeska. Matillija poppies grew there, white faces uplifted, and speckled trout swam in the stream beside me. '

Many years later, Butterfield re-visited the country of the Yorbas, of Juan Ontiveras and Jose Sepulveda, but the scene had changed by 1940. The mountain, old "Saddle Back," was still there and Orange County Park lay at the entrance to Santiago Canyon but the grape vines which had festooned the trees were gone, having lost their their water supply from the brook

The pepper trees still grew in Tustin, El Modina, Orange, and Santa Ana but some were beginning to show signs of age. The grevilleas, the elm, and the umbrella tree were there just as in his boyhood, yet the former simplicity of the open spaces was lacking.

Mission San Juan Capistrano

Butterfield: 'Passing by El Toro, situated on Canada de Los Alisos and established in 1866 by Dwight Whiting, one reaches San Juan Capistrano. The initial services were held on October 30, 1775. Father Serra said mass under an *enramada* of boughs. The first mission (Mission Vieja) was several miles to the northeast. The stone church was started in February, 1798, and completed in 1806, being one of the largest and handsomest in all California.'

'The 1812 earthquake destroyed the building and the church was never fully reconstructed. In 1858 only a few gardens remained. John ("Long John") Foster, an Englishman, married Pio Pico's youngest sister and later secured control of the old mission and the lands that surrounded it. A few old fruit trees, such as pears, peaches, figs, and olives remained there in 1858 but many were already afflicted with infirmities. Some of the old pear trees survive not far from the depot. Scions from these were taken to reproduce the pear trees for La Purisima's garden.'

The pepper tree once grew in the old San Juan Capistrano Mission Garden. Records tell about frost damage to some of the branches in the 1830's. Perhaps even then the swallows nested on the buildings in the vicinity. Today, with great precision the birds arrive on St. Joseph's Day (March 19) and usually depart on San Juan's Day (October 23).

In the modern era very enthusiastic volunteers from the city's garden club have filled the old mission courtyard with overflowing color and fragrance. Although this garden is highly anachronistic, the public is delighted and enjoys the charm and spectacle.

Venerable palm trees and fig trees may also be found in the community but the grapevines have fallen by the wayside. In 1890 Gustav Eisen reported, "Gigantic vines, which covered trellises and arbors, and which perhaps bore tons of grapes, with trunks as heavy as the body of a boy, were still there but without leaves or shoots, having surrendered to the vine disease." (Note 95)

CHAPTER 29

San Diego

A ccording to Butterfield: 'San Diego's gardens of memory are the oldest in California. After leaving San Juan Capistrano the highway soon reaches the ocean. There are tall palisades on the land side of the highway for several miles. Further along there is the Santa Margarita Rancho once owned by Don Juan (formerly John) Foster, but now a naval reservation.

Introduction of the pepper tree

The pepper tree (*Schinus molle*) was planted in the grounds of Mission San Luis Rey in about 1825. Seeds had been brought up from Mexico and the seedlings thrived, judging from records a little over thirty years later. In 1858 the trees were laden with their red berries. Only the female pepper trees have berries and both sexes are essential for the setting of berries. (Note 96)

In 1858 one of the pepper trees was fifteen inches in diameter, giving us some idea of its growth in a favorable coastal climate. The trees were not very old at that time. Nearly all the early California missions attempted to grow pepper trees from 1825 to 1830. The trees have given rise to a certain amount of legend, not always supported by the facts.

In 1958 the trees at Mission San Luis Rey were growing on artificial mounds, made by erecting strong circular adobe walls, three feet high and twelve feet across. The space in between was filled with soil and each tree was planted in the center. The wall of this large container was ornamented with various figures, either in relief or in fresco, similar to those on the fountains that may be seen at the mission today

Seeds of the pepper tree were found in adobe bricks from Mission Soledad founded in 1792, (Hendry). Santa Clara claimed that the seeds for the old trees at Mission Santa Clara and San Jose were brought up from southern California and planted early as noted elsewhere. There was an old pepper tree near the church in Los Angeles by the Plaza.

Recently a story has arisen at San Luis Rey Mission that a single tree now growing there is a remnant of the early planting. (1940s) This is highly unlikely. Any tree from the original planting would be enormous if still living. Unlike the trees at Purisima, Tustin, and San Jose,this one shows no great girth. The conditions at San Luis Rey would have been just as favorable for rapid growth.

By 1858, the ditches had overflowed into the old orchard because they had been neglected. The flooding killed all the trees. At that time, the flower garden was surrounded by century plants (probably *Agave americana*) which were still flourishing. About thirty of them had tall flower spikes. The State Agricultural society visiting committee reported, "Standing at a distance, and marking their outline against a bright morning sky, they irresistibly impress the stranger with the idea that he is approaching a forest of venerable pines."

Pala Chapel was known as Asistencia de San Antonio de Pala and was built as an outpost for San Luis Rey Mission about 1816. Its small garden and buildings provide a sense of neatness that lingers as we continue on our journey.

Colonel Couts

South from Pala Chapel near the present Vista is "Guajomita" (Big Frog), home of Colonel Cave Johnson Couts. Abel Stearns of Los Angeles and Los Alamitos Rancho, who married a sister of Colonel Couts' wife, is said to have given this rancho to his sister-in-law, Ysidora Bandini. Their father, Don Juan Bandini, was "one of the most prominent and responsible native gentlemen" and his daughter fulfilled the family tradition of giving a true welcome to visitors.

The one-story adobe building was laid out in Spanish style, forming a hollow square or patio which served as a private garden. This inner garden could be protected from cattle or marauders of all kinds. The house was built in 1852-3. This courtyard was about a quarter of an acre and originally had oranges, sweet lemons, *Acacia farnesiana*, *Myrtus communis*, and other ornamental plants that were popular in the 1850s.

Butterfield compared a picture of this garden taken in 1887 with one he took in 1935. Ornamental plants have been growing in Cout's patio for more than a hundred years. The Copa de Ora Vine (*Solandra guttata*) found there recently is probably a modern addition. Outside the adobe there is a row of old olive trees added shortly after it was constructed. Not too many animals really care to browse on olives, though deer will eat the leaves and birds occasionally take the fruit.

San Diego Old Town

On a summer day in 1935 Butterfield stood on Presidio Hill above Old Town, San Diego, not far from the large cross made of adobe bricks. These bricks may have been left from the first mission. Not far away was a lone remaining date palm believed to be the oldest exotic palm still growing in California. (Figure 52)

This palm tree probably marks the site of the first mission garden. Some may say that this palm would have been planted in the fruit garden but Father Gilbert of Santa Clara Mission believed that the Franciscans planted this date palm more as an ornamental tree than for its fruit. The fronds were used in religious ceremonies, as at Easter time. It is conceivable that this old palm tree is a remnant of the first planted garden in California.

Figure 52 Date Palm, Old Town, San Diego. Planted soon after Spanish arrived in 1769. It was the oldest exotic plant in California. Died and removed, June 6, 1957.
(Reproduced by permission of the Regents of the University of California)

Father Serra arrived on July 10, 1769. Visit the present Father Serra Museum, opened on July 16, 1929. Enjoy the garden, even though it was many years after the Franciscans came that a garden was created.

Conditions at Old Town in 1769-1775 were not entirely satisfactory for a mission garden so after six years a new site was selected six miles up the river where agriculture could be carried on more successfully. Old palm and olive trees still survive at that new location in spite of many years of neglect.

Old Town was incorporated in 1850 and streets were laid out a year later but the dream of this city was slow to materialize. The first charter was repealed but another was not granted until the 1870's. In 1867 A. E. Horton bought five quarter sections in the heart of downtown San Diego. At that time there were only twelve inhabitants.

On a tour through the Old Town try to picture the old Spanish gardens. Casa de Carillo (Pear Garden House) is remembered for the old pear tree planted by Francisco Maria Ruiz in 1807.

The adobe garden was not planted until three years later. Joaquin Carillo and Ignacio Lopez de Carillo lived there later.

The Estudillo Adobe is another one worth listing for its early garden. Jose Antonio Estudillo built the twelve room adobe in 1826. The garden had many varieties of trees and shrubs.

The Bandini House should be mentioned because there is so much sentiment attached to it. This adobe was built in 1826. After Abel Stearns died his widow, Dona Arcadia, married Colonel R. S. Baker for whom Bakersfield is named. Dona Ysidora married Lieutenant Cave J. Counts and lived at Guajomite near Vista. The other Bandini children were Dolores, Josefa, Jose Maria, Margarita who married James B. Winston, Juan de la Cruz, Alfredo, and Arturo.

Lorenzo Soto

Lorenzo Soto lived in Old Town on an acre of ground about which he erected a fence. He had an agave there which flowered in 1858. He also grew the Giant Reed used in thatching the roofs of the less expensive adobe buildings. Soto's garden was irrigated by a windmill pump, doubtless an American contribution. Pears, olives, pomegranates, figs, dates, peaches, and grapes grew in his early garden. His rancho was about thirty miles away.

Other Residents of San Diego's Old Town

Mrs. Wrightington, widow of an early American settler, lived quite near Lorenzo Soto's property in Old Town. She grew vegetables, such as corn, tomatoes and red pepper in her gardens. In 1858 the tomatoes had been growing for three to five years, truly perennials as viewed by members of the California State Agricultural Society.

George Lyons, Sheriff of San Diego County, had a small fruit garden in which there were a large number of peach trees, the fruit-laden branches touching the ground in 1858. He used mesquite as a hedge about his garden.

Garden plants in old San Diego

The older residents of San Diego recollected early garden ornamental plants. Many of the plants had to withstand some drought because of the scanty rainfall and limited supply of water for irrigation. One list included the pepper tree, geranium, petunia, date, fig, olive, and fan palm. Castilian roses and heliotrope were also planted in early San Diego gardens.

Early American settlers brought poinsettia, bougainvillea, lemon verbena, pampas grass, marguerite, lantana, rubber tree, Norfolk Island Pine (*Araucaria excelsa*), acacia, *Datura suaveolens* (Angel's Trumpet), and several others. A few of these such as Angel's Trumpet and lemon verbena may have been grown in the Mexican period but early records are so scarce we are not sure about all of the plants planted by Spanish and Mexican settlers.

Nurseries

Kate Sessions

Any survey of early gardens of San Diego would be incomplete without mentioning the work of Kate Oliva Sessions (1857-1940) (Figure 53. Kate Sessions was one of the first women to be graduated from the University of California. She went to San Diego in 1884 to teach in the high school. A year and a half later she left teaching because of impaired health and took up the nursery business at Coronado. At first she was in a partnership but a year later opened an office herself in San Diego after the partnership was dissolved. This office was at the corner of 5th Street and C Street where the Sefton Building was subsequently built.

Figure 53 Kate Olivia Sessions (1857-1940. The photograph shows her standing in the succulent garden planted in her honor in Balboa Park. (Reproduced by permission of the Regents of the University of California)

While in Coronado, she offered George F. Otto a position (in 1889), even agreeing to pay his fare from the north if he would stay two months. He accepted her offer but in 1893 he established his own nursery in Coronado. The Otto nursery survived until the 1950s.

Miss Session's property at Coronado became too valuable for nursery use and she had to move. Early in 1892 she leased thirty acres from the City of San Diego where Balboa Park now stands. She agreed to plant a hundred trees each year on this property as well as donate three hundred more to the city.

Kate Sessions started the new nursery on ten acres at the farthest northwest corner at Upas and 6th Street. Trees growing on 5th Street and at the old school grounds on B Street came from her nursery. At the close of her lease in 1915 she moved to the Mission Hills district and later to Pacific Beach. Kate Sessions planted the large Cocos Palms in the Plaza across from Hotel Grant by, on January 19, 1897

For many years Miss Sessions had great influence on the city's landscape, working her magic through her energetic voice and her domineering but loving way. The response of others inspired her to do more. She called attention to the great value of several native plants for garden used, such as the Matillija poppy, *Ceanothus cyaneus* , and of Fremontia. She introduced bougainvillea, acacia, eucalyptus, trumpet flower, *Cissus capensis*, and others to the area.

Kate Sessions was honored with the Meyer Medal and was awarded an honorary membership in California Garden Clubs, Inc. Her writings were always very practical.

Ernest Benard

Ernest Benard, a Frenchman, was once a foreman at the California Nursery Company at Niles, California. In 1889 he helped plant the grounds about Hotel Coronado. He liked the new area so well he bought land in Mission Valley and started his own nursery. He helped plant some of the trees seen today in Balboa Park.

Alfred Robinson

Mr. and Mrs. Alfred D. Robinson's Rosecroft Begonia Gardens at Point Loma were very well known. Through the efforts of Mr. Robinson, Kate Sessions, and a few others the San Diego Floral Association was formed in 1907. Mr. Robinson was the first president. The organization held its first flower show the same year. The publication, *The California Garden*, was started in July, 1909. In 1910 the Cook Memorial Library was founded. *The California Garden* is still published today.

In 1911 the organization planted twenty nine pepper trees in Golden Hill Park as a memorial to the same Mr Cook. They began preservation of the Torrey Pines in 1916. The Kate Sessions Aloe and Agave Planting in Balboa Park was started in 1932. The gardens we see in San Diego are memorials to these dedicated people.

Unlike San Francisco and Sacramento, nurseries were much slower to appear in San Diego. The city was developed more gradually. Gold rush fortunes did not percolate down so far south. Water was a serious problem. J. A. Asher started the first known nursery in San Diego in the 1880s. It was followed by Kate Sessions, Ernest Benard and George Otto,

Closing

Butterfield wrote: 'Many garden friends in San Diego County and elsewhere in California have always been willing to help explore early garden sites and to study early plant materials. No person working alone could hope to see all of the important things there are to see in old gardens.

Visits to many areas in California have been summarized with the hope of making a start in the history of California gardens. Many of the gardens are now gone and even some of those described are probably subdivided or removed. Any description is subject to such recent changes. It is hoped that others will supplement the records in this book so that a more complete reference list on the history of California gardens and the plants they contained will be available.'

There is much that can only be accomplished by organized effort. After more than forty years of affiliation with garden clubs and with the people who have founded such organizations, Butterfield felt that his greatest asset were the many friends he had made in such work.

By a wonderful chance, Harry Butterfield's manuscript was rescued from oblivion. I have attempted to fulfill his hope that more early gardens would be found and recorded. Butterfield described three hundred and twenty three gardens himself. I have added another fifty to the total, but am certain there are still more out there beng lovingly tended all unknown to the rest of us.

ACKNOWLEDGEMENTS

The author is exceedingly grateful to the following people who helped her unstintingly. If anyone has been inadvertently omitted from this list it is purely by an oversight and in no way intentional. The author remains solely responsible for any errors which may have crept into this work.

Pat Akre, Curator of Photographs, San Francisco History Center, San Francisco Public Library
Beverly Bastian, BelvedereTiburon Landmark Society
Jacqueline Beggs, ranger, East Bay Regional Parks system
Ben Braly ,docent, Bourn Cottage, Empire State Mine, Grass Valley
Janet Bryan, local historian, San Benito County
Diane Carpenter, archivist, Inverness
Joan De Fato, Librarian, Los Angeles County Arboretum
Thomas Dibblee, San Francisco
Phyllis Faber, botanist and consultant
Kathleen Fisher, Assistant Librarian, Helen Crocker Russell Library, Strybing Arboretum
William Gallagher, Nevada City
Evelyn Foote, Gardiner Grass Valley
Frances Grate, garden historian, Monterey
Louise Greenlaw, Calaveras County
Joseph Guida, St Josephs' Community Center, Grass Valley
Susan Haas, Registrar, Society of California Pioneers
Lynne Hanson, Harry Butterfield's granddaughter
Tanya Hollis, Librarian, California Historical Society
Patricia Keats, Librarian, Society of California Pioneers
Magaret Kirkham, San Francisco

Norma Kobzina, Librarian, University of California at Berkeley, Lifesciences Library
Sue Lloyd, San Mateo
Judith Marvin, historian, Calaveras County
Jocelyn Moss, Librarian, Marin County Historical Society and at the California Room, Civic
Center Library, San Rafael.
Barbara Pitschel, Librarian, Helen Crocker Russell Library, Strybing Arboretum
K. Quist, Monterey State Historic Park, Monterey
Michael Redmon, Santa Barbara Historical Society
Tania Rizzo, Pasadena Historical Museum
Dorothy Rucker, Harry Butterfield's daughter
Carolyn Singer, Grass Valley
John Skarstad, Archivist, University of California at Davis
Susan Snyder, Bancroft Library
Dorothy Soderholm, volunteer, Napa County Historical Society
Margaret Steele, Nevada City
Barden Stevenot, Calaveras County
Annabel Straus, Nevada City
William Sturm, Librarian, California Room, City of Oakland Public Library
Charlotte Tancin, Hunt Botanical Library, Pittsburgh
Dace Taube, Curator of Photographs, University of Southern California
Wendy Welker, Photographic archivist, California Historical Society
June Whitesides, Photographic archivist, Contra Costa Historical Society
Hazel Whitford, Nevada City

NOTES

[1] Coffin, Catherine Phillips 1932 *Portsmouth Plaza* San Francisco, California John Henry Marsh (page 29)

[2] A copy of Colonel J.L.Warren's 1853 catalogue is in the Bancroft Library. Mrs Gerald Kennedy of Stockton inherited another copy from her grandfather, Captain Charles Weber(page 32)

[3] John Butterfield ,whose company received an annual subsidy of $600,000 from the federal government to operate this stage from 1858-1861, was a grandson of Timothy Butterfield of Westmoreland, N.H. Timothy Butterfield was a brother of the writer's great-great-grandfather,also of Westmoreland (page 35)

[4] Professor Warren Tufts helped secure some of this information. Also see *The Daily Bee*, Sacramento, October 31, 1881, p. 3, Col. 1. James Saul reported on frost damage in his area in 1879 for Thomas Garey's book, *The Orange in California*. (page 43)

[5] List in *The California Horticulturist*, 1876. (page 45)

[6] Catalog in Mrs. Gerald D. Kennedy 's collection . (page 45)

[7] Copy of inventory in Mrs. Gerald D. Kennedy's. collection (page 45)

[8] Information from an interview with Charles Abraham's niece. (page 49)

[9] Two of Ludemann's catalogs for 1874 and 1875 are in the Bancroft Library, University of California at Berkeley. (page 51)

[10] Much of this information about Golden Gate Park and John McLaren was obtained in a personal interview, January 26, 1940. John McLaren retired in 1943. Eric Walther retired in 1957 and died in 1959. (page 62)

[11] See Report of the California State Agricultural Society for 1858,

p. 251. (page 70)

[12] See Albert Wilson's *Distinctive Trees, Shrubs and Vines in the Gardens of the San Francisco Peninsula,* 182 p. 1938. Menlo Park, California The author (page 72)

[13] Listed by William C. Walker of San Francisco in about 1859 (page 78)

[14] List from the *Pacific Rural Press,* San Francisco. (page 89)

[15] Toichi Domoto reported his father was not yet twenty years old when he arrived in California. (page 89)

[16] Patrick Barry, born near Dublin, Ireland, came to the United States at the age of twenty and worked first for Prince's nursery. In 1840 he helped found the nursery of Ellwanger and Barry at Rochester, N.Y. He was a famous horticultural editor and writer, and a pioneer in the field of pomology. Died at Rochester, N.Y. in 1890. (page 92)

[17] Date for plantings by G. P. Jones in *Pacific Rural Press* of 1876. For a biography of David Tisch see J.M.Quinn, *History of the State of California and Biographical Record of Oakland and Environs.* 2 volumes. Los Angeles, California Historic Record Co. (page 94)

[18] Letter to Harry Butterfield from Joseph Rowell, University of California archivist. (page 106)

[19] For full account by E.J.Wickson , see *Calif. Agr. Exp. Stat. Rept.* 1917-1918, pp. 35-103. (page 109)

[20] Account based on an interview with Mr Kieruff's son (page 111)

[21] Reported to Harry Butterfield in 1941 by a daughter of George Bailey. (page 113)

[22] Report of the California State Agricultural Society, 1858. p. 265. (page 118)

[23] Bishop Taylor Memorial Assoc. *Program Centenary Memorial Service,* p. 7, May 22, 1921. (page 119)

[24] Information largely from Dr. Kimball's daughter, Ruth. Statement on the Washington Navel Orange made at the Fruit Grower's Convention in Los Angeles in 1885. (page 124)

[25] Harry Butterfield learned this story from a distant relative of the

family in 1941. (page 128)

[26] A biography of Dr Strenzel with a picture was in Pacific Rural Press in the early 1900s (page 131)

[27] One of August Hemme's daughters told this story to Harry Butterfield. (page 132)

[28] Account in History of Santa Clara County. (page 135)

[29] The Charles Navlet Nursery Company was in business until fairly recently. Dorothy Rucker, Harry Butterfield's daughter, worked at a branch of this nursery. (page 140)

[30] The story of these palms appeared many years later in the Pacific Rural Press. The listing of plants in Prevost's nursery is from reports of the California State Agricultural Society. (page 142)

[31] An advertisement appeared in the Pacific Rural Press. (page 143)

[32] Quoted by permission of San Francisco Garden Club. (page 144)

[33] Report from California State Agricultural Society for 1858. (page 146)

[34] Letter to Harry Butterfield from Mrs. Cora Older in 1941. (page 147)

[35] Published by the San Francisco Garden Club. (Page 149)

[36] Reported by Woodbridge Metcalf, Extension Forester, University of California at Berkeley. (page 150)

[37] The history of the Pierce grape is found in the Report of the State Horticultural Society, 1891, see pp. 131-132. (page 155)

[38] See Smith, Sarah. *Adobe Days*. 217 p. 1926. Cedar Rapids, Iowa Toronto Press.. (page 165)

[39] Vallejo, Guadalupe. *Ranch and Mission Days in California*, Cent. Mag. 19: 183, Dec., 1890. (page 168)

[40] Bidwell, John. *Life in California before the Gold Discovery*. Cent. Mag. 19: 106. Dec. 1890. (page 170)

[41] The Monterey Chamber of Commerce has a leaflet covering "The Path of History." (page 171)

[42] See State Marker #574 at 219 York St., Vallejo. (page 179)

[43] Eliza Farnham recorded the difficulty of receiving fruit trees shipped round the Horn alive in her memoir "California Indoors and Out". (page 180)

[44] For a biography and picture of William H. Nash, see *The Blue Anchor*, Vol. 18, No. 2, p. 24, May, 1941. (page 186)

[45] E.J. Wickson in his *California Fruits* stated that the two men were the first to import fruit trees into the Napa Valley. Also see Camp, Charles. L. *William Alexander Peabody and the Overland Pioneers*, California Hist. Quarterly, Vol. XVI, No. 2, 1937. Reprint 22 p. Lawton R. Kennedy, San Francisco. (page 187)

[46] Site of Yount Blockhouse—State Marker #564, one mile north of Yountville. The Yount grave is State Marker #693 at Yountville. Blockhouse built 1836. House built 1837. (page 188)

[47] Wickson, E. J. *California Illustrated*, No. 1, 2nd ed. San Francisco, 1888 California View Co.,. (page 193)

[48] One account in the *California Farmer* for 1854. (page 197)

[49] Sacramento City Cemetery State Marker #566 (page 200)

[50] Account in Pacific Rural Press, 1877. (page 201)

[51] History of Bermuda grass (page 202)

[52] Old gardens first visited in 1940. The camellias continued to be healthy until 1957 (page 206)

[53] Site of farm located with State Marker #646 in Sutter Co. (page 206)

[54] See 1858 Report of California State Agricultural Society, p. 166. (page 208)

[55] Report of the California State Agricultural Society, 1858, p. 172. Mr. Beach was Secretary of the State Agricultural Society at the time.

For a fuller account of this orange tree, see Maslin, E. W. Report. Calif. Board Hort. 1887-88, p. 38. When Oroville Dam was started the old tree had to be moved. (page 209)

[56] State Marker #329 marks the site of the Bidwell adobe in Chico. Adobe built by native people in 1852. (page 210).

[57] State Market #312 in Chico—Bidwell Oak. (page 211)

[58] Reading Adobe built in 1847 by Major Pierson Barton Reading, located by State Marker #10 7 miles east of Cottonwood. (page 212)

[59] Old town of Shasta named Shasta June 8, 1850. (page 213)

[60] State Marker #668. Terminus of Oregon-California Trail. (page 214)

[61] State Marker #165. (page 216)

[62] Copy of William West's 1880 nursery catalog in collection of Mrs. Gerald D. Kennedy. (page 218)

[63] Copy of 1885 nursery catalog in collection of Mrs. Gerald D. Kennedy. (page 222)

[64] Statement of M. G. Vallejo before the Eighth Fruit Growers Convention, Santa Rosa, 1887. (page 264)

[65] See Vallejo, M. G. in Address before Fruit Growers Convention, State Board of Horticulture Report, 1888, p. 152. (page 281)

[66] Remarks of M. G. Vallejo before the 8th State Fruit Growers Convention at Santa Barbara, Dec. 5, 1887. Report Calif. State Board of Horticulture, 1888, pp. 152-153. (page 291)

[67] Also see his *Ornamental Trees and Shrubs*. Report State Board of Horticulture. 1888, pp. 228-239. (page 302)

[68] This and other estates were described in about 1940. (page 304)

[69] For pictures of several of the estates, see Dobyns, W. S. *California Gardens*, 1931. New York Macmillan Co. Also see Bissell, E. B. *Glimpse of Santa Barbara and Montecito Gardens*. 62 p. 1926. Schauer Printing Studio, Santa Barbara. (page 304)

[70] For the story of the Heath walnuts, see Heath, Russell, *The Hardshell Walnut*. California State Board of Horticulture Report, 1888. p 168. (page 308)

[71] See California State Board of Horticulture Report, 1893, Mrs. Theodosia B. Shepherd, *The Future of Horticulture in California*. p. 190. (She gives many of her personal experience.) Harry Butterfield owned a copy of Mrs Shepherd's1900 nursery catalog. (page 309)

[72] Pacific Rural Press, Nov. 22, 1899, p. 432, first column. Katherine Jones of the Universty of California, Dept. of Landscape Architecture (Design) gave this list to Harry Butterfield. (page 314)

[73] Description from Report of California State Agricultural Soci-

ety, 1857 and 1858. (page 324)

[74] For a fuller description of early Southern California, see: William Heath Davis . *Seventy-five Years in California*. 1929. John Howell J.A.Graves, J. A. *My Seventy Years in California*. . 1927. Times Mirror Press Harris Newmark . *Sixty Years in Southern California*. 1915 Knickerbocker Press. (page 324)

[75] Mathew Keller's article, *The Grapes and Wine of Los Angeles*, U.S. Patent Office Report for 1858, p. 346, clearly shows the intelligence of this pioneer. (page 325)

[76] H. Yosike's Japanese Nursery was at the corner of16th and Willow Streets (page 326)

[77] John Jacobs Thomas (1810-1895) famous pomologist and author *The American Fruit Grower* (1846). (page 331)

[78] Report in 1858 Report of California State Agricultural Society. (page 331)

[79] John Gralck advertised in the *Pacific Rural Press*. (page 332)

[80] For a complete account of exhibits, see Pacific Rural Press 1890. (page 333)

[81] Harry Johnson of the Johnson Cactus and Water Gardens, Paramount succeeded Sturtevant (page 333)

[82] Letter from Ernest Braunton to Harry Butterfield. (page 333)

[83] For a more complete list, see the report on the flower show exhibits in Los Angeles, Pacific Rural Press1890. Byron O. Clark's daughter reported her father germinated deodar cedar seeds. (page 340)

[84] See Calif. State Agr. Society Report for 1858, also California Citrograph ; *Oldest Orange Trees in California—Where?* Vol. 23, No. 3, Jan. 1938. pp. 106-107.. (page 343)

[85] *California – Where* vol 23 (3) January 1938 pp1016-107 (page 343)

[86] Mrs Lawles died in 1942. (oage 347)

[87] Also see mention of Father Zalvidea's garden in *Oldest Orange Trees in California*, Calif. Citrograph. Vol. 23, No. 3, p. 106. Jan. 1938. The Mission's orchard is also mentioned by William Spalding in *The Orange*, 1883, see p. 6-9. (page 351)

[88] Former president of the Southern California Historical Society

and well known landscape architect who restored several grounds about old adobes in southern California. Mr. Adams was also a past president of Calif. Garden Clubs, Inc. (page 351)

[89] Property described in Report of California State Agricultural Society for 1858. (page 351)

[90] Letter to Harry Butterfield from Fred Bixby describes Butterfield's father planting the old trees on Anaheim Road and in Recreation Park. (page 360)

[91] Hugh Evans to Harry Butterfield. (page 360)

[92] Also see Alexander, J. A. 1926 *The Life of George Chaffey*. Melbourne , Australia Macmillan Co., Ltd. (page 370)

[93] For the early history of Riverside, see Robert Hornbeck, 1913 *Robidoux's Ranch in the 'Seventies*. Riverside, California Riverside Press Printing Co. (page 371)

Others also obtained navel orange trees directly from William Saunders, including Dr. Edwin Kimball of Hayward and Alexander Craw when living at San Diego.

[94] For Crespi, see Herbert E. Bolton, 1927 *Fray Juan Crespi, Missionary Explorer on the Pacific Coast*. Berkeley California University of California Press (page 379)

[95] Eisen, Gustav. 1890 *The Raisin Industry*. San Francisco , California H.S.Crocker Co See pp. 190-193. (page 386)

[96] The date of planting is approximate only, since no accurate records have been found. Various reports of pepper trees elsewhere seem to indicate that1825 is probably correct. (page 387)

[97] For one list see E. C. W. *I Can Remember When*. California Garden. Vol. 30, No. 12. p. 11, 17. 1930. (page 419)

[98] Harvey Monroe Hall, Studies in ornamental trees and shrubs. U.C. Publications in Botany vol. 4 #1 March 10, 1910—see Plate 7. (page 423)

BIBLIOGRAPHY

California garden books

There are numerous delightful books about California's gardens which the reader may enjoy. Here is a selection:

+ Winifred Starr Dobyns *California Gardens* New York, New York MacMillan 1931
+ Priscilla Dunhill and Sue Freedman *Glorious Gardens to Visit in Northern California* New York Clarkson Potter 19193
+ Jere Stuart French 1993 *The California Garden* Washington D.C. Landscape Architecture Foundation
+ Carol Leigh *California Gardens-a nature lover's guide* Santa Barbara, California Capra Press 1993
+ Nancy Goslee Power *The Gardens of California; four centuries of design from Mission to Modern* New York, NY Clarkson Potter 1995
+ Victoria Padilla *Southern California Gardens* Berkeley, Los Angeles, London University of California Press 1961)
+Eric Sigg *California Public Gardens: a visitor's guide* Santa Fe, NM John Muir Publications 1991
+ David Streatfield *California gardens: creating a new Eden* Abbeville Press New York, NY 1994

California history

California has a very rich tradition of recording its own history. It would be impossible to list everything available. What follows is a brief listing of some key works, simply to get the reader started.

+ Hubert H. Bancroft's monumental history of the American West, with seven volumes devoted solely to California, remains the foundation of modern California studies.

A History of California (seven volumes) San Francisco, California The History Company 1894–1900

+ Kevin Starr's magisterial series about the history of California started with *"Americans and the California Dream"* in 1973. Next came *"Inventing the Dream"* 1985, then *"Material Dreams,"* 1990, *"Endangered Dreams"* 1996, *The Dream Endures* 1997 and *Embattled Dreams* 2002.

+ A useful, somewhat compressed one volume history is Warren A. Beck and David Wiliams *California: a history of the golden state* Garden City, New York Doubleday 1972

+ William Brewer *Up And Down California in 1860–1864* Berkeley University of California Press 1966

+ John S. Hittell *A History of San Francisco and Incidentally of the State of California* San Francisco, California A. L. Bancroft Company 1878

Two specialized monographs which give a strong flavor of the state in certain circumstances are:

+ J.S. Holliday *The World Rushed In* New York Simon and Schuster 1981

+ Harris Newmark *Sixty Years in Southern California* (Fourth edition) Los Angeles, California Zeitlin and ver Brugge 1970

+ The detailed specifics of the missions are covered by Father Zephyrin Engelhardt's
"Missions and Missionaries", San Francisco, California James H. Barry

Many historians of California deplore the rosy view of the state's history which vaunts the achievements of the conquerors, sets the native peoples at naught and neglects to comment on the despoliation of the land. Two representative books which attempt to set this record straight are:

+ Patricia Nelson Limerick *Legacy of Conquest* W.W. Norton (New

York) 1987

+ Richard White *It's Your Misfortune And None Of My Own: a new history of the American West* University of Oklahoma Press, Norman, Oklahoma 1991

San Francisco History

Raymond Clary *The Making of Golden Gate Park: the early years* San Francisco, California Don't Call It Frisco Press 1986

Raymond Clary *The Making of Golden Gate Park: the growing years* San Francisco, California Don't Call It Frisco Press 1987

Mel Scott *The San Francisco Bay Area: a metropolis in perspective* Berkeley University of California Press 1959

Frank Soulé, John Gihon and James Nisbet *Annals of San Francisco* (re-issued) Berkeley, California Berkeley Hills Press 1999 (Abridged)

Landscape History

John Brinkerhoff Jackson *Discovering the Vernacular Landscape* New Haven and London Yale University Press 1984

John R. Stilgoe *Borderland: origins of the American suburb* New Haven and London Yale University Press 1988

Garden History

Ulysses P. Hedrick *A History of American Horticulture To 1860* 1950 (re-issued 1988 Timber Press)

Joan Hockaday *San Francisco Gardens* Portland, Oregon Timber Press 1988

Anthony Huxley *An Illustrated History of Gardening* London Paddington Press in association with the Royal Horticultural Society 1978

Christopher Thacker *The History of Gardens* Berkeley Los Angeles University of California Press 1979

REFERENCES

Introduction

[1] Starr, Kevin 1973 *Americans and the California Dream* London New York Oxford University Press

Chapter 1

[2] Holliday, J.S. 1981 *The World Rushed In* New York Simon and Schuster

[3] Paxton, Sir Joseph 1840 *Botanical Dictionary Comprising the Names, History, and Culture of all Plants Known in Britain* London J. Andrews

[4] *Vignettes of Old San Francisco Homes and Gardens* 1935 San Francisco, California San Francisco Garden Club

[5] Clary, Raymond 1986/1987 *The Making of Golden Gate Park: the early years* and *The Making of Golden Gate Park: the growing years* San Francisco California Don't Call It Frisco Press

[6] Beatty, Russell A. 1970 "Metamorphosis in sand: the first five years of Golden Gate Park" Calif. Hort. J. *31* (2) 41-47

[7] McClintock, Elizabeth 2001 *The Trees of Golden Gate Park* Berkeley California Heyday Books

[8] Taylor, Judith M. 2002 "Sydney Stein Rich: Gardener and Pioneer, San Francisco 1906–1956" Western States Jewish History *34* (4) 291 – 307

[9] Hudson, Roy L. 1970 "John McLaren as I knew him" Calif. Hort. J. 31 (2) 47–50

[10] Aikman, Tom Girvan 1988 *Boss Gardener: the Life and Times of John McLaren* San Francisco, California Don't Call It Frisco Press

[11] Morey, R. 1970 "Japanese Tea Garden" Calif. Hort. J. *31* (2)
[12] Hockaday, Joan 1988 *The Gardens of San Francisco* Portland, Oregon Timber Press

Chapter 2

[13] Eyre, Florence Atherton 1933 *Reminiscences of Peninsula Gardens 1860–1890* San Francisco, California San Francisco Garden Club
[14] Santos, Robert Leroy 1997 *The Eucalyptus of California* Denair, California Allen-Cass Publications

Chapter 3

[15] Magee, Belle 1937 *Reminiscences of East Bay Gardens 1860–1890* San Francisco, California San Francisco Garden Club
[16] Scheuring, Anne Foley 1995 *Science and Service: a history of the land grant university and agriculture in California* Oakland, California University of California Division of Agriculture and Natural Resources Publication No. 3360
[17] Cockrell, Robert A. and Frederick Warnke 1976 *The Trees of the Berkeley Campus* Berkeley California University of California Division of Agriculture and Natural Resources
[18] Shaffer, Harry E. 1972 "A garden grows in Eden" San Leandro, California San Leandro Historical-Centennial Committee

Chapter 5

[19] *Vignettes of the gardens of San Jose de Guadalupe* 1938 San Francisco, California San Francisco Garden Club
[20] Taylor, Judith M. 2002 "A 'Lost' Rose Garden" Eden: Journal of the California Garden and Landscape History Society *5* (3) 5-6
[21] *Sunshine, Fruit and Flowers* 1896 (re-issued 1986) San Jose, California San Jose Mercury

Chapter 7

[22] Brown, Thomas 1988 "Gardens of the California Missions" Pacific Horticulture *49* (2) 8

Chapter 15

[23] Steinfeld, Charles 1996 *The Bourn Dynasty; the Empire Mine's golden era* Grass Valley, California Empire Mine Association

Chapter 16

[24] Boyd, Margaret Kittle 1934 *Remininscences of Early Marin County Gardens* San Francisco, California San Francisco Garden Club
[25] Mason, Jack 1973 "Last stage for Bolinas" Point Reyes, California Northshore Books re-issued 1982)
[26] Livingston, Dewey 1993 (July) "Ranching on the Point Reyes National Seashore" National Park Service (revised July 1994)
[27] Livingston, Dewey 1995 "Dairy Farming in the Olema Valley" National Park Service
[28] Kent, William 1929 *Reminiscences of an Outdoor Life* San Francisco, California A. M.Robertson
[29] Slosson, Elvenia 1951 Pioneering American Gardening New York Coward-McCann

Chapter 17

[30] Starr, Kevin 1990 *Material Dreams: Southern California in the 1920s* London New York Oxford University Press
[31] Hendry, George W. 1934 "The source literature of early plant introductions into Spanish America" Agricultural History *82* 64-71
[32] Padilla, Victoria 1961 *Southern California Gardens* Berkeley Los Angeles University of California Press
[33] Newmark, Harris 1970 *Sixty Years in Southern California* (Fourth edition) Los Angeles, California Zeitlin and ver Brugge .

Chapter 19

[34] Dakin, Susanna Bryant 1939 *A Scotch Paisano in Old Los Angeles* Berkeley Los Angeles London University of California Press

[35] Jackson, Helen Hunt 1912 *Ramona* New York, New York Grosset and Dunlap

[36] Higbie, Iris 1965 *William Wolfskill: frontier trapper to California ranchero* Spokane, Washington Arthur H Clark

[37] Hertrich, William 1949 *The Huntington Botanical Gardens* San Marino, California The Huntington Library

Chapter 26

[38] Stern, Norton 1983 "Louis Phillips of the Pomona Valley: rancher and real estate investor" Western States Jewish History *16* (1) 54-81

Chapter 27

[39] Snyder, Harold 2002 "Victoria Avenue" Pacific Horticulture 63 (1) 36-41

Chapter 28

[40] Jordan, Carol 1997 *The Landmark Trees of Tustin* Tustin, California Tustin Area Historical Society

TABLE

Some Popular Ornamentals with Approximate Dates

of First Listing

Compiled by H. H. Butterfield

Plant	Grower	Place	Date
Abelia triflora	Wm. C. Walker	San Francisco	1858
Abutilon striatum	Wm. C. Walker	San Francisco	1858
Acacia armata	Colonel Warren	Sacramento	1853
Acacia decurrens var. *dealbata*	Colonel Warren	Sacramento	1853
Acacia longifolia	Colonel Warren	Sacramento	1853
Acacia verticillata	Wm. C. Walker	San Francisco	1854
Acacias (first from seed)	Mrs. C. V. Gillespie	San Francisco	1854
Agapanthus africanus	Colonel Warren	Sacramento	1853
Agonis flexuosa	Stephen Nolan	Oakland	1871
Alstroemeria pulchella	Stephen Nolan	Oakland	1871
Archontophoenix cunninghamiana	Stephen Nolan	Oakland	1871
Arecastrum romanzoffianum	Woodwards Gardens	San Francisco	1877
Aucuba japonica	Colonel Warren	Sacramento	1853
Begonia manicate	Wm. C. Walker	San Francisco	1858
Begonia semperflorens	James Hutchison	Oakland	1874
Berberis darwinii	R. D. Fox	San Jose	1884
Bougainvillea glabra	R. D. Fox	San Jose	1884

Brunsvigia rosea	Colonel Warren	Sacramento	1853
Calliandra tweedii	Wm. C. Walker	San Francisco	1854
Callistemon citrinus	Colonel Warren	Sacramento	1853
Campsis chinensis	Commercial Nurseries	San Francisco	1854
Cassia tomentosa	Wm. C. Walker	San Francisco	1858
Casuarina stricta	Wm. C. Walker	San Francisco	1858
Cistus ladaniferus	Stephen Nolan	Oakland	1871
Convolvulus mauritanicus	Stephen Nolan	Oakland	1871
Cornus capitata	John Grelck	Los Angeles	1877
Cornus kousa	H. H. Berger	San Francisco	1887
Correa alba	Colonel Warren	Sacramento	1853
Coroderia selloana	James Hutchinson	Oakland	1869
Cotoneaster microphylla	Commercial Nurseries	San Francisco	1854
Cryptomeria japonica	Wm. C. Walker	San Francisco	1858
Cyca revoluta	James Hutchison	Oakland	1874
Cytisus racemosus	James Hutchinson	Oakland	1878
Cytisus scoparius	Stephen Nolan	Oakland	1871
Daphne odora	Stephen Nolan	Oakland	1871
Datura suaveolens	Wm. C. Walker	San Francisco	1854
Deutzia gracilis	Shell Mound Nurseries	Oakland	1856
Dolichos lignosus	Wm. C. Walker	San Francisco	1858
Duranta repens	Joseph Sexton	Santa Barbara	1879
Echeveria secunda glauca	James Hutchison	Oakland	1874
Erythrina crista-galli	Colonel Warren	Sacramento	1853
Escallania montevidensis	William C. Walker	San Francisco	1858
Escallonia rubra	Stephen Nolan	Oakland	1871
Eucalyptus sp.	Shell Mound Nurseries	Oakland	1856
Eucalyptus ficifolia	Charles Schurff	Pasadena	1873
Eucalyptus resinifera	William C. Walker	Oakland	1858
Eugenia paniculata var. *australis*	William C. Walker	San Francisco	1860
Euonymus japonicus	William C. Walker	San Francisco	1858

Euphorbia pulcherrima	William C. Walker	San Francisco	1854
Euphorbia splendens	William C. Walker	San Francisco	1858
Ficus repens	William C. Walker	San Francisco	1860
Fuchsia corymbiflora	Stephen Nolan	Oakland	1871
Fuchsia fulgens	William C. Walker	San Francisco	1861
Fuchsia procumbens	David Tisch	Oakland	1880
Gardenia jasminoides	William C. Walker	San Francisco	1858
Garrye elliptica	William C. Walker	San Francisco	1858
Gelsemium sempervirens	William C. Walker	San Francisco	1858
Gladiolus cardinalis	Colonel Warren	Sacramento	1853
Grevillea rosmarinaefolia	William C. Walker	San Francisco	1858
Hakea laurina	Stephen Nolan	Oakland	1871
Hakea saligna	William C. Walker	San Francisco	1860
Hardenbergia comptoniana	Stephen Nolan	Oakland	1871
Hebe (Veronica) andersoni	William C. Walker	San Francisco	1858
Hebe speciosa	R. D. Fox	San Jose	1885
Homolanthus populifolius	F. Ludemann	San Francisco	1874
Hoya carnosa	William C. Walker	San Francisco	1858
Iochroma tubulosum	Stephen Nolan	Oakland	1871
Iris unguicularis	H. H. Berger	San Francisco	1887
Jasminum grandiflorum	William C. Walker	San Francisco	1858
Jasminum humile	Commercial Nurseries	San Francisco	1854
Leptospermum laevigatum	William C. Walker	San Francisco	1858
Leptospermum scoparium	Stephen Nolan	Oakland	1871
Ligustrum lucidum	Stephen Nolan	Oakland	1871
Lilium longiflorum	Colonel Warren	Sacramento	1853
Lilium speciosum	Colonel Warren	Sacramento	1853
Livistona australis	Stephen Nolan	Oakland	1871
Lonicera japonica	Commercial Nurseries	San Francisco	1854

Magnolia grandiflora	Simpson Thompson	Suscol	1861
Magnolia stellata	H. H. Berger	San Francisco	1887
Melaleuca decussata	William C. Walker	San Francisco	1860
Melaleuca hypericifolia	William C. Walker	San Francisco	1860
Myrtus communis	William C. Walker	San Francisco	1858
Nandina domestica	Stephen Nolan	Oakland	1871
Narcissus-Soleil D'or	*Stephen Nolan*	*Oakland*	*1871*
Narcissus Von Scion	*Stephen Nolan*	*Oakland*	*1871*
Osmanthus fragrans	H. H. Berger	San Francisco	1887
Pandorea jasminoides	William C. Walker	San Francisco	1858
Passiflora manicata	William C. Walker	San Francisco	1858
Pelargonium— Mrs. Pollock	James Hutchison	Oakland	1874
Phoenix canariesis	Woodward Gardens	San Francisco	1874
Phormium tenax	William C. Walker	San Francisco	1858
Photinia serrulata	James Hutchison	Oakland	1874
Picea excelsa	William C. Walker	San Francisco	1858
Pimelia ferruginea	Colonel Warren	San Francisco	1858
Pittosporum crassifolim	Stephen Nolan	Oakland	1871
Pittosporum tobira	Colonel Warren	Sacramento	1853
Pittosporum undulatum	William C. Walker	San Francisco	1854
Plumbago capensis	William C. Walker	San Francisco	1858
Poinciana gilliesii	William C. Walker	San Francisco	1858
Polygala dalmaissiana	R. D. Fox	San Jose	1884
Prostanthera nivea	Stephen Nolan	Oakland	1871
Pyracantha coccinea	William C. Walker	San Francisco	1860
Pyrostegia ignea	William C. Walker	San Francisco	1858
Raphiolepis indica	Stephen Nolan	Oakland	1871
Raphiolepis umbellata	R. D. Fox	San Jose	1884
Rosa banksiae	Colonel Warren	Sacramento	1853
Schinus molle	Mission San Luis Rey	San Luis Rey	1825
Sequoiadendron giganteum	William C. Walker	San Francisco	1858
Skimmia japonica	John Rock	San Jose	1884
Sollya heterophylla	Colonel Warren	Sacramento	1853
Sparaxis tricolor	Colonel Warren	Sacramento	1853

Spartium junceum	William C. Walker	San Francisco	1858
Strelitzia augusta	R. D. Fox	San Jose	1884
Strelitzia reginae	Colonel Warren	Sacramento	1853
Syzygium jambos	Colonel Warren	Sacramento	1853
Tecomaria capensis	William C. Walker	San Francisco	1858
Tibouchina semidecandra	F. Ludemann	San Francisco	1874
Trachycarpus fortunei	Stephen Nolan	Oakland	1871
Vallota speciosa	Stephen Nolan	Oakland	1871
Viburnum odoratissimum	H. H. Berger	San Francisco	1887
Viburnum tinum	Colonel Warren	Sacramento	1853
Washingtonia filifera	Louis Prevost	San Jose	1858
Westringia rosmariniformis	William C. Walker	San Francisco	1858
Zantedeschia aethiopica	Colonel Warren	Sacramento	1853
Zantedeschia albo-maculata	James Hutchison	Oakland	1874
Zephyranthes alba	Stephen Nolan	Oakland	1871

With more complete records, the above dates might be pushed back in several cases. During the Spanish and Mexican period, records mention *Acacia farneschiana, Arundo donax,* hollyhock, lily, marigold, jonquil, nasturtium, oleander, pinks, pomegranate, *Rosa damascena* var. *triginitipetal,* sweet pea, violet, and wallflower. Also see Spanish Gardens for plants that may have been in California during the early period.

APPENDIX A

William Connell Walker

William Connell Walker's vines in 1858 included *Campsis chinensis, Cobaea scandens, Hova carnosa* and *H. bella, Jasminum officinale, Maurandia erubescence, M. barclaiana, Mandevilla suaveolens, Physianthus albens, Passiflora caerules, Sollya heterophylla, Solandra grandiflora,* and *Pandorea jasminoides.* A few selections of evergreen shrubbery from his nursery are: *Umbellularia californica,* Chinese arbor vitae, *Casuarina stricta, Cytisus nigricans, Eucalyptus resinifera, E. amygdalinus* var. *angustifolia, Escallonia montevidensis, Lagerstroemia indica, Myoporum acuminatum, Pittosporum tobira, Punica nana,* the Tea Plant (*lepstospermum*), *Veronica (Hebe) andersonii,* and *Westringia romaninifolius.*

APPENDIX B

The Trees of the Berkeley Campus

An old ginkgo tree (*Ginkgo biloba*) is growing to the east of Giannini Hall on the Berkeley campus. Formerly a Bald cypress (*Taxodium disticum*) grew nearby. Miss Kate O. Sessions stated in a letter many years ago that these trees were growing there when she graduated from the University in 1881. She also recalled the large Soap Bark tree (*Quillaja saponaria*) that is still growing near the walk at the Center Street entrance to the campus, on the south side of the driveway. Several of these old trees must have been planted around 1875-1880.

Near the creek at the Center Street entrance is a Kaki persimmon and just to the east is a specimen of *Litsea glauca,* a close relative of the camphor tree. It produces red berries in season. A little to the east of this tree is what may be the oldest living avocado tree in California, started from seed in 1878. The seed came from Guatemala. The small fruits are not important on this seedling tree. (Remember that Butterfield was writingin the mid 1940s or 1950s.)

Further east of the avocado tree is an old specimen of the Queensland Nut (*Macadamia ternifolia*). This tree was probably planted in the 1880's and forms round, hardshelled nuts which the squirrels now eat before fully ripe. South of the bridge on the creek is a specimen of *Persea lingue,* a relative of the avocado. Across on the north side of the creek bridge is an old camphor tree planted before 1880. (Harry Butterfield quotes a young man who later married one of Edward Gill's daughters saying that he had climbed this camphor tree as a boy in 1881).

The Soap bark tree (*Quillaja saponaria*) further west along the south side of the Center Street entrance was also planted in its present location before 1880. The New Zealand ash tree or Titoki (*Electryon excelsum*) found a little to the north of the camphor tree was moved from its original location near the Soap bark tree but it may date back to around 1880. The Ginkgo tree (*Ginkgo biloba*) growing near the creek to the north of the camphor tree, in earlier years grew on the south side of another bridge leading to the old Experimental Grounds of the Agricultural Experiment Station but the bridge was removed some time after 1917.

Still further up the creek on the west bank are specimens of *Persea indica* planted about 1920. The oldest cedar trees in the area were planted about the same time. All of the western area was graded down from a hill that stood up until after 1915. Pines and other trees were planted on this hill.

Passing to the east side and a little north of the eucalyptus grove we find eucalyptus trees planted toward the east, near the north entrance of the library. An excellent specimen of *Eucalyptus viminalis* or Manna gum stands to the north of the Life Sciences Building by the path and measures about six and a half feet in diameter breast high. This tree was pictured in the 1914 edition of L. H. Bailey's *Cyclopedia of American Horticulture* a good many years before the Life Sciences Building was constructed. This and the other old trees extending eastward were mostly planted from 1870-1871.

Near the creek to the north is an old tree of *Maytenus boaria*, one of several Chilean trees likely grown from seed imported by E. P. Rixford in the late 1870's. To the north of the Life Sciences building on the north bank of the creek is another of the Chilean Trees, *Cryptocaria miersii*, planted about 1876 according to Willis P. Jepson. This tree closely resembles an upright Grecian laurel, to which it is related. Also along the creek there were several Japanese cherries set out around 1920 as a gift of students from Japan. A list of their names was filed with the Extension Forester's office with a plan to show their location.

The road that leads to Haviland Hall passes by three more

Chilean trees. Near the intersection to the left is a specimen of *Peumus boldus* or Boldo tree that was growing in this location by 1885 and a specimen of *Lythraea caustica* once stood close to the north. It was removed in 1958. As the road turns eastward at the base of the slope to the right is a bushy specimen of *Lythraea mollioides* with a somewhat pinnate leaf.

The old Botanical Garden used to be in the depression extending from near the creek on the east well past the library. Except for a few trees, all the plants have been removed. In the group at the west will be found redwood trees, Bald cypress, and a specimen of *Eucalyptus angustifolia*.. On the east side of the road leading to Haviland Hall is a loquat tree and a *Grevillea robusta*.. Near the parking lot is a round-headed specimen of *Macadamia*' but perhaps the most notable tree still standing in the path leading north from the library is the Island ironwood (*Lyonothamnus floribundus* var. *aspelifolius*) planted in this location in 1895. (Note 97)

The old Lord and Burnham greenhouse was close to the parking area east of Haviland Hall. It had been erected in 1894 but was torn down some time after 1910. A specimen of *Eucalyptus ficifolia* grows at the east end of the parking area. Specimens of Tanbark oak (*Lithocarpus densiflorus*) and Mayten tree still grow along the south bank. Farther east near the bank is a fine specimen of the Torrey pine (*Pinus torrevana*).

A good many acacia trees planted about 1901 once grew near here. Acacias can stand poor soil, so the hollow to reach the Mining Building when it was constructed was filled with poor soil. Near the east end of the depression there was a specimen of *Colletia ephedra* from Chile. Before the Old Botanical Garden was planted in this hollow, it was used as a drill ground by students. Still other trees once grew near Harmon Gymnasium, such as *Abies venusta*, but they have now been removed.

An 1898 photograph of an E.D. Harmon's house in Berkeley 1898 survives. He may have been related to the A.F.K. Harmon who donated the gymnasium to the University of California. It looks substantial and comfortable, but not palatial. The garden is lush, with a palm tree to one side of the front walk and many smaller trees and shrubs crowded into a modest space.

There used to be a specimen of *Junipers cedrus.* south of Wheeler Hall. There are some Stone pines near the President's home on the north side of the campus. The Canary Island pines growing west of the tall eucalyptus grove and south of the Campanile were planted about in 1920. The Campanile was erected in 1917. A row of Bishop pines was once planted along Hearst Avenue as well as along the east side of Oxford Street. Old Monterey pines near the Power House on the campus were planted before students came in 1873.

APPENDIX C

Partial listing of contents of R D Fox's 1884 catalogue

(from page 15)

Cedrella sinensis
Cercis chinensis
Texas Umbrella
Prunus cerasifera var. *pissardi*
Berberia darwinii
Cryptomeria japonica var. *elegans*
Eucalyptus citriodora
Juniperis sabina var. *tamariscifolia*
Michelia fuscata
Pinus canariensis
Polygala dalmasiana
Chamaecyparis pisifera var. *plumosa*
Sciadopitys verticillata
Torreya californica
Veronica (Hebe) andersonii
Lonicera japonica var. *Halliana*

Hemerocallis fulva var. Kwanso
Bergenia (Saxifram) crassifolium
Alamanda nerifolia
Antigonon leptopus
Bougainvillea spectabilis and *B. glabra*
Clerodentron thomsonas
Alsophila australis
Dicksonia antartica
Ficus repens
Asystacia (Mackaya) Bella
Strelitzia augusta
Lilium aratum
Arecastrum romanzoffianum
(Cocus plumosa)

Fuchsias, such as Arora Superba,
Sunray, and *F. procumbens*
Garden geraniums such as
Happy Thought, New Life, Mrs.
Pollock, Mt. of Snow, and Lady
Plymouth
Anemone japonica

446

APPENDIX D

Plants in the Hillside Park, Santa Barbara

Select List of Ornamental Plants in Hillside Park

Acacia baileyana var. *purpurea*

Acacia elongata

Acacia pendula

Acacia pycnantha

Acacia scorpioides

Banksia integrifolia

Banksia litoralis

Bauhinia forficata

Callistemon viminalis

Casuarina fraseriana

Crinodendron dependens

Cupania anacardioides

Dombeya natalensis

Ehretia dicksoni

Ehretia elliptica

Erythina caffra

Erythrina crista-galli

Escallonia pulverulenta

Excallonia revoluta

Eucalyptus erythrocorys

Eucalyptus grossa

Eucalyptus preissiana

Eucalyptus stricklandi

Acronychia baueria (Scrub Yellow-Wood)

Agonis juniperiana (Australian Juniper Myrtle)

Aleurites fordii (Tung Oil Tree)

Angophora lanceolata (Gum Myrtle)

Banksia grandis

Ficus vogellii

Grevillea banksii

Hakea gibbosa

Hake trifurcata

Harpephyllum caffrum

Leptospermum ericoides

Melaleuca huegelii

Melaleuca parviflora

Peumus boldus

Phillyrea latifolia media

Pithecellobium pruinosum

Pittosporum erioloma

Pittosporum floribundum

Plumeria acuminata

Podaehaenium eminens

Pseudopanax lessonii

Regalia grandiflora

Sapindus rarak

Eugenia supra-exillaris
Ficus mysorensis
Spathodea nilotica
Stenocarpus salignus
Taiwania cryptomerioides

Schinus dependens
Schotia latifolia
Tupidanthus calyptratus
Vitex lucens

(Note 98)

APPENDIX E

Partial List of plants at the Bard Estate, Ventura

County

1915-1917
Vines

Bomarea caldasiana

Cissus rhombifolius

Deeringia amaranthoides

Kennedya rubicunda

Oxera pulchella

Solandra nitida

Rupidanthus calyptratus

Evergreen Shrubs (or small trees)

Acalypha wilkesiana var. *marginata*

Acokanthera spectabilis

Adhatoda vasica

Asystasia bella (Mackaya bella)

Berberis acinos; B. bergmanii;
  B. paynei; B. tricanthophora

Carissa edulis

Custus laurifolius

Convolvulus floridus

Citharoxylus barbinerve

Dryandra floribunda

Ficus chauvieri

Fontanesia phyllyraeoides

Gymnosporia serrata

Homolanthus populifolius

Leptospermum pubescens

Lithraea caustica

Melicope ternata

Melicytus ramiflorus

Myoporum acuminatum

Olearia haastii

Olearia paniculata

Pittosporum cornifolium

Rondeletia gratissum

Royana lubidae

Schefflera steltzneriana

Tecoma smithii

Halleria lucida   *Xylophylla angustifolia*

Evergreen Trees

Acacia mindenti   *Ficus australis*
Acacia robusta   *Ficus religiosa*
Calpurnia aurea   *Hemicyclia lasiogyne*
Cinnamomum hupehanum   *Maesa indica*
Citarexylum quadrangulare   *Maytenus boaria*
Crytocarya rubra   *Oreopanax nymphaefolium*
Dendrospanax japonicum   *Persica indica*
Dizogtheca reginas   *Quillaja saponaria*
Ficus altissum   *Triplaris americana*

Conifers

Araucaria columnaris   *Cupressus torulosa* (1905)
Araucaria cunninghamii   *Ginkgo biloba* (1905)
Callitris robusta   *Pinus canariensis*
Cedrus sargentii   *Podocarpus elongata*
Cephalotaxus drupacea
Cephalotaxus fortunei (1905)   *Podocarpus macrophylla*
Cunninghamia sinensis   *Podocarpus totara*
Cupressus fragrans

Deciduous Trees

Alectryon excelsum (evergreen with us) *Fagus sylvatica* var. *laciniata*
Castanospermum australe   *Fraxinus ornus* var. *juglandifolia*
Cithareylum dicksonii   *Fraxinus ornus* var. *rotundifolia*

Palms

Archontophoenix cunninghamiana   *Rhopalostylis sapida*
  (Seaforthia elegans)
Phoenix roebelenii   *Sabal minor*

Rhaphis flabelliformis   *Arecastrum (Cocos)* and *Howea* palm

Palm-like Plants

Cordyline australis, C. individa,   *Nolina longifolis*
   and *C. stricta*
Dasylirion acrotrichum   *Strelitzia augusta*
Dracaena draco   *Beaucarnea guatamalensis*

APPENDIX F

MONTEREY'S "PATH OF HISTORY"

One can pick up the "The Path of History" at Main Street where four buildings should be seen on the west side, north of Hartnell. First is Casa Gutierrez, built in about 1843-45. Notice the casuarinas or beefwood trees in the parking strip.' The State of California acquired the Gutierrez adobe in 1954, but since 1966, it has been used as a Mexican restaurant.

'A little to the north is the House of the Four Winds built in the late 1830s by Thomas O. Larkin. In recent years it has been restored by the Women's Civic Club but the old weather vane pointing to the four winds is still working with a rooster on top. *Coprosma baueri* is used as an edging and there are a few echeverias in the narrow garden strip.

A third small building just north of the Masonic Building and part of the Larkin grounds is Sherman's Headquarters . It is not much of a building, but it does bring up memories of the Lieutenant staying there in 1847. Ivy clings to the base of the front. Light blue*Plumbago capensis* flowers are attractive, as are the Lombardy poplar and buddleia. A large willow stands "weeping" in the Larkin garden just to the rear.

It was built in 1835 by Thomas Oliver Larkin to be both his residence and store. From 1842 to 1844 it housed the American Consulate. Jacobe Leese took it over after the gold rush.In 1850, the Larkin family moved away, first to New York, and then to San Francisco. They never returned to Monterey. Robert Johnson, once mayor, built the stone wall to the west which surrounds the garden.'

Many years after Thomas Larkin's death in 1858 his grand-daughter, Alice Larkin Toulmin, bought the Larkin house sight unseen, in honor of her grandfather. She later deeded it to the National Trust to ensure its future preservation. At the time Harry Butterfield visited Monterey, she still owned the house.

'Very graciously Mrs Toulmin showed me her garden' Butterfield wrote . 'A Cécile Brunner rose is behind the east wall, a redwood tree is near the south end of the front wall, and a cannon is in front. (The cannon served as a hitching post.) A Canary Island date palm peeks out above the rear. A rose overhangs the balcony. For a fine view, look at the garden from the west where Colton Hall Park is to be found.'

The history walk next takes one west via Jefferson, and Pacific Street (Calle de Estrada) to Madison where the Brown-Underwood Adobe is on the north side of the street. This adobe was built in 1843 and purchased by Jose Maria Sanchez a year later. Many years later, in 1931, the City of Monterey incorporated these premises into part of its administrative offices.

The last house of the four stands at the corner of Main and Jefferson. This is the Larkin House.

'Continue west to Dutra, then north on Dutra to Colton Hall. The building was dedicated on September 3, 1849 and the first state Constitutional Convention met in it . Among the delegates were eight "native" Californians, Pablo de la Guerra and Jacinto Rodrigues coming from Monterey, and *rancheros* such as Manuel Dominguez, Antonio Maria Pico, and others coming from the south. General M. G. Vallejo came down from Sonoma. Reverend Samuel Willey, who helped to establish the University of California, said prayers.

Captain Joseph Aram, fruit grower and nurseryman of San Jose, Captain Weber who founded Stockton, Hugo Reid, the "Scotch Paisano", who pioneered north of San Gabriel on what is now the State Arboretum, Don Abel Stearns who built the old adobe east of Long Beach now owned by the heirs of Fred Bixby, and John A. Sutter of Sacramento were also delegates at the Convention. The rather inappropriate front steps were added later. Monterey pines stand just in front of the building.

Colton Hall was taken over by the City of Monterey on September 28, 1948, and the second floor now houses administrative offices. A large Northern California black walnut tree looms up from the distance.

The paved highway from the east becomes Fremont Street after passing Del Monte. (See map) Follow this street west until it passes the old Protestant and Catholic cemeteries lying east of El Estero, an arm of Monterey Bay that thrusts itself inland.

Casa Buena is near this inlet and at one time was owned by L A Ross. There is a fine specimen of *Arbutus canariensis* (Canary Island Madrone) near the entrance. The roof is a good example of how an early Spanish or Indian laborer formed tiles.

The Borondo adobe stands in view to the west. Old Casa Bonifacio is next, on the east side of Mesa Road. This is where the so called Sherman Rose is supposed to be, but another rose seems have been substituted. The original Sherman rose was yellow but the rose that has been pointed out at the new location on Mesa Road is a different color.'

It is not clear exactly when Butterfield visited Monterey. The Borondo adobe no longer exists (early 2000). The original Casa Bonifacio was demolished in 1923. Some of the adobe bricks and roof tiles were used to construct a new house on Mesa Road. A bank stands on the earlier site. All this is very disappointing.

The adobe later known as Casa Bonifacio was initially built by Jose Rafael Gonzales in 1835, while he was a customs official. Carmen Pinto Bonifacio, the widow of an Italian stevedore, Giovanni Bonifacio, bought it in 1860. She and her daughter, Maria Ygnacia, made a living by renting out rooms.

One of their tenants was Fanny Osbourne, later Robert Louis Stevenson's wife. Stevenson courted her while he lived in another Monterey house. (v.i.) Maria Ygnacia stayed on in the house until 1916.

All this detail is important in understanding the charming legend which has grown up about the so-called "Sherman rose". A photograph of the Bonifacio house in 1900 reveals a huge yellow rose bush growing over the arbor in front of it.

William Tecumseh Sherman stayed in Monterey while on duty, in 1846-1847. He is supposed to have fallen in love with Maria Ygnacia. Regardless of the fact that she continually denied any such attachment, the rose was persistently known by Sherman's name. They are said to have planted it together. He was supposed to return and marry her when it bloomed. In fact, he had been betrothed before going to Monterey, and married his fiancee in due time, without any further ado.

The legend has reluctantly to be demolished, based on horticultural evidence from the plants themselves. There is no 1840s rose bush at the current Casa Bonifacio, but a modern hybrid tea rose. There had been a rose, *Chromatella* or Cloth of Gold, a yellow rose which was extant in 1843, a Noisette/ Tea variety, but it was not planted in Sherman's day.

That rose was planted a long time afterwards. Sherlock Harmon, a knowledgeable citizen, has left behind a record of what actually happened. His notes are stored in the Custom House Museum. The planting was in 1871. A man named Ross Morely gave the rose to Maria Ygnacia. She planted and tended it. Obviously this rose had nothing to do with Sherman.

The same variety of rose was found to be growing in the orchard behind another early adobe, the Cooper Molera house, according to Frances Grate, a dedicated garden historian in Monterey. Although that rose in its turn also died, Mrs Grate knew it had been budded earlier. A lineal descendant may still be found in the Cooper Molera orchard.

Butterfield found out the melancholy facts, writing: "I saw the yellow rose at Casa Bonifacio many years ago before it was moved to Mesa Road. The old adobe has since been replaced by a bank." Here is more cause for melancholy, in the harsh reality of development.

Next drive west on Fremont, and turn right one block west of El Estero to Church Street. Church Street runs past the Royal Chapel of San Carlos de Borromeo de Monterey founded by Father Serra in 1770 and completed in 1795. It is the only presidio church to survive in California and marks the southern boundary of the old Presidio grounds. As the visitor notes the old iron gates, all covered with ivy, try to imagine the original scene in June 1770.

Father Serra was accompanied by Juan Crespi, Captain Portola, Captain Rivera, Lieutenant Pedro Fages, and Jose Francisco Ortega while he said the initial mass. This old church has been in continuous use for more than a hundred and sixty years, an enduring example of strong faith.

The trunk of an old oak tree, another candidate for "Viscaino's Oak", used to be to the south of the Chapel . It had been moved there. Pause to look east across El Estero toward the old Catholic cemetery where so many early settlers are buried. McKinlay, Amesti, Vallejo, and Spence are some of the names inscribed on the gravestones.

Continue west to Abrego, then turn north on to Webster to see several other old dwellings with their gardens. Casa Pacheco, built in 1842 and remodeled in 1920, is at the southwest corner of Webster and Abrego. It is currently occupied by the Pacheco Club for men. Casa Abrego, built in 1835 by Don Jose Abrego, is across the street. Don Jose Abrego owned the land about Punta Pinos (now Pacific Grove).

Don Jose came to Monterey in 1834 and perhaps built the porch on Abrego Street side. It is also possible that he planted vines on the support. Today there is a willow near the north and sycamores in the parking area. Formerly this house had a typical patio. The Abrego family supplied the mantilla and shawl that can be seen in the Custom House Museum. Driving on west notice that ivy clings to the west wall of the old garden.

In the middle of the block west on Huston is "Stevenson's House", the old French Hotel where in 1879 Stevenson wrote such stories as *Vendetta of the West* and *Amateur Emigrant*.. He lived in a room on the second floor. Lilacs now grow behind the picket fence, and there are some Giant Reeds, waiting as of old to be used on some roof thatch.' The house is currently being renovated (early 2000.)

'Follow "The Path of History" via Huston, Webster, and Munras Avenue, to the northwest corner of Pearl and Tyler. Stop at the Chamber of Commerce on the site of the old *carcel* or jail and secure a map of the city. The triangle at the street intersection marks the site of the Mexican jail built in 1832.

General Jose Castro used the Casa Castro at this corner as headquarters. Some tree tobacco still lingers from an earlier planting on the east side. The bull and bear pits were at the rear of this building.

Turn west on Pearl one block to Alvarado. Near the northwest corner facing Alvarado is the first United States Post Office in Monterey. It once formed the northern boundary of the old Plaza.

Across Pearl to the south facing the triangle on Munras Avenue is the Cooper House, built in 1829 by Don Juan Batista R. Cooper for his bride, Dona Encarnacion Vallejo. Don Juan began life as John Rogers Cooper, Thomas Larkin's half brother. Larkin was the first and only US consul in Alta California. It was after John Cooper had settled in Monterey that he asked his brother Thomas to join him there. Here, too, is a portion of the old Plaza, the scene of fiestas and fandangos. The garden is a block wide. Also notice an old adobe wall south of the building and the barranca to the southwest.'

The property has been restored under the name Cooper/ Molera house. Don Juan Cooper's granddaughter, Frances Molera, deeded it to the National Trust. The latter in turn leases it to the California State Department of Parks for management. Frances Grate, a devoted member of the Old Monterey Preservation Society, oversaw the replanting of the orchard and other segments of the garden. There had always been an orchard and garden behind the Cooper homestead. Frances and her colleagues made sure that no anachronistic plants were introduced.

Butterfield recalled visiting Casa Amesti owned by Mrs. Frances Elkins. Mrs Elkins was the owner at the time he was writing. In 1953 Casa Amesti was given to the National Trust and is now leased by The Old Capital Club. It was built by Don Jose Amesti as a bridal gift for his daughter when she married Lieutenant James McKinlay in the late 1830s.

According to Butterfield the garden was in the French style with bordered walks and mixed plantings. 'In the extreme rear there was a fig tree marking the burial place of some member of the family long dead. I went out through the front entrance of Casa Amesti but turned to linger, glancing at the old pepper trees in the parking strip.' Harry Butterfield returned there often for a glimpse of a truly Spanish building.

Stop at the corner of Hartnell Street and Pearl Streets. Casa de la Torre, built by a Mexican captain, Gabriel de la Torre in 1841-42 is there. Notice the garden and barranca to the east behind the old "Blue Adobe." Box elders, willows, and tree mallows have grown in this garden.

The Stokes House or "Stokes Gray Adobe" lies across south on Hartnell Street opposite the end of Main Street. Main Street is the old Calle Principal of the Spanish. In present day Monterey, this street is once again named Calle Principal. 'This house was built in 1835 by Dr. James Stokes and was famous for its formal functions. See the garden and its barranca, lined with willows and an old fig tree. A cottonwood patriarch grows near the street. A fan palm and a rubber tree are near the house.' (In the modern era, the Stokes adobe has been turned into a restaurant and is privately owned.)

APPENDIX G

Santa Barbara's "Path of History"

'Coming in to Santa Barbara from the northwest off Highway 101 near Goleta, notice the Coast Live oaks (*Quercus agrifolia*) along a quarter of a mile at Serena Street . The American Legion planted them in 1926 as a living memorial to Santa Barbara County heroes who died in World War I. A little over half a mile further on, turn north on Mission Street and continue to 128 Mission where there is a specimen of *Phytolaca dioica*, an evergreen tree with a buttressed trunk, native to South America.

Go back two blocks to Los Olivos and on to Pueblo between De la Vina and Santa Barbara where there are two rows of Italian cypress trees that make a fine vista. Also notice the old olive trees from the early Mission orchard in the vicinity of Mission Santa Barbara. In front of Junipero Serra Hall is a specimen of *Caesalpinia echiata* (Brazil Wood), a small evergreen tree with pinnate compound leaves.

Turning north to the old Mission of Santa Barbara, try to picture the original orchard and vegetable garden bordered by Garden, Los Olivos, Laguna, and Padre Streets. There was also an orchard in the open area east of the Mission and about in line with Olivos Street as late as 1840. The old Settling Basin may still be seen near the turn of the street northeast of the Mission. Specimens of the Senegal Date Palm (*Phoenix reclinata*) are in front of the Mission building. They were planted in about 1901 or a little later.

In the fenced area to the south near the gate is a very tall specimen of *Myrtus communis*, perhaps the tallest in California. It was about twenty eight feet high in 1940. We might consider it to be very old until we learn how fast this ornamental grows in the local climate. Also within the confines of the garden area is the vegetable garden where Father Maynard Geiger (Franciscan scholar and historian) unearthed remnants of an old tile-lined irrigation ditch constructed as part of the orginal irrigation system. Portions of the old water *zanja* or ditch which Henry Chapman Ford sketched in 1890 may also be seen in places near where it approaches the mission on Mission Road.

The Cloister garden at the Mission is relatively new, having been planted by E. Denys Rowe since 1900. When he started there was nothing left growing from early Spanish days but today a visit is worthwhile. Readers will recall the visit of Sir George Simpson in 1841.

An olive tree planted by Crown Prince Leopold of Belgium in 1919 may be seen in the cemetery. The skull and crossbones imbedded over an archway are Indian bones, not those of "Poor Yorick," as an old priest jokingly suggested in answer to a silly question from a visitor.

Butterfield continues with his "Path of History": 'A seventy two-foot specimen of *Lagunaria patersoni* ("cow itch" tree, noted before in Monterey) may be seen in the former garden of the Clinton B. Hale Estate at the corner of Pedrogossa and Laguna. It is best seen from the Pedrogossa Street side. A large Mexican Grass Tree (*Dasylirion*) can also be seen. (These directions date from about forty years ago and the death of the owner's widow may have led to the subdivision of this property.)

Turning west to Islay, note some excellent specimens of *Pittosporum rhombifolium*, which bears beautiful orange berries, on the south side between Laguna and Garden. The specimen at 115 East Islay, north side, between Santa Barbara and Anacarpa, is said to be the original tree. E. O. Orpet has been given credit for the fine planting along Islay Street.

Next turn left to 1725 State Street where there is a fine specimen of the Surinam Cherry, known in past years as *Eugenia jambolana*, at E. Denys Rowe's house. He planted it in 1912. In front of the walk is a hybrid *Raphiolepis* introduced many years ago by Mr. Rowe.

Continue on for two blocks, then go in a westerly direction to 24 West Arrellaga Street where a fine old avocado tree is growing in the front yard. It was given to Dr. George A. White by Dr. Francheschi. White planted it as a seedling in 1895. It subsequently measured fifty six feet in height and had a spread of about fifty feet. In 1941 its trunk diameter in 1941 was ten and a half feet.

An Arlington Silk oak (*Grevillea robusta*), "Santa Barbara Lyre tree," so named because of its odd shape, is at 1309 State Street . It stands in what were once the Arlington Hotel grounds, built in 1875.

Turn west from State Street on Sola where there is a row of *Brachychiton populneum (Sterculia diversifolia)* trees, usually referred as Bottle trees. Opposite 122 West Victoria Street in the parking lot of the Board of Education is another species, *Brachychiton acerifolia*, known as the Flame tree because of its brilliant red flowers.

The official tree of Santa Barbara County, the ironwood, *Lyonothamnus asplenifolius*, was first brought from the islands off the coast of Santa Barbara in about 1895. There is a specimen growing on the ground of the County Court House, east of Anacapa between Anapamu and Figueroa, planted in honor of Windfield E. Metcalf, former county treasurer.

Every visitor should see Santa Barbara's Tree of Light, *Araucaria excelsa*, which stands in front of the Y.M.C.A. Building at Carrillo and Chappala. Each Christmas this tree is decorated and lighted.

Visitors may wish to go to Carrillo and Garden Street, north of Carrillo on the west side of Garden to see Santa Barbara's Orchid tree (*Bauhinia grandiflora*). It was forty three feet high in 1939. This is often referred to as Santa Barbara's Butterfly tree.

Go west on Ortega Street to 121 West Ortega, then glance across the street to see three fine camphor trees with branches extending across the street. Next on west to 735 Bath Street there is an exceptionally large Jacaranda tree with its lacy leaves and large blue flowers in late spring. Continuing west to Castillo Street we come to the "Hayward Hymenospermum" (*Hymenospermum flavum*) which was fifty one feet tall in 1939. It is noted for its fragrant yellow flowers that appear in early summer. The tree is in the parking strip near the corner. Small Cocos palms are growing on either side.

Driving east on Cota to De la Vina, then toward the ocean we come to 614 De la Vina, where there is a very large *Pittosporum tobira*, at least fifteen feet high and with a spread of twenty eight feet. Also notice on the west side in the 1200 block of De La Vina, two large *Araucaria excelsa* trees. There are more of these trees at 925 De La Vina.'

The next stop is at the southwest corner of State Street and Gutierrez where a very interesting tree may be seen, the Franceschi Flame tree sometimes referred to as *Sterculia greggorii*, but more properly *Brafhychiton populneum* var. *occidentalis*. This is on the site of an early nursery established by F. Franceschi in 1895, two years after he arrived in Santa Barbara.

While in this vicinity look for specimens of the Brazilian Cedarword tree (*Cedrella fissil)s)* on both sides of Gutierrez from Chapala to Santa Barbara. They resemble the *Ailanthus*, or Tree of Heaven. When ripe the large seed pods open to form a five-pointed star several inches in diameter.

Turning south toward the ocean one block to the southwest corner of Montecito and Chapella, the visitor will find the largest Moreton Bay Fig tree (*Ficus macrophylla)* in California. This specimen was planted by Mrs. Adeline Crabb Abraham in 1877. In 1939 it measured a hundred and thirty five feet in its crown spread and covered an area of 12,712 feet, estimated to be enough room for 9,500 people to stand. The large buttressed roots are almost as interesting as the tree's spread. The City now owns the property. It should be the pride of any city.

Turning west on Montecito to 412 Montecito Street, we come to a very old Cork Oak tree (*Quercus suber*), reported to have been planted in 1857. In 1940 it was seventy feet high and measured fifty one feet in diameter at four feet above the ground. This same area has two other worthy trees. The oldest Brisbane Box (*Tristanea conferta*) in Santa Barbara stands at the site of the old Joseph Sexton nursery that was established in 1868 on the northwest corner of Castillo and Montecito.

Looking southwest we may see a tall specimen of *Araucaria columnaris (A. cookii)* near the southwest corner of Catillo and Montecito. This is one of the few specimens of this species in California. It somewhat resembles *A. excelsa* but is not as refined. Some writers have considered it to be a form of *A. excelsa.*

Traveling east of Cabrillo Boulevard we come to a row of fine Canary Island Date Palms (*Phoenix canariensis*) between Bath and Chapala, marking the main entrance to what was the old Potter Hotel, burned down in 1921. Further north at 218 West Yanonali Street and forming a part of the old Potter Hotel grounds is a very fine Montezuma Bald-Cypress (*Taxodium micronatum*), said to be the largest in the Santa Barbara region. In 1939 it measured eighty one feet in height and had a trunk diameter of thirty three inches four feet from the ground. Also in this same district notice a Brazilian Pepper tree (*Schinus terebinthifolius*) in a vacant lot just west of 119 Los Aguajes Avenue, which is only about two blocks from the site of the old Sexton nursery already mentioned. It has had a spread of fifty eight feet and was twenty nine feet tall in 1940.

Our next tour takes us south to the scenic Cabrillo Boulevard and east along the ocean about a mile to Milpas Street, then north on Milpas about three blocks to the southwest corner of Cacique and Milpas. A large Jacaranda tree with a spread of fifty two feet in 1939 stands there. Fan palms planted along Cabrillo seem like sentinels near the breakwater.

Two blocks further up on Milpas, at the corner of Milpas and Quinientos, there is a stubby old sycamore (*Platanus racemosa*) now feeble in age, yet proudly tracing its life back to the days around 1800 when incoming sailing masters are said to have used this tree for sighting their anchorage. There is also the story that a lantern was hung in this tree to guide the sailors at night.

The tree was marked by the Daughters of the American Revolution in 1927. It now belongs to the Santa Barbara City Park Department. In 1941 it measured seventeen feet, with a nine and a half inches trunk circumference at four and a half feet.

APPENDIX H

Some Plants Imported by Hugh Evans

1924

Aster fruticosa
Baekia virgata
Bowkeri gerardiana

Chamaelaucium ciliatum
Drimys winteri

1925

Abelia schumanni
Chironia ixifera
Chironia baccifera
Correa pulchella
Correa speciosa
Correa ventricosa
Eucalyptus angulosa
Eucalyptus caesia
Eucalyptus constricta
Eucalyptus demodensis
Eucalyptus eremophylla
Eucalyptus erythorcorys
Eucalyptus forestiana
Eucalyptus grossa
Eucalyptus macrocarpa
Eucalyptus macrandra

Eucalyptus nutans
Eucalyptus odlfieldi
Eucalyptus preissiana
Eucalyptus pyreiforma
Eucalyptus sepulcralis
Eucalyptus spathulata
Eucalyptus steedmanni
Eucalyptus stricklandi
Eucalyptus tetraptera
Eucalyptus torquata
Grevillea obtusifolia
Grevillea leucopteris
Grevillea paniculata
Grevillea wilsoni
Strophanthus speciosus

1926

Aristea eckonis
Barcosma scoparia
Cassia splendida
Ceratostigma willmottiana
Coleonema pulchra

Crotolaria latifolia
Daviesia latifolia
Gossypium sturtii
Lasiandra laxa
Westringia rosmariniformis

1927

Bauhinia corymbosa
Clerodendrum mycroides
Hibbertia volubilis
Odonospermum sericium

Oxylobium lanceolatum
Pentas carnea
Clerodendrum mastacanthus

1929

Senecio confusus
Dimorphotheca spectabilis

Pentas longiflora
Sutera grandiflora

1930

Fuchsia alpestris

1931

Brachylaena elliptica

INDEX

Printed in the United States
15812LVS00001B/3